YOUR CHILD'S FIRST JOURNEY

A GUIDE TO PREPARED BIRTH
FROM PREGNANCY TO PARENTHOOD

YOUR CHILD'S FIRST JOURNEY

A GUIDE TO PREPARED BIRTH
FROM PREGNANCY TO PARENTHOOD

Second Edition

GINNY BRINKLEY · LINDA GOLDBERG · JANICE KUKAR

AVERY PUBLISHING GROUP INC.

Garden City Park, New York

PERMISSION CREDITS

Page

9-10   "The Pregnant Patient's Bill of Rights." Courtesy of Doris Haire, and the International Childbirth Education Association.

11   "The Pregnant Patient's Responsibilities." Courtesy of Doris Haire, and the International Childbirth Education Association.

13   "This Could Be the Start of Something Big." Used by Permission, Rosemeadow Publishing Corp. and Steve Allen, author of the song.

21, 22, 24   Photographs of Advancing Pregnancy. Photographs from *Pregnancy in Anatomical Illustrations.* Courtesy of the Carnation Company.

37-38   "The No-Risk Pregnancy Diet." Reprinted from *The Pregnancy After 30 Workbook* © 1978 by Gail Sforza Brewer. Permission granted by Rodale Press, Inc., Emmaus, PA 18049.

44-49   Nutrition chart from "Composition of Foods—Raw, Processed, Prepared." Reprinted by permission of the United States Department of Agriculture, Washington, D.C.

116   Regional Anesthesia in Obstetrics, Clinical Aid No. 17. Courtesy of Ross Laboratories, Columbus, Ohio.

143   Adapted from an illustration copyrighted © 1980 by Childbirth Graphics Ltd.

182   Mammary Glands and Breastfeeding, Clinical Aid No. 10. Courtesy of Ross Laboratories, Columbus, Ohio.

191   "A Hard Day's Night" (John Lennon and Paul McCartney) © 1964 Northern Songs Limited. All rights for the U.S.A., Mexico and the Philippines controlled by Maclen Music, Inc. by arrangement with Unart Music Corporation. Used by permission. All rights reserved.

204-205   Methods of Contraception chart, adapted from "Family Planning Methods of Contraception." Courtesy of DHEW Publication No. (HSA) 80—5646, Department of Health and Human Services, Public Health Service, Health Services Administration.

Cover photograph: Kathryn Abbe
Original illustrations: Melissa Brenner
Photographs: Terry Cuffel
Cartoons: Penny Banks
In-house editor: Joanne Abrams

Library of Congress Cataloging-in-Publication Data
Brinkley, Ginny.
    Your child's first journey.

    Bibliography: p.
    Includes index.
    1. Pregnancy. 2. Childbirth. I. Goldberg, Linda.
II. Kukar, Janice. III. Title.
RG525.B665   1988   618.2'4   87—33657
ISBN 0—89529—372—2 (pbk.)

Contents

A complete listing of options for pregnancy, labor, delivery, postpartum and cesarean birth to aid you in making informed choices. Also includes the Pregnant Patient's Bill of Rights and Responsibilities.

A detailed explanation of fetal development beginning with conception. The physical and emotional changes of each trimester, discussions of sexual relations, prenatal care, high-risk pregnancy and medical tests are presented.

Complete nutritional information emphasizing the pregnant woman's needs during each trimester. Presents the "no-risk" pregnancy diet. Also discusses use of non-food items and drugs, and provides general hints for better family nutrition.

A total exercise guide for pregnancy, designed to maintain physical well-being, prepare your body for birth and relieve discomforts.

Step-by-step guide to the Lamaze basics: relaxation to reduce tension and breathing techniques to cope with labor contractions. Also includes discussions of pushing positions and techniques, visualization, and acupressure.

Dedication

With much love, this is dedicated to our wonderful families: our husbands, Bill Brinkley, Bill Goldberg and Dave Kukar, who continue to stand by us with words of encouragement; our loving children, Scott and Brett Hewitt, Jeffrey and Rebecca Goldberg, and Bobby and Tommy Kukar, who joined us in experiencing the wonders of home computers (as compared to the many traumas endured—theirs *and* ours—during the cut-and-paste days of our first edition); and Jonathan Goldberg, whose birth provided the inspiration for our revised edition.

And to the more than 100,000 women and couples throughout the world who read and utilized the first edition of *Your Child's First Journey*.

Acknowledgements

It is with much happiness and a bit of amazement that we have revised *Your Child's First Journey* for publication of its second edition. To know that so many couples throughout the world have read and benefited from our initial effort brings great satisfaction. The numerous comments, suggestions and words of praise received from readers near and far are all appreciated, and each has been carefully considered in formulating the revised edition. With the help of our wonderful readers, the second edition contains the most current information available in 1988.

We would again like to thank all those who gave so much time and effort to assist us on the first edition. Much of their work continues to appear on these pages—Melissa Brenner's artwork, and Penny Banks's cartoons. In addition, some of the efforts of our original crew of contributors, rewriters and proofreaders can still be recognized throughout the text. These include the following workers:

Melissa Brenner
Mary Lee Buess
Audrey Burnsed
Linda Dunlap
Lani Ebert
Sally Edwards
Kris Goff
Mary Jane Green
Peggy Heifner
Jan Leary
Susan Patton

Betty Peck
Marilyn Rotchford
Barbara Teitelman
Alice Trainer

Many of the excellent photos from the first edition of the text continue to enhance the pages of this new edition. We would like to thank Mark Hildreth, Janet McIlroy and Mary Jane Green, who provided us with these photos. In addition, we greatly appreciate the artistry of photographer Terry Cuffel, whose work can be seen throughout this edition.

Special thanks go to Andrea R. Mann, M.S.N., and Anita Sherbanee, R.N., B.S.N., for their assistance on the new First Aid and Infant CPR sections, and to the following people who appear in our photos:

William and Kathy Aldridge
Terri and Carlton Allen
Pamela and Bradford Ames, Jr.
Peggy Bell
Carolyn and Amy Birch
Robert and Anna Blade
George and Deborah Blaylock
Patti Bradley
Clowtee and Caleb Brown
Terry Ann and Stephanie Cuffel
Leonard and Norma Danzler
Debbie Fischbach
Wayne Fonoti
Wayne and Wendy Gaff

Bill, Jeff, Becky and Jonathan Goldberg
Ashlen Harnett
Peggy, Heather, Derek and Alan Heifner
Howard and Pamela Hildreth
Mark and Janet Hildreth
Julie Huggins
B. Freeman Irby
Bobbie Johnson
Georgia and Gregory Johnson
Max Karrer
Joy King
Mary Lou Lawrence
Taffy Louis
Alice Marcinkoski
Victor, Casey and Jesse Leigh Mizzone
Majibullah Mojadidi

John and Josephine Oetjen
Mary and Natalie Pierce
Vickie Pope
Larry and Cheryl Ridley
Marisol and Santiago Rivera
Susan Robinson
Kenneth Sekine
Mark, Penny and Joshua Skenes

Again, much heartfelt appreciation belongs to the many expectant couples who have read *Your Child's First Journey* and have recommended it to their friends. These are the people who are ultimately responsible for the publication of our second edition.

About the Authors

Ginny Brinkley, B.S., M.B.A., is a graduate of Mary Washington College of the University of Virginia and has a Master of Business Administration degree from the University of North Florida. One of the original members of the Jacksonville CEA, she has served that organization as both Childbirth Education Coordinator and Executive Director, and has been a member of their Board of Directors since 1985.

Ginny's family includes her husband Bill and two sons, Scott and Brett Hewitt, both Lamaze babies and both breastfed.

Linda Goldberg, R.N., C.C.E., is a graduate of Helene Fuld School of Nursing at West Jersey Hospital. She has taught childbirth classes since 1977 and was Director of Instructor Training and Certification for the CEA of Jacksonville. She served as Vice President and President of that organization prior to moving to Winter Springs, Florida in 1984. Since 1985, Linda has taught childbirth education for an out-of-hospital birth center in Orlando.

Linda and her husband Bill have three children, Jeffrey, Rebecca and Jonathan, all delivered using the Lamaze method and all breastfed.

Janice Kukar, B.A., A.C.C.E., is a graduate of Michigan State University with a degree in home economics education and human development. An adult educator for ten years prior to adopting a baby, Janice has been an instructor with the CEA of Jacksonville since 1979. She has served as Volunteer Coordinator of that organization, as well as Associate Director, in charge of teacher training and evaluation.

Jan and her husband David have two sons, Bobby, adopted at four months, and Tommy, delivered using the Lamaze method and breastfed.

Ginny Brinkley

Linda Goldberg

Janice Kukar

Foreword

A WORD ABOUT CEA
OF JACKSONVILLE

On a March evening in 1971, seven enthusiastic couples gathered in a home on the southside of Jacksonville to discuss childbirth. Several of the couples had experienced shared Lamaze deliveries in other cities. The rest had heard or read about family centered maternity care and hoped to initiate the concept locally. At that time Jacksonville area hospitals were not allowing husbands in either labor or delivery rooms.

The little group of "fanatics" talked for long hours into the night organizing the CEA of Jacksonville and finally making the decision to begin sponsoring Lamaze classes. By June, an instructor was recruited to commute once a week from a nearby city, and the first class was filled through word of mouth with twelve expectant and eager couples.

Opposition from the medical community was strong as the prepared couples began requesting certain alternatives. One father-to-be made the comment that attending Lamaze classes and not sharing in his child's birth was like taking flying lessons and never being allowed to fly an airplane! Classes began every six weeks throughout the summer, as two CEA members became trained as instructors. A victory for consumerism was accomplished in November of that year when the first husband was permitted in the delivery room of a major local hospital. Within a few months other area hospitals had followed suit.

In less than ten years, CEA expanded to reach 2,000 couples per year through its classes. During that time, the organization was instrumental in bringing about such changes as rooming-in, bonding, husband-attended cesarean births, and sibling visitation in Jacksonville hospitals. In addition, four area hospitals have established birthing rooms in response to consumer requests.

Since 1983, CEA has been an agency of the United Way of Northeast Florida, which has made it possible to offer childbirth and parenting information to low-income expectant couples.

Along with its many class offerings, the CEA of Jacksonville provides a labor coaching service, breastpump rental, car seat rental and a support group for bereaved parents, and serves as a community resource center and referral service. Additionally, CEA promotes professional education through its extensive teacher training program and through regular workshops provided to nurses as well as childbirth educators. CEA is a member group of the International Childbirth Education Association (ICEA), which provides its members with the most current information on birthing issues.

The CEA of Jacksonville is a living testimony to the importance of consumerism and the far-reaching influence of a few enthusiastic couples. This book is a natural extension of CEA. It is a labor of love, to be provided to every couple desiring to make educated decisions on that most important event in their lives—their child's first journey.

Introduction

This book is designed to accompany the pregnant woman from her early months of pregnancy through the early months of parenthood. It provides the information needed to have a healthy, enjoyable pregnancy and an awake and aware childbirth experience, as well as helpful hints on parenting.

WHAT IS "FAMILY CENTERED MATERNITY CARE"?

The concept of family centered maternity care (FCMC) is promoted throughout the book, whereby the needs and feelings of mother, father and baby are of utmost importance, second only to the safety of mother and baby. FCMC stresses family togetherness during childbirth, rather than a woman laboring alone in an isolated room while her husband is somewhere else pacing the floor.

Family centered maternity care includes such concepts as fathers participating in labor, delivery and cesarean birth, bonding, rooming-in, sibling involvement, and the presence of other family members during labor and delivery, all of which are discussed in the book.

FCMC is promoted not simply for the emotional benefits. It also contributes to the physical health and well-being of mother and baby. Studies have shown that the presence of a support person (husband or other significant loved one) during labor tends to decrease the length of labor and the number of complications.[1]

ABOUT LAMAZE

The type of childbirth preparation provided here is termed Lamaze, (pronounced LeMahz) named for the French doctor, Fernand Lamaze, who discovered that laboring women could benefit from the conditioning techniques originated by the Russian scientist Pavlov. Lamaze preparation, however, is more than just a set of exercises. It is an attitude whereby the couple accepts responsibility for their childbirth experience. Lamaze, therefore, requires you to become familiar with many techniques and procedures, and to choose those which you feel will best contribute to the type of childbirth you desire. This is why there is no success or failure in Lamaze. Each childbirth is unique. The ultimate experience is achieved when you can make informed decisions concerning the management of your labor and delivery. This is accomplished through education and preparation. It also requires the knowledgeable seeking out of those birthing facilities and medical attendants which will most enhance the type of birth you desire.

The term *natural* childbirth is not appropriate when referring to Lamaze because natural does not include the concept of preparation. Lamaze implies prepared childbirth.

As in many scientific and medical fields, the techniques of Lamaze are constantly changing. The Lamaze of today is quite different from that of Dr. Lamaze's day, over 30 years ago. Aware childbirth educators are constantly updating and revising their teaching methods in order to incorporate those relaxation and breathing techniques which they have found to be most beneficial for the majority of couples. The techniques provided in this book are the most current of any taught in the U.S. today.

WHAT THE BOOK WILL DO FOR YOU

The purpose of the book is two-fold. First, it provides the tools to be utilized by you, the expectant couple, throughout pregnancy and birth, some of which must be studied and practiced many times for maximum benefit. Second, the book conveys an attitude—one of awareness and responsibility by which educated decisions may be made.

Whether this is your first baby or your first Lamaze baby, the information presented here will enable you to make this baby's birth a truly rewarding and memorable experience.

For the sake of clarity, the pronoun *she* is used in reference to the mother and the nurse, and *he* is used when referring to the labor partner, baby and doctor.

HOW TO USE THE BOOK

The book is intended to be used in conjunction with early pregnancy, Lamaze and new mothers' classes. The chapter on cesarean birth makes it an appropriate manual for cesarean preparation classes. When being used individually, rather than in a class setting, the book should first be read briefly from cover to cover. Then the various sections should be studied in more detail appropriate to the different stages of pregnancy: for example, the nutrition chapter during the early months, relaxation and breathing during the later months, etc.

[1]John Kennell, ICEA Convention, Detroit, July 2, 1980.

Chapter 1

The Rights and Responsibilities Involved in Achieving An Optimum Birth Experience

or "This is not Intended to Drive Your Doctor Crazy"

Pregnancy is a time of heightened awareness. You become aware of the changes in your body, in your way of thinking and in your priorities. You must also become aware of the choices which may help to determine how you feel about your birth experience, your baby and yourselves as parents. You have the right, as consumers and parents, to know about the different options available. You have the responsibility, as well, to learn as much as possible, through classes, your doctor or midwife, and independent reading, in order to make informed, considered choices concerning your own birth experience.

THE FIRST STEP— CHOOSING YOUR BIRTH ATTENDANT

Your birth attendant is that person whom you select to provide prenatal care and deliver your baby. The choice of this important person may have a significant effect on the type of birth experience you have. The question, "How do I find the best birth attendant?" should be discussed before becoming pregnant, if possible. Early in pregnancy you have sufficient time for interviewing and exploring the options. However, even late in pregnancy, couples have found it appropriate to change their birth attendant. It is best if both husband and wife can be present for the interview.

According to Dr. Silvia Feldman in her book, *Choices in Childbirth*, the "Choice of a birth assistant should be determined by three things: his or her expertise, philosophy, and personality."[1] Dr. Feldman

recommends, in cases of projected normal pregnancy and childbirth, that couples should interview several birth attendants using an organized list of specific needs and wishes. It is important to be assertive in an interview, and to watch the prospective birth attendant for body language and tone of voice. Be wary if he is too easy going and quick to go along with every request without reservation. A physician who is truly supportive provides more than just yes or no answers. He takes time to discuss his feelings and encourages you to attend pregnancy and birth classes. A good exchange of views without sarcasm or hostility establishes a good rapport and a feeling of mutual trust and sincerity. You may also want to verify the credentials of the doctor or midwife. For example, find out if the midwife is a certified nurse midwife or simply a lay midwife.

A conscientious, up-to-date birth attendant will bring up nutrition and give advice on dietary planning for pregnancy. A rigid attitude about weight gain is not desirable. Rather, he should have enthusiasm about getting enough protein and calories in the diet to allow for healthy development in the mother and baby. Questions concerning his practice of family centered maternity care are also important. In addition, information about his cesarean rate, reasons he considers absolute for cesarean, and his willingness to discuss options with you can provide you with adequate knowledge for choosing the correct birth attendant.

Many American women prefer the obstetrician as a birth attendant because of his training in han-

Choose your options wisely.

dling problems that may arise. Other doctors in family or general practice also deliver babies. A certified nurse midwife's experience and training are in handling the normal, uncomplicated birth. Because of this training, as well as her outlook, a midwife is less likely to use medical interventions in the course of labor and delivery. In the event of any problems, the nurse midwife refers the woman to an obstetrician. If you are considering employing a midwife, you may also want to have a consultation with her medical back-up.

OPTIMUM BIRTH— THE OPTIONS INVOLVED

The following is a list of options in which many couples have shown an interest. Not all of these options will be appropriate for you. Some may not be currently available in your area, but all of them are possibilities to be discussed and reasoned through with your birth attendant. If any of these options appeal to you, and your birth attendant refuses your request, encourage him to tell you why. If you feel strongly that a lack of communication or understanding exists between you and any member of your medical team, you have the option of seeking care elsewhere. But be sure that you inform all those involved and state the reason for your decision. The only way to get people to change their minds or their behavior is to let them know you are not satisfied!

These options are listed according to pregnancy, labor, delivery and postpartum. They are geared to the **low-risk woman experiencing a normal, uncomplicated labor and birth**. Also included is a section devoted entirely to cesarean couples, with options for them to discuss with their doctors. With the rising cesarean rate, *every* couple should be prepared for a vaginal *or* a cesarean birth, and the options for both should be thought through long before birth occurs. Read the list and check those options which are important to you. Then add any other desires which you may have for your birth experience. This will be your birth plan. Take it with you to be discussed thoroughly when choosing or consulting with your doctor or midwife.

After you and your birth attendant have agreed on your birth plan, you may want to make several copies of it—one to be kept with your record, one for your labor partner and one to give to the nursing staff when you enter the hospital. It is often recommended that you have your physician or midwife sign or initial all copies of your birth plan to indicate their agreement with your desires.

PREGNANCY

OPTIONS	REASONING
☐ **Optimum nutrition**	The "no-risk" pregnancy diet can reduce the danger of complications, for yourself and your baby, to the lowest possible level.[2] See Chapter 3.
☐ **Supportive medical attendant willing to be flexible in your labor and delivery choices, including birth place (birth center or hospital)**	Careful selection of your attendant can eliminate the stress of trying to change the attitudes of a doctor or midwife who will not consider your individual wishes. Some low-risk women feel more at home in an out-of-hospital birth center. Others feel safer within the hospital environment.

PREGNANCY (continued)

OPTIONS	REASONING
☐ **Consumer oriented childbirth classes**	Consumer oriented classes inform you about all available options rather than the routine of a particular hospital or doctor. This enables you to make educated decisions about what options you want in your childbirth experience, and provides you as well with thorough training for labor and delivery.
☐ **Refrain from smoking, drugs and alcoholic beverages**	These have been shown by authorities to have adverse effects on the baby. See Chapter 3.
☐ **No routine use of ultrasound during pregnancy**	The FDA and NIH have stated that ultrasound has not been *proven* safe for use during pregnancy and should only be used when medically indicated. See Chapter 2.

LABOR

OPTIONS	REASONING
☐ **Presence of a support person during admission procedures and examinations if desired**	Presence of partner during admission procedures eliminates the stress of separation.
☐ **Presence of a support person for labor and birth**	A trained partner supplies the necessary physical and emotional support so vital during labor and delivery. His presence enhances bonding of the family.
☐ **Presence of other family members or friends during labor and/or delivery**	They can provide additional support for the laboring woman and her partner. Incidence of infection has not increased as long as those present have no signs of illness (runny nose, diarrhea, etc.).
☐ **Presence of professional labor support person (childbirth instructor, R.N. or midwife not associated with hospital in which birth is taking place)**	A knowledgeable professional who has a strong commitment to the type of birth you desire can provide you with additional information when circumstances arise.
☐ **Freedom to move about and assume a position of comfort**	Walking stimulates the uterus to work more efficiently. Labors conducted in this manner are documented to be shorter, and less pain medication is needed.[3] Sitting up, lying on side, or on hands and knees may be most comfortable.
☐ **Liquid nourishment or light snacks in early labor**	Supplies energy needed for more advanced labor.
☐ **Ice chips or sips of water**	Mouth becomes very dry doing the breathing patterns.
☐ **Personal items of choice (nightgown, music, flowers, etc.)**	Familiar articles enhance the birth experience by encouraging relaxation and comfort.
☐ **No prep (shaving of the pubic hair) unless desired**	Shaving of the pubic area does not decrease the incidence of infection, and the regrowth of hair is uncomfortable. See Chapter 6.

LABOR (continued)

OPTIONS	REASONING
☐ **No enema unless needed**	An enema is unnecessary if you have had a good bowel movement or have experienced diarrhea within 24 hours.[4] A soapsuds enema can be very uncomfortable for the laboring woman. If you have been constipated, an enema may be desired, but a small fleet enema will suffice. See Chapter 6.
☐ **Intravenous fluids only if medically indicated**	I.V.'s restrict mobility and interfere with relaxation. Clear liquids in early labor reduce the chance of dehydration. Hemorrhage is rare when the birth is unmedicated and spontaneous, and when immediate breastfeeding is initiated. See Chapter 8.
☐ **Electronic fetal monitor only if medically indicated**	In a low-risk woman, frequent auscultation (listening to the fetal heart rate) by a trained nurse has been shown to be as effective in detecting fetal well-being or distress as the electronic monitor.[5] The fetal monitor restricts movement, can be uncomfortable, and sometimes women are instructed to lie on their backs. As an alternative to being monitored throughout the labor, the monitor can be used for only a short period of time to determine the baby's response to contractions, then removed. See Chapter 8.
☐ **Spontaneous rupture of membranes**	The amniotic fluid contained in the membranes has a cushioning effect, equalizing pressure which results in less molding of the baby's head. Artificial rupture of the membranes provides a passageway for infection and creates a "time limit" for delivery. See Chapter 8.
☐ **Medication administered only as requested by you, and with full information as to the possible effects on you, the baby, and the labor itself**	You should actively seek information on which drugs your particular birth attendant uses most often. You should discuss your feelings prior to labor, and you should have the option of changing your mind once you are in labor. You may refuse medication! But you should be able to state your reason for doing so. See Chapter 7.
☐ **Pitocin, used to induce or augment labor, only if medically indicated**	Contractions induced by pitocin are more difficult to handle, for both you and the baby, than natural contractions. The risks of induction include reducing the baby's oxygen supply and of birthing a premature baby. These risks are not warranted solely for the convenience of mother or doctor (elective induction). Complications that may develop in a labor involving pitocin can increase the chances of cesarean delivery.[6] See Chapter 8.

DELIVERY

OPTIONS	REASONING
☐ **Use of a birthing room or laboring and delivering in the same bed**	Avoids stress and discomfort involved during the expulsion stage when a woman is hurriedly transported to the delivery room and then awkwardly moved to the delivery table. You are often told not to push until everything is "in position," while having contractions in which the urge to push is overwhelming. See Chapter 6.

DELIVERY (continued)

OPTIONS	REASONING
☐ **Comfortable and efficient pushing and delivery position**	Semi-reclined at a 70° angle, side-lying, or kneeling may be more comfortable than being flat on your back. Lying flat on your back reduces the pelvic outlet to its smallest diameter,[7] may be uncomfortable, and the weight of the uterus may impede blood flow. In the squat position, the birth canal is shortened, the pelvic outlet is at its widest, and the contractions are more efficient as the uterus is assisted by gravity.[8] See Chapter 5.
☐ **Avoid use of stirrups**	Lithotomy position with legs up in stirrups works against gravity and results in the woman pushing the baby uphill. Wide stirrups, while giving the birth attendant a good field of vision in which to work, cause the perineum to be stretched taut and increase the need for an episiotomy.[9] See Chapter 5.
☐ **Episiotomy (small incision in vaginal outlet to enlarge the opening) done only if needed**	By allowing the baby's head to emerge slowly under uterine force alone, perineal tissue has a better chance to stretch, and this minimizes tearing. The decision to do an episiotomy should be made as the baby's head distends the perineum; many doctors, however, routinely do an episiotomy whether or not the woman needs one. If an episiotomy is needed, it should be done at crowning. Healing of the episiotomy may be very uncomfortable during the postpartum period. It can cause muscle scarring which may negatively affect sexual pleasure.
☐ **Use of regional anesthesia if medical or surgical intervention becomes necessary**	Anesthesia is unnecessary in an uncomplicated delivery. If an episiotomy is done, a local anesthetic may be given after the delivery for the repair. Regional anesthesia is compatible with an awake delivery; general anesthesia (gas or sodium pentothal) is not. See Chapter 7.
☐ **Leboyer delivery (gentle birth)**	A gentle birth decreases the sensory and physical trauma to the infant as he is delivered. This is an attitude as well as a procedure. See Chapter 8.
☐ **Delay cutting the cord until it stops pulsating**	Allows baby to receive extra blood which decreases the chance of anoxia. Allows infant to continue to receive oxygen through the cord while his respiratory system begins to function. See Chapter 6.
☐ **Father permitted to cut umbilical cord**	Increases his participation in the birth.
☐ **Infant placed immediately onto your bare abdomen or into your arms**	Immediate skin-to-skin contact is beneficial. When both mother and baby are covered with a blanket, the infant's temperature can be maintained. See Chapter 6.

DELIVERY (continued)

OPTIONS	REASONING
☐ **Allow infant to breastfeed as soon as possible**	Baby's sucking stimulates oxytocin which aids in the release of the placenta and decreases postpartum bleeding. Infant's sucking reflex is strongest at birth. Colostrum acts as a laxative, cleansing the intestinal tract of mucus and meconium, and also gives the infant antibodies.
☐ **Delay antibiotic ointment or silver nitrate drops until after bonding**	These can interfere with the baby's vision which is so important during the attachment period. See Chapter 6.
☐ **Allow placenta to detach from the wall of the uterus spontaneously**	Strong traction or massaging may cause placental tissue to be retained which can cause postpartum bleeding. See Chapter 6.
☐ **Bonding**	The first hour after birth is very important in developing maternal and paternal attachment to the newborn. See Chapter 6.
☐ **Take snapshots, videotapes, tape recording of birth**	Provides a wonderful way to relive these unforgettable moments.

POSTPARTUM

OPTIONS	REASONING
☐ **Breastfeeding**	Nutritionally, it is the perfect food for your baby. It is an emotionally satisfying experience for you and the infant. Breastfeeding is economical. Nursing aids in returning the uterus to its prepregnant state faster.
☐ **No supplements (water or formula) if breastfeeding**	Drinking from a rubber nipple can confuse baby (milk comes out easily, and he may get lazy and won't nurse). Baby will not be hungry when he comes to you for feeding and not nurse well if fed supplements between nursings. See Chapter 11.
☐ **You and your baby discharged from the hospital within 24 hours after birth**	Reduces hospital costs; decreases chances of hospital-induced infections. Decreases separation time from other children.
☐ **Flexible rooming-in**	Allows both parents and baby close contact to enhance the bonding process as you desire, depending on your postpartum condition. Permits breastfeeding on demand rather than on a rigid schedule. You are able to acquire skills in baby care under supervision of hospital staff. See Chapter 6.
☐ **Sibling visitation with mother and baby**	Helps reassure other children that you are fine. Encourages acceptance of the new baby by the siblings. See Chapter 6.

POSTPARTUM (continued)

OPTIONS	REASONING
☐ **No circumcision unless desired**	Circumcision is part of a Jewish tradition. There is no medical reason for doing it routinely.[10] It is preferable to delay this procedure until 12-24 hours after birth to allow the infant time to adjust to extrauterine life. May cause bleeding or infection. See Chapter 10.

CESAREAN BIRTH OPTIONS

A cesarean delivery can be a very rewarding experience for those couples who prepare and participate in the birth. Even an unexpected or emergency cesarean birth can be family centered if you prepare ahead "just in case."

If you have chosen a nurse midwife as your birth attendant, these options should be discussed with her physician back-up. See Chapter 9.

CESAREAN BIRTH

OPTIONS	REASONING
☐ **Supportive physician, hospital, and agreeable anesthesiologist, willing to allow a family centered Cesarean birth**	Careful selection will insure family participation in the event of a cesarean delivery.
☐ **Participation in the birth process by support person (special classes may be required)**	A support person provides emotional security during this special experience.
☐ **Admission on day of surgery/ birth for planned cesareans**	Gives you one more night at home. Can mean a better night's sleep and extra time with husband and other children.
☐ **Permission to wait for labor to begin before a planned cesarean is performed**	Labor is nature's way of telling you it is time to have your baby (lessens chance of premature baby).
☐ **Partial prep (shaving from abdomen to pubic bone)**	Minimizes the uncomfortable feeling while pubic hair is growing back in.
☐ **No preoperative sedation**	All medication may affect the baby. Relaxation techniques can be used prior to surgery. Medication may also affect your ability to interact with the baby at birth.[11]
☐ **Choice of anesthesia which allows you to be awake for the surgery/birth**	Except in the case of an acute emergency, adequate time for regional anesthesia to be given is usually available. This allows you to be awake when your baby is delivered and facilitates bonding.
☐ **Knowledge of different procedures associated with cesarean birth (lab tests, prep, catheter in bladder, etc.)**	Awareness of what is to be done fosters a more relaxed birth experience.

CESAREAN BIRTH (continued)

	OPTIONS	REASONING
☐	**Lowering of drape during the delivery**	Allows mother and father to view the birth of their baby.
☐	**Judgment of baby's condition on an individual basis**	A pediatrician's evaluation and approval of a baby's condition can mean contact with mother and father soon after birth. Rooming-in may begin sooner. Placement in the newborn nursery instead of intensive care may be indicated if there are no respiratory problems.
☐	**Permission to nurse baby on delivery table or as soon as possible**	Allows baby and mother the same advantages of early nursing as following a vaginal delivery.
☐	**Bonding to take place as soon after birth as feasible (ideally, in recovery while the regional anesthesia is still in effect)**	Holding and touching the baby can reduce parental anxiety along with providing the benefits of early bonding.
☐	**Rooming-in on a flexible basis**	Allows you to care for your baby as you are able. Enhances bonding and breastfeeding. A cesarean mother benefits from her support person's additional help, as well as the hospital staff's assistance.

THE PREGNANT PATIENT'S BILL OF RIGHTS AND RESPONSIBILITIES

Included in this chapter are "The Pregnant Patient's Bill of Rights" and "The Pregnant Patient's Responsibilities." These have been prepared by the International Childbirth Education Association (ICEA), to expand your awareness of what rights and responsibilities you have as expectant parents.

Your obstetrician has the legal obligation of obtaining your "informed consent" prior to treatment. "Informed consent" means you have received information regarding the treatment as to what is involved, including whether the treatment is new or unusual, the risks and hazards, chances for recovery after the treatment, necessity of the treatment, and the feasibility of alternative methods of treatment. This information must be explained so that you understand it thoroughly. Reasons such as "the patient may prefer not to be told the unpleasant possibilities of the treatment;" that "full disclosure might suggest infinite dangers to a patient with an active imagination, thereby causing her to refuse treatment;" or that "the patient, on learning the risks involved, might rationally decline treatment" are not sufficient reasons to justify failure to inform. [12]

If medical or surgical intervention is discussed with you during your pregnancy, labor, delivery and postpartum, it is important that you be aware of your rights and also your responsibilities in either accepting or refusing the suggested treatment.

THE PREGNANT PATIENT'S BILL OF RIGHTS

American parents are becoming increasingly aware that well-intentioned health professionals do not always have scientific data to support common American obstetrical practices and that many of these practices are carried out primarily because they are part of medical and hospital tradition. In the last forty years many artificial practices have been introduced which have changed childbirth from a physiological event to a very complicated medical procedure in which all kinds of drugs are used and procedures carried out, sometimes unnecessarily, and many of them potentially damaging for the baby and even for the mother. A growing body of research makes it alarmingly clear that every aspect of traditional American hospital care during labor and delivery must now be questioned as to its possible effect on the future well-being of both the obstetric patient and her unborn child.

One in every 35 children born in the United States today will eventually be diagnosed as retarded; in 75% of these cases there is no familial or genetic predisposing factor. One in every 10 to 17 children has been found to have some form of brain dysfunction or learning disability requiring special treatment. Such statistics are not confined to the lower socioeconomic group but cut across all segments of American society.

New concerns are being raised by childbearing women because no one knows what degree of oxygen depletion, head compression, or traction by forceps the unborn or newborn infant can tolerate before that child sustains permanent brain damage or dysfunction. The recent findings regarding the cancer-related drug diethylstilbestrol have alerted the public to the fact that neither the approval of a drug by the U.S. Food and Drug Administration nor the fact that a drug is prescribed by a physician serves as a guarantee that a drug or medication is safe for the mother or her unborn child. In fact, the American Academy of Pediatrics' Committee on Drugs has recently stated that there is no drug, whether prescription or over-the-counter remedy, which has been proven safe for the unborn child.

The Pregnant Patient has the right to participate in decisions involving her well-being and that of her unborn child, unless there is a clearcut medical emergency that prevents her participation. In addition to the rights set forth in the American Hospital Association's "Patient's Bill of Rights," (which has also been adopted by the New York City Department of Health) the Pregnant Patient, because she represents TWO patients rather than one, should be recognized as having the additional rights listed below.

1. *The Pregnant Patient has the right,* prior to the administration of any drug or procedure, to be informed by the health professional caring for her of any potential direct or indirect effects, risks or hazards to herself or her unborn or newborn infant which may result from the use of a drug or procedure prescribed for or administered to her during pregnancy, labor, birth or lactation.

2. *The Pregnant Patient has the right,* prior to the proposed therapy, to be informed, not only of the benefits, risks and hazards of the proposed therapy but also of known alternative therapy, such as available childbirth education classes which could help to prepare the Pregnant Patient physically and mentally to cope with the discomfort or stress of pregnancy and the experience of childbirth, thereby reducing or eliminating her need for drugs and obstertic intervention. She should be offered such information early in her pregnancy in order that she may make a reasoned decision.

3. *The Pregnant Patient has the right,* prior to the administration of any drug, to be informed by the health professional who is prescribing or administering the drug to her that any drug which she receives during pregnancy, labor and birth, no matter how or when the drug is taken or administered, may adversely affect her unborn baby, directly or indirectly, and that there is no drug or chemical which has been proven safe for the unborn child.

4. *The Pregnant Patient has the right* if Cesarean birth is anticipated, to be informed prior to the administration of any drug, and preferably prior to her hospitalization, that minimizing her and, in turn, her baby's intake of nonessential pre-operative medicine will benefit her baby.

5. *The Pregnant Patient has the right,* prior to the administration of a drug or procedure, to be informed of the areas of uncertainty if there is NO properly controlled follow-up research which has established the safety of the drug or procedure with regard to its direct and/or indirect effects on the physiological, mental and neurological development of the child exposed, via the mother, to the drug or procedure during pregnancy, labor, birth or lactation — (this would apply to virtually all drugs and the vast majority of obstetric procedures).

6. *The Pregnant Patient has the right,* prior to the administration of any drug, to be informed of the brand name and generic name of the drug in order that she may advise the health professional of any past adverse reaction to the drug.

7. *The Pregnant Patient has the right* to determine for herself, without pressure from her attendant, whether she will accept the risks inherent in the proposed therapy or refuse a drug or procedure.

8. *The Pregnant Patient has the right* to know the name and qualifications of the individual administering a medication or procedure to her during labor or birth.

9. *The Pregnant Patient has the right* to be informed, prior to the administration of any procedure, whether that procedure is being administered to her for her or her baby's benefit (medically indicated) or as an elective procedure (for convenience, teaching purposes or research).

10. *The Pregnant Patient has the right* to be accompanied during the stress of labor and birth by someone she cares for, and to whom she looks for emotional comfort and encouragement.

11. *The Pregnant Patient has the right* after appropriate medical consultation to choose a position for labor and for birth which is least stressful to her baby and to herself.

12. *The Obstetric Patient has the right* to have her baby cared for at her bedside if her baby is normal, and to feed her baby according to her baby's needs rather than according to the hospital regimen.

13. *The Obstetric Patient has the right* to be informed in writing of the name of the person who actually delivered her baby and the professional qualifications of that person. This information should also be on the birth certificate.

14. *The Obstetric Patient has the right* to be informed if there is any known or indicated aspect of her or her baby's care or condition which may cause her or her baby later difficulty or problems.

15. *The Obstetric Patient has the right* to have her and her baby's hospital medical records complete, accurate and legible and to have their records, including Nurses' Notes, retained by the hospital until the child reaches at least the age of majority, or, alternatively, to have the records offered to her before they are destroyed.

16. *The Obstetric Patient,* both during and after her hospital stay, has the right to have access to her complete hospital medical records, including Nurses' Notes, and to receive a copy upon payment of a reasonable fee and without incurring the expense of retaining an attorney.

It is the obstetric patient and her baby, not the health professional, who must sustain any trauma or injury resulting from the use of a drug or obstetric procedure. The observation of the rights listed above will not only permit the obstetric patient to participate in the decisions involving her and her baby's health care, but will help to protect the health professional and the hospital against litigation arising from resentment or misunderstanding on the part of the mother.

Prepared by Doris Haire

THE PREGNANT PATIENT'S RESPONSIBILITIES

In addition to understanding her rights the Pregnant Patient should also understand that she too has certain responsibilities. The Pregnant Patient's responsibilities include the following:

1. The Pregnant Patient is responsible for learning about the physical and psychological process of labor, birth and postpartum recovery. The better informed expectant parents are the better they will be able to participate in decisions concerning the planning of their care.

2. The Pregnant Patient is responsible for learning what comprises good prenatal and intranatal care and for making an effort to obtain the best care possible.

3. Expectant parents are responsible for knowing about those hospital policies and regulations which will affect their birth and postpartum experience.

4. The Pregnant Patient is responsible for arranging for a companion or support person (husband, mother, sister, friend, etc.) who will share in her plans for birth and who will accompany her during her labor and birth experience.

5. The Pregnant Patient is responsible for making her preferences known clearly to the health professionals involved in her case in a courteous and cooperative manner and for making mutually agreed-upon arrangements regarding maternity care alternatives with her physician and hospital in advance of labor.

6. Expectant parents are responsible for listening to their chosen physician or midwife with an open mind, just as they expect him or her to listen openly to them.

7. Once they have agreed to a course of health care, expectant parents are responsible, to the best of their ability, for seeing that the program is carried out in consultation with others with whom they have made the agreement.

8. The Pregnant Patient is responsible for obtaining information in advance regarding the approximate cost of her obstetric and hospital care.

9. The Pregnant Patient who intends to change her physician or hospital is responsible for notifying all concerned, well in advance of the birth if possible, and for informing both of her reasons for changing.

10. In all their interactions with medical and nursing personnel, the expectant parents should behave towards those caring for them with the same respect and consideration they themselves would like.

11. During the mother's hospital stay the mother is responsible for learning about her and her baby's continuing care after discharge from the hospital.

12. After birth, the parents should put into writing constructive comments and feelings of satisfaction and/or dissatisfaction with the care (nursing, medical and personal) they received. Good service to families in the future will be facilitated by those parents who take the time and responsibility to write letters expressing their feelings about the maternity care they received.

All the previous statements assume a normal birth and postpartum experience. Expectant parents should realize that, if complications develop in their cases, there will be an increased need to trust the expertise of the physician and hospital staff they have chosen. However, if problems occur, the childbearing woman still retains her responsibility for making informed decisions about her care or treatment and that of her baby. If she is incapable of assuming that responsibility because of her physical condition, her previously authorized companion or support person should assume responsibility for making informed decisions on her behalf.

Prepared by Members of ICEA

FOOTNOTES

Chapter One

1. Silvia Feldman, *Choices in Childbirth* (N. Y., Grosset and Dunlap, 1978), p. 160.
2. Gail Sforza Brewer, *Pregnancy After 30 Workbook* (Emmaus, Pa., Rodale Press, 1978), p. 43.
3. "Maternal Position During Labor and Birth," *ICEA Review,* Vol. 2, No. 3 (Summer, 1978), pp. 2,3.
4. Nancy Whatley and Esther Mark, "Are Enemas Justified in Labor?", *American Journal of Nursing* (July, 1980), p. 1339.
5. David Banta and Stephen Thacker, "Electronic Fetal Monitoring: Is it a Benefit?", *Birth and the Family Journal* (Winter, 1979), p. 247.
6. Diony Young and Charles Mahan, *Unnecessary Cesareans, Ways to Avoid Them* (Minn., Mn.,ICEA,1980), p. 4.
7. Brewer, p. 61.
8. Brewer, p. 61.
9. "Maternal Position During Labor and Birth," pp. 2,3.
10. David Grimes, "Routine Circumcision Reconsidered," *American Journal of Nursing* (January, 1980), p. 108.
11. Young and Mahan, p. 18.
12. Introduction to "The Pregnant Patient's Bill of Rights; The Pregnant Patient's Responsibilities " (Minn., Mn., ICEA).

Chapter 2

Pregnancy

or "This Could Be the Start of Something Big"

Pregnancy begins with conception (fertilization) and continues until the moment of birth. It is that special time in your life when your body totally encompasses the growth of a new being. Everything you do, everything you eat, and even your emotional condition, may have an effect on the development of that new life. It is, therefore, very important that you are aware of those actions to take which will most benefit this development, as well as the detrimental factors which you should avoid. Your knowledge of the normal course of pregnancy will aid you in acquiring this awareness.

Each woman's pregnancy differs in some ways from every other woman's. In fact, different pregnancies in the same woman usually vary. However, some aspects of pregnancy are common to all women. Certain physical and emotional changes can be seen in every pregnant woman, resulting in similar physical and emotional needs. These common factors, experienced in all pregnancies, are discussed in the following sections.

FERTILIZATION

Every baby is formed by the union of an egg cell from a woman's body and a sperm cell from a man's body. This union is called fertilization and marks the beginning of pregnancy. The egg and sperm cells each contain one half of the genetic material, or chromosomes, necessary to begin human life. Each chromosome contains thousands of sections called genes, which determine the various characteristics of

the child. The mother and father each contribute 23 chromosomes to their child, making a total of 46. Because of the billions of possible combinations which can be produced from these 46 chromosomes and their thousands of genes, every child is unique.

The mother's biological contribution begins in one of two ovaries where an egg follicle ripens and swells. The ripening of the egg cell is initiated by a pituitary hormone. The walls of the follicle surrounding the ripening egg begin to produce estrogen, which causes the lining of the uterus, or womb, to thicken. The follicle thins out at one point, and an egg is released near the fringed end of the fallopian tubes. The release of an egg from an ovary is called ovula-

May the best sperm win!

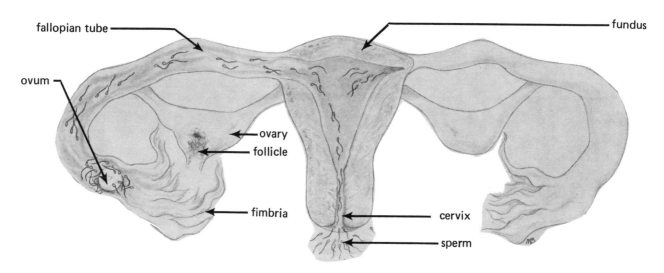

Female reproductive organs showing fertilization.

tion. The usual time for ovulation to occur is fourteen days before the next menstrual period, or about midway through the cycle.

The fallopian tubes are muscular canals lined with fine hairs (cilia) which move with a wave-like action, drawing the egg into the tube and then through it toward the uterus. Meanwhile, the follicle, stimulated by a pituitary hormone, begins producing progesterone, another hormone, which causes the uterine lining to thicken. (See illustration.)

The biological contribution the father makes to the baby begins with the production of sperm cells in his testes, two organs hanging outside of his body in a sac of skin called the scrotum. (See illustration) Sperm cells (or spermatozoa) are produced in the seminiferous tubules within the testes and are then propelled into the epididymis for storage until ejaculation. As the spermatozoa pass from the epididymis through the vas deferens to the urethra, secretions are added. These secretions are produced in glands: the seminal vesicles, the prostate and Cowper's glands. The purpose of the secretions from these glands is to provide a nourishing and fluid material to help the spermatozoa move through the vagina, where they are deposited during intercourse.

The penis becomes erect during sexual excitement as blood pours into its layers of spongy material, and the vessels leaving the penis constrict. When excited further, the muscles around the seminal vesicles, the vas deferens and the prostate gland contract, driving the semen into the urethra. The muscles in the penis contract and push the semen

through the opening of the urethra. About half a billion sperm are ejaculated.

For fertilization to occur, the sperm must reach the egg within 24 hours of ovulation. The sperm may remain viable for up to 72 hours. It takes the sperm from 30 minutes to two hours to swim from the upper vagina, where they are usually deposited, to the outer third of the fallopian tube, where fertilization takes place. The sperm may reach an egg, however, even if they are deposited externally on the vulva. Only one sperm cell, out of the thousands that may reach the egg, actually fertilizes it. The rest of the sperm are kept from penetrating the fertilized egg cell, for a reason which is still unknown.

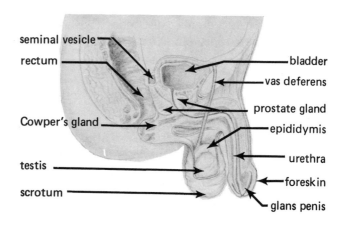

Male reproductive organs.

IMPLANTATION

The fertilized egg cell, now called an ovum, divides into two cells, then into four, and so on repeatedly. By the fourth day it is a cluster of 3 dozen cells called the morula. By the time it reaches the uterus by way of the fallopian tubes, 3-4 days later, it is a hollow ball of 150 cells separated into three layers and is known as a blastocyst. The blastocyst implants in the wall of the uterus, usually on the upper back wall, about ten days after fertilization. Projections on the outside of the blastocyst help it to attach to the thick inner lining of the uterine muscle. It then can tap into the mother's blood supply for nourishment.

FETAL DEVELOPMENT

Most of the development of the fetal organs takes place during the first trimester. At the beginning of this phase, it is a single cell. By twelve weeks the fetus is recognizable as a human, and the placenta is functioning fully to exchange nutrients and waste products.

First Week: The single cell, or "ovum" as the developing being is called for the first two weeks, divides again and again and forms a hollow ball of three cell layers. Projections called villi, appear on the outside of the ovum. These villi help the ovum to burrow into the uterus, usually on the upper back wall.

Second Week: The hollow space in the ovum now has two parts: an amniotic sac, filled with fluid, and a yolk sac, which will produce small blood vessels and cells. The yolk sac degenerates as the developing embryo is able to produce its own blood cells. The amniotic sac or "bag of waters" serves three functions: it protects the developing embryo from shocks, it keeps the temperature constant, and it serves as a barrier to infection from the outside.

Third Week: The developing being is called an "embryo" from the third to the eighth week of life. It is now the size of a pencil dot. There are buds that will grow into lungs, a tube that will become a heart, and the beginning of the central nervous system, all growing from the three layers of cells.

Fourth Week: By the end of this week, the embryo is ³⁄₁₆ of an inch long. The nervous system and brain are beginning to grow. A face is forming with a mouth, lower jaw, and dark circles where the eyes will be. The heart is beating 65 times per minute by the end of the fourth week, pumping blood around the developing blood vessels.

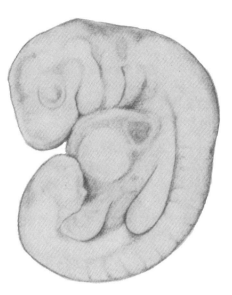

Embryo—4 weeks, actual size 3/16".

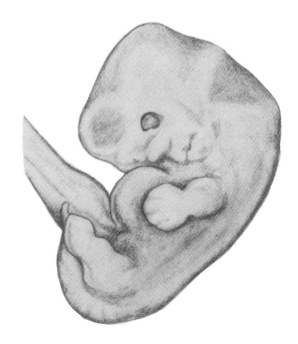

Embryo—5 weeks.

Fifth Week: The brain, spinal cord and nervous system are now more developed. From eight to ten vertebrae of the backbone are in place. Two folds of tissue that will be ears, little buds for the arms and legs, and the lenses of the eyes are appearing.

Sixth Week: By the end of this week the embryo is ¼ inch long. The brain is growing rapidly and the backbone is formed. The mouth is closed now, and dark hollows appear where the eyes and ears will be. The heart is still outside the body; the digestive tract is developing. The germ cells that will grow into the ovaries or testes are present. A skeleton made of cartilage, not real bone, has appeared. A tail is apparent at the end of the spinal cord.

Seventh Week: The embryo is ½ inch in length by the end of this week. The brain is large. The heart has moved inside the chest. The stomach, intestines and other organs are forming. The face is flattening, openings for the nose appear and eyes can be seen through the closed lids. The body may begin to move as small muscle fibers grow. Buds for fingers and toes appear. The tail has almost disappeared. The embryo is now uniquely human and has most of his internal organs.

Eighth Week: From now until birth the developing baby is termed a "fetus." At the end of this week the fetus is almost an inch long and weighs about two grams (1/15 ounce). The jaws and other facial features are now more clearly developed. Teeth are forming. Stubby fingers are present and the toes are forming. The arms are long enough for baby to touch his face. If the baby is a boy, his penis is now apparent. If the baby is a girl, her clitoris has developed.

Ninth Week: The fetus now looks more human and measures one inch in length; it weighs six grams (1/5 ounce). The heart is forming four chambers and beats 117-157 times per minute. Major blood vessels develop. The scrotum appears.

Tenth Week: The eyes move to the front of the head from the sides. The head is almost half of the fetus.

Embryo—6 weeks, actual size ¼".

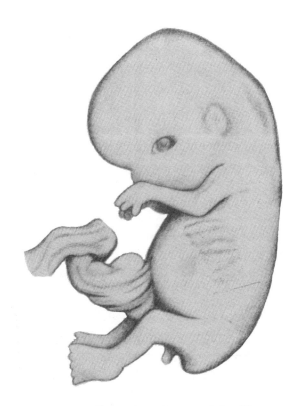

Fetus—9 weeks, actual size 1".

End of the Third Lunar Month* (12 Weeks): The baby is now about three inches long and weighs 30 grams (1 oz.). The face is well developed. Eyelids are present, but they are fused together. The baby can move the muscles of his face to squint, purse his lips or open his mouth. Amniotic fluid may be swallowed and passed out as urine. Arms, hands, fingers, legs, feet and toes are fully developed. The baby can make a fist and kick with his feet, although the mother cannot feel it yet.

End of the Fourth Lunar Month (16 Weeks): The fetus is about eight and one half inches long, and weighs 180 grams (6 ounces). The essential body systems are complete now. Most of the remaining changes will be in size. To facilitate this growth, the placenta also grows rapidly during this month. The baby's skin is getting thicker and less transparent and is forming several layers. Eyebrows and eyelashes appear. The sex of the baby is easily distinguished. He may suck his thumb. The heart can be heard with a stethoscope, and the mother begins to feel faint fluttering movements between her pubic bone and navel. She may confuse these movements with gas at first. But this is "quickening," the earliest felt movements of her child. The fluttering is first perceived from sixteen to eighteen weeks.

End of the Fifth Lunar Month (20 Weeks): His length is twelve inches and he weighs about 480 grams (1 lb.). Hair appears on the head and some fat is deposited under the skin, but the baby is still quite thin.

End of the Sixth Lunar Month (24 Weeks): The length of the fetus reaches fourteen inches. His weight is 960 grams (2 lbs.). Vernix caseosa, a cheese-like coating that protects the baby's skin from its watery environment, has developed. The eyes open and the fetus can hear. Fingerprints and footprints form. One baby in ten born by the 24th week survives.

End of the Seventh Lunar Month (28 weeks): The baby is sixteen inches long and weighs about 1,440 grams (3 lbs.). Fine downy hair, called lanugo, has appeared all over the baby and helps to protect him from the amniotic fluid. A baby boy's testicles have descended into his scrotum. More than half the babies born at seven months survive, and every day after that increases the baby's chance of survival.

*A lunar month equals 28 days.

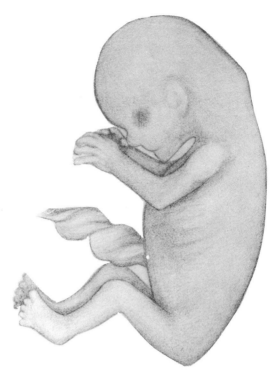

Fetus—12 weeks, actual size 3".

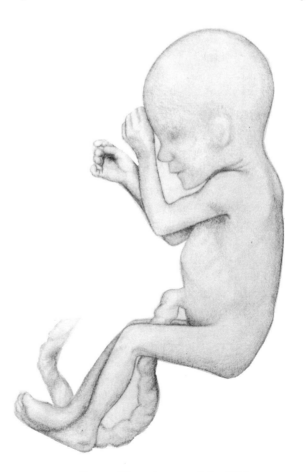

Fetus—16 weeks, actual size 8½".

End of the Eighth Lunar Month (32 weeks):   His length averages eighteen inches and his weight is 2,400 grams (5 lbs.) or more. The baby gains about an ounce a day during the last two months of fetal life. This is important in providing a layer of fat under the skin to keep his temperature constant in his life outside of the uterus. His skin is still red, but is less wrinkled. The fingernails are long. The baby's chance of survival, if born now, is better than ninety percent.

End of the Ninth Lunar Month (36 Weeks):   The baby is 19 inches long, and weighs around 2,880 grams (6 lbs.). The skin is smoother and the redness has faded to pink. Lanugo drops off, remaining only on the arms and shoulders. Fat continues to be deposited. The lungs are maturing and producing lecithin necessary for respiration.

The Tenth Lunar Month (36-40 Weeks):   The brain greatly increases its number of cells. This growth continues for the first five to six months of life outside of the uterus. During this month, 96% of all babies are head down. During the last two to four weeks the head or other presenting part settles down into the top of the pelvis. During the last month the baby gains about one half pound per week. At 38 weeks he averages 20 inches in length and weighs 7-7½ lbs. The baby is ready to be born!

FETAL EMOTIONS

We now know that even as all of this physical development is occurring, the unborn child is becoming an aware, reacting human being. As early as 8 weeks, he can express his likes and dislikes with well-placed kicks and jerks. At 28 to 32 weeks, his emerging sense of awareness transforms his physical responses into feelings. His mother's emotional state can, and does, have an effect on the way the growing fetus perceives his world—warm and friendly, or cold and hostile. That is not to say that fleeting anxiety or doubt about your health will negatively affect your unborn child. But it does mean that chronic anxiety or stress, especially of a personal nature, or deep ambivalence about motherhood may affect the personality of your baby.

Recent studies show that the unborn child hears well from the 24th week. The kinds of sounds

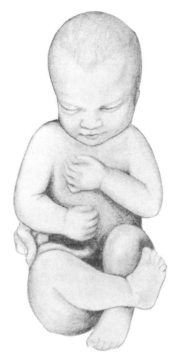

Fetus—38-40 weeks.

that he hears definitely affect him emotionally. Soft, soothing sounds or music calm him; rock-and-roll can make him kick violently. For further information on this topic, see *The Secret Life of The Unborn Child* by Thomas Verny with John Kelly.

The exciting aspect of this new knowledge is that you can begin shaping a positive relationship with your child before birth. Take the time to talk soothingly to your baby and send him loving thoughts. This is also a good way to get your partner involved in the pregnancy. Encourage him to gently massage your abdomen and talk to his baby as well. Try to spend a portion of each day in a relaxed, anxiety-free state of mind. Both you and your unborn child will benefit.

THE PLACENTA

By the time the fetus is two weeks old, the placenta, or afterbirth, is developing. The villi, embedded in the lining of the uterus, are forming primitive blood vessels that tap into your blood supply. The function of the placenta is to supply the growing fetus with the oxygen and nutrients it needs from your blood system, and to pass to you the waste products it does not need.

The fetal blood is always separate from your blood. Substances are passed back and forth through a semi-permeable membrane. Formerly, the placenta was thought to act as a barrier to materials that might hurt the fetus. It is now known that almost everything that enters your body, including viruses, drugs, nicotine and alcohol, is passed to the fetus.

The placenta continues to grow until about two months before delivery, when it reaches its maximum size. It is about the size and shape of a dinner plate (eight to nine inches in diameter), but thicker and heavier, weighing one to two pounds at birth. The side that is attached to the uterine wall is dark red and has sections in it, like circular puzzle pieces. Scar-like areas of tissue may appear in it. These are areas of calcification and denote places which have degenerated. More of them occur in placentas of mothers who smoke during pregnancy. The side that is next to the fetus is white and smooth, being covered by a membrane (the amniotic sac).

The nutrients coming from the mother are passed to the blood vessels in the placenta. From the placenta they reach the fetus by way of the umbilical cord, and then move into the blood circulating within the fetus.

Inside the umbilical cord are three blood vessels: one large vein and two smaller arteries. Nutrients travel from the placenta to the fetus through the vein. Waste products return to the placenta through the arteries to be passed to the mother's system. A jelly-like substance, called "Wharton's jelly," surrounds the blood vessels and helps to protect them.

The cord begins developing during the second week of life and usually grows to about two feet, although it is possible for the cord to grow anywhere from seven inches to four feet. After the birth of the baby the cord is clamped and cut. A stump remains, which dries up and falls off in seven to ten days.

LENGTH OF PREGNANCY

The length of an average pregnancy is about 280 days; this is about nine months by the calendar, or ten lunar months. A lunar month is the time it takes for the moon to go from full moon to full moon (28 days).

Your doctor has calculated an estimated due date by adding seven days to the first day of your last normal menstrual period, and then counting back three months. For example, if the first day of your last menstrual period was February 15, add seven days to that giving you February 22. Subtract three months and you get November 22 as the expected due date, or about 280 days from February 15. The baby is only about 266 days old at that point, but the date of the last menstrual period is used since the actual date of conception is usually unknown and could be as early as day five or six of the menstrual cycle. Only about four percent of all women carry their babies exactly 280 days, but two-thirds deliver within ten days either way of their due date. The due date is only an estimate, an average of all pregnancies. Your baby may take more or less time to develop, in the same way that some babies take more time to get their first tooth.

PHYSICAL AND EMOTIONAL CHANGES

Pregnancy is generally divided into three trimesters, or three three-month periods, for purposes of discussion. This is done because women usually experience the same general kinds of changes during each of the trimesters.

During pregnancy, two kinds of development go on at once: the physical changes in you, the mother-to-be, and the physical changes in your fetus. Along with the physical changes you experience, some emotional changes take place. You and your partner can use these changes as an opportunity to grow, to expand your awareness of yourselves, to deepen your sense of responsibility and to become aware of what millions of other parents have experienced.

First Trimester

Physical Changes in the Mother

Uterus: For many women a missed menstrual period may be the first sign of pregnancy. Other women continue to have very light periods for two or three months even though they are pregnant. Many women spot slightly on the day the ovum attaches to the uterine wall; this is called "implantation bleeding." The lack of menstrual periods results from the continued high levels of estrogen and progesterone which maintain the uterine lining to nourish the developing embryo.

By the time the fetus is twelve weeks old, the top of the uterus is just above the pubic bone and the placenta, or afterbirth, has formed. The uterus itself

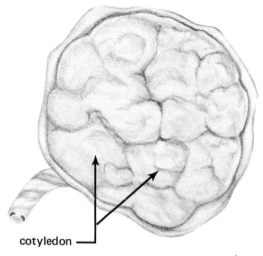

cotyledon

Maternal side (attached to wall of the uterus).

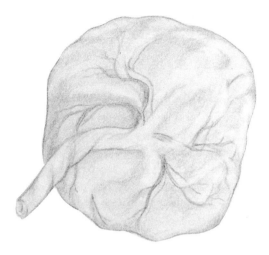

Fetal side (amniotic sac originates from this side).

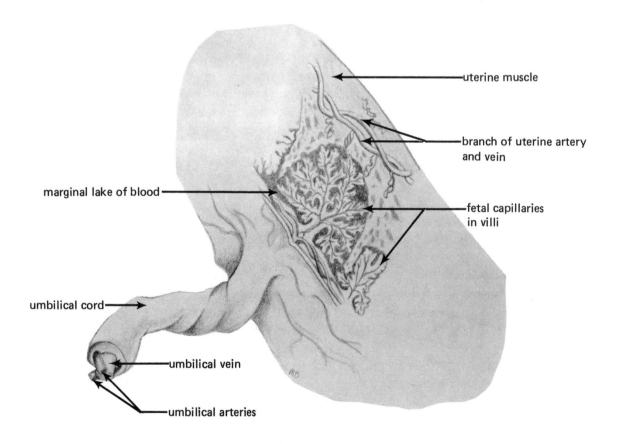

uterine muscle

branch of uterine artery and vein

marginal lake of blood

fetal capillaries in villi

umbilical cord

umbilical vein

umbilical arteries

Cross section of placenta showing blood supply and circulation.

The Placenta

increases in size and weight throughout the pregnancy. By twelve weeks, it is the size of a grapefruit. The cervix is softer.

Vagina: The vagina thickens and softens because of the increase in maternal hormones. It becomes blue to violet in color as the result of an increased blood supply to the area. Vaginal secretions become more noticeable, increasing in amount as pregnancy progresses.

Breasts: A tingling or prickling sensation in the breasts is often felt during the early weeks of pregnancy. This is the result of an increasing blood supply and growth of the milk secreting glands. After a few weeks or months, the tingling or prickling disappears, but your breasts usually continue to enlarge until the third trimester. Around the eighth week, the veins may become visible under the skin. Small round elevated areas appear about the same time on the dark part of the nipple, the areola. These are oil glands (glands of Montgomery) which enlarge during pregnancy. Their oil helps to keep the nipples soft and pliable in preparation for breastfeeding.

Urination: The need to urinate more frequently may be felt as the enlarging uterus presses on your bladder. This need usually eases during the second trimester as the uterus rises out of the pelvis. Even though it means more trips to the bathroom, it is very important to drink plenty of fluids in order to maintain good kidney function and to provide the water necessary to metabolize the protein you eat.

Digestion: About half of all pregnant women feel nauseated and may vomit during early pregnancy and sometimes even later. This may occur in the morning and/or at other times during the day. "Morning sickness," as it is called, has been attributed to an increase in hormone levels in the woman, lack of sufficient vitamin B_6, and/or low blood sugar. Eating foods high in vitamin B and eating small, high protein meals throughout the day usually help this condition. (See Chapter 3.)

In addition to nausea, you may have trouble with indigestion and heartburn. The hormones relaxin and progesterone relax smooth muscles in the body. One of the muscles affected is the sphincter at the top of the stomach, which keeps food in the stomach. Progesterone is also responsible for relaxing the intestines somewhat, thereby slowing digestion and making constipation more likely during pregnancy. Eating a diet high in fiber (fresh fruit and vegetables and whole grains), drinking plenty of fluids and exercising regularly minimize this problem.

Fatigue: Pregnancy brings changes to every system in your body, and these changes may require a great deal of physical and emotional energy. Proper rest is extremely important for an expectant mother. You need not feel guilty about resting during the day, or about going to bed early. Rest is needed for your body to adjust to pregnancy.

Emotional Changes

The first trimester is usually a time of affirming the fact of conception and what it implies. This is true for other family members as well as yourself. You may draw inward and focus on the changes in your body and on your fears and dreams. You may feel increas-

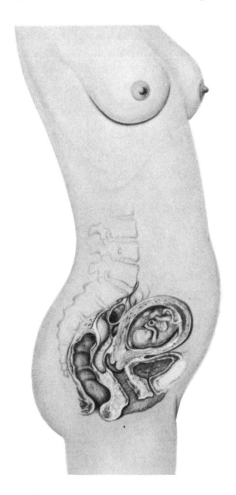

End of first trimester.

ingly vulnerable to danger and may also fear miscarriage.

Even when the pregnancy is wanted, expectant parents usually have many questions: Can we afford a child? Will I quit work? How will our lifestyle change? Will we have jealousy problems with our other children? Both of you may feel a sense of panic at additional responsibility. It is very common to have ambivalent feelings toward the pregnancy in the early months. These feelings are not bad or wrong; by acknowledging and talking about them, you and your partner will find that you are better able to cope with them and finally accept the pregnancy. Facing your own doubts and fears about pregnancy aids in emotional growth.

Sexual activity may increase or decrease during this time of adjustment. (See section on sexual relations.) There is a real need for you to talk to each other openly about your feelings, in order to keep your pent-up fears from damaging your relationship.

By the end of this trimester you may begin to sort out feelings toward your own parents and examine them. Think about how you will be different from or similar to your own parents.

Other feelings during the first trimester may include excitement, increased creativity and an increased sensuality. You may feel "special" during this time.

Mood swings sometimes become more extreme during pregnancy. You may find yourself laughing or crying over insignificant things. This is probably related to the increasing levels of the hormones of pregnancy. Researchers state that these hormones do not cause moods, but they probably increase the intensity of the feelings.[1] Some evidence shows that the expectant mother feels more anxiety if the baby she is carrying is a boy, but the reason is not known.

Women experiencing a second, or later pregnancy often find that they are less preoccupied with this pregnancy than with their first. The major adjustment to parenthood seems to come with the first pregnancy. With later pregnancies, there is less time available and less need is felt to ponder the meaning of the physical changes.

Second Trimester

Physical Changes in the Mother

Uterus: The uterus begins to expand out of the pelvis into the abdominal cavity by the 14th week. By the middle of the second trimester (20 weeks) the uterus is usually at the level of the navel.

The movements of the fetus are felt during a first pregnancy (primigravida) at 16-18 weeks. They are often noticed earlier by women who have already borne at least one child. The fetus is about 8-12 inches long and weighs one pound when the movements are first perceived. Mild uterine contractions, called Braxton-Hicks, may become apparent.

Vagina: The tissues soften and become more elastic, preparing for the baby's passage.

Pelvis: The joints of the pelvis loosen up. Softer cartilage replaces some of the bone so that it allows a large baby to pass through more easily.

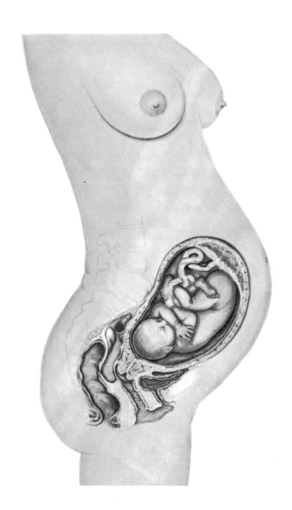

End of second trimester.

Breasts: Colostrum, a clear yellow fluid which precedes breastmilk, is often present by sixteen weeks. Some women are able to express (gently squeeze out) a little of it; some are not.

Circulatory System: By the end of the second trimester the blood volume increases by 40-60% and the heart actually pumps more blood per beat. Edema, or swelling, is common because of the increased blood volume, pressure from the enlarging uterus, and the increase in estrogen.

The fluid tends to pool in the feet and hands when standing for long periods. If the swelling is sudden and involves the face, the doctor should be notified as this may be a sign of toxemia. Resting on your side improves circulation and helps to relieve this discomfort. Increasing your protein intake will also help to decrease swelling.

Linea Nigra: A dark line from your navel to the pubic hairline may appear as a result of hormone activity. It fades after delivery, but may continue to be visible.

Stretch Marks (Striae Gravidarum):   These appear when the connective tissue of the skin is stretched to the point that it ruptures. The lines are red or pink during pregnancy and may appear on the abdomen, thighs, or breasts. They fade to white after delivery. Massaging with oil or lotion may help prevent stretch marks although heredity seems to be a more important factor.

Mask of Pregnancy: Dark blotches may appear on the face which usually disappear after pregnancy. This pigmentation results from increased levels of a hormone called MSH (melanocyte stimulating hormone) whose production drops after pregnancy.[2] It may also be caused by folic acid deficiency. Your prenatal vitamins should include folic acid (a B vitamin) to meet your increased requirement.

Emotional Changes

For most women, the second trimester is a more positive experience than the first as you begin to feel the movements of the life within you. This trimester may be the most pleasurable of the pregnancy. The pregnancy becomes obvious to other people and you are frequently the center of attention in groups of your friends. Fatigue and nausea are usually less of a problem now. Your body, although larger, is not cumbersome, and it is fairly easy for you to move around.

Your husband, too, by this time has often accepted the fact of the pregnancy and is excited about the movements of the baby. During this trimester, men frequently become more aware of their wives' growing dependence on them. As your pregnancy progresses, you may feel more vulnerable, need his attention more, and want him to become involved with the pregnancy and the baby. You may become overly concerned for your husband's safety. Meanwhile, he may share your interest in the pregnancy, or he may feel an increased creative interest in his work or hobby. He may gain weight or show other symptoms of pregnancy. All of these things are ways that both husband and wife deal with the stress and changes that are occurring. It is important for you to be aware of and talk about your feelings especially when friction exists between you and your partner.

Dreams become very real and are sometimes disturbing for many women. They are a way of bringing fears to consciousness where they can be dealt with more easily. Dreaming about misfortune to the baby or yourself or about giving birth to animals is common. If fears remain unacknowledged, they may cause increasing anxiety.

Third Trimester
Physical Changes in the Mother

Uterus: Towards the end of pregnancy, the uterus reaches the breastbone (sternum) and measures about eleven by fourteen inches. In a primigravida, lightening occurs from one to six weeks before delivery. This means that the uterus settles downward into the pelvis and the baby's head may engage in the pelvic inlet.

Braxton-Hicks contractions become stronger and more apparent as the time for delivery approaches. (See Chapter 6, false labor.) The cervix becomes softer in the last few days or weeks before the baby is born and may begin to thin out and open up a little in preparation for labor.

Vagina: Much more mucus is passed vaginally, preparing for the passage of the baby. Increased vaginal swelling at this time may result in discomfort during sexual intercourse. (See sexual relations during pregnancy.)

Digestion: The growing uterus puts pressure on the stomach and intestines, pushing them up and back. Heartburn may occur. Eating more small, high-protein meals throughout the day may help this condition. Some women find that taking papaya enzyme with meals can aid digestion and prevent heartburn.

Breathing: Shortness of breath is common, since the uterus pushes up on the diaphragm. This improves after lightening.

Circulatory System: Varicose veins may develop in the legs, the vulva, or the rectum (hemorrhoids). They result from increased pelvic pressure exerted by the uterus and growing fetus as well as the decreased blood return from the lower body and limbs.

Urination: The need to urinate usually increases, especially after lightening occurs.

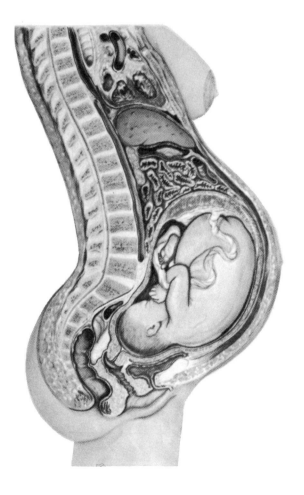

End of third trimester.

Fatigue: Carrying around the extra weight causes fatigue to return during the last trimester.

Emotional Changes

During the third trimester, you focus more and more on the baby, and on labor and delivery. For husband and wife, naming the baby becomes an important pastime. An area in the house is prepared for the baby. Almost all women now accept the fact of pregnancy and are able to differentiate the baby as a real person, separate from themselves.

Time during the third trimester seems endless. Many women count on their due date to bring the end of their discomfort, and may be very discouraged if they go a week or more beyond the expected time.

Because of their large size, many women feel their self-esteem drop during this trimester. It is important for the people around you, especially your husband, to reassure you that you are still attractive.

Your preoccupation with labor and delivery can be used to your advantage by gathering as much information about the experience as possible. Reading books, taking classes, and talking to other people who have recently had babies are good ways to learn. If you are in your third trimester, try to avoid talking with people who repeatedly attempt to discourage you from taking childbirth preparation classes, or who dwell on their own negative birth experiences. It is important for you to keep a confident, relaxed attitude toward your own birth experience. Don't avoid your own fears, but don't allow negative thinking to dominate you. Your chances of a positive birth experience are to a great extent determined by your attitude. It is fear and anxiety that create negative experiences.

SEXUAL RELATIONS DURING PREGNANCY

During pregnancy you undergo many changes, both physical and emotional. How you react to these changes, how openly you can talk with your partner and whether or not your physician or midwife makes you feel comfortable discussing your lovemaking, all play a role in your attitude as a couple towards sexual relations during pregnancy.

Your husband may find you more desirable with the realization that your body carries his child. Or, he may be concerned about the effects sexual intercourse might have on the growing baby in terms of miscarriage or harm. Unless you have a history of miscarriage or other problems, this is an unnecessary concern. Check with your doctor to be reassured about a healthy pregnancy. The beginning of your pregnancy is an extremely important time to decide together to remain physically close, even if times of lessened sexual activity occur. Touching, snuggling, caressing or massaging, without necessarily leading to sex, can keep you feeling open, warm and loving towards one another. Accepting both positive and negative feelings is a necessary part in dealing with and coming to terms with the pregnancy. Open communication with each other and, of course, with your birth attendant, will help insure that your pregnancy gets off to a good start.

Early pregnancy classes, if offered in your community, may afford a chance to talk about sexuality and your changing body in relation to your love-making. Prepared childbirth classes may also be a good place for such an exchange of information, although much of your pregnancy will be behind you by this time. Often these classes have a lending library. An informative book on this subject is *Making Love During Pregnancy* by Elisabeth Bing and Libby Colman.

The first trimester of pregnancy can be an exciting time with both partners feeling very good about themselves and their bodies. You may feel beautiful, exhilarated with the thought of a new life growing within you and very close to your mate. You may also find yourself easily fatigued, nauseated, anxious and very emotional. Your husband may be proud and excited about the new life he helped to create. At the same time, he may be anxious or feeling a personal rejection that your love and attention are now concentrated on the growing child.

The first three months can certainly be a time of adjustment for the two of you. Wide mood swings are normal for you both. You will also experience changes in your body and in your relationship. While you continue to love each other as much or even more, the physical expression of that love is often altered—sometimes to a surprising degree! Please be assured that this is not unique to you. Whatever your feelings, desires, needs, or concerns are, they have been shared and experienced by countless other couples. Be aware that there is a wide range of these emotions, needs and concerns. Some women experience increased sexual desires during the first

trimester; others (especially if nauseated and fatigued) have a decreased desire. Even if you are nauseated, you will appreciate the touching and caressing from a good back rub by your husband. Both of you will enjoy a warm hug and kiss.

During **the second trimester**, the growing uterus begins to bulge the abdomen, though not usually to the extent that it is in the way or makes sex uncomfortable. Some women experience a decline in sexual enjoyment as the pregnancy advances, while others feel increased pleasure. Again, if you are open with each other and responsive to each others' sexual needs, you can eliminate many of the problems.

Some of the initial complaints have disappeared by the third or fourth month. Generally, the nausea

and fatigue have passed, and you feel more comfortable with the pregnancy now that the chance of miscarriage has diminished.

As you move into **the third trimester**, you may find simple movement such as getting in and out of bed, bending forward, even standing, walking and sitting, very awkward and difficult. These physical changes may keep you from enjoying sexual intercourse, and your partner may also feel these restraints. On the other hand, increased pelvic congestion may arouse sexual desires that are relieved by orgasm. Your husband may be uncomfortable feeling the baby moving while he is making love to you.

You may have already tried a **variety of positions** to increase your comfort during intercourse. If your pregnancy has advanced to being almost "in the way," you may find having your partner on top, but slightly to the side, relieves the weight pressing on your abdomen. It also gives you more mobility and lessens penetration of the penis. You might find the position with the woman on top to be more comfortable as you can control the degree of penetration. Some couples, however, find this position results in penetration that is too deep and causes discomfort.

You might be comfortable and satisfied with side-lying positions. The man can enter from behind, either in the side-lying position or with the woman kneeling or standing, using the bed for support. This position controls the extent of penetration and relieves abdominal pressure. You can also lie close to the edge of the bed and have your partner support your legs with his arms or rest them on his shoulders as he enters. Needless to say, experimenting so that both of you are comfortable and satisfied is important, along with a sense of humor!

Many couples find **alternatives to sexual intercourse** at this time. Remember that massaging, touching and caressing give close physical contact which is equally important to both of you. Perhaps genital manipulation and mutual masturbation will be most sexually gratifying for you. Even self-masturbation can be relieving. Some couples enjoy oral sex and continue this during pregnancy. **A word of caution** is necessary concerning cunnilingus or oral stimulation of the female genitals during pregnancy. Air should *not* be forced into the vagina at any time, as a rare phenomenon called air embolism can result. Because of increased vascularity during pregnancy, air passing into the uterus can enter the wom-

an's blood stream and cause serious problems and even death. If you enjoy this form of sex play, it is all right to continue it as long as you are aware of this one restriction.

Unless you are spotting or have a history of miscarriages, you should consider pregnancy a sign of physical health and continue your life as normally as possible, keeping in mind that intercourse will not harm your baby and can be continued throughout pregnancy. If you are leaking fluid from your vagina, experience pain in your pelvic region or are bleeding vaginally, you should contact your physician or midwife immediately. Orgasms do cause the uterus to contract. However, the uterus contracts in the same manner with Braxton-Hicks contractions which are a perfectly natural occurrence during pregnancy. Intercourse without orgasm will not initiate labor. However, if your doctor advises against orgasm, it's important to realize this means orgasms via masturbation as well. Your physician or midwife should let you know if there is some medical problem which may require altering your position or frequency of intercourse, or curtailing it altogether. Otherwise, most physicians state that intercourse can continue until labor begins or until your water breaks. Therefore, experiment and enjoy!

PRENATAL CARE

Prenatal care should begin the moment you suspect you are pregnant. All of your baby's vital organs have already begun forming by this time. The person you choose as your birth attendant will be the one providing this care. (See Chapter 1 on choosing your birth attendant.) He will chart your progress during pregnancy and watch for any signs indicating potential problems.

When you visit the office for your first prenatal examination, a complete medical history and physical examination will be done. This could be very complete with counsel on the need to stop smoking, to cease using alcohol and drugs indiscriminately, and the need for better nutrition habits. You may be advised on the benefits of exercise, and counseled about sex, hygiene or any other topics that may be bothering you. Expect this first exam to take about an hour and feel free to explore any subjects of concern that are not brought up in the course of the exam. The physical will consist of:

1. a breast examination
2. a pelvic or vaginal exam which:
   • confirms pregnancy
   • allows for a pap smear
   • allows for a smear for gonorrhea
   • estimates the size and shape of the pelvis
   (This is usually not done again until the last month of pregnancy.)
3. blood tests to check:
   • blood type and Rh factor
   • complete blood count with tests for anemia
   • VDRL test for syphilis
   (Some clinics or offices also provide other blood chemistry checks for a more complete analysis of the mother's health.)
4. urine tests which involve:
   • a complete urinalysis
   • a culture to check for infection
   • a pregnancy test even if you are already sure you are pregnant

Following the first examination, you will usually have check-ups monthly, then bi-weekly starting with the seventh month, then weekly in the ninth month. These check-ups will usually involve:

1. weighing
2. recording blood pressure
3. checking urine for:
   • protein which may indicate toxemia
   • sugar which may indicate diabetes
   • infection

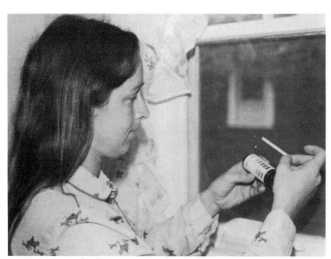

Pregnant woman doing her own urinalysis.

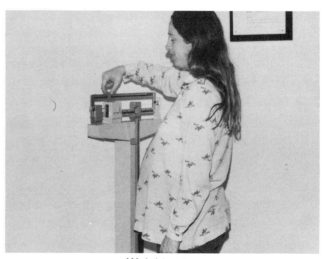

Weighing in.

4.   checking your abdomen for:
   • the growth of the uterus in order to estimate the progress of the pregnancy
   • the size and position of the fetus

Some doctors and midwives encourage women to participate in their care by doing their own weight, urine and hemoglobin checks during their office visits.

Several important things to do for yourself and your baby during your pregnancy are: (1) eat well and avoid alcohol, drugs, and tobacco, (2) get enough moderate exercise to strengthen your body and maintain your energy, and (3) get good medical care beginning early in pregnancy from a qualified doctor or midwife.

Your birth attendant will probably discuss the things he or she wants you to report, but below is a list of common signals for your reference. They may or may not indicate a serious complication, but your doctor or midwife should be the one to decide. Do not worry about bothering your birth attendant. It is his job to answer questions about your physical well-being.

Danger Signals: Notify your doctor or midwife immediately for any of these symptoms; do not wait for office hours.

1.   vaginal bleeding; it is never normal to bleed during pregnancy
2.   sharp abdominal pain or severe cramping
3.   loss of fluid from vagina

Warning Signals: For any of these signals notify the doctor during office hours, but do not wait longer than 24 hours (as on a weekend).

1.   frequent dizzy spells
2.   visual disturbances: dimness, blurring, flashes of light or dots in front of the eyes
3.   nausea or vomiting that persists
4.   sudden and excessive swelling of face, hands, and feet
5.   headache that is severe and does not let up
6.   painful or burning urination
7.   marked decrease in the amount of urination
8.   fever higher than 100°F. orally or chills and fever
9.   vaginal discharge that is irritating

These signs should be taken as a warning of possible illness, infection, or threatened miscarriage. It is important to remain calm, as nothing may be wrong. Just speaking with your birth attendant can be reassuring. Genital sores, discharges from the vagina or penis, or other genital discomforts may be a warning of a venereal or sexually transmitted disease. Your baby is at risk if you contract a venereal disease while pregnant. Not only gonorrhea and syphilis are serious, but also herpes virus and chlamydia trachamatis may cause serious problems if the baby becomes infected. Inform your doctor or midwife of any problems or previous venereal disease, so that you may be tested and treated, if necessary, during your pregnancy. In addition, recent studies indicate that pregnant women who have been exposed to the AIDS virus may have an increased risk of passing it on to their unborn children.

Another condition to be aware of is toxoplasmosis, a disease which can be contracted by eating raw or rare meat or by coming in contact with a cat, particularly the feces of a cat, which has the disease. It can cause brain damage, malformation, blindness or death to the unborn child. Therefore, avoid changing a cat's litter box and eating meat that is not well-cooked while you are pregnant.

Several work-place situations have been cited as possibly being hazardous during the first few months of pregnancy. One investigation showed that certain employees in a semiconductor plant—those working in a room where computer chips were etched with acids and gases—had a miscarriage rate of 39 percent, nearly twice the national average.[3]

High miscarriage rates have also been reported among users of video display terminals (VDTs). VDTs emit certain wavelengths of ionizing radiation.

Further studies are needed to verify or refute these findings. Until then, it may be advisable to avoid such situations during pregnancy.

HIGHER-RISK PREGNANCY

Some pregnant women are considered "higher-risk." This includes women who have previous medical histories of diabetes, heart disease, high blood pressure, or develop these conditions during pregnancy or labor. Also included are those women who are carrying their fifth or later child, carrying twins, triplets, etc., are under eighteen, over 35, or over 30 and carrying their first child. The degree of risk varies with each of these conditions and should be thoroughly explained to you by your doctor. If you find you are in one of these categories, the management of your pregnancy and labor may vary somewhat from that of a low-risk pregnancy. Consequently, some of the options discussed in this book may not be available to you.

TESTS USED IN PREGNANCY

Various tests and procedures are sometimes used in cases of pregnancy complications. Like all medical procedures, they offer advantages but may carry risks. Therefore, they should be applied *only* when medically indicated and not routinely for your or your doctor's convenience, or to satisfy your curiosity. When deciding whether or not to undergo one of these tests, you might ask your doctor if the results will in any way alter his care of you and if so, how. If the answer is no, you might question if the test is necessary. Be aware of the risks and benefits involved with each procedure.

Amniocentesis

During this test, a sample of amniotic fluid is obtained to detect abnormalities in the baby or to judge gestational maturity. A local anesthetic is given and then a long, hollow needle is inserted through the abdominal and uterine walls so that fluid can be withdrawn for analysis. It should be done in conjunction with ultrasound to outline the location of the fetus, the placenta and the umbilical cord. This procedure is very valuable, but according to many experts, it can be misused. Risks include some chance of blood exchange between the mother and the baby (creating greater Rh incompatibility while testing for it), infection of the amniotic fluid, peritonitis, blood clots, placental hemorrhage, injury to the baby, or even premature labor.[4] Amniocentesis should definitely not be used just to satisfy your curiosity about your baby's sex ahead of time, but it may be needed to assess the fetal lung maturity in judging when a cesarean delivery may safely be performed. To determine fetal lung maturity, the amniotic fluid is examined for specific phospholipids which are present when the baby's lungs are mature.

Amniocentesis is also done for genetic testing. But unless you plan to terminate the pregnancy if an abnormality is found, or unless this knowledge alters your prenatal care, it is questionable to have this done just for the information.

Chorionic Villi Sampling

A new test which can detect genetic abnormalities earlier than amniocentesis has been developed. This test, called chorionic villi sampling (CVS), is usually done between the eighth and tenth weeks of pregnancy.

The chorionic villi are finger-like projections that cover the developing embryo and contain cells that have the same genetic composition as the embryo. CVS involves the insertion of a suction catheter into the uterus under the visual guidance of ultrasound. A small sample of chorionic tissue—one about the size of a grain of cooked rice—is removed. The procedure takes about a half hour to complete.

Advantages of this test are the quickness of the results and the ability to perform it early in pregnancy. Amniocentesis cannot be performed as early, and three to four weeks may pass before results are known. Possible risks from CVS include "infection, maternal or fetal bleeding, spontaneous abortion, Rh immunization, birth defect[s] and perforation of the membrane surrounding the embryo."[5] Another disadvantage to this procedure is its lack of availability.

Ultrasound

Ultrasound was developed for the space program to project the sound reflected off objects through the use of high frequency sound waves. One form of ultrasound, the sonogram or B-scan, directs intermittent sound waves towards the pregnant woman's abdomen. An outline of the baby, placenta, and other structures involved in the pregnancy are transmitted to a video screen. A sonogram is often used to determine fetal position, estimate the maturity of the baby or confirm a multiple pregnancy. The location of the placenta can also be pinpointed when placenta previa (low implanted placenta) is suspected. It is also used to visualize the baby and placenta when amniocentesis or CVS is being performed. Since X-rays are now considered dangerous to the developing baby, ultrasound is being used instead.

Many physicians (especially those who have the equipment in their offices) use B-scans routinely to determine your due date. The determination of due date is most accurate when done in the first trimester, but warnings have been issued that ultrasound should be avoided during this time until more information on its safety is available.[6]

When performed between 14–20 weeks, the test is accurate between one week before and after the estimated due date. Later in pregnancy and especially after 32 weeks gestation, sonograms are inaccurate in determining due dates because of variations in fetal growth.[7]

In a high-risk pregnancy, it is important to have an accurate due date to make sure the infant is delivered at the best time. In a normal low-risk pregnancy, the risk of routine sonograms may outweigh the benefit.

Ultrasound can also be directed in a continuous wave to check the baby's heart rate during routine examinations with the "Doptone." Most often, it is used during labor as a part of monitoring. There is some concern over this long exposure (6–8 hours) to ultrasound when long term effects are unknown. (See Chapter 8 on interventions for more information on fetal monitors.)

Diagnostically, ultrasound is preferred over X-rays. However, more and more physicians are using ultrasound routinely during labor and involving their patients in one or more B-scans during pregnancy. As with any procedure, the use of ultrasound should be medically justified, and you have the legal right to refuse it. The U.S. Food and Drug Administration has issued a warning that ultrasound during pregnancy has not been proven safe for routine use and that it should only be used when medically indicated. The concern is that damage may oc-

cur to the baby's chromosomes and developing gonads, resulting in birth defects (in your child's children) and possible infertility.[8] This has not been proven, but it would not become evident until those children who are now being exposed to ultrasound are of childbearing age.

In 1984, the National Institutes of Health (NIH) released a statement following more than a year of data gathering. The NIH study concluded that current available information does "not allow a recommendation for routine screening at this time."[9] This supports the FDA warning against the routine use of ultrasound. More studies of possible long-term effects were recommended by the NIH.

The International Childbirth Education Association (ICEA) has issued a position paper on ultrasound which states that "Before an ultrasound examination, expectant parents should be given information about the procedure, its benefits and known risks, gaps in knowledge about biological effects, and alternative tests which might be done and their benefits and risks."[10]

Doris Haire of the National Women's Health Network has prepared a "Certification and Consent Form for Ultrasound Exposure," which can be obtained from the Network.[11] Ms. Haire has stated that "those who contend that ultrasound used for fetal monitoring is harmless should be reminded that many men and women now have cancer as a result of X-ray therapy for acne, enlarged tonsils, etc., because X-rays were once considered harmless."[12] DES (diethylstilbesterol) is another example of a medication that was given to pregnant women and considered safe. It took twenty years to discover that many of the exposed daughters are now victims of cancer of the reproductive organs.

X-ray

X-ray pelvimetry measures the size of the woman's pelvis and the size and position of the baby's head to determine the cephalopelvic relationship. It is seldom used except at the end of the pregnancy, and much less now that ultrasound has been developed. X-ray carries a risk of being carcinogenic (cancer producing).[13]

Estriol Excretion Studies

Estriol is an estrogen type hormone made by the placenta and excreted in your blood and urine. This test

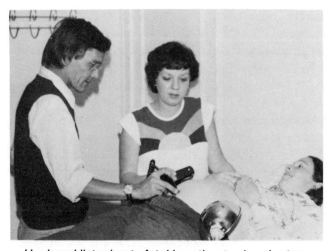

Husband listening to fetal heartbeat using doptone.

helps to determine the functioning of the placenta and the baby's well-being. Urine may have to be collected by you for 24 hours or a single sample of your blood may be taken. A drop in the estriol level indicates the placenta's functioning is declining. Several consecutive studies may need to be done to assess the degree of placental function. The results are used, along with other tests, to determine the best time for delivery of the baby in cases of diabetes or other difficulties in the pregnancy.

Non-Stress Test

This can be a very reliable test for fetal well-being without drug intervention, such as in the oxytocin challenge test (OCT). Fetal well-being is determined by measuring the fetal heart rate response to the baby's activity. The examiner first takes the heart rate when the fetus is still, and then stimulates the baby to move by pushing or pressing on your abdomen, by making a loud tone close by or by watching for spontaneous fetal movement. An increase in fetal heart rate is a positive sign indicating fetal well-being. If the test is negative, then an OCT usually follows. This test may be affected by low blood sugar (so it is best to make sure you have eaten before the test) and sleepiness of the fetus.

Oxytocin Challenge Test (OCT or Stress Test)

This test is done in the hospital to help determine how well your baby will undergo the stress of labor. While reclining at a 45° angle, you are given oxytocin intravenously until you repeatedly have three contractions within a ten minute period for a full half hour. Your baby's heart rate is electronically monitored to check the effect of the contractions on him. This test is positive when the fetal heart rate appears abnormal during the stress of the contraction. In this case, a cesarean birth may be planned as the baby may not tolerate the stress of labor. In a negative result, the heart rate stays normal during contractions, which is a good sign and an indication that the baby may do well during labor. Avoid lying flat on your back as this can cause your blood pressure to drop, decreasing oxygen to the baby and possibly causing the appearance of fetal distress on the monitor.

These procedures should be discussed thoroughly with your doctor or midwife if the necessity for any of them arises. Continue to ask questions and to request explanations until you feel comfortable. Understanding the benefits can help to relax you and free you from concern about the procedure. Or, you may decide to ask for an alternative.

THINGS TO DO BEFORE YOUR DUE DATE

The following are suggestions of things to complete four to six weeks before your baby is due.

Take a Hospital Tour

This will familiarize you with your labor setting. It will also give you the opportunity to discuss your desires with the staff and to acquaint yourself with hospital policies.

Pre-register

Pre-register at the hospital. In order to complete the required forms, you will need to bring insurance information and possibly a deposit. This will shorten your admittance procedure when you arrive in labor. If you are given blanket consent forms concerning medication, circumcision, etc., read them carefully at this time and modify them according to your desires before signing. You may have neither the interest nor the time to make these decisions once you are in active labor.

Prepare Your Home for the Baby

Get the baby equipment and furniture set up and ready to use. Assemble the baby clothes, wash them and put them away. The last months of pregnancy are a good time to reorganize your home, making it safe for a small child. Lock up medicines and poisons. Ask friends who have small children to help you spot potential hazards. (See Chapter 10 for specific suggestions.)

Get Your Household Organized

Get your household organized for your absence and the work simplified for your return. If a relative or friend is coming to help out, be sure they understand that they are to help with the housework, not take care of the baby. Organize your shopping and cleaning list on a weekly or monthly basis. Buy ahead and store as many items as you have room for. Try to make double portions of casseroles and dishes like spaghetti sauce so you can freeze half of them for later use. Stock up on disposables such as paper plates and napkins.

You may want to locate a drug store that will deliver to your home. Some will only send out prescriptions. Others have a minimum purchase policy. You will need to have plenty of sanitary pads at home for the first two weeks. If you plan to nurse, you may want to purchase nursing pads. Men's handkerchiefs and squares of old diaper material also serve this purpose well.

Plan for the Next Two Months

It will save you a lot of effort if you can buy any family gifts and cards now, that you will need during the two months after your delivery. If you are going to buy presents for your preschooler, do that now too. You may also want to pick up some "busy things" for the other child(ren) (coloring or punch out books, marking pens, sewing cards, etc.) to bring out on a rough day. (See Chapter 12 on siblings for more suggestions.) Write down a schedule of meals, naps, bedtimes, school, carpools and after-school activities. Be sure to list absolute "no-no's."

You can address and stamp envelopes for your birth announcements before you go to the hospital. Then you will only need to fill them in while you are there.

Don't forget to pack your bags for the hospital. Listed below are suggested items that you should pack.

Lamaze Bag
(For Use During Labor)

- this book, with your completed birth plan
- object or picture—to use as a focal point
- watch with second hand—to time contractions
- playing cards, books, games—to use if admitted in early labor
- paper and pencil—to record contractions (labor record from back of book)
- extra pillows—to give needed support and comfort during labor
- small paper bag—to use if hyperventilation occurs

- tennis balls placed in sock—to lie on in case of backache
- cornstarch, talcum powder or lotion—to reduce friction while doing effleurage and back rub
- chapstick or lipgloss—to soothe dry lips
- washcloths—to suck on if ice chips are unavailable and to cool face
- plastic spoon—to get ice chips out of cup easily
- sour lollipops—to prevent a dry mouth (if staff permits)
- toothbrush, toothpaste, mouthwash—to cope with a dry mouth
- heavy socks—to warm cold feet
- snack and beverage—to give labor partner energy to keep him from having to leave to get food
- camera with closed flash attachment, movie camera, tape recorder—to record the birth
- baby book—to have staff record baby's footprints in it
- list of phone numbers to be called; change if needed

Hospital Bag for Woman
(Leave in Car Until After Birth)

- nightgowns—front buttoning or special nursing gowns for ease in breastfeeding
- robe and slippers

- nursing bras (2–3)
- *sanitary pads and belts (if you have a preference); beltless if cesarean birth is planned
- usual cosmetic and grooming aids
- shower cap
- birth announcements
- BIRTH REPORT—to fill out and mail to instructor while experience is fresh in mind
- going home clothes—loose fitting dress or maternity clothes; it will be some weeks before you regain your prepregnant figure
- radio, clock—optional
- *items for peri-care—squeeze bottle, Tucks, anesthetic spray

*These are usually supplied by the hospital and charged to your bill. If you have inadequate or no insurance, it will be cheaper to purchase them yourself and inform nursing staff of your choice so you won't be billed. DOUBLE CHECK YOUR BILL FOR EXTRA CHARGES WHEN IT ARRIVES.

Hospital Bag for Baby
(Pack and Take to the Hospital
On the Day of Discharge)

- going home outfit
- disposable or cloth diapers, pins, and waterproof pants (hospital may supply disposable diaper)
- booties and/or cap (optional)
- receiving blanket, outside blanket if necessary
- dynamically tested car seat to be used for the ride home

Emergency Birth Kit

If you have a history of rapid labors, live some distance from the hospital, or just want to be prepared in case your baby arrives unexpectedly, pack an emergency birth kit. Below is a list of items you may need in the event of an emergency delivery. Keep them wrapped tightly in a clean plastic bag and put it in a convenient place. Don't forget it as you leave for the hospital.

- flashlight
- blankets (including one baby blanket)
- clean towels, newspapers or crib pad
- clean handkerchiefs
- new ear syringe
- new shoe strings

(See Chapter 8 for details on emergency childbirth.)

FOOTNOTES

Chapter Two

1. Arthur and Libby Colman, *Pregnancy: The Psychological Experience* (N.Y., Seabury Press, Inc., 1978), pp. 9–11.
2. Constance Lerch, *Maternity Nursing* (St. Louis, Mo., C.V. Mosby Co., 1970), p. 61.
3. "Companies Wrestle With Threats to Workers' Reproductive Health," *The Wall Street Journal* (February 5, 1987), p. 23.
4. Silvia Feldman, *Choices in Childbirth* (N.Y., Grosset and Dunlap, 1978), pp. 63–64.
5. Jean Caldwell, "CVS: An Early Test for Genetic Problems," *American Baby* (February, 1985), p. 21.
6. Margot Edwards and Penny Simkin, *Obstetric Tests and Technology, A Consumer's Guide*, p. 5.
7. Edwards and Simkin, p. 5.
8. M.E. Stratmeyer, "Research in Ultrasound Bioeffects: A Public Health View," *Birth and the Family Journal*, Vol. 7:2 (Summer, 1980), pp. 98–99.
9. "Diagnostic Ultrasound Imaging in Pregnancy," National Institutes of Health Consensus Development Conference Consensus Statement, Vol. 5, No. 1, 1984, p. 4.
10. "ICEA Position Paper: Diagnostic Ultrasound in Obstetrics," International Childbirth Education Association, Minneapolis, Minn., 1983, p. 1.
11. "Certification and Consent Form for Ultrasound Exposure," National Women's Health Network, Washington, D.C., 1984.
12. Feldman, p. 65.
13. Edwards and Simkin, p. 4.

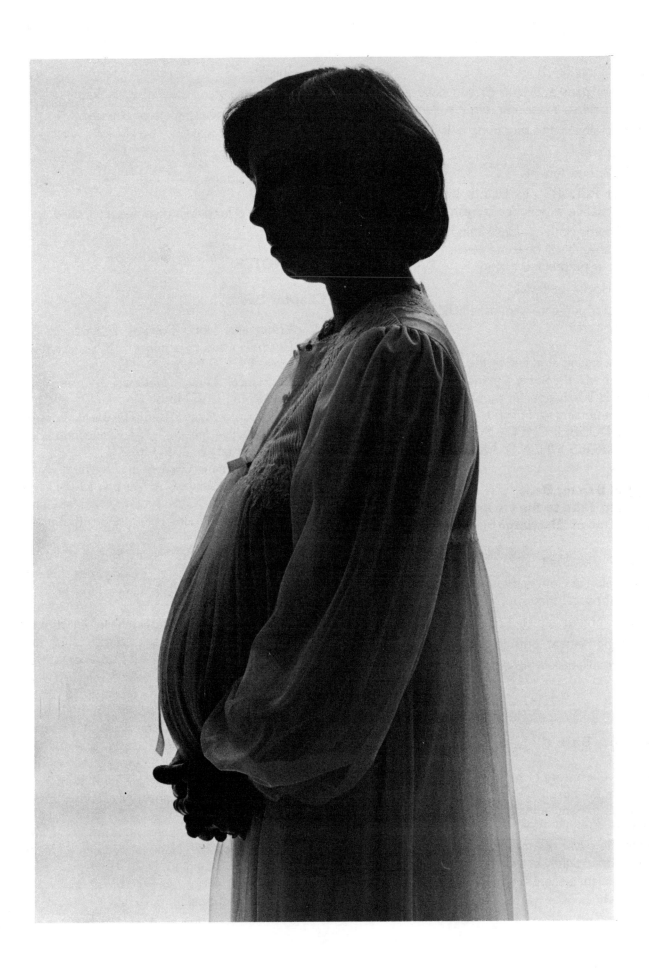

Chapter 3

Nutrition During Pregnancy
or "Food for Thought"

Because Americans are among the wealthiest people in the world, they are often thought to be the most well-nourished. Unfortunately, this is not true. Much of the average American diet is made up of sugar, highly processed foods and unnecessary fat. This "junk food" provides only empty calories—that is, high caloric content with no corresponding nutritional value. A diet of this type is not healthy for anyone, but for a developing fetus it is disastrous! Your baby's entire body—his liver, his heart, his bones, and his brain—are formed completely from the nutrients you provide him. He is not a parasite drawing from your body's reserves. Only the nutrients which you consume are available for his formation and growth. In order that he develop to his full potential, both physically and mentally, it is essential that you eat properly throughout your pregnancy. Even his I.Q. in later life can be affected by your protein intake since his tiny brain cells need adequate protein from which to develop. Remember this as you plan your meals every day.

If you are already nutrition conscious and eating a healthy diet, your main concern will simply be to increase your protein intake. However, if you have previously been a "junk food junkie," now is the time to change. By eliminating the empty calories as well as increasing your protein consumption, you can be confident that you are providing your baby with the optimum building blocks. And, as a bonus, *you* will feel better, too!

Fortunately, many women do begin to pay closer attention to the nutritional content of their diets during pregnancy. You may be motivated by a desire to do everything possible to insure a healthy child. Problems with constipation, heartburn, morning sickness or fatigue may also motivate you to make changes in your diet. An expanding abdomen and weight gain are factors which negatively concern some women, fearing that the added pounds may never be lost. It is important to realize that gaining weight is necessary and that it will go away after pregnancy.

A poor diet during pregnancy can result in anemia, infection, placental malfunction, a difficult labor, cesarean delivery, poor postpartum healing and failure at breastfeeding. The effects of a poor diet on the baby run from prematurity and low birth weight to brain damage and stillbirth.[1]

This chapter is designed to give you usable information which will explain exactly why you need certain food substances and how to go about planning your diet to get them.

Needs of the Pregnant Woman

You are not only growing a baby but a **placenta** as well. It needs to be adequately nourished to insure proper implantation and development for efficient functioning. The placenta carries out many essential life functions for your baby as it grows within you. Along with the umbilical cord, the amniotic sac and the uterus, the placenta is a life support system for this tiny person.

The placenta, in providing nourishment for the baby, works very much like a fuel pump. If the fuel quality is poor or of the wrong octane for the particular engine, the pump will work ineffectively or even stop completely. Also, if the pressure or volume of fuel coming through the pump is affected, the pump's efficiency will be altered. If you think of the nutrients in the bloodstream as fuel, you can see that a poor diet results in a poor quality of nutrients moving through the "placenta-pump." If the volume of fluid in the bloodstream is inadequate, then the pressure of blood coming through the "placenta-pump" will be low and the nutrients will not be able to get through in sufficient quantity to nourish the fetus adequately.

Your **blood volume** needs to increase more than 40 percent[2] during the last half of pregnancy to make the placenta an efficient pump. This requires an adequate **intake of salt** or sodium. Many women experience an increase in their taste for salt during pregnancy. This is the body's way of insuring an adequate supply and thereby helping to increase the total blood volume. Thus, restricting salt may inhibit your body's ability to perform this vital function. Intrauterine growth retardation can result from a low sodium content in the diet.[3]

Many women and physicians are overly concerned about swelling or edema. Some degree of **swelling is normal** for the pregnant woman. The increasing weight of the uterus pressing on the leg veins will cause dependent edema if you have been standing or sitting for long periods. Also, estrogen, manufactured by the placenta during pregnancy, causes your tissues to retain extra fluid. You may have noticed this water retention prior to your menstrual period or if you have taken birth control pills. This was caused by the increased amount of estrogen in your body.

Occasionally a doctor will treat even this normal swelling with a drug classified as a **diuretic (water pill),** and he will restrict salt from the diet. Fortunately, this practice is being eliminated because of the potential side effects, and almost all current obstetrical authors warn that diuretics can actually increase the symptoms, and can cause more serious side effects, including a rise in the blood pH, reduced placental exchange, decreased tolerance for carbohydrates, generalized edema, severe loss of calcium through the urine, and salt depletion.[4] If the swelling is a result of hypovolemia (low blood volume), diuretics may drive salt and water from the circulation and lower the blood volume even further. This could actually cause or accentuate toxemia, the disease the diuretic was supposed to prevent. Diuretics may be indicated in pregnancy if the mother has abnormal swelling because of heart or kidney disease.

Rather than resort to diuretics and salt restriction, the normal pregnant woman should be certain she is obtaining ample protein (75–100 grams) in her diet, and her salt intake should be about 25 grams (5 tsps.) a day.[5] Much of this is contained naturally in the foods you eat. "Salt to taste" is a good rule to follow.

Your **liver** is also helping to maintain a sufficiently increased blood volume by providing albumin, a protein which keeps water in circulation. An inadequate intake of protein during pregnancy prevents the liver from producing enough albumin to hold the water in the blood stream, and thus fluid leaks out into the mother's tissues causing abnormal puffiness.

Filtering the highly increased levels of hormones produced during pregnancy (equal to 100 birth control pills daily) and ridding the body of toxins normally produced in the lower bowel are also jobs performed by your liver, along with approximately 500 others. Your liver is under increasing stress as the baby grows, so you need increasing amounts of protein, calories, vitamins and salt in your diet in the last half of pregnancy to counteract the stress on your liver.[6]

Your baby's brain grows most in the last two months, and an adequate intake of protein, mandatory for building brain cells, is essential at this time. So even if your diet has been unstructured up to your seventh month, a change is still a great benefit. Conversely, if your diet has been adequate up to your seventh month, and you begin restricting calories or protein in particular, your baby may suffer greatly from your attempts not to gain any more weight before birth.[7]

Weight gain varies from woman to woman, along with the pattern of weight gain. Total weight gain will be determined by your pre-pregnant weight, eating habits, daily activities and your individual metabolism. Since every woman is unique, it is difficult to say a certain number of pounds is the correct weight gain for all pregnant women.

Even for **overweight women,** dieting during pregnancy is risky for both mother and child. Usually changing the woman's diet to include only nutritionally beneficial foods and eliminating high calorie "junk foods" will provide the baby with nourishment and may even bring about a weight loss for the woman. A diet providing less than 2300 calories will neither provide the nutrients necessary for the growth of the baby, nor an adequate gain in weight. A report from the Maternal and Child Health Branch of the California Department of Health recommends a "smooth and progressive weight gain of at least 24 pounds, just as would be expected in a non-obese woman."[8]

During the last weeks of pregnancy, your baby is laying down stores of vital minerals and body fat, essential for his survival. He puts on a layer of insulating body fat and builds his **stores of iron** because his diet for the first six months of extrauterine life will be low in iron. Even the iron supplement in infant formula is poorly absorbed by the infant, so it is very important that you eat foods that will provide you and your baby a sufficient supply of iron in the last months of pregnancy. For the breastfeeding mother, the small amount of iron in breastmilk is efficiently absorbed by the baby and does not diminish the infant's iron supply as quickly as in a formula fed infant.

If you are carrying **twins,** your nutritional needs will increase further than those of a woman carrying a single baby. Your protein intake should be 110–130 grams while taking in at least 3100 calories per day.[9] Physiologic swelling is even more ex-

aggerated as you may have two placentas or one larger placenta producing a larger quantity of estrogen. The larger and heavier uterus adds more restriction on the venous return, increasing dependent edema. Weight gain in a woman carrying twins can be as much as 50–60 pounds if she is encouraged to eat right. Women who follow this diet regime along with not restricting salt often find their babies are of normal weight at birth (not less than 5½ lbs.) and arrive at term, not prematurely as is usually expected.[10]

The direct relationship between a nutritious diet during pregnancy and a healthy baby has only been established in the last few years. For this reason, some doctors who attended school ten years ago or more may not be aware of this important correlation. In addition, as of 1985, no U.S. medical school required that its students study applied human nutrition to graduate, and no obstetrical departments required residents to study nutrition as part of their training.[11] If you find that your doctor is unaware of current findings on nutrition as presented in this book, perhaps you can supply him with helpful information. An excellent book on this topic is *What Every Pregnant Woman Should Know, The Truth About Diets and Drugs in Pregnancy.* (See reading list.) If you and he continue to disagree on the management of your pregnancy, you may desire to seek care elsewhere.

Dr. Tom Brewer devised the "no-risk" pregnancy diet, which includes a daily/weekly food pattern geared towards supplying those foods which will provide you and your baby with adequate building materials and reserves.

THE "NO-RISK" PREGNANCY DIET

When you are pregnant, you need more of good-quality foods than when you are not pregnant. To meet your own needs and those of your developing baby, you must have, *every day*, at least:

1. One quart (four glasses) of milk—any kind: whole milk, low-fat, skim, powdered skim, or buttermilk. If you do not like milk, you can substitute one cup of yogurt for each cup of milk

2. Two eggs

3. Two servings of fish, shellfish, chicken or turkey, lean beef, veal, lamb, pork, liver, or kidney

Alternative combinations include:
   Rice with: beans, cheese, sesame seeds, milk
   Cornmeal with: beans, cheese, tofu, milk
   Beans with: rice, bulgur, cornmeal, wheat noodles, sesame seeds, milk
   Peanuts with: sunflower seeds, milk
   Whole wheat bread or noodles with: beans, cheese, peanut butter, tofu, milk

For each serving of meat, you can substitute these quantities of cheese:

Brick	— 4 oz.	Longhorn	— 3 oz.
Camembert	— 6 oz.	Muenster	— 4 oz.
Cheddar	— 3 oz.	Monterey Jack	— 4 oz.
Cottage	— 6 oz.	Swiss	— 3 oz.

4. Two servings of fresh, green leafy vegetables: mustard, beet, collard, dandelion or turnip greens, spinach, lettuce, cabbage, broccoli, kale, Swiss chard

5. Five servings of whole-grain breads, rolls, cereals or pancakes: Wheatena, bran flakes, granola, shredded wheat, wheat germ, oatmeal, buckwheat or whole wheat pancakes, corn bread, corn tortillas, corn or bran or whole wheat muffins, waffles, brown rice

6. Two choices from: a whole potato (any style), large green pepper, orange, grapefruit, lemon, lime, papaya, tomato (one piece of fruit or one large glass of juice)

7. Three pats of margarine, vitamin A-enriched, or butter, or oil

Also include in your diet:

8. A yellow- or orange-colored vegetable or fruit five times a week

9. Liver once a week, if you like it

10. Table salt: **SALT YOUR FOOD TO TASTE**

11. Water: drink to thirst

It is not healthy for you and your unborn baby to go even 24 hours without good food!

Note: Vitamin supplements are in routine use in prenatal care; they do not take the place of a sound, balanced diet of nutritious foods.

BASIC FACTS OF NUTRITION

Proteins are the building blocks of all cells and are composed of amino acids. They are necessary for the growth and repair of tissue, for building blood and amniotic fluid, and they help in forming antibodies for both you and the baby. There are two kinds of protein, complete and incomplete. The complete protein supplies all eight of the essential amino acids. Animal sources of protein are usually complete. Vegetable protein is usually incomplete. If you are a vegetarian, detailed knowledge of protein composition is necessary to plan menus that insure a balanced diet and provide all eight essential amino acids. Including both animal and vegetable sources of protein is the best insurance that you will be getting all of the essential amino acids in your diet. Some good sources of protein are: meat, fish, poultry, eggs, milk, cheese, dried beans and peas, peanut butter, nuts, whole grain bread and cereals.

Carbohydrates come in two forms. Sugars, the simpler ones, are found in fruit and milk. Starches, the more complex carbohydrates, are found in vegetables and cereals. Their intake during pregnancy supplies energy making it possible for protein to be "spared" to do the important work of building tissues, rather than supplying energy to the mother. Many snacks (chips, cookies, candy) are largely carbohydrates which supply empty calories and little else. Vegetables and fruits supply not only energy, but vitamins and minerals that are beneficial to both you and your developing baby. Some carbohydrates also provide fiber to help minimize the problem of constipation. Good sources of carbohydrates are: fresh fruits and vegetables, whole grain bread and cereals.

A small amount of **fat** is essential for the body's processing of certain fat soluble vitamins (A, D, E, K). Vegetable fat is thought to be more beneficial than animal fat in the human body. Corn oil margarine contains less saturated fat and no cholesterol. Good sources of fat include: oils used for cooking, butter and margarine, nuts, peanut butter, and bacon.

Rather than concentrating on the number of **calories** you are eating, you should be certain you are obtaining the proper nutrients in the correct amounts.

A higher caloric intake is usually needed during pregnancy, unless you have been eating junk foods in abundance. By eliminating the junk calories, some women can actually lower their caloric intake and still get sufficient nutrients if they were overeating to begin with.

For the moderately active woman, an increase of 300–400 calories is needed to elevate her caloric intake to at least 2600 calories daily during the second half of pregnancy. If you are carrying twins, the figure is at least 3100 calories. If you follow a weight control diet, and especially if you are carrying twins, a deficiency of energy and protein will result. The protein you eat will be burned for energy and will not be available for building the baby's body and brain.

Calcium builds bones and teeth, aids in clotting blood, regulates the use of other minerals in the body and functions in muscle tone and relaxation. An imbalance of calcium and phosphorus can contribute to the discomfort of leg cramps in pregancy. One bottle of soft drink may contain enough of other minerals to have a negative effect on the availability of calcium to your body's cells.[12] Eliminate soda from your diet and eat good sources of calcium. Decreased amounts of calcium in the diet are associated with decreased strength in infant bones.[13] Good sources of calcium are: dairy products, broccoli, dark-green leafy vegetables and some seafood.

Iron is essential in the formation of hemoglobin, the element which carries oxygen to the tissues and cells of the body. Because of the increase in your total blood volume during pregnancy, the ratio of hemoglobin to blood volume will go down in the last trimester. This is normal and sometimes confused with true anemia. During pregnancy your body demands an increase in iron intake in order to build the baby's supply and prevent anemia in you.

It is important to eat enough iron rich foods on a daily basis to obtain this needed amount of iron. To insure this, many doctors recommend an iron supplement along with the prenatal vitamins so commonly prescribed. Iron supplements can have a constipating effect and make some women nauseated. Talk with your doctor or midwife and find a form of iron that will agree with you and also fulfill the requirements. Good sources of iron in the diet are: liver, red meats, egg yolk, oysters, shellfish, bread and cereals (enriched and wholegrain) and dried fruits.

The best way of obtaining **vitamins** is through a diet that includes both the water-soluble B-complex and C vitamins and the fat-soluble vitamins A, D, E and K. Vitamin supplements are essentially just that, supplements. They will not compensate for an inadequate diet, and should not be thought of as the best way to obtain vitamins. They contain only those vitamins for which nutritional requirements are known. There are many trace vitamins in a well balanced diet for which requirements have not been set or are not even known.

The chart that follows summarizes those nutrients that are known to be important to the pregnant woman. It includes functions, amount needed and sources of each in the daily diet.

DAILY NUTRITIONAL REQUIREMENTS DURING PREGNANCY

Nutrient	Requirement	Function	Sources	
Calories	2600 calories a day during second half of pregnancy	to spare protein for building tissues	proteins fats carbohydrates	
Protein	75-100 grams (gms)	for development and growth of fetus, amniotic fluid, placenta, maternal tissue and maternal stores for labor, delivery and lactation	milk cheese eggs meat poultry fish dried beans and peas	peanut butter nuts soybeans whole grain bread and cereals
Calcium	1200 milligrams (mgs)	forms fetal skeleton and tooth buds	milk cheese yogurt dark green vegetables	nuts oysters clams sardines
Phosphorus	1200 milligrams	helps in bone and tooth formation and for normal muscle function	Good sources of protein are good sources of phosphorus	
Iodine	175 micrograms (mcgs)	normal thyroid function	iodized salt salt water fish	
Magnesium	450 milligrams	needed for energy and protein metabolism, muscle action and tissue growth	nuts soybeans cocoa seafood green vegetables	whole grain cereals dried beans and peas
Iron	36 milligrams	to increase hemoglobin as maternal blood volume expands and to provide for fetal liver iron storage	liver red meat dried fruits dark green vegetables oysters	enriched and whole grain bread and cereals egg yolk shellfish
Vitamin A	1000 micrograms (1 milligram)	essential for cell development, tissue growth, and tooth bud formation	butter margarine cantaloupe peaches	dark green and yellow vegetables
Vitamin D	10-12 micrograms	absorption of calcium, and phosphorus, bone and tooth formation	fortified milk fortified margarine sunshine	

DAILY NUTRITIONAL REQUIREMENTS DURING PREGNANCY

Nutrient	Requirement	Function	Sources
Vitamin E	10 micrograms	promotes tissue growth and healthy red blood cells	vegetable oils eggs green leafy vegetables milk cereals
Vitamin C	80 milligrams	necessary for tissue formation and increases absorption of iron	berries citrus fruits melons green peppers tomatoes green leafy potatoes vegetables
Vitamin B$_6$	2.6 milligrams	necessary for protein metabolism	meat bran wheat germ corn liver
Vitamin B$_{12}$	4 micrograms	formation of red blood cells	milk eggs cheese meat liver
Folic Acid	0.8 milligrams	prevents certain anemias	liver lean beef fish asparagus green leafy vegetables lima beans
Niacin	15 milligrams	necessary for energy and protein metabolism	meat peanuts enriched bread and cereals dried beans and peas
Riboflavin	1.5 milligrams	necessary for energy and protein metabolism	milk liver enriched bread and cereals
Thiamine	1.3 milligrams	metabolism of carbohydrates, maintenance of healthy nerves	legumes enriched and whole pork grain bread and beef cereals liver
Sodium (Salt)	25 grams	necessary for expansion of maternal blood volume and efficient functioning of placenta	iodized salt naturally present in many foods
Fluids	at least eight 8 oz. glasses	to maintain increase in maternal blood volume, and to insure good kidney function	water milk juices

NUTRITIONAL CHANGES TRIMESTER BY TRIMESTER

First Trimester—Months 1–3

During the early weeks of pregnancy, you may not be aware of the baby within your body. Therefore, an adequate diet is important even before you consider becoming pregnant. Once the pregnancy is discovered, you may experience nausea or "morning sickness" which minimizes your thought of food. But even this early in the pregnancy, you need to be sure that you are eating a good diet, although your nutritional requirements are essentially the same as for a non-pregnant healthy woman.[14]

Lack of certain nutrients in the diet, primarily lack of vitamin B_6, is thought to contribute to morning sickness.[15] If you are bothered by this problem, try some of these natural non-drug remedies.

- Eat dry crackers or toast before rising in the morning.
- Avoid greasy, fried or highly spiced foods.
- Drink teas made from small amounts of herbs— such as raspberry leaf, peppermint or chamomile.
- Increase your intake of B vitamins, especially B_6, or eat foods rich in vitamin B.

Morning sickness may occur because of low blood sugar after not eating all night. Some women experience this nausea throughout the day, especially if they go for long periods without eating. Eating frequent high protein snacks during the day and at bedtime may eliminate or lessen the severity of the symptoms. If none of these remedies help and nausea and vomiting become a severe problem, your doctor can prescribe medication. Gratefully, this symptom passes by your fourth month.

Second Trimester—Months 4–6

During the second trimester, you need to follow the increased allowances for calories, vitamins and minerals recommended by the National Research Council. (See chart, page 40.) Your baby puts on very little weight during the second trimester. However, maternal tissues greatly increase. You begin to lay down a store of fat, which your body will utilize during lactation. Your uterus and breasts enlarge, the volume of amniotic fluid increases, the placenta grows in size and your blood volume increases greatly. Therefore, increased fluid and protein intake are essential.

Third Trimester—Months 7–9

During the last trimester, your baby begins gaining weight rapidly. His brain grows at its greatest rate during the last two months, and he builds his store of iron. Make sure you are following the "no-risk" pregnancy diet during this time, and beyond if you breastfeed your baby. Protein (75-100 grams) and sufficient calories are vital for optimum development of the baby's brain and body. Dieting at this point is not beneficial to you or your baby, and should not be encouraged. Fasting before doctors' appointments in order to minimize weight gain is foolish. Be certain that you are eating well, and the weight you gain will insure the health of both you and your baby.

If you are experiencing increased swelling, try adding more protein to your diet. In rare cases, this swelling puts pressure on the nerves in the wrist, resulting in tingling, numbness and pain in the hands and fingers. This is called carpal tunnel syndrome. Additional B_6 may help to relieve or prevent further development of this condition. It will gradually subside following delivery.

Remember Throughout Your Pregnancy

- Not to restrict salt unless your doctor can give you documented proof that this is necessary in your case.
- Not to take diuretics for "normal swelling" in pregnancy.
- Not to restrict calories in the last trimester to "hold down" weight gain. This is harmful for both you and your baby!
- Not to go even 24 hours without *good food!*

NUTRITIONAL HINTS

Vegetables

Buy fresh vegetables when they are in season. Use a steamer or cook them quickly in a small amount of water to preserve the nutrients, and only until tender. Frozen vegetables can add greater variety to your menus when fresh are not available. Cook them the same as fresh using little water (½ cup per box) and be careful not to overcook. Canned vegetables are only slightly less nutritious if prepared properly. Because they have already been fully cooked during the canning process, they should only be warmed. Further cooking will decrease their nutritional value.

To insure the maximum benefit from the vegetables you prepare, save all vegetable cooking water. This water often contains more vitamins and minerals than the vegetables themselves. Use this water in spaghetti sauce, chili, gravies, soups, stews, casseroles, stuffing, cream sauces, pot roasts, etc. Mild tasting vegetable water (corn, peas, green beans) may be used in any recipe that calls for water—cakes, muffins, etc. You can even use it as a drink for a pre-dinner appetizer. If you have no immediate use for the water, freeze it.

Wheat Germ

Wheat germ is a versatile and nutritious addition to almost any dish. Its concentration of protein, thiamine, iron and vitamin E can be used to fortify cake, muffin and pancake mixes. Add about ½ cup of wheat germ per box of mix. You can also use it as a topping for casseroles. And you can add it to most ground beef recipes, at the rate of about ½ cup per pound of meat. Mix it with peanut butter for a nutritious sandwich spread. It can be used in almost all cookie recipes, in addition to, or in place of, nuts. Use it as your cereal, served with milk, or add it to your baby's mashed bananas. In fact, you can add it to all cooked and cold cereals for extra nutrition. Its nut-like flavor will enhance the taste of most foods. Let your imagination create new uses for wheat germ.

Brewer's Yeast

Brewer's yeast is a natural vitamin B complex concentrate, which can be purchased in health food stores. Because its flavor is somewhat strong, you may need to begin by using it in recipes which require cooking. This seems to produce a milder flavor. You can add it, for example, to all dark cookie recipes, about one tablespoon per batch. You can also add it to pancakes, cake mixes and breads. For instant energy, stir 1 to 3 tablespoons of brewer's yeast into a 12 oz. glass of tomato, pineapple or other vegetable or fruit juice.

Powdered brewer's yeast is the most valuable nutritionally, but instant flakes dissolve better and have a milder taste. Ask for a tasteless brand. Tablets are available at drug stores, but huge quantities must be consumed to be of value.

Honey

Honey is a natural form of sugar which is slightly more nutritious than processed sugar. It does contain 1 mg. of calcium per tablespoon but brown sugar contains more, nearly 12 mg. per tablespoon. One tablespoon of honey contains 65 calories as compared to 40 in granulated sugar. As with all sweets, honey should have a limited place in your diet. The best way to get sugar is in the fruits, vegetables and milk you consume each day.

DO NOT give raw honey to a baby under one year of age. He could develop infantile botulism from spores that may be present in the honey.

If you do prefer using honey in cooking, you can replace half of the sugar in a cake recipe with honey. In puddings, custards and pie fillings, honey may be used instead of sugar. Use about two-thirds as much. For more recipe ideas, send for the booklet, "Honey—Some Ways to Use It," from the U. S. Dept. of Agriculture, Washington, D. C.

Peanut Butter

Peanut butter is a very rich source of protein, as are all nut butters. It is easily homemade in the blender, or you may buy the natural, old-fashioned variety or that freshly ground at the store. Commercial manufacturers add too much salt, extra fats (often unhealthy ones), and unnecessary sugar, as well as other additives.

General Hints

Get in the habit of fortifying almost everything you cook. Add wheat germ, powdered milk, brewer's yeast, or anything else that is nutritious. For example, a boxed pizza can be doctored up with wheat germ, a fresh sliced tomato, ¼ pound of hamburger, and extra cheese. Cooking nutritionally is a challenge and it's fun. The additional cost can be compensated for by not buying the "valueless" foods such as soft drinks, cookies, and potato chips. In time, fewer doctor and dentist bills will demonstrate even greater savings.

If your family has well-established, but poor eating habits, make changes slowly. You will neither reach your nutritional goal nor have a happy family if your try to change a lifetime of eating habits in one week. Make only one change at a time, and don't comment on it. Gradually, as the weeks change into months, you will find that your family is eating and enjoying truly nutritious foods. The highly refined and valueless foods will simply fall by the wayside, forgotten and not missed.

Read *The Supermarket Handbook* for a more overall view. There are many paperbacks on nutrition at book stores and health food stores which are also valuable. Most of them contain recipes which are easy to prepare as well as nutritionally superior.

The following chart is designed to help you calculate the amount of protein, calcium and iron you are eating each day. Although these are not the only nutrients you need, they are very important and you need to plan carefully to make sure you are obtaining them. By eating sufficient quantities of protein, calcium and iron, plus a vitamin C rich food each day, you can be sure you are getting all the necessary nutrients for a balanced diet. Follow the "no-

risk pregnancy diet" when planning your meals.

To use the chart, write down everything you eat and drink for a 24 hour period. Then add up the amount of protein, calcium and iron you have consumed. Compare it to the daily requirement for a pregnant woman to see how you are doing. If there is a specific area you are deficient in, refer to the chart to find which foods are high in that nutrient.

The calorie column is included to help you determine which foods supply the most nutrition for the amount of calories consumed.

NUTRITION CHART

	Serving Size	Protein	Calcium	Iron	Calories
Daily Requirement		*75-100 grams*	*1200 mg.*	*36 mg.*	*2600*
Dairy					
Milk					
whole	1 cup	9	288	0.1	160
2%	1 cup	9	288	0.1	145
skim	1 cup	9	298	0.1	90
buttermilk	1 cup	9	298	0.1	90
Cheese					
natural (cheddar,	1 in. cube	4	128	0.2	70
swiss, etc.)	1 oz.	7	213	0.3	105
pasteurized process	1 wrapped slice (¾ oz.)	5	149	0.2	79
	1 tbsp.	3	80	0.1	45
Cottage cheese					
creamed	½ cup	15	106	0.4	120
uncreamed	½ cup	19	101	0.4	98

NUTRITION CHART (continued)

	Serving Size	Protein	Calcium	Iron	Calories
Daily Requirement		*75-100 grams*	*1200 mg.*	*36 mg.*	*2600*
Custard, baked	½ cup	7	139	0.5	148
Ice cream	1 cup	6	175	0.1	295
Ice milk	1 cup	6	292	0.1	285
Yogurt (using partially skimmed milk)	1 cup	8	295	0.1	120
Eggs (large)	1 egg	6	27	1.1	80
Meat, Poultry, Fish					
Bacon (broiled or fried crisp)	2 slices	5	2	0.5	95
Beef					
lean ground beef	4 oz. (½ cup)	23	10	2.9	185
sirloin (broiled)	4 oz. (lean only)	36	14	4.4	230
Chicken (fried)	½ breast	25	9	1.3	155
	2 drumsticks	24	12	1.8	180
Chile con carne, canned					
with beans	1 cup	19	80	4.2	335
without beans	1 cup	26	97	3.6	510
Liver, beef	4 oz.	30	12	10.0	260
Pork	1 chop	16	8	2.2	260
	3 oz. ham	18	8	2.2	245
Lunchmeat, boiled ham	2 oz.	11	6	1.6	135
Hot dog (8 per 1 lb. package)	2 hot dogs (4 oz.)	12	6	1.6	340
Sausage	2 links (1 oz.)	5	2	0.6	125
	1 patty	5	2	0.6	125
Fish (baked)	3 oz.	22	25	0.6	135
Fishsticks	5	19	13	0.5	200
Oysters (raw)	1 cup (13-19 medium)	20	226	13.2	160
Shrimp, meat only	3 oz.	21	98	2.6	100
Tuna	3 oz. (½ can)	24	7	1.6	170

NUTRITION CHART (continued)

	Serving Size	Protein	Calcium	Iron	Calories
Daily Requirement	*75-100 grams*	*1200 mg.*	*36 mg.*	*2600*
Dry Beans and Peas, Nuts, Peanuts					
Almonds	½ cup	13	166	3.4	425
Beans (canned Great Northern, Navy)	½ cup	8	37	2.3	115
Pork & Beans	½ cup	8	70	2.4	155
Limas, cooked	½ cup	8	28	2.8	130
Cashew nuts, roasted	½ cup	12	26	2.6	380
Blackeye peas, dry (cooked)	½ cup	7	21	1.6	95
Peanuts	½ cup	19	54	1.5	420
Peanut butter	1 tbsp.	4	9	0.3	95
Vegetables					
Asparagus	6 canned spears	2	18	1.8	20
Green beans	½ cup	1	31	0.4	15
Broccoli	½ cup	3	66	0.6	20
Brussel sprouts	½ cup	3	21	0.7	23
Cabbage, cooked	1 cup	2	75	0.5	35
Carrots, raw	1 whole	1	18	0.4	20
Coleslaw	1 cup	1	52	0.5	varies with seasoning
Corn on cob	1 ear, 5 in. long	3	2	0.5	70
Corn, canned	½ cup	3	5	0.5	85
Cucumber	6 (⅛ in.) slices	trace	8	0.2	5
Lettuce	¼ head	1	23	0.6	15
Okra	8 pods	2	78	0.4	25
Peas, cooked	½ cup	5	19	1.5	58
Potato					
baked	1 potato	3	9	0.7	90
french fried	10 (ea. 2 × ½ × ½ in.)	2	9	0.7	155
frozen, heated in oven	10	2	5	1.0	125
Spinach, cooked	½ cup	3	84	2.0	20
Tomatoes	1 medium	2	20	0.8	35

	Serving Size	Protein	Calcium	Iron	Calories
Daily Requirement		*75-100 grams*	*1200 mg.*	*36 mg.*	*2600*
Fruits					
Apple	1 medium	trace	8	0.4	70
Apple juice	1 cup (8 oz.)	trace	15	1.5	120
Apricots					
raw	3	1	18	0.5	55
dried, uncooked	20 small halves (½ cup)	4	50	4.1	195
Bananas (3 per lb.)	1	1	8	0.7	85
Cantaloupe, raw	½ medium	1	27	0.8	60
Grapefruit	½	1	22	0.6	55
Orange, raw Florida variety	1 cup	1	67	0.3	75
Orange juice, fresh Florida or frozen reconstituted	1 cup	2	25	0.5	110
Prunes					
raw	4	1	14	1.1	70
cooked	½ cup	1	30	2.3	148
Prune juice	1 cup	1	36	10.5	200
Raisins	½ cup	2	50	2.8	230
Strawberries, fresh	1 cup	1	31	1.5	55
Grain Products					
Biscuits	1	3	46	0.6	140
Bran flakes	1 oz. (1 cup)	3	20	1.2	95
Bread					
rye	1 slice	2	17	0.4	55
white	1 slice	2	19	0.6	60
whole wheat	1 slice	2	23	0.5	55
Corn flakes	1 cup	2	5	0.4	110
Corn muffin	1	3	50	0.8	150
Crackers, saltines	4 crackers (2 in. square)	2	4	0.2	70
Macaroni, spaghetti (enriched)	1 cup cooked	5	11	1.3	155
Oat cereal	1 cup	3	44	1.3	115

NUTRITION CHART (continued)

	Serving Size	Protein	Calcium	Iron	Calories
Daily Requirement		*75-100 grams*	*1200 mg.*	*36 mg.*	*2600*
Oatmeal	1 cup	5	21	1.4	130
Pancakes	1 (4 in. cake)	2	27	0.4	60
Pizza, cheese	1 slice (⅛ of 14 in. pie)	7	107	0.7	185
Popcorn					
plain	1 cup	1	1	0.3	25
with oil	1 cup	1	1	0.3	65
Rice					
cooked	1 cup	3	17	1.5	185
instant	1 cup	5	6	0.3	156
Rice flakes	1 cup	2	9	0.5	115
Waffle (enriched flour, milk, egg)	1 waffle (7 in. diameter)	7	179	1.0	210
Wheat cereal	1 large biscuit	3	12	1.0	100
	1 cup flakes	3	12	1.3	105
Wheat germ	½ cup	9	25	3.2	123

Miscellaneous

	Serving Size	Protein	Calcium	Iron	Calories
Beverages					
cola	12 oz.	0	0	0.0	145
gingerale	12 oz.	0	0	0.0	115
root beer	12 oz.	0	0	0.0	150
Cookies					
brownies (from mix)	1	1	8	0.4	95
chocolate chip	1	1	4	0.2	50
sandwich (vanilla or chocolate)	1	1	2	0.1	50
Doughnuts (cake type)	1	1	13	0.4	125
Fats					
butter, margarine	1 tbsp.	trace	3	0.0	100
cooking oil	1 tbsp.	1	0	0.0	125
Pie					
apple	⅐ of 9 in. pie	3	11	0.4	350
cherry	⅐ of 9 in. pie	4	19	0.4	350
pumpkin	⅐ of 9 in. pie	5	66	0.7	275

	Serving Size	Protein	Calcium	Iron	Calories
Daily Requirement		**75-100 grams**	**1200 mg.**	**36 mg.**	**2600**
Soup					
beef boullion	1 cup	5	trace	0.5	30
chicken noodle	1 cup	4	10	0.5	65
clam chowder	1 cup	2	36	1.0	85
vegetable with beef broth	1 cup	3	20	0.8	80
split pea	1 cup	6	32	1.5	140

NON-FOOD ITEMS AND DRUGS DURING PREGNANCY

We are a drug oriented society. We as adults, routinely consume, and encourage our children to consume, many medicines without considering that even most "over-the-counter" substances are drugs.

Virtually all drugs and medications which you take during pregnancy cross the placenta and reach your baby. The baby will often get an equal amount of the drug dosage although the drug is taken with your age and weight in mind. Such rapid fetal growth and development goes on during pregnancy that a drug may have a profound effect on your baby even though the drug is considered mild. Many drugs may only be harmful if used at a particular time in pregnancy, or only if used in conjunction with other drugs or agents. It is difficult to trace exact connections between some drugs and birth defects, since humans are not used as experimental subjects. Therefore, you should be cautious about taking or using *any* drug during pregnancy. No drug is *known* to be safe, even though it may not be considered harmful. Always weigh the possible risks against the possible benefits before taking any medication.

Often a drug-free treatment can provide relief. For example, a headache may be caused by tension or going for long periods without eating. Try lying down with some relaxing music or use an ice bag. Eating frequent small meals may also help. Some women have found headache relief by applying firm fingertip pressure to the following acupressure points: the temples; the area midway between the eyebrows; and the back of the neck, along the hairline. You may find that circular massage is more effective than direct pressure. Keep in mind that the area should be tender to the touch. This will help

you in locating the correct pressure points. (See page 83 for a discussion of acupressure.)

Backaches are often caused by poor posture. Using good body mechanics and the pelvic rock (see Chapter 4 on exercise) may be more beneficial than a pill. Constipation can be avoided by a high fiber diet, plenty of fluids and exercise. Medications for colds or flu are not a cure and only relieve the symptoms. Your cold will not go away faster by taking them and these drugs can be harmful to your baby. Try getting plenty of rest, extra fluids and using a vaporizer for stuffy nose.

If you do develop a medical problem during pregnancy, such as a urinary infection, or have a pre-existing condition (diabetes, heart disease), you may need to take medication. If a problem is not treated, it could be more dangerous to the fetus than the medication prescribed. Your doctor will use the medication or treatment he feels is safest during pregnancy.

The following non-food items are presented in greater detail.

Tobacco

The toxic substances in cigarette smoke are harmful to both you and your unborn child. While pregnant, your best bet is to stop smoking or to cut down as much as possible, and to avoid being around others who are heavy smokers. A direct relationship exists between the number of cigarettes you smoke per day and the degree to which your baby is affected.

Pregnant smokers give birth to smaller babies, have a greater chance of premature birth and placental malformations, and have more premature rupture of membranes and stillbirths. They also have a higher incidence of sudden infant death syn-

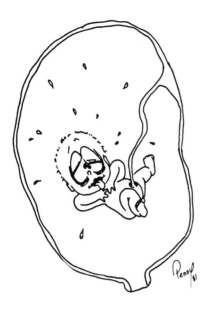

"Those cigarettes are killing me."

drome among their babies,[16] and have been shown to have babies intellectually three to five months behind the children of non-smokers.

In addition, some effects have been found to be lasting. Follow-up studies have shown that seven-year-old children of mothers who smoked during pregnancy were shorter in average stature, tended to have retarded reading ability, and rated lower in "social adjustment" than children of mothers who had not smoked during pregnancy.[17] Offspring of heavy smokers experience more behavioral problems. These are in part related to impaired hearing caused by the toxic effect of smoking on the inner ear.[18]

Marijuana and Hard Drugs

Marijuana affects your baby as much as it does you. In animal studies, temporary brain cell alterations occurred in the fetuses of rats exposed to marijuana smoke.[19] Some reports have indicated that pregnant women who smoke marijuana in excess and those who take LSD may cause chromosomal damage in their babies.[20]

Pregnant women who are addicted to drugs give birth to babies who are also addicted and who must suffer the horrors of withdrawal. The long-term effects of drugs are not known. Don't risk ruining your child's development. Stay away from marijuana and other drugs while you are pregnant.

Alcohol

Current research has proven that alcohol has a toxic effect on the developing fetus. If you drink during pregnancy, the alcohol quickly crosses the placenta and saturates the fetal blood supply with the same concentration that is present in your blood. There is no known safe level of alcohol consumption. Therefore, you would be wise to give up drinking alcoholic beverages during pregnancy or to limit yourself to an occasional drink.

Babies born to women who are heavy drinkers have a 50% chance of having fetal alcohol syndrome, which involves mental retardation, a slowing of body growth and other abnormalities in the infant. Even two drinks a day may cause a lowered birth weight in your baby. Be sure to avoid any type of drinking "binge" during pregnancy, or even if you just suspect you are pregnant. One big party is not worth the risk of interfering with the rapid growth and development which your baby undergoes during those first few weeks.

Caffeine

Caffeine is a stimulant present in coffee, tea, cola drinks, chocolate and some over-the-counter drugs. Numerous studies on pregnant animals have shown birth defects, such as cleft palate and missing bones, resulting from doses of caffeine equivalent to three to four cups of coffee a day.

"I wish I could tell her what those drinks do to me."

In August 1980, the FDA issued a warning to pregnant women urging them to limit their consumption of coffee and other caffeine containing substances. Michael Jacobson, executive director of the Center for Science in the Public Interest, feels that a pregnant woman should limit her consumption of caffeine "to a minuscule fraction of a cup of coffee a day."[21] In other words, consume no caffeine at all. One or two cups of coffee a day may not harm your baby. On the other hand, you are only pregnant for nine months and should do everything possible to insure a healthy child.

Many good tasting decaffeinated coffees are on the market today which you can substitute. Milk, water and fruit juices should make up the bulk of your fluid intake for maximum nutrition. Coffee has no nutritional value. Below are common sources of caffeine and the amount in one serving.

Caffeine Levels in Common Sources

5 oz. cup of brewed coffee	85–110 mg.
5 oz. cup of instant coffee	66 mg.
5 oz. cup of black tea	50 mg.
5 oz. cup of instant tea	30 mg.
5 oz. cup of decaffeinated coffee	3 mg.
12 oz. cola drink	50 mg.
12 oz. Mellow Yello	51 mg.
1 cup of cocoa	6–42 mg.
1 chocolate bar	20 mg.
1 Excedrin, Anacin tablet	60 mg.

Food Additives

Food additives such as saccharin, nitrates, nitrites, artificial colors and flavors, preservatives, PCB and PBB (industrial chemical wastes found in fresh water fish) are possibly related to an increased susceptibility to cancer and birth defects.[22]

Saccharin presents a special risk to the male fetus if consumed by his mother. The FDA reports studies that indicate a positive correlation (60–100% increased risk) between saccharin ingestion during pregnancy and bladder cancer in male offspring.[23] Aspartame—which is marketed as Nutrasweet, an artificial sweetener of soft drinks and packaged foods, and Equal, a granulated sugar substitute—has not had time to be fully tested. The FDA has recommended moderation in its use during pregnancy. For optimum safety, you may want to eliminate all artificially sweetened substances from your diet at this time.

Medicines

Over-the-counter and prescription drugs all pass through the placenta to your baby. You should check with your doctor or midwife before taking any medication during pregnancy. Drugs used to treat such symptoms as pain, nervousness, sleeplessness, runny nose, heartburn, nausea, coughs and constipation may be avoided by using common sense, good nutrition and relaxation techniques. Avoid taking aspirin, sedatives, antihistamines, barbiturates, diuretics, hormones, diet pills, antacids, cough medicines or tranquilizers. Some of these substances are thought to be associated with jaundice, bleeding and cleft palates in babies.[24]

The drug Accutane, used to treat severe acne, has recently been found to cause major birth defects when taken during the first three months of pregnancy.[25] Avoid taking this drug if there is any chance that you may be pregnant.

FOOTNOTES

Chapter 3

1. Gail Sforza Brewer, *What Every Pregnant Woman Should Know, The Truth About Diet and Drugs During Pregnancy* (N.Y., Penguin Press, 1985), p. 22.
2. *What Every Pregnant Woman Should Know*, p. 25.
3. *What Every Pregnant Woman Should Know*, p. 25.
4. Madeline Shearer, "Malnutrition in Middle Class Pregnant Women," *Birth and the Family Journal*, Vol. 7:1 (Spring, 1980), p. 30.
5. L. Jean Bogert, Ph.D., George M. Briggs, Ph.D., Doris Howes Calloway, Ph.D., *Nutrition and Physical Fitness, 9th Ed.* (Philadelphia, W.B. Saunders Co., 1973), p. 380.
6. Gail Sforza Brewer, *The Pregnancy After 30 Workbook* (Emmaus, Pa., Rodale Press, 1978), p. 31.
7. *The Pregnancy After 30 Workbook*, p. 32.
8. Bogert, p. 380.
9. *What Every Pregnant Woman Should Know*, p. 23.

10. *What Every Pregnant Woman Should Know,* p. 36.

11. *What Every Pregnant Woman Should Know,* p. 114.

12. Bonnie Worthington, *Nutrition in Pregnancy and Lactation* (St. Louis, C.V. Mosby Co., 1977), p. 49.

13. Worthington, p. 48.

14. Eva May Hamilton and Eleanor Whitney, *Nutrition Concepts and Controversies* (St. Paul, West Publishing Co., 1979), p. 445.

15. Adelle Davis, *Let's Have Healthy Children* (N.Y., Harcourt Brace Jovanovich, Inc., 1972), p. 45.

16. "Recent Advances in Research," *Florida SIDS Information Exchange,* No. 5 (March, 1979), p. 2.

17. "Lesser Known Facts," *American Cancer Society Fact Sheet,* Jacksonville, Fla., 1980, p. 1.

18. "Lesser Known Facts," p. 1.

19. A. Jakubovic, T. Hattori and P. McGee, "Radioactivity in Suckling Rats After Giving C-14-Tetrahydrocannabinol to the Mother," *European Journal of Pharmacy,* 22 (1973), pp. 221–223.

20. Cynthia W. Cooke and Susan Dworkin, *The Ms. Guide to A Woman's Health* (N.Y., Doubleday, 1979), p. 184.

21. Paul Jacobs, "Caffeine Warning Set for Pregnant Women," *Florida Times Union and Jacksonville Journal,* August 3, 1980, p. A-4.

22. Nikki Goldbeck, *As You Eat, So Your Baby Grows* (N.Y., Ceres Press, 1978), p. 13.

23. Cherry Wunderlich, "Unborn Males, Children at Risk with Saccharin," *ICEA News,* Vol. 18, No. 3 (1979), p. 1.

24. Silvia Feldman, *Choices in Childbirth* (N.Y., Grosset and Dunlap, 1979), p. 35.

25. *Physicians' Desk Reference, ed. 41* (Oradell, N.J., Medical Economics Co., Inc., 1987), p. 1641.

Chapter 4

Exercise

or "More Bounce to the Ounce"

Most experts agree that women who exercise during pregnancy feel better, look better, and get back into shape faster after their babies are born. Many women have an uncomfortable pregnancy. They move laboriously from chair to chair, feeling tired, constipated and depressed. They look at the rippling fat on their legs and sigh, not realizing that with a good exercise program it doesn't have to be this way.

There are two basic types of exercise. One is called sustained; the other, conditioning. During **sustained exercise** (running, walking, bicycling), your heart rate increases and thus strengthens the heart and lungs (cardiopulmonary system). Also, during sustained exercise you breathe deeper, getting more oxygen into the bloodstream. This means that more oxygen gets to the baby as well.

Conditioning exercises, such as calisthenics or isometrics, improve muscle tone by using a muscle over and over again. Using muscles during exercise also keeps fat deposits from building up in that area and keeps muscles stretched out. Doing a combination of both types of exercise, sustained and conditioning, gives you the best overall benefit. Together, they use calories, tone the muscles, develop the cardiovascular system and saturate the body with oxygen.

In this chapter you will learn specific exercises to prepare your body for labor and delivery, as well as proper body mechanics and measures to relieve the minor discomforts of pregnancy, all of which can help you feel better *right now.*

SOME CAUTIONS

When exercising, you must **make some concessions to your pregnancy.** Because your circulatory and other systems have more work to do when you are pregnant, you may find that you are not able to exercise for as long at one time as you did before you were pregnant. You may also find that you require more time to rest and recover after exercise. You should never exercise to the point of breathlessness. If you are out of breath, your baby may be low on oxygen. You should always be able to talk as you exercise. If you cannot talk while exercising, then slow down and catch your breath.

Stop exercising if your feel pain and consult your doctor. Perhaps you are just doing the exercise incorrectly, or you may have overdone it a bit. Discontinue any exercise if you are bleeding or cramping. Get your doctor's okay before beginning to exercise again. Finally, be careful not to overstretch while doing any exercise, or even while doing some everyday activity like getting out of bed. During pregnancy, your body secretes a hormone that slightly loosens joints and ligaments in preparation for birth. This makes it easier to strain ligaments or muscles.

Jogging at 7½ months.

Doctors usually advise that it is fine to continue any activity that you were doing before you became pregnant, even something as strenuous as jogging. According to Dr. Evelyn Gendel, Director of the Kansas Division of Maternal and Child Health, "There is no reason for women not to continue in athletics during pregnancy, if they are continuing what is customary for them. Assuming a normally implanted pregnancy, physical activity is not only permissible but desirable. It not only increases the joy of living; it also maintains cardiopulmonary efficiency and muscle tone, and prevents back problems."[1] Begin slowly, as early in pregnancy as possible, and gradually increase your stamina.

Another benefit of exercising regularly throughout pregnancy may be an increased secretion of the "well-being" hormones, called endorphins, discussed in Chapter 7. It has been found that women who exercise regularly have higher levels of endorphins while exercising than do women who exercise irregularly. It would follow that by exercising during pregnancy, a woman could increase the level of natural painkillers that she will have in her body during labor.[2]

PROPER BODY MECHANICS

Good posture is essential. During pregnancy, your center of gravity changes as your baby grows and your uterus enlarges. You will be tempted to compensate for this growth by slumping. The same good posture you had before pregnancy should be maintained. This lessens back discomfort, improves digestion and enhances your body image.

While **standing,** the way you hold your head influences the position of the rest of your body. If you let your head hang forward, your body will droop like a wilted flower. Instead, think tall! Hold your head up with your chin tucked in and neck straight. Lift your shoulders up and pull them back. This position will keep you from cramping the rib cage, which can make breathing difficult and possibly cause indigestion. Your pelvic area, containing the weight of the growing baby, requires special attention for continuous body adjustments. Think of your pelvis as a bowl filled with liquid. To prevent the liquid from spilling out, tilt the "bowl" back by tightening the abdominal muscles and tucking your buttocks under. (See pelvic tilt exercise.) By keeping the pelvis tilted back, you can prevent excess tension in the muscles of your lower back. This is an important back care measure. By bending your knees slightly and keeping your body weight over your feet, you can maintain the proper pelvic alignment. Place your body weight on the center of each foot, never putting it on the inside of the foot. If you stand for a long time, put one foot on a small stool to flex the hip.

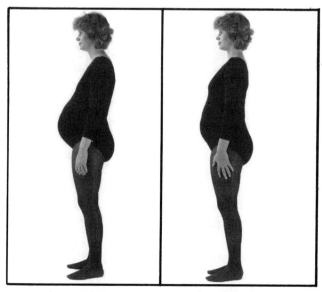

Poor posture.   *Good posture.*

While **sitting in a chair,** use the back of the chair to avoid slumping forward. It is preferable to sit in a straight back chair. Pillows placed behind your neck and the small of your back will increase comfort. The entire length of your thigh should rest on the seat of the chair. The chair seat should be high enough to keep your knees even with your hips.

Tailor sitting or sitting "Indian style" is an excellent position during pregnancy. It is comfortable and improves the circulation in your legs, while stretching and increasing the flexibility of your inner thigh muscles. Sit this way whenever possible (watching T.V., reading, folding clothes, peeling potatoes). If your legs become tired in this position, stretch them out in front of you.

Lying down flat on your back (supine) for an extended period of time is not recommended after the fourth month of pregnancy. This position puts the increasing weight of the baby on the major vessels and compresses them. This can lower your blood pressure and thereby reduce the amount of blood traveling to the placenta and the baby. If it is necessary to lie on your back (during an examination, for example), you can modify the position by supporting the small of your back with a pillow and bending your knees. Refrain from doing exercises which require that you lie on your back.

Side-lying is a position that takes the weight of the baby off the back and groin and allows the joints to be flexed loosely. A pillow placed lengthwise between your legs will make it easier to relax. Another pillow under your abdomen takes the strain off the lower back.

You may feel comfortable lying further over on your abdomen in a three-quarter position. Your lower arm can be behind your back and your upper arm and leg forward, supported by pillows.

To get up from a supine position, roll over onto your side, and push yourself to a sitting position with your arms. Then swing your legs over the side of the bed. Be careful not to twist your body as you get up. This technique will help you avoid strain, both on your back and abdominal muscles.

When **walking,** remember all the points of correct posture described above. Bring your legs straight forward from the hip. Don't swing them sideways in a "waddle."

Be careful when **climbing stairs.** Use your legs to lift your body up, rather than pulling yourself up with your arms. Lean slightly forward as you go

Proper posture while sitting.

Tailor sitting.

Getting up from supine position.

up, placing your foot completely on each step. In the postpartum period, climb steps slowly, tightening abdominal and pelvic floor muscles, and use the leg muscles to do the work.

Many women, especially those with small children or toddlers, find that some **lifting** is necessary during pregnancy. Incorrect lifting can put excessive strain on the back and the pelvic floor. Therefore, it is important that you learn how to lift correctly.

Avoid lifting heavy objects. Lift only what you can lift easily with one arm. To lift, get close to the object and go down into a squat, bending at the knees, not at the waist. With your feet parallel, keep your back straight, and as you lift, straighten your legs without twisting your body. An alternate method is to place one foot in front of the other and lower yourself slowly to one knee. Keeping your back straight, push yourself up with your rear foot.

Small children can climb onto a stool or chair, enabling you to lift them without straining your back.

Lifting incorrectly.

Lifting correctly.

CLOTHING

The kind of **shoes** you wear can affect your posture. During pregnancy, it is best to wear a flat shoe with good support. A high heeled shoe thrusts your body weight forward, putting strain on your lower back and the ligaments of the hips and knees. The high heel can also cause difficulty in maintaining your balance. The calf muscles tighten into a knot and will actually shorten if you wear high heels habitually. If you have been wearing them, progress gradually to lower heels and then to flat shoes to allow your calf muscles to stretch slowly.

Support hose may give relief to tired leg muscles and help prevent varicose veins. Avoid the use of garters to hold stockings as they constrict the circulation in the leg and cause varicose veins.

A good **bra** is important during pregnancy to provide support for your breasts as they increase in weight. This support will minimize upper backache as well as improve your posture. If your breasts don't have this support, the tissue will stretch and they may sag. Select a maternity/nursing bra with wide, non-elastic straps to provide support during pregnancy and which can be used later while breastfeeding.

Cotton panties are preferable to nylon because they absorb moisture and help prevent irritation and infection.

Maternity clothing should be made of absorbent fabric which does not trap body heat (cotton rather than polyester), because pregnant women often feel warmer than non-pregnant individuals. Clothing should be loose fitting and allow for growth.

SUSTAINED EXERCISES

If you have not been exercising, then begin with something like **walking.** This is an excellent exercise for a pregnant woman. A brisk walk of fifteen to twenty minutes each day develops cardiovascular strength and uses almost every muscle in the body. Even if you have little extra time, you can usually find time to walk. **Bicycling** is another excellent exercise. In addition to improving cardiovascular strength, it develops the abdominal muscles which support the baby. **Swimming** is unique in that the buoyancy of the water helps support the baby while allowing you to use your leg, arm and back muscles. Swimming for fifteen to twenty minutes several times a week builds muscle tone and strength.

CONDITIONING EXERCISES

These exercises are designed to improve the muscle tone of specific areas (especially those areas involved in childbirth) and to relieve tension and minor discomforts of pregnancy. Do all exercises slowly and smoothly to avoid jerky movements which could overstretch the tendons and ligaments and possibly dislocate joints. Do each exercise only 2–3 times per session to start; gradually increase to recommended repetitions. For maximum benefit have two exercise sessions per day. Be sure to continue breathing normally as you exercise. Don't hold your breath. For ease of practice, do the exercises in the order they are given.

Rib Cage Stretch

Benefits: Relieves tension in the shoulders and under the ribs. Strengthens the upper back and helps relieve indigestion.

Cautions: Don't arch your back while doing this exercise. Raising your arms above your head will *not* harm the baby, as an old wives' tale suggests.

Directions: Inhale slowly while raising both arms over your head to the count of 5. As you exhale, slowly lower both your arms and continue the motion until arms are behind your back to the count of 5.

Frequency: 5 times per session and whenever you feel tension in your upper body or have indigestion.

Arm Circles

Benefits: Strengthens the upper back and upper arm muscles, and relieves tension.

Directions: Stretch your arms out to the side with your palms up. Make small circles, gradually increasing the size of the circles to the count of ten. Then reverse the direction of the circles, and make large circles, gradually decreasing their size to the count of ten.

Frequency: 2 times per session.

Rib cage stretch.

Arm circles.

Shoulder Rotating

Benefit: Helps to relieve upper backache caused by poor posture or heavy breasts.

Directions: Place your fingers on your shoulders and move your elbows in circles from front to back, so that you make backward circles.

Frequency: 10 circles per session and whenever you have upper backache.

Calf stretching.

Calf Stretching

Benefits: May help to decrease leg cramps and improve circulation.

Directions: Stand facing the wall or your partner with one leg well forward (in the lunge position) and hands pressed against the wall or your partner's hands. The rear leg should be outstretched so that knee is straight and foot is flat on floor. Bend front leg at knee to cause stretching. Stretch gradually.

Frequency: Do for 1–2 minutes per session.

Pelvic Tilt or Rock

Benefits: Improves posture, relieves back discomfort, increases abdominal muscle tone and relieves pelvic congestion.

Directions: This exercise can be performed in several positions. All are done with a rocking motion and constant rhythm.

Shoulder rotating.

Pelvic tilt on all fours (erasing the curve).

On All Fours (hands and knees) the weight of the baby is off your back and this further provides relief from backache. Align your head with your spine. Do not let the spine sag. Tuck in your bottom and pull up abdominal muscles. Press up spine at lower back just enough to erase the curve—do not hump your back. Hold for a few seconds and return to starting position. Continue motion.

Stand in front of a mirror to check your side view. Assume correct posture. With one hand on your pubic bone and the other at the small of your back (to help you get the motion), rotate your pelvis forward, tucking in your bottom and abdomen. Then, relax. Continue motion. (This exercise is exhibited by belly dancers to a degree.)

Frequency: 10 times per session.

Tailor Press

Benefits: Stretches and increases elasticity of ligaments and muscles on the inside of the thighs, which promotes comfort during the birth of your baby. Practice of this exercise will help you relax and feel at ease in this position while giving birth.

Cautions: Do not bounce knees. Discontinue if you feel pain in the area of the pubic bone. This may indicate some separation at the joints. Do not tailor sit after birth until the episiotomy incision heals.

Directions: Sit with the soles of your feet together and pull them towards your body. Using only the muscles of your legs, press knees downward. You will feel the muscles in your inner thigh pull slightly.

Frequency: Do 10 presses per session.

Isometric Tailor Press

Benefits: Strengthens the muscles of the inner thighs and the pectoral muscles which support the breasts.

Cautions: Same as for Tailor Press.

Directions: While tailor sitting, place your hands *under* your knees and pull up with your hands while pushing down with your knees. Hold for a count of 5. Now place your hands *on top* of your knees and press down while pulling up with your knees. Hold for a count of 5. In both of these exercises there should be no movement, only stationary counterpressure.

Frequency: Do 10 (five of each) per session.

Isometric tailor press.

Tailor stretch.

Tailor Stretch

Benefits: Same as Tailor Press plus stretches lower back and calf muscles.

Cautions: Same as Tailor Press.

Directions: Sit on floor with your legs stretched out in front and angled apart. Lean forward with your hands outstretched and reach for your ankles. Variation: Sit with legs angled to each side and move both hands down your right leg and reach your toes. Repeat with left leg.

Frequency: 10 times per session.

Kegel Exercises

The Kegel exercises (pronounced kee' gull) are named after Dr. Arnold Kegel, the physician who developed them. They are designed to restore or improve muscle tone and increase your control of the pelvic floor muscles.

The muscles of the pelvic floor can be pictured as a sling that attaches to the pubic bone in front and the coccyx in back. Another name for this muscle group is pubococcygeus, named for its position. Part of this group, the sphincters, forms a figure eight around the urethra and vagina anteriorly (situated in front) and the anus posteriorly (situated toward the back). See illustration. Voluntary control of the pelvic floor can be achieved by exercise and will allow you to release the area consciously during the time of birth. This relaxation of the pelvic floor allows the baby an easier passage during expulsion and perhaps reduces the need for an episiotomy.

During birth, the pelvic floor muscles are stretched. Kegel exercises eliminate problems which could otherwise result from this stretching—a prolapsed (sagging) uterus, a prolapsed bladder, and possible urinary stress incontinence (an uncontrolled leaking of urine with sudden movement, like coughing or sneezing). See illustration.

By contracting the muscles of the pelvic floor soon after birth, you are shortening the muscle fibers that have been stretched, thus aiding their restoration. If you had an episiotomy, this exercise will increase the blood flow to the area which will reduce swelling and aid in healing.

An added bonus which you will receive with the continued practice of Kegels is an increased sensitivity in the vagina during sexual intercourse. With improved muscle tone, the vagina becomes more snug, and the response from the nerve endings beneath the vaginal walls is improved. Your husband, too, will appreciate this extra snugness! The benefits, then, of Kegel exercises are not limited to the period of birth, but extend into the immediate postpartum period and continue throughout your life.

Your first step in exercising the pelvic floor is to **locate the muscles.** To do this, contract the muscles around the urethra as if you are trying to hold back the flow of urine. Then, try urinating when your bladder is not full, **stopping and starting the flow of urine** several times. Progressively allow a smaller amount of urine to escape each time. Be aware that stopping the flow tightens the pelvic floor while releasing the flow relaxes the pelvic floor.

Another way of checking for pelvic floor tension and relaxation is to **tighten the muscles of the vagina around the penis** during sexual intercourse. Your partner can give you feedback on the effectiveness of this exercise.

Make sure you are aware of the difference between your abdominal muscles and your pelvic floor muscles. You can contract both at the same time, but don't mistake one for the other. It is easiest to isolate the pelvic floor muscles if you practice with your legs apart.

Once you achieve awareness of the pelvic floor muscles, you should discontinue practice during urination. Now **contract and release pelvic floor muscles quickly and firmly,** starting with ten per session, five times a day, increasing to ten sessions

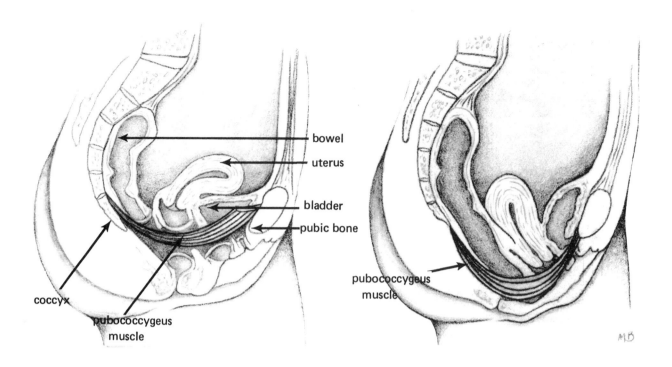

Good muscle tone.   *Poor muscle tone.*

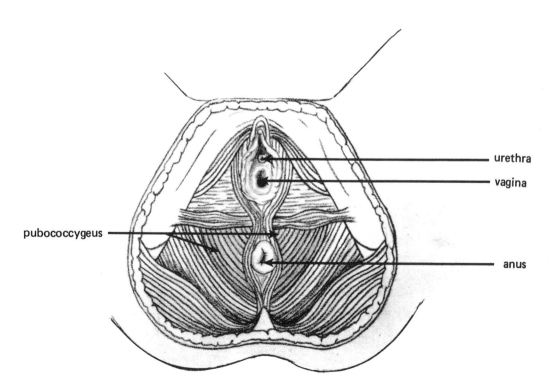

Pelvic floor muscles (cross section).

per day. Hint: Use an everyday activity such as washing dishes or stopping at red lights to remind yourself to do a series of Kegels. After the baby comes, doing Kegels with every diaper change will insure plenty of practice. This particular Kegel exercise increases awareness and strength of the pelvic floor muscles.

The elevator exercise is done by **imagining the pelvic floor as an elevator.** Contract the muscles upward, from the first floor to the fifth floor, stopping at each floor and getting tighter as you go higher. Then, release downward, releasing tension (letting people off) at each floor, from the fifth to the first.

With continued practice you should be able to develop enough control to **lift the elevator ten floors.** Make sure you are not holding your breath while doing this. This Kegel exercise helps you achieve deeper muscle control.

The next step in learning control over the pelvic floor muscles is to **release them completely to a basement level by giving a slight push.** This is the degree of relaxation you need to achieve while pushing the baby down the birth canal. Practice this with your bladder empty. Always return to the second level to maintain a constant degree of tension, just as a hammock returns to a higher position when you get up.

The final Kegel exercise is designed to develop elasticity of the pelvic floor muscles. Sit on a low stool or chair with your knees apart. Lean forward and rest your elbows on your knees. Begin by **tensing the muscles around the urethra, then the vagina and backward to the rectum** in a wave-like pattern. Release in the opposite direction.

All of these exercises should be done for the rest of your life to maintain optimum muscular condition of the pelvic floor.

Daily Practice Session

1. Firmly and quickly contract and release pelvic floor muscles 10 times a session, 5–10 times daily.
2. Elevator exercise: Work up to 10th floor. Do slowly, 5 times a session, at least 3 times a day.
3. Add basement level to elevator.
4. Tense from front to back, then release back to front. Do this 5 times a session, 3 times a day.

PERINEAL MASSAGE

Just as you exercise to tone and prepare your muscles for delivery, it is also important to prepare the perineum for the stretching which will be required to accommodate the baby's head. This is especially important if you desire to avoid an episiotomy. Many birth attendants feel that prenatal preparation of the perineum will increase your chances of delivering with an intact perineum. Prenatal preparation includes several steps. The most important is to determine your birth attendant's philosophy concerning episiotomies. Is he willing to support you in your desire to deliver without one? Secondly, excellent nutrition will contribute to healthy tissues that stretch and heal rapidly. Some feel that taking a supplement of vitamin E will also enhance your tissues' ability to stretch. Practicing relaxation, pushing and Kegels will give you additional control over the perineal area which is so important during labor.

Perineal massage can be performed by you or your partner. It should be started about your thirty-second week. You may use your body's secretions, some K–Y Jelly, vitamin E oil or any other oil as a lubricant. Insert your thumbs into the vagina about one inch and press toward the rectum. Use your thumbs and index fingers to stretch the perineal tissues outward toward the thighs. You should feel a stinging or burning sensation. Do this for five minutes every day. If perineal massage is done by your partner, he should insert his index fingers into the vagina with his thumbs on the outside.

Do *not* perform perineal massage if you have active herpes lesions.

EXERCISES FOR RELIEF OF DISCOMFORT

The following exercises are designed to provide relief of specific discomforts. Become familiar with them so that you can use them if needed.

Rib Cage Stretch

Benefits: Relieves indigestion and tension in upper body. See page 57.

Neck Circles

Benefits: Relieves tension in the neck and shoulder area.

Caution: Do very slowly and carefully if you have ever had a neck injury.

Directions: Rest your chin on your chest. Slowly rotate your head to the right, then back, left and forward in a continuous motion, completing the circle. Totally relax the muscles of your neck as you do this. Repeat 3 times, then rotate to the left 3 times.

Frequency: Whenever you feel tension in your neck or shoulders.

Shoulder Rotating

Benefit: Relieves upper backache. See page 58.

Foot Bending and Stretching

Benefits: Improves circulation of legs. May help to eliminate varicosities, swollen ankles and leg cramps.

Caution: Do not point toes. If you develop leg cramps, pull toes toward you until you have relief.

Directions: Elevate legs while in a sitting or lying position. Flex your ankle and draw toes up toward you. Rotate both feet in a circle, first out, then down, in and up. Reverse.

Frequency: When, sitting repeat the rotation 3–4 times per hour.

Calf Stretching

Benefit: Relieves leg cramps.

Directions: Partner should press down on knee of your cramped leg. With other hand, have him grasp your foot and pull toes towards your head.

Frequency: Whenever you have leg cramps.

Calf stretching.

Passive Pelvic Rock

Benefit: Relieves backache during labor.

Directions: Lie on your left side with partner behind you. Partner should place his left hand on your hipbone and his right hand on your tailbone. Have him exert pressure by pushing with his right hand while pulling with his left hand to tilt your pelvis. He should then release. Continue in a rocking motion. (If you are on your right side, have labor partner switch hands.)

Frequency: Whenever needed for comfort.

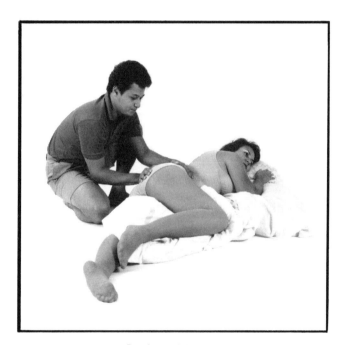

Passive pelvic rock.

FOOTNOTES

Chapter 4

1. "Running in Motherhood," *Runner's World,* May, 1973, as quoted in *The Complete Runner* (N.Y., Avon Press, 1978), p. 160.
2. Diana Korte and Roberta Scaer, *A Good Birth, A Safe Birth* (N.Y., Bantam Books, 1984), p. 217.

Chapter 5

Relaxation and Breathing
or "Practice Makes Perfect"

Lamaze childbirth training prepares you for childbirth on three levels: physical, mental and emotional. You prepare mentally by learning all you can about the natural process of labor and birth and how to deal with complications, should they arise. Emotionally, you are encouraged to think positively about your birth experience and openly face your anxieties and fears. Physically, you practice exercises that promote comfort during pregnancy and birth, as well as techniques of relaxation, distraction and attention focusing to be using during labor.

Fernand Lamaze, a French obstetrician, first became aware of the importance of preparation for childbirth while observing the labors and deliveries of Russian women using the techniques of *psychoprophylaxis*. Psychoprophylaxis literally means "mind prevention" or using the mind to reduce the awareness of pain sensations. Upon returning to France, Dr. Lamaze modified the techniques and began practicing them in his clinic. (The technique has since become synonymous with his name.) Marjorie Karmel introduced the method into the United States in the 1950s after having a baby under the guidance of Dr. Lamaze in France.

The method is based primarily on the principles of conditioned response training discovered by the Russian physiologist Pavlov during his experiments with dogs. Each time Pavlov fed the dogs he would ring a bell. When the dogs saw the food they naturally salivated. After a period of time whenever the dogs heard the bell, they would salivate. In other words, they were conditioned.

Using this theory in childbirth preparation, you will learn new, positive responses to the contractions of labor. When you feel a contraction begin, you will consciously relax and breathe in a patterned, controlled way (rather than holding your breath and tensing muscles as an unprepared woman does).

Your preparation also breaks the fear-tension-pain cycle, first identified by Dr. Grantly Dick-Read as a major contributor to pain in childbirth. This cycle accurately describes the labor experience of the unprepared woman. She enters labor full of fear— fear of the unknown, fear of the expected (as presented by T.V., books, friends, family, etc.) and fear of being alone. Her natural response to fear is tensing her muscles. (Consider how you have reacted to narrowly missing a traffic accident or watching a terrifying movie.) This muscular tension creates painful contractions which make her more fearful of the next contraction, which is then more painful because of the increased tension. The cycle continues, increasing in intensity throughout her labor.

With Lamaze preparation, the fear is eliminated by gaining information about labor and birth, which promotes a positive attitude. Tension is relieved by using relaxation techniques, and the painful sensations of labor are reduced by using the breathing techniques. You thus eliminate the fear-tension-pain cycle before it begins to function in your labor.

In France, during the early days of Lamaze, the laboring woman was accompanied and aided by a *monitrice,* the woman who had taught her the techniques. In the United States this labor companion is usually someone emotionally close to the woman (husband, mother, sister, or close friend) who is also trained in the techniques. The love and support of this person provide another important factor in creating a confident, positive attitude toward the childbirth experience.

In Chapter Four you learned physical exercises which enhance your comfort during pregnancy and prepare your body for giving birth. In Chapter Six you will learn about the physical process of labor and birth and normal hospital and birthing center procedures. In this chapter your attention is focused on the conscious relaxation techniques and breathing patterns that will become your response to the contractions of your uterus during labor.

RELAXATION

Learning how to relax your body consciously and deliberately is the single most important skill you will develop as you prepare yourself for the activity or work of labor. Labor *is* hard work. The uterine muscle will contract intermittently over a period of hours to cause the cervix to open up and move the baby down the birth canal. It takes a great deal of energy to accomplish this task. One source estimates that it is the equivalent of a non-stop 12–18 mile hike. By relaxing all of your muscles except the one that needs to contract, the uterus, you will be freeing more energy and oxygen for its use. In addition, relaxation has other benefits:

1. Decreases pain perception; tension increases it.

2. Reduces fatigue; tension causes fatigue which increases pain perception.

3. Lessens muscle resistance to the opening cervix which enhances comfort and may speed up labor; tension increases muscle resistance which causes pain and may lead to prolonged labor.

4. Breaks the fear-tension-pain cycle.

When you hear the word *relaxed*, certain images probably come to mind: rag doll, jello, spaghetti, limp, and floppy. These are all images of extreme passiveness. A sleeping child is the picture of passive relaxation. What you will be learning is a more active, conscious form of relaxation, in which

the mind is alert while the body is relaxed. It involves the awareness and release of tension. Do the following exercise to illustrate this point: slowly contract the muscles of your right arm. Now let it flop. That's *passive relaxation.* Again slowly contract the muscles of your right arm. Now slowly, with concentration, relax the parts of your right arm. Feel the biceps, lower arms, hands, and fingers gradually relax. That's *active relaxation!* As you prepare for labor, you will learn to relax your body consciously. This process is technically called neuromuscular control (mind control of the muscles). You will learn a number of exercises that will help you develop skill in controlled relaxation.

The first step in learning active relaxation is to develop a sense of body awareness as well as the feeling of muscle tension. The following series of exercises are designed to help you recognize and reduce unnecessary body tension.

Relaxation Basics

1. **Assume a comfortable position** with all parts of your body completely supported; otherwise, the force of gravity will cause unsupported body parts to do muscle work (contract). Here are several positions in which to practice:

   A. For ease of checking for tension by partner, initial practice should be done in a *semi-reclining* position at a 45° angle. Place pillows under head, back, knees and arms.

   B. *Lie on your side* with a pillow under your head, under your upper leg and foot, and under your abdomen.

Sims' position.

C. *Lie in Sims' position* (¾ over) with body positioned more on front than sidelying. Place your lower arm behind your back with pillows supporting your head, front shoulder and upper arm, front leg and abdomen. This is an excellent position for rest during pregnancy and when experiencing back labor, as it takes all of the weight of the uterus off the back.

D. As you develop skill in relaxation, you can also practice *sitting up* and *on your hands and knees.*

2. **Keep all joints bent** as this relieves the mechanical tensions that activate the body's "stretch reflex," a state of readiness for muscle action.

3. **The supporting surface should be firm.** If it sags, such as a very soft mattress, the support will be lost and strain and muscle tension will follow.

4. **The physical environment should be conducive to relaxation:** comfortable and warm surroundings, loose clothing, and no shoes. A quiet place is good at first; add noise to simulate a busy labor suite as you develop skill in relaxation.

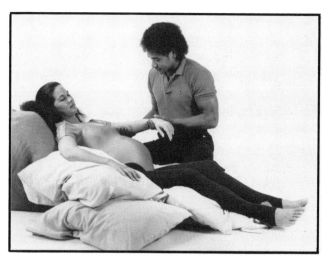

Checking arm for relaxation.

Labor Partner: How to Check for Relaxation

A very important part of your role is checking your partner for relaxation. During labor, she may be so involved in what her body is doing that she becomes tense without even being aware of it. You must check her for relaxation both during contractions and, as her labor progresses, between contractions to assure that she is resting completely.

First, **make a visual check** of your partner's appearance. Is she frowning? Do her shoulders and neck look rigid? Are her toes flexed back or curled? Are her fingers tightly clenched?

Second, **check her physically for relaxation** by doing the following:

1. Gently pick up her arm, supporting it under the elbow and wrist. The upper arm, lower arm and wrist should each move separately and feel heavy in your hands. If it is rigid and stiff and/or she lifts it for you, it is tense. Gently lower the arm to the floor or bed. *Never drop it!* She won't trust you and will tense rather than relax to your touch.

2. Check the other arm in the same way.

3. In the same manner lift a leg, supporting it under the knee and ankle. A relaxed leg will be very heavy and the parts will move separately, the same as the arm. Gently lower the leg. The knee should flop to the side when set down on the pillow.

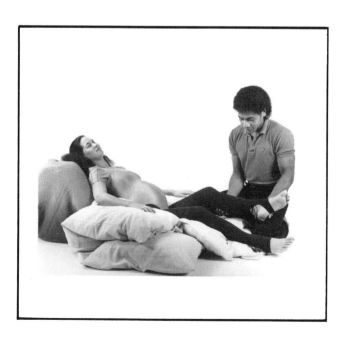

Checking leg for relaxation.

4. Check the other leg in the same way.

5. Check for tension in the neck by gently rotating her head from side to side.

6. Check for tension in the shoulders by placing your hands on both shoulders and gently moving them from side to side. Tense shoulders stay put; relaxed ones move easily.

7. Check hips by placing your hands on the outside of each hip and moving the pelvis from side to side. Relaxed hips move easily.

If in your checking you find parts that are not completely relaxed, do one or more of the following:

1. Quietly repeat "Let your arm, leg, etc. relax."

2. Tell your partner to tense the part as tightly as possible, then slowly release it to the count of 10.

3. Use light circular massage or firm stroking (whichever your partner prefers) on the tense part.

Preliminary Routine for Controlled Relaxation

The goal of this exercise is to create an awareness of the different feelings of body tension and relaxation. When you practice this at home, your partner will give the verbal cues.

Continue this exercise by following the instructions given with each muscle group below. Remem-ber to tense the muscles while inhaling and relax while exhaling. Partner should continue checking for relaxation.

- Squeeze thighs together
- Tighten buttocks
- Arch back
- Pull in abdomen
- Expand chest
- Press shoulder blades back
- Tense hands by making fists
- Tighten neck muscles
- Tense lips
- Frown
- Tense cheeks
- Tense over nose
- Tense eyes (wide open)
- Lift eyebrows

Gradual Release

Repeat the above exercise but relax muscles slowly to the count of 10. If you are practicing alone, count to yourself silently. When your partner is working with you, he can count out loud for you. After each tension-relaxation sequence, your partner should check that muscle group for complete relaxation. Spend more time working on muscle groups that are especially hard for you to relax.

CONTROLLED RELAXATION GUIDE

Verbal Cue	Woman's Action	Partner's Reaction
"Pull up toes."	Breathe in slowly through nose and tense toes. Breathe out slowly through mouth and relax toes.	Observe physical appearance of tense/relaxed muscles, then physically check for relaxation.
"Turn ankles out."	Breathe in—tense ankles. Breathe out—relax ankles inward.	Same as above.
"Bend knees."	Breathe in—flex knees with feet on floor. Breathe out—straighten legs and let knees flop outward.	Same as above.

TOTAL BODY RELAXATION

The next step in refining your relaxation skills is to work on total body relaxation. Below is one routine that will help you work on total body relaxation using verbal and mental images.

TOUCH RELAXATION

Another technique that can aid dramatically in developing your skill in relaxation is touch relaxation. You will learn to respond to your partner's touch by re-laxing tense muscles toward his hand. By practicing this non-verbal form of communication, you will find your partner's touching, stroking, or massage in labor an effective stimulus to promote relaxation.

As with all relaxation exercises, get into a comfortable, relaxed position. You will contract a set of muscles and then your partner will rest his hand on the contracted muscle. As soon as you feel your partner's touch, begin to release your muscles toward his hand. With his continued touching, you will relax each muscle group completely.

TOTAL BODY RELAXATION GUIDE

Partner's Cue	Woman's Action	Partner's Reaction
"Tense your entire body, starting at the bottom and moving up: toes, ankles, lower leg, thighs, etc."	Tense toes, then gradually move tension up the body to the top of the head.	Observe spread of body tension.
"Relax your body, starting at the top: scalp, forehead, face, lips, neck, etc."	Relax body slowly, one muscle group at a time.	Observe the relaxation of body parts. Check for relaxation.
"Relax your body even more: close your eyes, feel eyelids becoming heavy, eyes sinking back into head."	Relax all muscles surrounding eyes, lids, temples, forehead.	Same as above.
"Feel your shoulder blades opening outward, like a dress falling off a hanger."	Relax neck, shoulder and upper arm.	Same as above.
"Concentrate on breathing; with each out breath release a little more tension."	Be aware of tension release.	Same as above.
"Breathe in through nose and out through mouth, making each breath a little longer until you feel very relaxed. Try to feel as if you are breathing right down your back."	Focus on breathing and use it as a signal to relax further.	Same as above.
"Feel every limb as heavy: your ankles, your thighs, your arms, your shoulders."	Experience a feeling of heaviness.	Same as above.
"The force of gravity is pulling you down into the earth."	Become so relaxed you feel yourself sinking.	Same as above.
"Your knees are so heavy they flop apart to the sides."	Legs are limp and open to sides.	Same as above.
"Your whole body is melting and spreading across the floor."	Feel sensation of tension flowing outward.	Check partner for *total* relaxation.

Partner—Be sure to touch with a relaxed, but firm hand, and slowly mold your hand to the shape of the body part. If touching the part does not result in complete relaxation, stroke or massage the body part until it relaxes. Touch relaxation is one of the best techniques to use for relaxation during labor.

TOUCH RELAXATION GUIDE

Verbal Cue	Woman's Action	Partner's Reaction
"Contract forehead."	Frown; wrinkle forehead.	Rest hand on her forehead. Feel muscle relax.
"Tense face."	Grit teeth—clench jaws together.	Place hand on either side of her jaw. Feel jaw drop.
"Tense scalp."	Raise eyebrows.	Place hands on either side of her scalp. Feel eyebrows lower.
"Tense right arm."	Clench fist and stiffen entire arm.	Rest hands on fist, then slowly move hands up both sides of arm until shoulder is reached. Press shoulder firmly. Relaxation should move up arm slowly.
"Repeat with left arm."	Same as above.	Same as above.
"Tense abdomen."	Pull abdomen in toward spine.	Rest hand on curve of upper abdomen. Abdomen will expand outward.
"Tense shoulders."	Press shoulder blades back against floor/bed.	Rest hands on front of shoulders. Feel forward movement.
"Tense thighs."	Press upper legs together.	Touch outside of each leg. Feel legs fall to the sides.
"Tense thighs again."	Press legs and knees against floor.	Rest hands on top of thigh. Legs will rise and fall to the sides.
"Tense right leg."	Straighten and stiffen leg, pointing toes up.	Firmly touch foot on instep (foot relaxes); slowly move hands up to knee (feel relaxation from knee down), then continue stroking up to top of leg (thigh falls outward).
"Repeat with left leg."	Same as above.	Same as above.
"Tense neck."	Raise chin in the air and contract back of neck.	Rest hand on the nape of her neck. Chin falls forward and muscles relax toward your hand.
"Tense back."	Arch the small of back.	Rest both hands on either side of sacrum. Back will drop towards floor.
"Tense any other body parts of your choice."	Tense muscle.	Touch tensed body part and feel it rel .

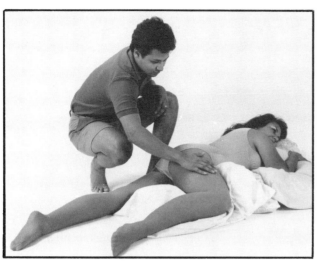
Using touch relaxation.

SELECTIVE RELAXATION

Once you have developed skill at total body relaxation using all the above techniques, you are ready to learn a more complex form known as *selective relaxation*. It requires greater concentration and mental activity. The technique will develop your ability to maintain general relaxation while one or more parts of your body are tense. In this practice, the tense part will be an arm, leg, etc. In labor it will be the uterus. This is a practice *for* labor; you will not perform this exercise during labor.

Begin by contracting the muscle groups for a few seconds; gradually extend the amount of time a muscle group is contracted to 60 seconds, the length of an average labor contraction.

SELECTIVE RELAXATION GUIDE

Note: During your first practice sessions, concentrate on the single muscle group contractions. As you develop skill, you can add the more difficult routines.

Verbal Cue	Woman's Action	Partner's Reaction
"Contract right arm."	With arm extended, make a fist of right hand.	Check left arm and both legs for relaxation.
"Relax right arm."	Unclench fist.	Check for total relaxation in contracted limb.
"Contract left arm."	Same as for right arm.	Same as for right arm.
"Relax left arm."	Same as for right arm.	Same as for right arm.
"Contract left leg."	Flex foot toward body; tighten muscles of leg as if to raise it.	Check both arms and right leg for relaxation; check to see if buttocks are tense (hard).
"Relax left leg."	Unflex foot and let leg roll to side.	Check leg for relaxation.
"Contract right leg."	Same as for left leg.	Same as for left leg.
"Relax right leg."	Same as for left leg.	Same as for left leg.
"Contract right arm and right leg."	Make fist and flex foot.	Check for relaxation in left arm and left leg.
"Relax right arm and right leg."	Unclench fist and unflex foot.	Check right arm and right leg for relaxation.
"Contract left arm and left leg."	Same as for right arm and right leg.	Same as for right arm and right leg.
"Relax left arm and left leg."	Same as for right arm and right leg.	Same as for right arm and right leg.

Partner's Cue	Woman's Reaction	Partner's Reaction
"Contract right arm and left leg."	Tighten right fist and flex left foot.	Check left arm and right leg for relaxation.
"Relax right arm and left leg."	Unclench right fist and unflex left foot.	Check right arm and left leg for relaxation.
"Contract left arm and right leg."	Same as for right arm and left leg.	Same as for right arm and left leg.
"Relax left arm and right leg."	Same as for right arm and left leg.	Same as for right arm and left leg.
"Contract both arms."	Tighten both fists.	Check for relaxation in neck, face and legs.
"Relax both arms."	Both arms fall loosely to sides.	Check for relaxation in both arms.
"Contract both legs."	Flex both feet.	Check both arms, head, and neck for relaxation.
"Relax both legs."	Both legs should go limp.	Check legs for relaxation.
"Contract both shoulders."	Shrug shoulders.	Check hands and both legs for relaxation; observe face for relaxed appearance.
"Relax shoulders."	Let shoulders fall back against support.	Check neck for relaxation, ease of shoulder movement.

Contracting right arm, checking left arm.

POINTERS FOR LABOR PARTNER

By doing these exercises together you are developing teamwork, as well as learning specific skills. The ability to work together as a team, to communicate clearly and to trust each other, is as important to your labor experience as the skills you are learning. All of this takes time to develop, so encourage each other and give positive feedback first; then discuss where you need improvement. **TAKE TIME EACH DAY TO PRACTICE TOGETHER.** The quality of your labor experience is greatly dependent upon the quality and amount of time you prepare together.

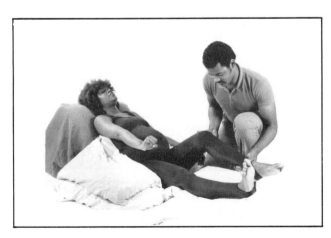

Contracting right arm and right leg.

RELAXATION GAMES

When you have become proficient in relaxation, there are a few games you can try to test yourself and your labor partner.[1]

Release with Motion

This tests your ability to relax your body consciously while one part is in motion. Remember, tension spreads, so it will take concentration to remain relaxed.

Directions: Consciously relax your entire body. Put one part of your body in motion as you concentrate on keeping the rest of your body relaxed. Your labor partner should check you for relaxation.

Examples: Tap one finger, open and close hand, move your toes, wink your eye, do Kegels, etc.

Tension-Release Switch

This activity will help you gain greater control over your ability to release tension.

Directions: Consciously relax your body. Contract one muscle (right arm). Make sure the corresponding muscle (left arm) is relaxed. As your labor partner gives you the command, "switch," relax your right arm and tense your left. Labor partner checks for relaxation.

Examples: Contract left leg, contract right arm and right leg, contract left arm and right leg (difficult).

Hidden Tension

This game tests the ability of the labor partner to find tension, which is very important in labor.

Directions: Consciously relax your body. Tense a muscle or joint that is not obvious. Your labor partner searches for the tension by sight and touch. Do not give him verbal clues. He should look for sudden movement (however slight), hardening of a muscle or rigidity of a joint.

Examples: Jaw, one finger, buttocks, neck, shoulder. No fair doing Kegels!

BREATHING TECHNIQUES

For some women, active relaxation is sufficient to cope with the sensations of their labors. Others need more complex mental activities which are provided by special breathing patterns and attention focusing techniques. You should learn them all; then use those tools that you need during your unique labor situation, modifying them as you desire.

The breathing patterns you will learn are designed to do several things:

1. Serve as an attention focusing technique.
2. Aid in relaxation.
3. Keep the diaphragm off the contracting uterus to reduce pressure and discomfort during contractions.
4. Maintain a constant, balanced exchange of oxygen and carbon dioxide which wards off hyperventilation and insures a good oxygen supply to the working uterus, placenta and baby.

In addition to breathing techniques, you will learn two additional attention focusing/distraction tools: *effleurage* (a form of massage) and the use of a *focal point* on which to concentrate during contractions. As you will discover while practicing, it takes a great deal of concentration to relax your body, breathe a special way, massage your abdomen, and focus your eyes on one spot in the room for a full minute. All these tools serve to keep your mind busy and decrease the amount of pain sensations from the uterus that are assimilated by the brain as you concentrate on something other than the uterine contraction.

BREATHING BASICS

Several elements that are consistent with all of the breathing patterns are:

1. As each contraction begins and ends, you will inhale (take in a smooth, deep breath) through your *nose* and exhale (let the air out like a sigh) through your *mouth*. This is known as a **cleansing** or **releasing breath**. This breath does three things for you: it gives you a good

boost of oxygen for the baby and uterus at the start of the contraction; it is a signal to your partner that the contraction has begun and ended; and it is your cue to relax your body.

2. You may focus your eyes on some object or spot in the room during the entire contraction. This is called your **focal point**. If you can find a particularly pleasing object to use for practice at home (a picture of a baby, a bright design, a happy scene, or a religious symbol), take it with you to the hospital. This gives you something outside of yourself to concentrate on and thus lessens your awareness of the strength of your contractions.

 Some women are more comfortable keeping their eyes closed during contractions because it helps them to be in tune with their bodies.

3. You may use **effleurage**, which is a light fingertip massage, during some or all of your contractions. It is an added form of distraction, as well as a source of comfort and aid to relaxation. To do effleurage, place the fingertips of both hands on your abdomen just above the pubic bone. Using light pressure, slowly bring your hands upward to a point near the top of your abdomen, and then draw them downward and outward to the beginning point. Continue drawing circles on your abdomen for the duration of the contraction. Usually, effleurage is done in rhythm with your breathing. Your partner can do effleurage for you in the same manner, or he can do it with one hand in a circular pattern on your abdomen, your back or your inner thighs.

4. The verbal cues **"contraction begins"** and **"contraction ends"** should always be used in practice by your labor partner. In labor, your practiced responses will automatically transfer from the verbal cues to the physical sensations of the uterine contractions.

To summarize, the pattern of practice for all of the breathing techniques which follow is:

1. Your partner says "contraction begins."
2. You take a cleansing breath and relax.
3. Concentrate on a focal point, if desired.

Doing effleurage.

Partner doing effleurage.

4. Begin breathing pattern and do effleurage.
5. Partner says "contraction ends."
6. Take cleansing breath, totally relax and rest!

BREATHING PATTERNS

Now that you are familiar with the common elements of all the breathing techniques, you may begin learning the individual patterns. Keep in mind that each person's breathing rate is different, and that the patterns should be modified to your own comfort. Have your partner count your breaths for one minute to determine your normal resting rate. With all the patterns, you can either take air in through your nose and let it out through your mouth, do all nasal breathing, or do all mouth breathing. If you experience nasal congestion, you may find mouth breathing easiest.

Do not begin using any of the special breathing techniques until you really need them. As long as you are able to walk and talk through your contractions, you won't need to do anything special except stay relaxed. As the contractions begin to get stronger, use effleurage as a distraction even before starting with the first breathing pattern. Once you begin using the special breathing techniques, you will feel committed to continue using them. The faster techniques require more energy and make it more difficult to stay relaxed. The longer you can comfortably wait before starting your special techniques, the more energy you will save.

Slow-Paced Breathing

This is the first, and possibly the only, breathing pattern you will use in labor. It is done by breathing at approximately half your normal rate, in a relaxed and comfortable manner.

Modified-Paced Breathing

When and if slow-paced breathing is no longer effective in keeping you relaxed and comfortable, you can begin using modified-paced breathing. This is more rapid, but no faster than twice your normal breathing rate. Since this is a more fatiguing pattern, you should return to slow-paced breathing when possible. (See Figure 2.)

If you are mouth breathing, reduce dryness by placing your tongue behind your lower teeth as you use the breathing pattern. You are working for light, effortless, quiet breathing, taking in and letting out

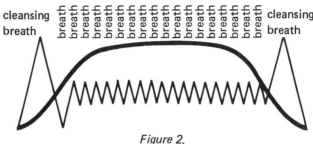

Figure 2.
Modified-paced breathing.

the same amount of air. Making a "he" or "ha" sound on the exhale as you begin practicing may help you to get the rhythm. Later, your breathing should be quiet.

Don't work for speed—rather, try to develop a slow, even rate. You may want to breathe in a 4/4 rhythm by mentally counting your breaths up to four, and then starting again. Or think of a nursery rhyme (example: Jack and Jill went up the hill . . .) and use that to pace yourself. Your breathing will accelerate naturally in response to the sensations of your labor. You might find that you start the contraction with slow-paced breathing, gradually increasing the rate as the contraction builds, and then slowly decreasing the rate as the contraction subsides. (See Figure 3.)

Breathing too fast is not only exhausting, it could make you hyperventilate. This occurs when you exhale too much carbon dioxide. You may feel dizzy or experience numbness or tingling in your fingertips, nose or tongue. To combat this, breathe into your cupped hands or a small paper bag (rebreathe the same air) and slow down your breathing rate.

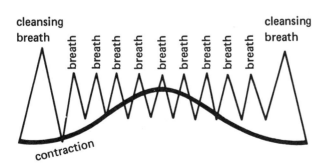

Figure 1.
Slow-paced breathing.

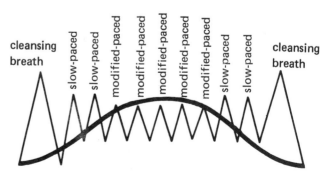

Figure 3.

Accelerated-decelerated breathing
(slow-paced and modified-paced).

Patterned-Paced Breathing (Pant-Blow)

The last breathing pattern is especially designed to cope with the long, strong and often erratic contractions of transition. You should wait to use it until modified-paced breathing is no longer effective. It is the most tiring pattern, and will prove exhausting if you use it too early. Most women find that mouth breathing is easiest with this pattern.

As with the other breathing patterns, begin with a cleansing breath. You may need to make it a shorter breath if you find the contractions peaking quickly. Otherwise, the contraction will get ahead of you and may cause you to lose control. (If the contraction peaks immediately, forget the cleansing breath and start the breathing pattern at once.)

The pattern is composed of 3 (4,5 or 6) shallow breaths or pants (in and out mouth) followed by a short blowing out breath through pursed lips. Don't forget to inhale before you blow out!! The blow should be only a short accent—don't overemphasize it by breathing too slowly. You should feel it lightly on your hand about 12 inches away (like candle blowing). Repeat the pattern until the end of the contraction. Work for a light, even rhythm.

Try several of the variations (3 pants/1 blow, 4 pants/1 blow, 5 pants/1 blow, 6 pants/1 blow) and decide which is most comfortable for you. Practice it for use in labor. (See Figure 4.)

You may find yourself moving in rhythm with your breathing when you begin practicing this pattern; this uses extra energy unnecessarily. Your shoulders and face should remain relaxed and quiet while doing patterned-paced breathing.

You can also practice a more complicated form of this breathing pattern that demands even greater concentration. You can increase and then decrease the number of pants before each blow. For exam-

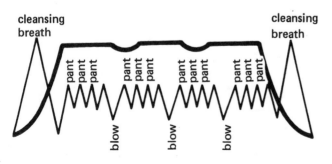

Figure 4.
Patterned-paced breathing (pant-blow).

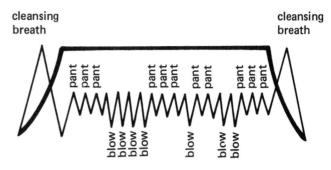

Figure 5.
Patterned-paced breathing
with premature urge to push.

ple: 2 pants/blow, 3 pants/blow, 4 pants/blow, 3 pants/blow, 2 pants/blow, or any other combination that you choose to develop.

BLOWING FOR PREMATURE URGE TO PUSH

If during a contraction you should feel a strong urge to push, repeatedly and forcefully blow out until the urge passes, remembering to breathe in air before you blow out. It is difficult to bear down or push effectively when you blow out strongly. When the urge to push is gone, return to the breathing pattern you were using. (See Figure 5.)

BREATHING FOR PUSHING

When your cervix has completely effaced and dilated, you can actively help the uterus move the baby down the birth canal by pushing or bearing down with the contractions. Most women feel a strong desire to push, but a few do not. If you do not immediately feel an urge to push, continue to breathe through your contractions until the urge begins. It has been noted that if a woman continues to breathe through several contractions (it may be as long as an hour), the urge will eventually be felt. But if the woman is instructed to start pushing without the urge, it may never appear. This makes the pushing stage more difficult and less satisfying.

Use your body's natural messages, and bear down only as your uterus directs. This may be mild bearing down accompanied by grunts and groans or, if you feel the need, a stronger push. It is important to assume the position *you* prefer, not necessarily the one practiced in childbirth class or the one demonstrated in childbirth films. Side-lying, squatting, standing, kneeling or on hands and knees may be the position you desire, and may be the one most advantageous to your baby's descent. While this natural pushing may not produce results as quickly as forceful breath holding, there is no evidence that a longer second stage is harmful to a baby not in distress. It may be more beneficial to your baby to experience a slower, more gentle birth than a forceful surge down the birth canal.[2]

Two types of pushing patterns will be discussed to help you prepare for the birth. The first is less work, and is therefore less tiring. For some women it is sufficient to move the baby down the birth canal. Others may need to use the second breathing technique to make any progress. Long breath holding and forceful pushing (the Valsalva maneuver) are not recommended since they can lower the mother's blood pressure and thus decrease the amount of oxygen the baby receives.

Gentle Pushing

As the contraction begins, take cleansing breaths until you feel the urge to push. Then exhale through pursed lips slowly and steadily as you bear down using the diaphragm. When you need another breath, inhale quickly while continuing to bear down; then exhale through your mouth. Repeat this pattern until the end of the contraction. When the contraction ends, take several cleansing breaths and completely relax until the next contraction.

Modified Valsalva Pushing

As the contraction begins, take cleansing breaths until you feel the urge to push. Then inhale, let a little air out, and hold the breath in the back of your throat, not your cheeks. This reduces the tension in your face and neck and lessens the chance of breaking small blood vessels from unnecessary straining. While you hold your breath and push, your partner will count slowly to 6 to pace your breath holding and pushing effort. When he reaches the count of 6, ease breath out slowly. This maintains abdominal pressure and keeps the diaphragm down on top of the uterus. Straighten your neck and inhale again, let a little out, hold, and push while your partner counts. Repeat the pattern as many times as needed during the contraction. When the contraction ends,

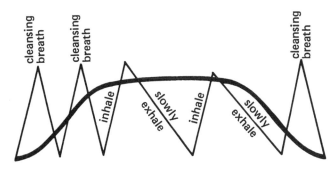

Figure 6.
Breathing for gentle pushing.

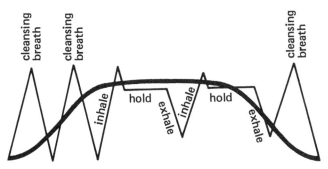

Figure 7.
Breathing for modified Valsalva pushing.

gradually stop pushing as you exhale slowly. Take one or two cleansing breaths and relax completely; you want to save all of your energy for your pushing effort. (See Figure 7.)

Once you feel comfortable with the breathing patterns, you can add the elements of the pushing effort and practice them in various positions (which will be described in the next section). As you slowly exhale or hold your breath, bear down by doing the following:

1. Push using your natural urge as a guide. If you are instructed to push and do not experience a strong urge during the contraction, use two cleansing breaths, then start bearing down on the third breath until the contraction is over.

2. Keep the diaphragm down on the uterus through your breath holding or slow exhalations.

3. Bulge your lower abdominal muscles down and forward.

4. Totally relax your perineum (pelvic floor) by

doing "basement Kegels" so it feels like your perineum is bulging out.

5.   As the contraction ends, slowly reduce pushing effort. This will help to maintain position of your baby and avoid his receding.

Don't push forcefully during practice—only enough to get the feeling of the proper sensations. It may help to think of pushing as if you are trying to empty your bladder forcefully. Also visualize your baby coming down lower and lower as you push and consciously relax your legs and bottom. A tight perineum can cause a longer, more difficult birth and almost certainly insure the need for an episiotomy.

Your first pushes will move your baby gradually down the birth canal. Your partner may even see a little hair showing as you push. But the hair will disappear as the baby moves back up at the end of the contraction. When the top part of his head stays in view between contractions, it is called crowning. Your birth attendant may ask you to stop pushing. Use pant-blow breathing or continuous blowing to keep from pushing at this time. Doing this will allow your baby's head to gradually stretch the birth outlet and perineum, resulting in a more controlled delivery of the baby's head and reducing the need for an episiotomy.

POSITIONS FOR PUSHING

The position(s) that you use during your pushing effort is largely determined by your comfort and your birth attendant's preferences. The possibilities include lithotomy, squatting, semi-reclining, side-lying, kneeling or on hands and knees. Most nurses and doctors prefer and encourage use of the semi-reclining position for pushing in the labor bed. But it may not prove to be the position of greatest comfort for you. Discuss all of the positions described below with your birth attendant to learn his preferences and to share your desires with him. Then practice pushing in all of the positions so that you can use what feels best when you are in labor.

Many American women give birth in the **lithotomy position**, lying flat on their backs with their feet up in stirrups. While this position has advantages for the physician, such as enabling him to observe your abdomen and perineum, check for fetal heart tone, apply forceps when necessary and

manage postpartum hemorrhage, it has definite disadvantages for you.

Pushing in this position reduces your pelvic outlet to its smallest diameter, and the contractions are irregular and less frequent. With your legs in stirrups, the strength of the contraction may actually lift your hips off the table, resulting in your pushing the baby uphill and against gravity. Episiotomies are done more frequently as there is a narrowing of the vaginal opening, along with a perineum which is stretched taut. The weight of the uterus on your vena cava (large blood vessel) may lower your blood pressure (supine hypotension) and thereby decrease the amount of oxygen your baby receives.[3] In an experiment using a device which continuously monitors fetal oxygenation, a pregnant woman was made to roll onto her back. Within two minutes, the oxygen level was in the danger range. The woman was immediately rolled onto her side and given oxygen. It took eight minutes for the fetal oxygen level to return to a safe range.[4] This position also results in increased back strain from the wide separation of your feet in stirrups.[5]

If you do deliver in the lithotomy position, make sure that the stirrups are adjusted for comfort and are not strapped on too tight. If you are a primigravida, most of your pushing will occur in the labor room where one of the alternative pushing positions can be used.

To simulate the lithotomy position:

1.   Lie on your back.
2.   Place your legs on a chair or sofa seat.
3.   Have your partner raise your back to a 70° angle when you are ready to
4.   **PUSH** (follow breathing pattern for pushing).
5.   Recline and relax between contractions.

If you are able to labor and deliver in the same bed, any one of the following can be employed.

Squatting is physiologically the best position to use while pushing. Keeping your feet flat on the floor, you can support yourself in a squat by holding on to the bedrail or your partner. A comfortable squat can be accomplished by having your partner sit on a chair. Squat between his legs, placing your arms over his thighs. Women delivering in birth centers are often encouraged to sit on the toilet to

Squatting with partner sitting in chair.

achieve the squat position. A birthing stool may also facilitate pushing in this manner.

Because most American women are not comfortable in a full squat position, and because it presents physical and visual difficulties for the birth attendant, many women have adopted a **modified squat at a 70° angle**. This can be used in the labor bed or even in the conventional delivery room by not using stirrups and placing your feet on the delivery table. In this position, your uterus is assisted by gravity so your contractions are more efficient, longer and come more frequently. Your pelvic outlet is at its widest, your birth canal is shortened and episiotomies are needed less frequently. As this position is very comfortable, the need for pain medication is reduced. Delivery time is shortened as you are able to push more effectively.[6] Do not squat before the presenting part is engaged as this may prevent descent and engagement.[7] In case of complications, a full squat may present some manual and visual inconvenience for the birth attendant, whereas the modified squat eliminates this problem.

To practice in the modified squat or semi-reclined position, you will need your labor partner to sit or kneel behind you and be your back support. Placing pillows between your partner's legs and your back will add to your comfort. To get into the proper position, do the following:

1. Raise your head and back to make a 70° angle with the floor or bed.

2. Be sure to sit on the small of your back, not your rectum.

3. Bend your knees, spread your legs apart, and place your feet flat on the floor/bed.

4. Rest your hands on your inner thighs. This encourages the continued relaxation of the legs and perineum.

5. If you must hold on while pushing, grasp your inner thighs and draw them toward you.

6. **PUSH!**

The **lateral Sims'** or side-lying position is very comfortable for most women, especially if they are experiencing back labor or leg cramps. It may also be helpful in aiding the rotation of your baby's head during labor if he isn't in a face down position already. Lateral Sims' is advantageous for breech delivery as well.

While lying on your side, the uterus is not pressing on the vena cava, thereby decreasing the chance of supine hypotension. Fewer episiotomies are needed as the perineum is loose. If one is needed, a shallow one can be performed. This position does not utilize the force of gravity as well as squatting, and your view of the birth is not as good. If a difficult forceps delivery or repair of lacerations is necessary, this position is not suggested.[8]

To push in side-lying or lateral Sims' position, do the following:

1. Turn on your side with one or more pillows supporting your head. The left side is preferable because it results in improved blood flow.

2. Curve your upper body into a C-shape. This will happen almost naturally as your begin to bear down.

3. Your upper leg will need to be supported by your partner's arms or lower rung of the bed rail. (Pad it with a pillow.)

4. **PUSH!**

5. Between contractions let your leg relax on the bed.

A **kneeling** position is preferred by some women. Physiologically, this is a good position for pushing as it takes advantage of the force of gravity. It may be especially helpful if your baby is slow in coming down the birth canal or if you experience

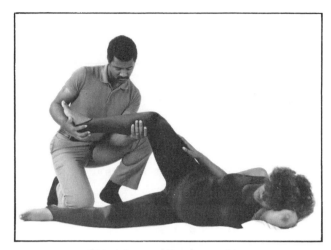

Side-lying position for pushing.

Kneeling position for pushing.

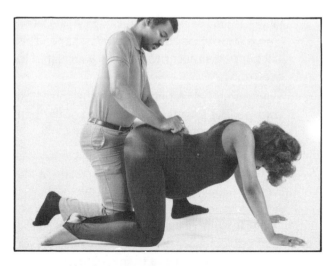

Hands and knees position for pushing with husband applying pressure.

back labor. As you push, tilt your head to "look for the baby." This will improve the angle of your pelvis.

To push in a kneeling position, do the following:

1. Kneel on the bed facing your partner.
2. Put your arms around your partner's shoulders for support and
3. **PUSH!**

Variation: Lean against the raised head of the labor bed for support.

Another position that can be both comfortable and effective is the all fours or **hands and knees** position. In this position you can arch your back, or rock back and forth doing pelvic rock as you feel the need. Women whose babies are in a posterior position often find this position eases their discomfort.

PRACTICE FOR LABOR

You should practice your conditioning, relaxation, and breathing exercises every day. If possible, get in two practice sessions each day; one alone and one with your labor partner. You may choose to do the conditioning exercises (found in Chapter 4) at the same time or separately at another time of day. Try to practice at a time when you are rested and can give your full concentration to your practice effort.

Rehearse in your mind the labor and birth of your baby. Start with early labor and continue, through transition, pushing and birth. Learn your role so completely that you will automatically begin a breathing pattern and relax your body as each contraction begins during labor.

Below is a suggested sequence for practice of your exercises, relaxation and breathing techniques. Begin with the first step and add to your routine as you learn new techniques.

1. Do each of your conditioning exercises in a series of 10, at least once, preferably twice a day.
2. Practice the selective relaxation exercise. Contract various muscle groups for 30–60 seconds while keeping the rest of your body relaxed. Be sure that your partner checks to be sure you *are* relaxed.
3. Do slow-paced breathing in a series of 3 contractions lasting 60 seconds each with a minute rest between them. Use effleurage or back

rubs as a comfort measure during the practice contractions.

4. Add 3 modified-paced contractions. Have them last 60–90 seconds. Maintain a steady, even breathing rate throughout the contraction. Then practice accelerated-decelerated breathing while your partner applies manual pressure.

5. Add 3 patterned-paced contractions. Have the contractions last 90 seconds with a 30-second rest between them. During one or more contractions have your partner call out one or more 15-second periods of a premature urge to push. You should blow out forcefully until your partner signals that the urge to push has passed.

6. Practice both gentle pushing and modified Valsalva pushing, 3 times each. Have the contractions last 60 seconds with 1–2 minutes of rest between them. Use the different positions for pushing so you will be comfortable in all of them.

Once you become familiar with all of the breathing patterns, practice your relaxation and breathing in various positions: semi-reclined, tailor sitting, side-lying, or on hands and knees. This will insure maximum comfort and relaxation in all positions during labor.

Simulate various kinds of labor situations as you practice. This will enable you to cope better with any type of labor. Some examples include: back labor, induced or very rapid labor, loss of control, and hyperventilation.

Helpful Hints for Labor Partners

1. **Simulate contractions** during practice by applying enough manual pressure to the bony part of your partner's wrist, elbow or knee to cause discomfort. Increase and decrease pressure in varying patterns so she can learn to respond to different sensations. For example, slowly increase pressure to a peak, then rapidly decline. Or peak quickly and maintain strength through most of the contraction, or give contraction multiple peaks. This technique is especially helpful when practicing accelerated-decelerated breathing.

Using manual pressure to simulate a contraction.

2. **Call out the passing seconds** in 15 second intervals. Pacing the contraction helps your partner keep her perspective.

3. **Check for tension** both during and between contractions. The longer that labor continues, the greater the chance of slowly spreading tension. Use both touch and verbal cues as needed to help her relax.

4. Help your partner maintain her breathing rhythm by **counting or breathing with her.** Tapping on a hard surface or moving your hand in front of her face may also keep her on track.

5. Encourage her to take advantage of **Braxton-Hicks contractions** as signals to practice her relaxation and breathing skills.

VISUALIZATION

Another helpful technique to prepare you both mentally and emotionally is birth visualization. This uses your imagination to picture the process of labor and delivery. Prenatally, it can help you develop a positive attitude for birth. During labor, it can help you focus in on your body and can aid in relaxation.

Visualization should be done following a relaxation practice, when you are calm and receptive to suggestion. Your partner can make up his own, or he can read the one below. The practice sessions will be most effective when your partner uses a soft and soothing tone of voice, increasing in volume and speed as the contractions accelerate, and becoming softer and slower as the contractions recede. He should speak slowly and pause frequently to allow the images to develop. Soft background music is also beneficial. When using this visualization, have your partner pause for a count of one whenever he sees a dot; for example " . . . " would be a pause of 1,2,3.

Let your attention be on your breathing . . . . breathing deeply and peacefully . . . with each breath allow yourself to let go more and more . . . . As you relax, picture in your mind a special place where you would like to have your baby . . . . . . Take yourself there and become comfortable . . . . . Notice the surroundings . . . . What do you see? . . . . Are there any scents? . . . . . What textures do you feel? . . . . . Do you hear any sounds? . . . .

As you continue to breathe slowly and deeply, picture the uterus in your mind . . . large and pear shaped . . . round and full at the top . . . tapered and narrow at the bottom . . . . a strong muscular organ, capable of much hard work.

See the round, healthy, red placenta on the back of the uterine wall . . . See the pulsating umbilical cord sending oxygen and food to your baby . . . . Watch your baby floating freely and peacefully in the warm, clear amniotic fluid . . . . His head is down in the pelvic cradle, just waiting for the day when he will be born . . . . Hear your baby's heartbeat—strong and sure . . . . See the downy lanugo hair . . . . Look at the vernix covering his body like a protective coat . . . . Count his fingers and toes . . . Look how long his nails have grown . . . It may be a boy . . . it may be a girl . . . but it is *your* baby continuing to grow and waiting to be born.

From your baby's point of view, look down on the cervix . . . See it puffy and soft with the mucus plug sealing its opening . . . much like a cork in the neck of a bottle . . . which protects your baby from infection until it's time to be born.

Now take yourself forward in time to the day labor begins . . . . . See the cervix . . . . The mucus plug is gone and it's getting shorter and shorter as your uterus begins to contract . . . . Feel your baby's head pressing firmly against the cervix . . . helping it to stretch and become thinner and thinner and slowly open up.

You feel a contraction starting, much like a train approaching on a distant track . . getting closer and closer and the contraction is getting stronger and stronger. Your baby's head is pressing harder and harder on the cervix; the cervix is stretching more and more and the baby's head is coming down and down and you open and open more and the contraction begins to fade and fade—just as the train moves off into the distance . . . . Feel your body relax . . . Let all tension go . . . Gather strength from within for the next contraction . . . Rest and your baby also rests. *(Pause. Repeat this paragraph two more times.)*

As the next contraction comes, feel its rising intensity much like a large wave, building, building, building. Feel the cervix stretching and stretching as you feel the baby's head moving down, down, down into the cervix. Now feel the contraction subsiding . . . just as the wave comes to shore, as you know it always will . . . And you rest and your baby rests . . . . *(Repeat.)*

Quickly another contraction begins to build, getting stronger and stronger and stretching the cervix further and further as the uterine muscles pull it up and back over the baby's head. Feel your baby straining to get through as the bag of waters bulges into your vagina, and feel relief and warmth as the water gushes out onto the bed and the contraction subsides as the baby slips back.

Now you feel another contraction. It is very hard and builds rapidly—see your vagina unfold to receive the rapidly advancing head, just as the petals on a flower open up. Feel the baby's head moving through the pelvis and under the pubic bone. Then the contraction begins to fade . . . and you rest and your baby rests.

And still another contraction comes, massaging your baby's skin—preparing him to breathe on his own very soon—very soon. Feel the pressure of your baby's head on the perineum . . . . As it stretches more and more you feel burning and stinging and you are panting, panting—relaxing your bottom so your baby can ease his way out. Slowly, very slowly here comes the head . . . and now the top shoulder . . then the bottom shoulder . . . Hear your baby breathe . . . . You are reaching down, then lifting your baby onto your chest . . . . Feel his warm wetness against your skin . . . . Watch his chest rise and fall as he begins to breathe and his color turns from blue to pink . . . . He looks intently at your face . . . then begins rooting for your breast till he finds it and begins to suck vigorously . . . . Such peace and joy . . your baby has been born!!

And now, as you are enjoying the sensations of touching, seeing, hearing and smelling your new baby, you are aware of another contraction, a milder contraction as your placenta is delivered . . . Your uterus continues to contract very firmly to prevent bleeding, just as it should.

Now bring yourself back to the present and know that your baby is growing and getting ready for that day when he will be born . . . It is still a few weeks off but getting closer with each passing day.

Continue to breathe deeply and relax and in a moment you can open your eyes, feeling renewed and refreshed knowing that your body will perform just as it should when the baby's birthday arrives.[9]

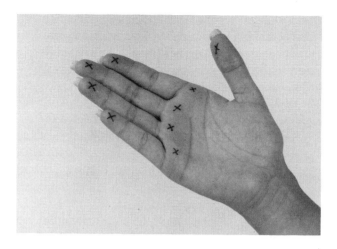

Acupressure points are located on the fingertips and on the palm, at the base of the fingers.

ACUPRESSURE

Although acupuncture and its finger-pressure variations have been in use in the Far East for thousands of years, they have only recently come into use in Western cultures. One of these techniques, acupressure, is a method of stimulating certain points on the body in order to provide pain relief in other specific areas.

Because you can perform this technique on yourself, you can utilize the most effective method of applying pressure, guided by the feelings and sensations you obtain. You may want to use your thumbs, your fingertips or another object. Since the points are in pairs, on both sides of the body, remember to treat both sides. Deep pressure on some points may reveal tenderness or produce a tingling sensation, which will help in locating the correct points. The pressure should be applied for at least 20 to 30 seconds.

During labor you may want your labor partner to assist you in applying pressure. The following photos illustrate acupressure points for relief of labor pain.

Use a comb as shown to apply pressure to points using both hands.

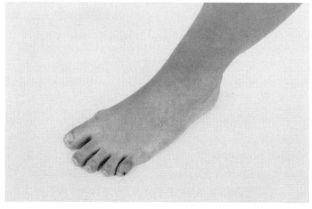

Apply strong pressure to the little toe as shown. Use your fingernail, or tape a BB, a ball bearing, or a small fishing weight to the area and press with your finger.

FOOTNOTES

Chapter 5

1. Adapted from *Parents' Guide to the Childbearing Year*, Peg Beals, ICEA, Milwaukee, Wisconsin, Sixth Edition, rev., May, 1978.

2. Roberto Caldeyro-Barcia, "The Influence of Maternal Bearing-Down Effort During Second Stage on Fetal Well-Being," *Birth and the Family Journal*, Vol. 6:1 (Spring, 1979), pp. 17–21.

3. M. Hugo, "A Look at Maternal Position During Labor," *Journal of Nurse Midwifery*, XXII (Fall, 1977), pp. 26–27 (as cited in "Maternal Position During Labor and Birth," *ICEA Review*, Vol. 2, No. 3 [Summer, 1975], p. 2).

4. Katherine Camacho Carr, "Obstetric Practices Which Protect Against Neonatal Morbidity: Focus on Maternal Position in Labor and Birth," *Birth and the Family Journal*, Vol. 7:4 (Winter, 1980), p. 251.

5. Hugo, pp. 26–27.

6. Christman Ehrstrom, Personal Correspondence, Aug., 1978 (as cited in "Maternal Position During Labor and Birth," *ICEA Review*, Vol. 2, No. 3 [Summer, 1978], p. 1).

7. Morris Notelovitz, "Commentary," *ICEA Review*, Vol. 2, No. 3 (Summer, 1978), p. 6.

8. W. I. Hampton, "Practical Considerations for the Routine Application of Left Lateral Sims' Position for Vaginal Delivery," *American Journal of Obstetrics and Gynecology*, 131 (May 15, 1978), pp. 129–133 (as cited in "Maternal Position During Labor and Birth," *ICEA Review*, Vol. 2, No. 3 [Summer, 1978], p. 3).

9. Adapted from Gayle Peterson, *Birthing Normally, 2nd Ed.* (Berkeley, Mindbody Press, 1984), pp. 57–72.

Chapter 6

Guide to Labor and Birth
or "I Gotta Get Out of This Place"

UNDERSTANDING LABOR AND BIRTH

Labor is the process by which the products of conception (the baby, placenta, amniotic sac and fluid) are expelled from your uterus to the outside world. Each labor is unique, differing from one woman to another and even from one labor to the next in the same woman. It is most important that you go into labor trusting your body. Remember, your body was built to carry, nourish and safely deliver your baby. Some of the factors that affect the course of labor include your health, nutrition, and emotional makeup, size and shape of your pelvis, size and presentation of the baby, your preparation for labor and birth through education in the birth process, and the practice of exercises, relaxation and breathing techniques. During labor, the emotional support you receive, along with medical interventions, may also affect the course of labor.

Labor is a process that, once begun, moves ahead in a fairly predictable fashion to its ultimate conclusion—the birth of a baby. For ease of explanation it is divided into four stages. The first stage of labor begins with the onset of labor and ends with the complete effacement and dilatation of the cervix. The second stage of labor (expulsion) begins with complete dilatation and ends with the birth of the baby. The third stage of labor is the delivery of the placenta. The fourth stage of labor is the first hours after birth, or the recovery period.

WARM UP SIGNS OF LABOR

Prior to the onset of labor, some signs become apparent that will indicate that labor is approaching. Some of them are noticeable several days or even weeks in advance; others signal that labor is imminent.

Lightening or "dropping" refers to the settling of the fetus' head into the true pelvis. After lightening the abdomen usually appears lower and more protruding. You may notice a greater ease in breathing, relief from heartburn and an ability to eat more at one time. However, lightening increases pressure in the pelvis causing more awkwardness in walking and **greater frequency of urination.** It may happen from two to four weeks before labor begins in the primigravida (first pregnancy); often not until labor begins in the multigravida (second or later pregnancy). The lower position of the fetus, together with its greater size, can lead to **increased backache and sacroiliac discomfort.** You may have difficulty finding a comfortable sleeping position; try using relaxation techniques and extra pillows.

Vaginal secretions increase in amount during the last weeks of pregnancy as the body prepares for the passage of the baby through the vagina. **Effacement and dilatation** (the thinning and opening) of the cervix may start prior to the onset of labor and cause the release of slightly brown, pink, or **blood-tinged mucus** as the mucus plug is released from the cervix.

Anxiety and depression are very common as the "due date" approaches or passes without labor beginning. Try to keep occupied and active.

A loss or leveling off of weight may be noticed in the last few days before labor begins. As much as two to three pounds may be lost due to excretion of body water. About 24 to 48 hours be-

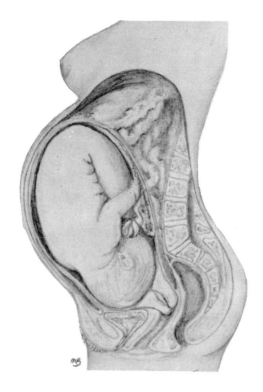

Before lightening.

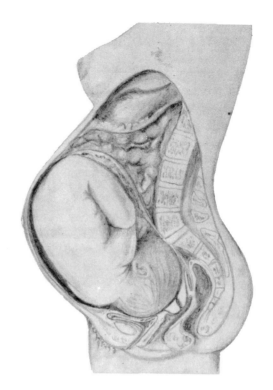

After lightening.

fore delivery, some women notice a **spurt of energy**. If you experience this, you may want to clean the entire house, wash floors or carpets, clean closets, etc. **DON'T!!** Nature gives you this extra energy to help you during labor. **Frequent bowel movements** may be experienced within 48 hours of labor, cleansing the lower bowel in preparation for birth.

An increased frequency of Braxton-Hicks contractions may be noticed. Braxton-Hicks contractions, named after the man who first described them, may be felt as early as the fourth month of pregnancy. Their purpose is to facilitate return of blood to the placenta and so aid the oxygenation of

fetal blood.[1] These "practice" contractions prepare the uterus for labor and may cause some of the effacement and dilatation that can occur during the warm-up period. They do not ordinarily cause pain but may be sufficiently strong and regular during the last weeks of pregnancy to be confused with true labor. This is referred to as false labor.[2]

True or False Labor

False labor can only be differentiated from true labor by an internal examination. Generally, if your contractions are not uncomfortable, are irregular, are af-

True Labor	False Labor
• Contractions often felt more in the back	• Contractions felt more in abdomen
• Contractions become stronger, longer, and closer together over time	• Contractions do not change in intensity (even though sometimes strong and close together)
• Usually bloody or pink show present	• No bloody show
• Activity change or warm shower increases intensity	• Activity change or warm shower usually decreases intensity

fected when activity is changed and do not last more than 45 seconds, then you are probably experiencing false labor.

True labor contractions will become stronger, last longer and become closer together as labor progresses. These will effect changes in the cervix, causing it to thin out and open while encouraging the descent of the baby through the pelvis.

ONSET OF LABOR

Several theories exist as to why labor begins:

1. The physical aging of the placenta may cause insufficient nutrients to reach the fetus.[3]

2. The uterus reaches a crucial point of distension which may cause tension on muscle fibers and stimulate their activity.[4]

3. Nerve impulses from the uterus to the posterior pituitary gland may bring about release of oxytocin (a hormone which causes the uterus to contract).[5]

4. Changes in the level of hormones may render the uterus irritable. (Progesterone drops.)[6]

5. Adrenal glands of the fetus, when mature, may release a substance to stimulate labor.

6. The release of prostaglandin from the wall of the uterus may initiate labor.

What are Contractions and How to Time Them

Contractions are the periodic tightening and relaxing of the uterine muscles. They can be felt in different ways. Most commonly, a contraction is perceived as starting in the back and radiating to the front. **The abdomen becomes very hard** to the touch. Some women state that they feel all the contractions or discomfort in the lower back area. You may also experience exaggerated menstrual cramps or severe gas pains which may be confused with flu symptoms or intestinal disorders.

A contraction gradually **builds in intensity** until it reaches its peak (the strongest point), then gradually subsides. It is described by many women as a **wave action.** Contractions are intermittent, with a rest period following each contraction. When **timing contractions,** time from the beginning of one contraction to the beginning of the next.

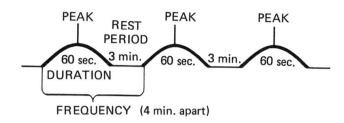

Contraction pattern.

Time Contraction Starts	Duration of Contraction
10:00	45 sec.
10:10	45 sec.
10:15	60 sec.
10:20	55 sec.
10:25	60 sec.
10:29	60 sec.
10:33	65 sec.
10:37	60 sec.
10:40	60 sec.
10:43	65 sec.
10:47	60 sec.

Chart of timed contractions.

The easiest way to time contractions is to write down on paper the time each contraction starts. The duration (seconds the actual contraction lasts) can also be noted. (See above example.)

True Signs of Labor

The following are signs that labor has begun. They may occur in any order.

Progressive Contractions: Contractions will get longer, stronger and closer together as labor advances. There should be some regularity or pattern when timed. Persistent contractions that have no rhythm but are 5–7 minutes apart or less should be reported to your doctor or midwife.

Loss of Mucus Plug from the Cervix: This is also known as "bloody show." It appears as thick mucus, usually tinged with blood from the breaking of small capillaries as the cervix begins to dilate. Although the mucus plug usually is lost 24–48 hours before labor begins, it may be passed as much as a week in advance. A few women do not notice a bloody show until labor is well established.

Rupture of Membranes (bag of waters): This may be noticed as a gush or uncontrollable leakage of fluid from the vagina. Amniotic fluid is easily distinguished from urine. It is colorless, odorless and cannot be stopped by doing Kegel exercises. Contractions will generally start within 6–12 hours following the rupture of the amniotic sac. Your doctor will need to be notified as soon as the membranes rupture because there is a passageway for infection. Therefore, you should not douche or have intercourse after this time.

Although most physicians insist that babies be delivered 24 hours (or less) after the rupture of the membranes to prevent infection, some physicians allow women to labor longer with good results. Frequent temperature checks and white blood cell counts can be used to monitor for infection. Of utmost importance is the avoidance of vaginal exams to prevent the introduction of bacteria into the vagina.

There is no such thing as a "dry birth." Approximately one third of the fluid is replaced every hour.[7]

Once labor is well established, notify your doctor or midwife. Be prepared to tell him:

1. how far apart the contractions are, their length, and their intensity and if you are using breathing techniques;

2. whether or not the bag of waters has broken; note its color;

3. if there is a bloody show present.

You will be instructed when to leave for the hospital or birth center.

GOING TO THE HOSPITAL OR BIRTH CENTER

Sometime during early or active labor you will decide to go to the hospital or birth center. Whether you are a primigravida or multigravida, the distance to the hospital, your previous labor history, and your doctor's opinion will enter into your decision. Learning to recognize the signs of the various labor phases will enable you to judge your progress and thus **avoid arriving too early.**

Leave all valuables at home. **Take your suitcase,** but leave it in the car, and don't forget your **Lamaze bag and class certificate.** Generally during the day you will go to the admissions office; at night you will go to the emergency room entrance. On admittance, many hospitals automatically reserve a postpartum room for which you are charged. A day's charges begin at 12:01 a.m. If you arrive at the hospital close to midnight and are not in really hard labor, you may want to wait until after midnight to avoid an extra day's charge.

After showing your pre-registration form, you will be taken to the labor-delivery area. Your labor partner will be taken to the father's waiting room and you will be escorted, via wheelchair, to the labor suite.

When you arrive in the labor room **you will be asked questions** concerning your medical history, allergies to medication, whether breast or bottle feeding, circumcision if the baby is a boy, and your present labor symptoms. If a contraction starts during the questioning, stop talking and go into your breathing pattern. The attendant will wait to resume questioning. **A vaginal exam will be done** to determine the cervical dilatation, effacement and station of the presenting part.

After labor has been verified and you have been admitted, **certain procedures may take place** depending on your doctor, your desires and your progress in labor. None of these procedures should be considered routine. Depending on your circumstances they may or may not be necessary.

"Now let's see . . . did I forget anything?"

"Couldn't we just talk first?!"

Prep: This refers to the shaving of the pubic hair. Rarely is a full prep or shaving of all the pubic hair done. It has been found to be unnecessary and very uncomfortable for the woman as the hair is growing back in. Some doctors do a "mini" prep involving the area from the vaginal outlet to the rectum (the area where the episiotomy is done). Others only trim the hair with scissors doing a "clip." Still other birth attendants feel shaving the area is not necessary at all, stating studies showing that there is no increase in infection and the mother is spared the itching and discomfort associated with the regrowth of the hair.[8]

Enema: This may either be a soapsuds enema (about one quart of water with a soap solution added) or a fleet enema. The second is more acceptable to the laboring woman because of the smaller amount of liquid used. Many physicians feel the enema is unnecessary, especially if the woman had a good bowel movement within the preceding 24 hours. An enema is given routinely by some physicians to empty the lower bowel and colon. It may be helpful if you have been constipated during pregnancy or if you feel you will not be able to relax your bottom effectively during the pushing stage of labor for fear of soiling the bed. If you arrive at the hospital and labor seems to be progressing rapidly, the enema might be cancelled. After an enema, the contractions can intensify.

A **fetal monitor may be applied or an I.V. started** at this time if indicated. (See Chapter 8.)

Labor Partner's Role

After approximately 30–45 minutes of anxious waiting you will be reunited. Prior to entering the labor area, you will be given a **protective cover gown** to put on over your street clothes. The labor and delivery suite is considered a clean area and street clothes are considered "dirty." If you leave the area, you must remove the cover gown and put on a clean gown when you return. If you are kept in the father's waiting room for over 45 minutes **call back to the nurse's station** to remind the staff that you are still waiting. They may have thought someone else notified you or may just have forgotten if they are busy.

When you join your partner in the labor room, you may find her tense and losing control. Immediately **start encouraging her to relax** and help her with her breathing techniques. Some couples who desire not to be separated at all during their labor, **request to be together during the admission procedures** so that the labor partner can assist the woman in remaining relaxed and cooperative and also avoid the panic some women feel when left alone.

A few doctors still request that the labor partner leave during exams. Your feelings about this should be discussed with your birth attendant in advance.

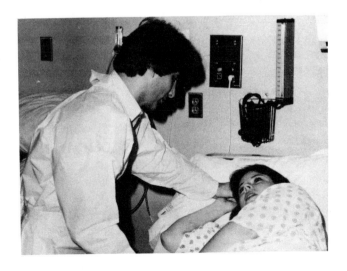

Working through a contraction.

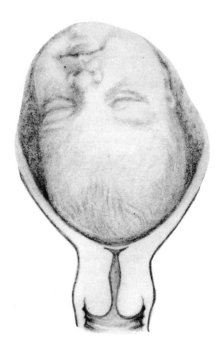

No effacement or dilatation.

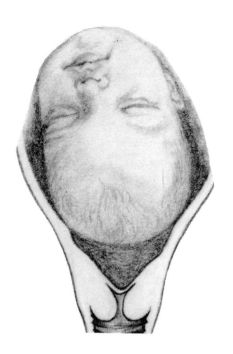

Effaced 60%.

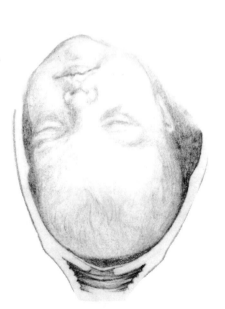

Effaced 100%—dilated 2 cm.

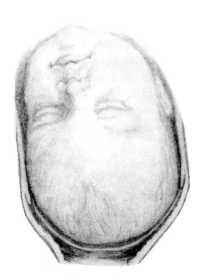

Effaced 100%—dilated 10 cm.

THE FIRST STAGE OF LABOR

During the first stage of labor the contractions of your uterine muscles will cause the cervix to efface and dilate. **Effacement** refers to the shortening or thinning of the cervix. This is expressed in percentage, from 0% (long and thick) to 100% (completely thinned out).

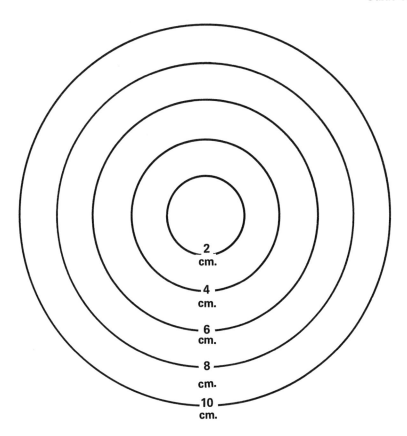

Dilatation chart (actual size).

Dilatation refers to the opening of the cervix. This is expressed in centimeters (cm.), 0 (closed) to 10 cm. (dilatation complete). Dilatation may also be expressed in fingers, 5 fingers being equal to 10 cm. (approximately 4 inches in diameter).

Another term used to indicate labor progress is **station**. This refers to the location of the presenting part (usually the head) in relation to the level of the ischial spines of the pelvis. This indicates the degree of advancement of the baby through the pelvis. Stations are expressed in centimeters above (minus) and below (plus) the level of the ischial spines (zero station). The head is usually engaged when it reaches the level of the ischial spines.

Your progress during labor is determined by your physician, midwife or nurse by vaginal examinations which measure the effacement and dilatation of the cervix and the station of the baby. These examinations, although sometimes uncomfortable, help you and your partner to assess your progress in labor.

The first stage of labor is divided into three phases: early, active, and transition. These will be discussed individually.

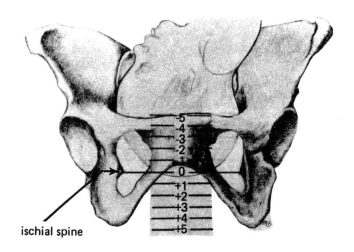

Station of presenting part.

LABOR PARTNER'S SUMMARY

		What's Going On?	How is She Feeling?
	Before Labor Begins	Lightening Increased frequency of Braxton-Hicks Early effacement and dilatation Increased vaginal discharge Leveling off or loss of weight (1-3 lbs.) Baby less active	Excited, sense of anticipation Depressed Has difficulty sleeping—very tired Has spurt of energy
STAGE I	**Beginning of Labor**	She may experience any or all of the following: —contractions —loss of mucus plug —leaking or rupture of membranes —frequent bowel movements	Excited Apprehensive Talkative
	Early Phase	Effacement and dilatation of the cervix from 0-4 cm. Contractions 5-20 min. apart, lasting 30-60 sec., becoming longer, stronger, and more frequent	Confident Sociable
	Active Phase	Dilatation from 4-8 cm. with more effacement Contractions 2-4 min. apart, lasting 45-60 sec. with greater intensity and longer peaks	Anxious Apprehensive—doubts ability to handle labor Serious mood—birth oriented Attention turned inward Not talkative
	Transition	Dilatation from 8-10 cm. Contractions 1½-2 min. apart, lasting 60-90 sec., extremely strong and erratic, possibly with more than one peak	She may experience one or more of the following: —Panicky, feels like giving up —Irritable —Desires not to be touched —Forgetful, disoriented, amnesia —Rectal pressure, premature urge to push —Nausea/vomiting —Alternating hot/cold feeling —Trembling of the legs
STAGE II	**Birth**	Dilatation complete Baby moves down birth canal Head crowns Delivery of head, shoulders, and then rest of body Contractions 3-5 min. apart, lasting 60-75 sec., like those in earlier labor	Has strong urge to push Relieved to be able to push Renewed energy level Feels great deal of pressure Burning, splitting sensation Is sociable again between contractions
STAGE III	**Delivery of Placenta**	Mild uterine contractions Separation and expulsion of placenta	Exhilarated Possibly fatigued
STAGE IV	**Bonding and Recovery**	Perineal repair if episiotomy was done Identification procedures for baby Move to bonding and / or recovery room Intermittent uterine contractions Checking of mother's physical status Removal of baby to nursery after bonding	Emotionally high, proud Happy Tired Motherly Hungry and thirsty

LABOR PARTNER'S SUMMARY (continued)

What Should She Do?	How Can I Help Her?

Simplify housekeeping.
Pack suitcase and Lamaze bag.
Conserve energy—take naps.
Pre-register at hospital.
Practice exercises, relaxation, and
    breathing techniques DAILY.
	Assist with housekeeping chores.
	Encourage her to rest.
	Provide diversion—take walks, eat out, etc.
	Practice relaxation and
	    breathing techniques with her.

Try to sleep if at night. Continue normal daytime activities. Take a walk. Take a shower, wash hair, shave legs. Eat light snack.	Time contractions. Reassure her (of her readiness for labor). Call babysitter. If at night—encourage her to sleep and sleep yourself.
Relax with contractions. Begin slow-paced breathing if necessary. Assume upright position as much as possible. Empty bladder every hour. Call doctor or midwife. Drink clear liquids.	Time and record contractions. Remind her to relax, use touch relaxation. Give encouragement, praise her. Help her with breathing, if necessary. Encourage walking. Remind her to urinate. Use distractions—play cards, games, go to a movie.
Continue relaxation and breathing techniques. Use focal point. Do effleurage as desired. Change position frequently. Continue to urinate hourly. Adjust pillows for comfort. Go to hospital or birth center.	If walking, support her body during contractions. Assist with effleurage or back rubs. Provide cool wash cloth for her face. Give ice chips (if available) or wet wash cloth to suck on. Remind her to change positions and urinate. Keep her informed of her progress. Encourage relaxation and assist with breathing. If breathing seems ineffective, suggest changing pattern. Watch for signs of transition.

Remember this phase is intense, but SHORT.
Take one contraction at a time.
Change breathing technique as needed.
Eliminate cleansing breath if contraction
    peaks immediately.
Blow with premature urge to push.
Use slow-paced breathing between
    contractions.
	Don't leave her for any reason.
	Remind her it is transition—LABOR IS ALMOST
	    OVER—Baby is coming.
	Praise her lavishly for her efforts.
	Communicate with medical staff.
	Keep calm, don't argue.
	Apply back pressure.
	Call nurse if urge to push is felt.
	Breathe with her—have her mimic you.
	Help her catch contractions at start.
	Help her relax between contractions.
	BE POSITIVE!!

Assume comfortable pushing position. Use most comfortable pushing technique. Push only when feeling urge. Pant or blow as head is delivered. Relax perineum. Keep eyes open.	Help her assume a comfortable position for pushing. Count if using modified Valsalva to pace her pushing. Remind her to relax bottom, check her face for relaxation. Coach her to pant or blow as head is delivered. Remind her to keep eyes open. Be sure she can see in mirror. Take pictures as baby is born.
Push with contractions as instructed. Hold and soothe your new baby. Initiate breastfeeding. Use breathing techniques if necessary.	Take pictures of mother and baby. Hold baby.
Undress, examine, caress, nurse, and talk to baby. Make eye contact with baby. Take pictures of father and baby. Massage fundus of uterus. Eat and drink.	Share in bonding with baby. Take more pictures. Make telephone calls.

EARLY LABOR

This is the **easiest but the longest** part of labor. It usually lasts from 2–9 hours. Along with effacement, **the cervix is dilating from 0–4 centimeters.** Contractions during this phase are from 30 to 60 seconds long. They usually start 20–30 minutes apart and get progressively closer, until they are about 5 minutes apart. The **contractions start out mild to slightly uncomfortable,** becoming stronger and longer as labor progresses. During the rest period between contractions, you should feel good, be talkative and be able to walk around and **continue your normal activities**. You will probably be at home for most of this phase. Prepared women generally **feel very confident** during this time and are able to handle labor well. Some women express anxiety, realizing that once labor has begun, it will not stop.

If labor starts during the day, **activity or walking** will help stimulate the contractions. If labor begins at night, it is advisable to **get some sleep** or rest so you can better handle the active phase. Be assured that when your contractions become strong you will awaken!

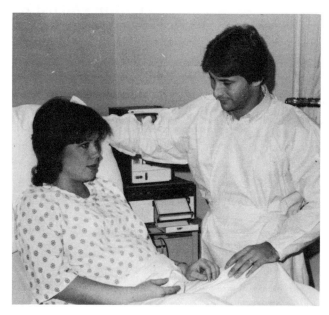

Practicing breathing techniques.

Clear liquids (tea, jello, apple juice, broth, popsicles) may be taken during early labor. Light nutritious snacks, such as crackers, fruits and toast, may also be eaten at this time to provide the nourishment needed during labor. Digestion slows during active labor, as does the laboring woman's desire for food. Eating during labor remains controversial because of the possibility of vomiting and aspirating the stomach contents into the lungs if general anesthesia has been given. This could result in serious complications. On the other hand, general anesthesia is seldom used and if vomiting does occur when awake and alert, it is not harmful.

Labor Partner's Role

This is the time to **become familiar with the contractions.** If you place your hand on your partner's abdomen, you can feel the uterus become very hard. Sometimes you can feel a contraction beginning even before your partner is aware of it and can help her prepare for it. **Assist in timing the contractions** and make sure your partner is relaxing with them. If you notice her tensing or expressing discomfort during the contractions, **encourage her to relax, change position or urinate.** (Possibly a full bladder is causing her discomfort.) If these measures fail to produce relaxation, then begin slow-paced breathing.

Early labor.

Active labor.

ACTIVE LABOR

During active labor the **cervix is dilating from 4–8 cm.** Labor can progress very rapidly after 5 cm. Your labor is more than half over when you reach this point. **Contractions are becoming stronger and peaking faster**, with the peak lasting longer after 5 cm. The contractions usually last 40–60 seconds and are 2–4 minutes apart. If the membranes rupture at this point, it is usually with a gush. You may notice an increased intensity in the contractions after the water has broken.

During this phase your **mood becomes serious** and very "birth-oriented." You may not want to be distracted and **may begin to doubt your ability to cope** with the contractions. You will no longer desire to play cards or games, will be **less talkative** between contractions, and may need more help in maintaining relaxation. You or your partner may do effleurage to give added comfort.

Labor Partner's Role

Continue with **reassurance and encouragement**. It is important that you **keep her informed of her progress**. Help her to maintain control during the contractions and assist her with breathing if necessary. You may want to use each other's eyes as a focal point. **Commands should be kept short** as she is not interested in long conversations. Continue to remind her to empty her bladder every 1–2 hours.

Use comfort measures as needed. If her mouth is dry, she may benefit from sipping ice chips, sucking on a washcloth, brushing her teeth or rinsing with mouthwash. For dry lips, she may want to apply chapstick or lip gloss. A cool cloth may feel refreshing to her face. If you are walking during labor, you may need to stop and support her during a contraction. If she is in bed, have her **change positions often** (every 20–30 minutes) and adjust the bed for comfort.

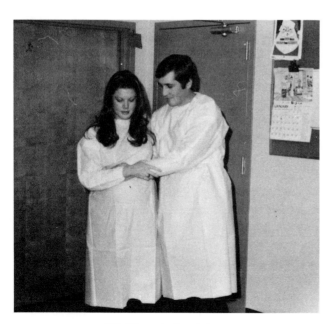

Walking during labor.

Stopping for a contraction.

TRANSITION

The transition from the first stage of labor to the second stage is **the shortest phase**, but it is **also the most intense.** The **cervix is dilating from 8 to 10 cm.** The contractions are usually 60 to 90 seconds in duration; they **peak very suddenly and may peak more than once.** Contractions may also be as close as 1½ to 2 minutes apart. Even though there is a short rest period, some women say the contractions feel as though they are right on top of each other with no relief. Transition may last 10 minutes to 1½ hours. **Think positive—labor is almost over!**

Certain signs will alert your labor partner to the fact that you are in transition. Be assured that you will not experience all of these signs:

1. Premature urge to push or bear down. This may be mistaken for the need to have a bowel movement.
2. Belching or hiccups.
3. Nausea and/or vomiting.
4. Shaking or uncontrollable trembling of legs or body.
5. Chills and/or extreme warmth.
6. Loss of modesty (may throw off covers).
7. Cramps in legs and buttocks.
8. Sensitivity to touch (may not want to be touched).
9. Spontaneous rupture of membranes now if not before, usually with a gush.
10. Dopey feeling, amnesia between contractions, sleeping between contractions.
11. Increased bloody mucus discharge.
12. Confusion, tendency to give up ("I can't do it,"; "I can't take another contraction.")
13. Feeling of getting nowhere, that labor will never end.
14. Panic if left alone.
15. Susceptibility to suggestion, especially if offered medication.
16. Inability to comprehend direction and the need for your labor partner to do breathing with you.
17. Irritability and restlessness.
18. Feeling of being out of control—easy to lose contraction.
19. Flushed face.

Transition.

Labor Partner's Role

During transition your encouragement and presence are vital. **DO NOT LEAVE YOUR PARTNER DURING THIS TIME FOR ANY REASON!** Very often she will panic if left alone even for a short period. If offered medication at this point, she will more than likely accept anything that is offered or even state that she wishes to be put out. You will want to **do most of the communicating with the medical staff** at this time because of her intense involvement with her labor. Therefore, it is important that you are aware of her desires.

If your labor partner expresses the desire to move her bowels or begins to bear down, inform the birth attendant so she can be examined. **If she is not fully dilated, you will have to instruct her to blow out forcefully** during the urge to push. If pushing is begun too soon, it could cause the cervix to swell, thereby prolonging labor and possibly even tearing the cervix.

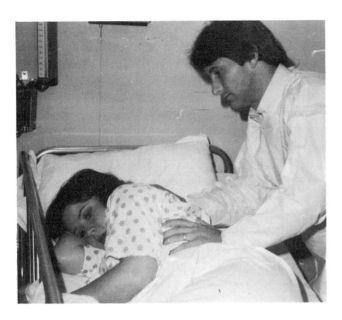

Coaching through transition.

It is necessary for you to **make sure that your partner "catches" each contraction.** If she is sleeping or has amnesia between the contractions, you must make sure she starts her breathing in time. Let her know when the contraction ends and help her relax in between. **Remain calm!** Even if she yells at you, don't argue. Make your commands short and precise. If she becomes confused, have her sit up in bed.

If she expresses the desire to give up, keep reminding her that this is the shortest phase and that labor is almost over.

What do I do if she Panics? You may notice that she is not using a focal point, is rocking her head from side to side or is gripping the sheet, your hand, or bedrail. She may stop the breathing pattern and may hold her breath, moan or cry out, and may even thrash around in the bed. To help her gain control you should first **stand up.** This puts you in an authority position. **Grasp her face or wrists** with your hands. **Call her name** and **bring your face close to hers** and **do the breathing with her.** You may need to be firm with her during this time and take full command of the situation. Generally, when the contractions become unbearable, **transition is almost over** and she may only have a few more contractions left. Be sure to tell her this!

Continue with the other comfort measures as needed. If her back is uncomfortable, use pressure, massage the area, or apply a warm or cool cloth.

Warm socks may be worn for cold feet. To aid trembling legs, lightly massage her inner thighs or firmly grasp her legs. Keep a cool cloth on her forehead. Tell her she is doing wonderfully and keep her informed of her progress. Above all else, keep a positive attitude!

SECOND STAGE OF LABOR

The second stage of labor **begins when the cervix reaches complete dilatation and effacement and it ends with the birth of the baby.** The contractions are more like those experienced earlier in labor, lasting approximately 60–75 seconds. During the peak of the contraction, **a strong urge to push is felt;** occasionally a woman does not feel this urge and needs guidance in her pushing effort. Contractions slow in frequency and are usually 3–5 minutes apart. The second stage of labor may last from 10 minutes to 2 hours. For the multigravida, this stage is generally short.

Your **mood greatly improves.** You become sociable, even talkative, and feel more positive about your progress in labor. If you have been blowing to combat a premature urge to push, it is a tremendous relief to be able to work actively with the contractions. Many women feel a great satisfaction even though **working very hard,** while pushing the baby down the birth canal. Some women even relate this part of labor to an orgasmic experience as the baby emerges from the vagina. As the baby descends the

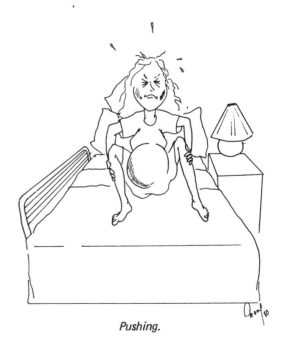

Pushing.

birth canal, you may experience increased show or discharge, a burning or splitting sensation, or leg cramps. Your face may be red, perspiring, and have a **look of intense concentration.** You may make involuntary grunting or groaning noises as you actively work with the contractions. These normal responses may be misinterpreted by your partner as expressions of pain. A minority of women may express discomfort or pain with pushing, which is usually associated with an unusual presentation or position of the baby, the position of the mother, a large baby or an unrelaxed pelvic floor. A strong feeling of **needing to have a bowel movement may be felt,** to which some women respond by tightening the pelvic floor so they won't soil the bed. This is a normal sensation as the baby's head presses against the bowel. Do not react to this sensation by tensing; rather, concentrate on relaxing your bottom for max-

imum comfort and progress. (If your jaw is relaxed, your pelvic floor will also be relaxed. As you practice the Kegel exercises, you will note that if you tense your jaw, you will feel a tightening in the pelvic floor. Conversely, as you relax your jaw, your pelvic floor will also relax.)

A large amount of pressure or a burning sensation is felt as the baby nears the perineum. You may notice the baby's head during the contraction at the vaginal outlet along with some bulging of the perineum and separation of the vaginal lips. The head may appear wrinkled, and covered with wet hair. It will recede between contractions until, finally, the top part of the baby's head is visible between contractions. This is known as **crowning**. With the next few contractions, the head is born. It will then rotate, the face looking toward your thigh. The shoulders are delivered, and the body slides out

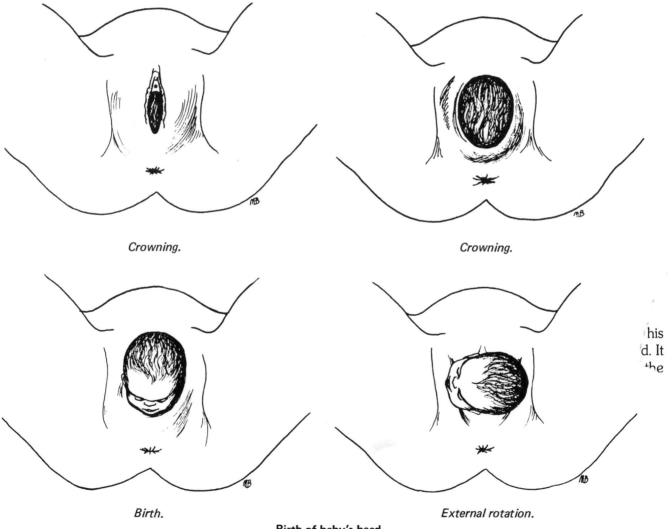

Crowning.

Crowning.

Birth.

External rotation.

Birth of baby's head.

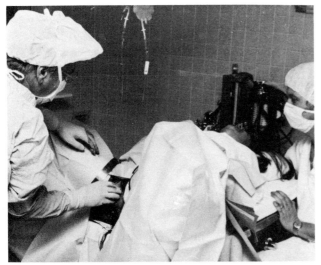

Lithotomy position.

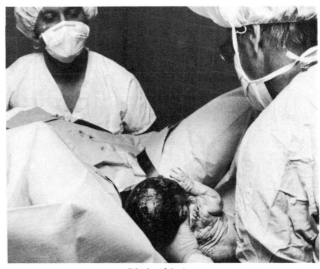

Birth of baby.

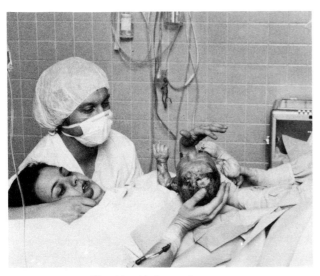

Greeting their newborn.

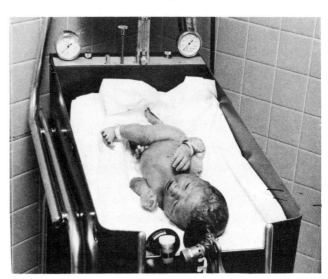

Infant in warming bed.

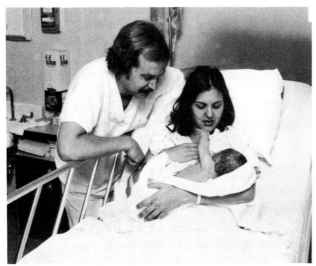

Bonding.

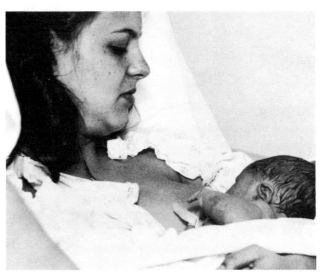

First nursing.

Conventional Hospital Delivery

Photographed by Mark Hildreth

THIRD STAGE OF LABOR

This is the shortest stage of labor, lasting from 5–20 minutes. Following the birth of the baby, the uterus continues contracting, although with less intensity than that of labor contractions. The **placenta spontaneously separates** from the wall of the uterus and is expelled. You may be asked to push with the contractions to deliver the placenta, or the birth attendant may guide the placenta out by using firm fundal pressure. The placenta should be allowed to separate without strong traction or pulling on the cord. The danger in pulling is the possibility of retained placental tissue inside the uterus which can result in postpartum hemorrhaging. Once the placenta is delivered, the physician or midwife will examine it to determine if it is intact. If necessary, the physician may do an internal examination of the uterus to be sure there is no retained placental tissue. This is uncomfortable and you will need to do your breathing to reduce the discomfort.

FOURTH STAGE OF LABOR

During this stage, the birth attendant will be **repairing the episiotomy** (if done) or any vaginal or perineal lacerations that may have occurred. If this becomes uncomfortable, ask for another injection of local anesthetic. You **may be aware of uterine contractions** if medication has been given to contract the uterus, or if you have started breastfeeding.

You may **feel exhilarated** and very excited about the baby. If labor has been long or difficult, you may experience a feeling of relief or exhaustion. Involuntary trembling of your legs and/or body may occur.

BONDING

Bonding refers to the attachment which a mother and father develop towards their new baby. This process actually begins before birth as you feel your baby's movements and anticipate his arrival. The feeling is heightened at the first sight of your newborn. For centuries, new mothers have felt the desire to hold and cuddle their new babies as soon as possible after birth. Recent studies confirm that this really is best for babies!

The current emphasis on bonding is the result of the research done in connection with battered, abused and "failure to thrive" children. (Failure to

Bonding.

thrive means a baby does not grow, gain weight or develop behaviorally at a normal rate even though there is no organic disease present.) A profound number of these infants had been separated from their mothers at birth for a period of time. A significant correlation was found between this early separation and subsequent development of these disastrous conditions.[11] It is well documented in the animal kingdom that separation of a mother and baby results in abandonment or rejection by the mother. As a result of these studies, neonatal intensive care nurseries now encourage families to visit, touch and even assist in the care of their premature or sick newborns while they are hospitalized.

In their research, Marshall Klaus and John Kennell found the quality of mothering was more positive in women who were able to bond immediately after birth and receive five extra hours of contact with their newborn daily while in the hospital. A control group of women were subjected to the conventional hospital routine: a glimpse of the baby at birth, brief contact after six to eight hours, and then short visits of 20–30 minutes every four hours for feeding. These mothers were followed at periodic intervals up to five years.

At one month, more mothers who bonded picked up and cuddled their crying babies, rather than allowing them to "cry it out." They were also more reluctant to go out and leave their infants behind. During an examination they showed more soothing behavior when their babies cried. While feeding their infants, it was observed that the mothers who had received extended contact with their babies fondled them more and exhibited more eye-to-eye contact.[12]

At one year these toddlers cried less and smiled more. After two years, the mothers spoke to their children with more descriptive language and used fewer commands. When tested at five years of age there was a high correlation between advanced speech development and the speech patterns used by these mothers when their children were two.[13]

Because of these findings and other similar research, Drs. Klaus and Kennell suggest that the father, mother and infant be allowed a minimum of 30–60 minutes alone after birth, and that the mother and baby be allowed to stay together as much as the mother desires while in the hospital. During the first hour of life, the baby is in a *quiet alert* state. This is followed by a deep sleep for 3–4 hours. After this time, the quiet alert state can last for periods as short as a few seconds. In the quiet alert state, the baby is awake and responsive to his environment. He will look intently at your face and gaze into your eyes. Contrary to popular belief, **your baby can see at birth**. Interestingly, he can focus best on an object 12–15 inches away—the length from his face to yours when being held in your arms or when being breastfed.[14] It is suggested that the **antibiotic ointment or silver nitrate drops be de-**

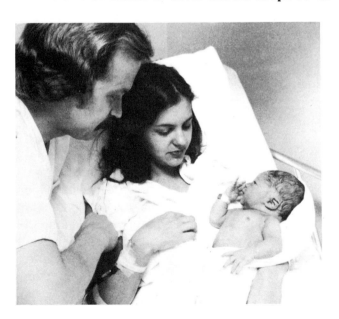

Baby in the quiet alert state.

layed until after the initial bonding period so as not to interfere with his vision.

Ideally, **breastfeeding should be initiated at this time** as your baby's sucking reflex is strongest at birth. This reflex diminishes after a few hours and may not return for 24–48 hours. The colostrum received by your baby during that first nursing provides him with protection against infection and acts as a laxative, cleansing his system of mucus and meconium. You also benefit from this early nursing. The baby's sucking releases the hormone prolactin into your system which enhances your maternal feelings. Oxytocin, which is also released, causes the uterus to contract and reduces the blood loss following birth.

Many hospitals today offer a **special bonding room,** although any private area will suffice (labor room, delivery room, recovery room). In complete privacy, you, as a couple, can explore and marvel at your new creation. You can hold your naked infant close to your bare breast, provide skin-to-skin contact, and begin the nursing relationship. By covering you and the baby with a blanket, you can prevent a drop in the baby's temperature, even without a heat lamp.[15] Both you and your partner can hold, talk to, and caress your baby. Don't be surprised if you find yourselves talking to your newborn in a high-pitched voice. It is almost instinctive to do this and you will find the baby responds very positively to these sounds.

When you hold your baby in your arms, you will notice that he is especially attracted to your eyes and facial features. He will respond by gazing, listening, imitating, possibly crying (which can be soothed), and following with his eyes. He is so new, yet so alert!

A positive childbirth experience usually fosters the bonding process. Similarly, a negative childbirth experience may adversely affect a mother's feelings toward her child for a while, and thus cause a delay in maternal attachment. Additionally, some parents simply take a little longer to develop loving emotions towards their newborns. In these cases, bonding takes place in the weeks following birth, rather than during the first few minutes. It is important to realize that the newborn stage is not the *only* time in a baby's life when the strong parent-to-baby bond can be established. The initial bonding period can be compared to a honeymoon—if the couple become ardent, completely satisfied lovers, then so much the better. But a less-than-perfect honeymoon does not doom the marriage. Nor does a less-than-perfect birth/bonding experience doom the parent/child relationship.

The use of medication during labor and delivery may also adversely affect your bonding experience. If you are heavily sedated, you will not have the opportunity for immediate interaction with your baby. In this case, bonding should take place as soon as you are able. The father may arrange to bond with his baby even though circumstances may prevent you from doing so right after delivery.

The baby who has received medication via the placenta may be sleepy and less responsive. This medication may remain in his system as long as 30 days[16] and affect his responses and sucking ability. Bonding is more difficult in this case.

Active participation in the birth of your child enhances the strong feeling of attachment towards your baby for both you and your husband. In addition, when you work together to bring about the birth of your baby you will feel a closeness towards one another that is not easily forgotten. The bonding between mother and father can be tremendous. This close feeling should be maintained especially during those difficult first six weeks after birth.

Happily, the unnatural routine of separation right after delivery is changing to provide a time together after the birth. However, you need to discuss this with your doctor prior to delivery to insure that time for bonding will be provided. Bonding is such a positive step in the framework of family centered maternity care, a step that enables you to enjoy your right to love and cuddle your new baby as you welcome him into your lives.

RECOVERY ROOM

After the delivery room procedures are completed and the bonding period is over, your baby is placed in the newborn nursery for observation and bathing. You are closely observed for a period of one to two hours in the recovery room. This is the time it usually takes for your vital signs (blood pressure, pulse and respiration) to become stable. If you deliver in a birth center, you and your baby will not be separated during this time.

The nursing staff checks your uterus for firmness and for its position in the abdomen. The **fun-**

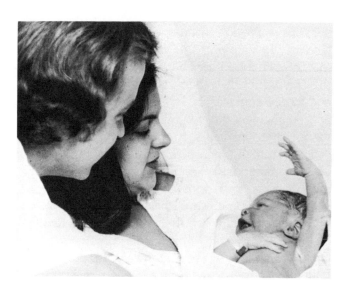

Responsive newborn, minutes after birth.

dus is massaged to keep your uterus in a contracted state. You can do this yourself. The **amount and consistency of the lochia** (normal flow of blood, excess tissue, and fluids from the uterus) is also closely watched. **You will be asked to urinate** before you leave the recovery room because a distended bladder can force the uterus up and out of position and cause it to relax. You may not feel the need to urinate since other sensations after birth can mask the awareness of a full bladder. If necessary, a catheter is inserted into your bladder to empty it.

A blanket helps alleviate any trembling of your legs, a common experience postpartum. Ice bags on your perineum may relieve any burning sensation or discomfort in that area. Using slow-paced breathing helps you deal with the afterbirth contractions you may feel as your uterus continues to contract and grow smaller. These afterbirth pains are more noticeable after second and subsequent births.

During the period in the recovery room, you should try to contract the pelvic floor muscles (**Kegel exercises**). This increases the blood flow to the area, which reduces swelling and speeds the healing of the episiotomy site. If an episiotomy was not done, you should still Kegel to help restore the muscle tone of your pelvic floor. You may be hungry and thirsty and should be provided with some well-deserved nourishment. If it's not offered, ask! You will both be experiencing an emotional high, feeling proud of your accomplishment. Together, you will probably be reliving the details of your birth, over and over again.

ROOMING-IN

Rooming-in is an option that is available in many hospitals and should be initiated as soon after birth as possible. It allows you to keep your baby in the room with you for all or part of the day. Complete or 24 hour rooming-in means you have your baby day and night, while partial rooming-in means the baby stays with you from morning until evening and returns to the nursery for the night. Your baby may be brought to you for the night-time feeding if you desire. Flexible rooming-in provides you the option of returning your baby to the nursery as you wish (for visitors, naps, etc.).

Even with complete rooming-in, most hospitals return the baby to the nursery for a short period of time each morning to allow for a pediatric examination and bathing. This time also allows you to shower and receive any required nursing care.

The bond of affection formed immediately after birth can grow and deepen during the days of the hospital stay. The close association and interaction between you and your baby continue as you care for your infant. You will feel more confident and competent in caring for your baby than mothers who are separated from their babies by traditional hospital routines.

Doctors Klaus and Kennell believe that the mother should have complete care of the infant for a long period during the day (at least five hours) with nurses available as consultants. As a result of this extended contact with the baby, rooming-in mothers seem to develop maternal feelings more quickly and resume physical activities earlier than mothers who don't room-in. The baby who can interact with just one care-giver, his mother, appears to be more content. He cries less and organizes his sleep-wake rhythm and feeding pattern more quickly than babies who interact with several, different care-givers and are fed on a rigid schedule.

The rooming-in stay also provides a time when your baby's father can hold, care for, and enjoy his baby before he brings you both home. This continues the strengthening of the paternal bond and aids in his adjustment to the new baby.

SIBLING VISITATION

Your ability to adjust to a home situation that includes other children will be greatly improved if they are allowed to visit you in the hospital. This visit also reduces the separation anxieties your children experience. Many hospitals provide a special time for children to visit with their mother and observe their new brother or sister through the nursery window. If you are rooming-in, your baby is usually returned to the nursery for sibling visitation. Some hospitals do allow children to visit with their mother and the new baby in the mother's room. In birth centers, siblings are encouraged to interact with the new baby from the moment of birth. Early involvement by all family members enhances the bonding of your new family unit.

HOSPITAL STAY

The **length of your hospital stay** is determined in part by the health of you and your baby. Other considerations include the needs of siblings at home and monetary concerns. Some mothers choose to discharge themselves hours after birth and others choose to stay for a full period of three days. Most birth centers allow mothers to go home within hours after delivery. Women experiencing a cesarean birth can expect a hospital stay of three to six days.

During the hospital stay the nursing staff provides medical care for you and the baby. You will be instructed in **perineal care** to prevent infection and promote healing of the vagina and perineum. If an episiotomy was performed or if hemorrhoids are present, you will be offered some or all of the following to relieve soreness: medicated pads (Tucks), anesthetic spray, heat lamp treatments, and a warm soaking of the perineum called a **sitz bath.** In the first 24 to 48 hours after delivery, the fluid that was retained during pregnancy begins to be eliminated. The nursing staff may ask you to urinate into a container the first day postpartum to insure you are **emptying your bladder** adequately.

Because of the relaxation of the abdominal muscles, soreness of the perineum, and perhaps hemorrhoids, you may have difficulty **moving your bowels.** If proper diet (fresh fruits and vegetables, whole grain, and sufficient water) doesn't help, a stool softener may be prescribed. Be sure to wipe from front to back to avoid fecal contamination and infection.

Your **vital signs are monitored** by the nursing staff along with observation of the height and tone of your fundus, type and amount of lochia and condition of the episiotomy site. You can expect a daily visit from your obstetrician and the baby's pediatrician.

If you are an **Rh negative mother** who has given birth to an Rh positive infant, you will receive an injection of RhoGam within 72 hours after birth. This injection prevents your body from producing antibodies which could endanger subsequent babies during pregnancy. RhoGam should also be given following a miscarriage or abortion as the blood type of the fetus is usually not known. In addition, the American College of Obstetrics now recommends that RhoGam be given preventatively at 26 to 28 weeks of pregnancy. This injection prevents the sensitization that occurs in rare cases during the third trimester. Some doctors and midwives are reluctant to offer this additional immunization during pregnancy because of "marginal benefits, great costs and the lack of adequate fetal safety studies."[17]

It is hoped that the first few days of your baby's life can be utilized to the fullest in establishing a close family bond. Up-to-date hospitals have policies which promote mother-father-baby-sibling contact. If your hospital allows family involvement, be sure to make use of it. If your hospital doesn't allow such interactions, request them anyway. It is *important* to make your wishes known. Perhaps allowances can be made to accommodate the type of experience you desire. Opportunities for family members to interact and bond during this period will help promote a loving, thriving family.

Parental infant bonding.

FOOTNOTES

Chapter 6

1. Constance Lerch, *Maternity Nursing* (St. Louis, C. V. Mosby Co., 1970), p. 59.
2. Lerch, p. 59.
3. Lerch, p. 148.
4. Lerch, p. 148.
5. Lerch, p. 148.
6. Lerch, p. 148.
7. Lerch, p. 161.
8. Silvia Feldman, *Choices in Childbirth* (N.Y., Grosset and Dunlap, 1978), p. 55.
9. Feldman, p. 55.
10. Frederick Leboyer, *Birth Without Violence* (N.Y., Alfred A. Knopf, 1976), p. 50.
11. Marshall Klaus and John Kennell, *Maternal-Infant Bonding* (St. Louis, C. V. Mosby Co., 1976), p. 2.
12. *Maternal-Infant Bonding*, p. 56.
13. Marshall Klaus and John Kennell, *Parent-Infant Bonding* (St. Louis, C.V. Mosby Co., 1982), p. 46.
14. *Maternal-Infant Bonding*, p. 71.
15. *Maternal-Infant Bonding*, p. 76.
16. Avis Ericson, *Medications Used During Labor and Birth* (Milwaukee, ICEA, 1978), p. III (foreword by Murray Enkin).
17. Paul A. Hensleigh, "Preventing rhesus isoimmunization," *American Journal of Obstetrics and Gynecology*, Vol. 146, No. 7 (August 1, 1983), p. 755.

Chapter 7

Medications and Anesthesia
or "How Do You Spell Relief?"

The avoidance of the use of medication throughout your pregnancy has been thoroughly discussed in Chapter 2. Therefore this chapter will deal with those medications or anesthetics that may be available during your labor, delivery and postpartum.

In a normal, uncomplicated labor and delivery, the use of medication is often unnecessary. The relaxation tools and breathing techniques, if practiced regularly, are very effective in combating the sensation of pain. In addition, acupressure may be useful for pain relief. (See discussion of acupressure on page 83.) **The presence of a loving support person is probably the best tranquilizer available.** Also, the support given by the hospital staff and your birth attendant may affect your need for medication. If you are given positive reinforcement ("You're doing great!"; "It's almost over!"), are permitted to move about freely, and interventions are kept to a minimum, you will probably experience very little need for medication. On the other hand, if you are frequently asked if you need anything for "pain," are made to lie in one position, and medical interventions are used (amniotomy, pitocin or an enema which intensify contractions; a monitor or I.V.'s which restrict movement), you may have an increased desire for some type of medication.

Nature has provided its own painkiller for the laboring woman. During labor, as during any activity causing extreme exertion, a chemical release of the "well-being" hormones called **endorphins** takes place. These are narcotic-like natural pain relievers which are said to be several times more potent than morphine.[1] Current research is just beginning to discover the full effects of these amazing substances, which produce a sensation of enormous pleasure after the tremendous exertion of labor. It has been found that any drug given to the woman during labor disturbs the production of this natural painkiller.[2]

Your knowledge of the labor and birth process will also enhance your ability to cope with labor. **Before deciding to take medication in labor, find out how far your labor has progressed.** If you are in transition and labor is almost over, you may want to work with a few more contractions that may complete the first stage of labor. By the time the nurse goes out, draws up the medication and returns with it, you may have reached 10 cm., and the need for medication would be gone. If given at this time, it may have a strong effect on your baby, and may cause you to be sleepy, resulting in not pushing well and in having diminished bonding ability at birth.

It is important to discuss with your birth attendant what medications and types of anesthesia you will be offered if the need arises. It is also important that your labor partner be well informed as to your desires long before labor begins. Labor is a stressful period and is not the time to decide what medication is best for you. If you wait until you are in active labor or transition to make a decision, you may agree to something that is totally unacceptable to you. **Know your alternatives** and how they will affect both you and your partner's participation in your labor and birth. In discussing medication, or prior to accepting either medication or any prescribed treatment, you should ask your health care professional the following questions:

"How will this medication (or treatment) affect my labor, me, and my baby?"

"What are the benefits and risks?"

"If I decide not to take this medication, what will happen?"

"Is there an alternative form of treatment?"

Even though the relaxation and breathing techniques work extremely well for many women, you may find that these tools do not provide adequate relief of pain or promote maximum relaxation. In a prolonged or difficult labor, some women may feel the need to rely on medication to help them cope with their contractions. In the event of a complicated delivery, where forceps or the vacuum extractor is necessary, the availability of anesthesia is beneficial. In case you need a cesarean section, anesthesia is a necessity.

No one perfect medication exists for all circumstances. Since you cannot foresee what your labor will be like, except in the case of a planned cesarean, you must remain flexible in your attitude. Each medication or anesthetic has benefits and risks. It is important that you are aware of these in order to make an informed decision. **Only when the benefits of using the medication outweigh the risks, should you consider using that particular medication.** Your doctor's preference and skill will also enter into your decision. Certain types of anesthetics (epidurals and paracervicals) require technical expertise. If your physician is unfamiliar with their application, you will feel more comfortable using a different method.

BENEFITS

In a difficult labor, small amounts of medication can decrease some of the pain sensations, and may aid in relaxation, especially between contractions. You should realize that analgesics will not take away *all* pain sensations, but the effect may be sufficient to help you cope with the contractions, and still utilize your Lamaze techniques.

In a prolonged labor, demerol may relax the cervix so that your labor will progress more rapidly. If surgical intervention is necessary (forceps or cesarean), regional anesthetics provide for pain relief while allowing you to be awake for your baby's birth.

RISKS

In discussing the risks involved, many factors must be considered. While the dosage of medication used is geared to the mother, we are dealing with two individuals, one much smaller than the other. All medications, in one way or another, affect the fetus. The American Academy of Pediatrics Committee on Drugs has warned that there is *no* drug which has been proven safe for the unborn child.

The fetus may be affected either directly or indirectly by medication used during labor and delivery. Both effects are highly influenced by the dose and time the medication is administered prior to birth. If sufficient time has passed, much of the medication will be metabolized by you, thereby decreasing some of the side effects in the infant. But, if birth occurs while a large amount of the medication is in the baby's system, his immature liver will have to excrete this on its own. Liver enzyme activity is immature in the fetus and newborn, taking four to eight weeks after birth to reach adult capacity.[3] In a premature infant, the effects of these drugs will be even greater.

Direct effects of medications include toxicity or alteration of the fetal central nervous system, respiration, muscle tone and temperature regulating centers.[4] Indirect effects are caused by the influence of the drug on the mother's physiology. If the mother's respiration or blood pressure is depressed as a result of medication, the amount of oxygen the infant receives is reduced.

The use of one medication or anesthetic may increase the need for further intervention. For example, the use of oxytocin in labor intensifies the contractions, thereby increasing the possibility that you may need pain medication. These stronger contractions may also decrease the amount of oxygen the fetus receives. Conversely, some medications may slow down or prolong labor, thus encouraging the use of oxytocin. Certain anesthetics diminish your urge to push which can increase the need for a forceps delivery.

The decision to either accept or refuse medication is not an *easy* one. Inform yourself of what is available and then, if the need arises, choose that which you are most comfortable with. If you have a known allergy to medication, make sure your birth attendant is aware of this and writes it on your chart. Also, prior to accepting any medication, ask, "What are you giving me?'' If you are very sensitive to medication (become sleepy with cold capsules), alert your doctor to this and ask for a very small dose of the medication. If this small dose is not sufficient, you can always ask for more. But if it is too strong, you may not be able to handle your contractions effectively. Remember, once it's been given it can't be taken back! The chart on page 110 summarizes those medications and anesthetics that are commonly used in childbirth.

"Even better than Mom's chicken soup!"

MEDICATIONS CHART[5]

Type	Examples	How They Are Given	When They Are Given
Sedatives Hypnotics	**Barbiturates** Seconal Nembutal Phenobarbital **Nonbarbiturates** Chloral hydrate	Orally Intramuscular injection (IM) Intravenously (IV)	Early labor (Usually unnecessary in prepared women)
Tranquilizers	Vistaril (Atarax) Valium Librium Miltown (Equanil) Thorazine Compazine Sparine Phenergan Largon	Orally IM IV	(Oral dose in early labor, usually unnecessary in prepared women) Active labor or transition— alone or in combination with analgesics
Analgesics	Demerol Morphine Talwin Stadol	IM IV	Active labor
Narcotic Antagonists	Nalline Lorfan Narcan	IM or IV to mother IM or in umbilical vein in baby	During 2nd stage After birth
Anticholinergics	Scopolamine (Scope, Twilight Sleep) Atropine	IM IV	Active labor As preoperative medication prior to cesarean

MEDICATIONS CHART

Benefits or Use	Possible Risks or Side Effects to Mother	Possible Risks or Side Effects to Baby
Effect dependent on drug dose Sedatives allay anxiety or excitement and induce rest Hypnotics can induce sleep Do not relieve pain	Can slow labor if given too soon Disorientation Drowsiness Lowers blood pressure	Accumulates in tissues Respiratory depression Decreased responsiveness Poor sucking ability Cord level–70%*
Relieves tension and anxiety Promotes relaxation Vistaril, phenergan and largon used to prevent nausea and vomiting when used with analgesics–also potentiates effects of analgesics	Drowsiness and confusion Blood pressure and heart rate changes Urinary retention	Affects heart rate Poor sucking ability Poor muscle tone Low body temperature Less attentive, more restless Increased jaundice Cord level–95%-100% Valium–100%-200%
Reduces or alters your perception of pain Demerol may relax the cervix and hasten dilatation	Dizziness Dry mouth Euphoria Nausea Respiratory depression Lowered blood pressure Large dose may make you drowsy; may have difficulty concentrating on breathing or pushing Sleepy during birth	Respiratory depression Poor sucking Altered behavioral responses for several days or weeks *FDA requires warning label that demerol may have adverse effects on infant* *Safety has not been proven*[6] Cord level: Demerol–80%-130%. Talwin–40-70%.
Reverses respiratory depression caused by analgesics	If lorfan is used without narcotics, may cause respiratory depression Lorfan not effective against respiratory depression due to nonnarcotic agents or pathologic causes	Little is known about long-term effects Except for narcan they may increase mild depression or depression which is not drug induced (birth trauma) Effects of antagonists are of shorter duration than analgesics and depression may reoccur
Sedation and amnesia Given in combination with analgesics Helps to dry air passage for general anesthesia (prior to cesarean)	Has no place in prepared childbirth Results in disorientation, loss of control, inability to utilize Lamaze techniques Reactions vary from sleeping to hallucinating,[7] to requiring physical restraint Delirium can occur if not used with an analgesic[8] Depresses central nervous system Labor partner is required to leave **Avoid if you want to share your birth experience**	Same as analgesics Increased heart rate Depression Delayed newborn reaction time

* Cord level indicates the amount of drug in the baby's blood stream as compared to that in the mother.

MEDICATIONS CHART

Type	Examples	How They Are Given	When They Are Given
Oxytocics (Synthetic hormones to contract uterus)	Pitocin Syntocinon Oxytocin Ergotrate Methergine	IM IV Dosage best controlled when diluted in IV fluid	Prior to or during labor Postpartum
Regional Anesthesia	Uses "caine" drugs (ex.: Xylocaine, Marcaine, Procaine) (See below)		
	Local Infiltration	Injection into perineum	2nd stage or prior to repair of episiotomy
	Pudendal Block	Injection into pudendal nerves via vagina	2nd stage
	Paracervical Block	Injection into nerves on both sides of cervix via vagina	Active labor
	Epidural	Continuous—insertion of catheter into epidural space (low spine area) or as single injection Done in sitting or side-lying position	Active labor (after 5 cm.) 2nd stage Prior to cesarean birth
	Caudal	Same as epidural but placed in caudal canal (base of spine) Done in sitting or knee-chest position	Same as epidural

MEDICATIONS CHART

Benefits or Use	Possible Risks or Side Effects to Mother	Possible Risks or Side Effects to Baby
Induces or stimulates contractions when medically indicated Postpartum to control bleeding	Drop in blood pressure Anxiety Increased heart rate Edema Severe water intoxication Tetanic (very strong) contractions or rupture of the uterus Increased desire for pain medication Increased need for coaching and support *FDA warning states oxytocics should not be used for elective inductions for convenience of doctor or mother* If breastfeeding, oxytocin is released naturally; if ergotrate or methergine is given postpartum, it can increase blood pressure or cause severe "after pains"	Slower or faster heart rate Fetal asphyxia due to tetanic contractions Increased jaundice
You are awake and can observe delivery Cough reflex is not depressed—less danger of aspiration if vomiting occurs Labor partner can participate		
Numbs perineum for repair of episiotomy or lacerations Response time–3-4 minutes Duration–1-2 hours	Anesthetic not necessary for episiotomy because of natural anesthesia of the perineum during birth (is necessary for repair!) Burning or stinging on administration	Decreased muscle tone[9]
Numbs birth canal and perineum for forceps delivery, episiotomy and repair Response time–2-3 minutes Duration–1 hour	Urge to push is not felt—need coaching Large dose is required—may result in toxicity	Large amounts may cause fetal depression
Relieves discomfort caused by dilatation of the cervix Response time–3-4 minutes Duration–1-2 hours	Slows labor temporarily	Slowing of fetal heart rate Drug crosses placenta in 2-4 minutes Convulsions and death result from direct fetal injection
Complete pain relief for uterine contractions, birth and repair, depending on dosage No spinal headaches if done correctly Response time–10-15 minutes Duration–1½ hours, repeated injections with continuous epidural	Technically difficult—may not work, or take only on one side Prolongs labor May cause a drop in your blood pressure Diminished urge to push prolongs 2nd stage, increasing the need for forceps Increased need for frequent medical supervision and interventions (IV's, fetal monitor, pitocin) Increases chance of a cesarean delivery[10]	If your blood pressure drops, this may cause a decrease in oxygen received by the baby and drop in fetal heart rate Subtle behavior alterations Poor muscle tone
Same as epidural Response time–15-20 minutes Duration–same as epidural	Similar to epidural	Similar to epidural

MEDICATIONS CHART

Type	Examples	How They Are Given	When They Are Given
Regional Anesthesia Cont'd	Spinal	Single injection into spinal fluid Done in side-lying position	Prior to cesarean birth
	Saddle Block (low spinal)	Same as spinal only lower Done in sitting position	2nd stage
General Anesthesia (Gas)	Penthrane Ether Nitrous oxide Cyclopropane Trilene Fluothane	Inhaled through mask	Active labor (Trilene) 2nd stage
Lactation Suppressants	*Hormonal* Deladumone OB Diethylstilbesterol (DES) TACE	Deladumone—IM Orally	Deladumone—immediately prior to or just after birth Postpartum
	Nonhormonal Parlodel	Orally	Postpartum

MEDICATIONS CHART

Benefits or Use	Possible Risks or Side Effects to Mother	Possible Risks or Side Effects to Baby
Numbs area from above navel to toes for cesarean birth Response time–1-2 minutes Duration–1-3 hours	Drop in blood pressure Spinal headache Difficulty with urinating	A drop in your blood pressure may decrease oxygen to baby and result in depression
Numbs pubic area to toes for forceps delivery Response time–same as spinal Duration–same as spinal	Same as spinal Urge to push is lost	Same as spinal
Relieves pain, larger doses will render you unconscious Appropriate for emergency cesarean when there is not time to administer a regional anesthetic	Nausea, vomiting—may aspirate vomitus Deep anesthesia produces: 　Skeletal muscle weakness 　Depression of central nervous system—requires constant supervision 　Cardiac and respiratory depression, irregular heart pattern, lowered blood pressure 　Depression of liver, kidney, and GI tract function Not compatible with prepared childbirth Labor partner is unable to be present	Crosses placenta rapidly Effects are same as those of deep anesthesia in mother Cord levels vary up to 85%; with trilene it may be greater than 100%
Inhibits milk production and prevents breast engorgement; not always effective	Pain at injection site Nausea, diarrhea *FDA warning—may be cancer-causing agents*	Nursing may be reinstated after drug is given; effects unknown TACE is reported to be excreted via breastmilk. No information present on others
Same as above; engorgement may occur when discontinued Nonestrogenic	Lowered blood pressure Dizziness Headache Nausea	

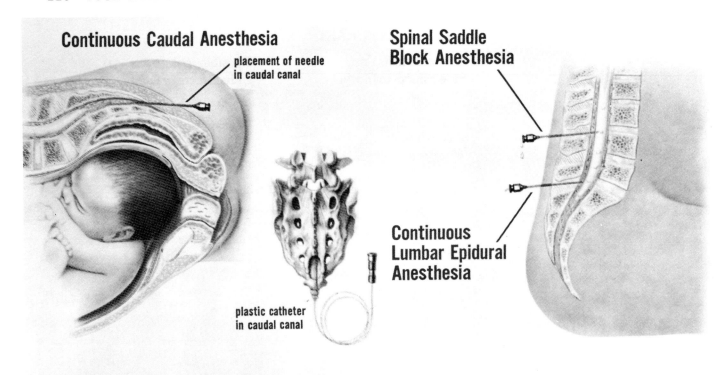

Continuous Caudal Anesthesia

placement of needle in caudal canal

plastic catheter in caudal canal

Spinal Saddle Block Anesthesia

Continuous Lumbar Epidural Anesthesia

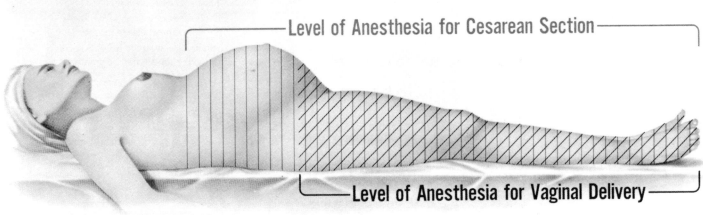

Level of Anesthesia for Cesarean Section

Level of Anesthesia for Vaginal Delivery

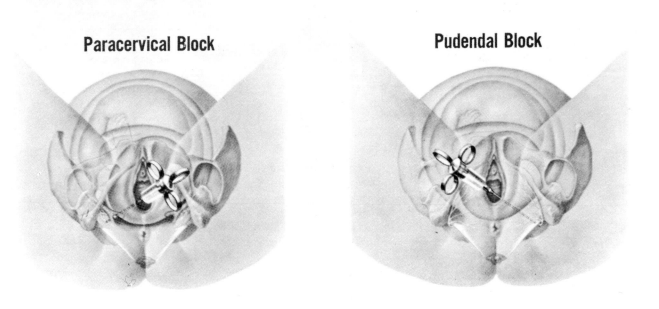

Paracervical Block

Pudendal Block

Regional anesthesia in obstetrics.

FOOTNOTES

Chapter 7

1. Diana Korte and Roberta Scaer, *A Good Birth, A Safe Birth* (N.Y., Bantam Books, 1984), p. 31.
2. Korte and Scaer, p. 223.
3. Avis J. Ericson, Pharm. D., *Medications Used During Labor and Birth: A Resource for Childbirth Educators* (Milwaukee, Wis., ICEA, 1977), p. 5.
4. Ericson, p. 4.
5. Information from *Medications Used During Labor and Birth*, Avis J. Ericson, ICEA, Milwaukee, Wis., 1978; *To Have and To Hold*, Joyce Kieffer (Training Resource Association, Harrisburg, Pa.); *Physician's Desk Reference*, Medical Economics, Inc., Oradell, N.J., 1987.
6. *FDA Consumer*, HEW Publication No. (FDA) 79-1057, U.S. Dept. HEW, Public Health Service, FDA Office of Public Affairs, May, 1979, p. 1.
7. Tracy Hotchner, *Pregnancy and Childbirth* (N.Y., Avon Books, 1979), p. 430.
8. Betty Bergerson and Elsie Krugen, *Pharmacology in Nursing* (St. Louis, C.V. Mosby Co., 1966), p. 374.
9. Tim Chard and Martin Richards, *Benefits and Hazards of the New Obstetrics* (Suffolk, England, Lavenham Press, LTD., 1977), p. 112.
10. Charles Mahan and Diony Young, *Unnecessary Cesareans, Ways to Avoid Them* (Minneapolis, Minn., ICEA, 1980), p. 6.

"It's okay nurse, I brought my own 'SCOPE' with me!"

Chapter 8

Variations and Interventions in Labor and Birth
or "Any Which Way You Can"

The type of labor you experience may be considered "normal" and yet not progress exactly "by the book." Each woman's labor is unique, and you need to be prepared for any situation which may arise. A modification or adjustment of the techniques you have learned may be necessary. In some cases, specific additional measures are required. The following discussion of some possible variations and interventions should provide you with further tools and thus enhance your preparation.

FETAL PRESENTATION AND POSITION

Presentation

The term presentation refers to the way the baby is situated in the uterus. The part of the baby that is closest to the cervix is called the presenting part. As you already know, in a normal birth the head is lowest, and is, therefore, the presenting part. This is called **vertex or cephalic presentation.** A very small percentage of births involve a **transverse lie or shoulder presentation.** In this case, a cesarean delivery is mandatory as the baby is lying sideways in the uterus.

Another presentation, known as **breech,** in which the buttocks present first, accounts for 3–4% of all deliveries. Labor may be longer than in the vertex presentation because the buttocks are not as efficient a dilating wedge as the top of the head. The most common variations are complete breech, in

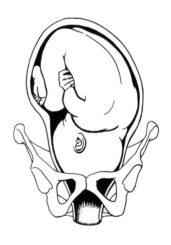

Cephalic presentation.

Shoulder presentation.

which the fetus sits cross-legged in the bottom of the uterus, and frank breech, where the legs are straight up with feet near the face. A less common variation is the footling breech, which is similar to the complete breech but one or both feet present first. The knee breech, the rarest form, has the knee instead of the foot presenting at the cervix.

Risk to the baby is greater in a breech delivery, thus increasing possible obstetrical intervention. Some physicians routinely perform a cesarean in the case of a breech presentation in a primigravida since the pelvis has not been tried. The buttocks may easily pass through the pelvis, whereas the larger head may cause problems. Ideally, your physician will consider the following factors in determining the method of delivery: fetal size; your pelvic dimensions and architecture; the type of breech presentation; adequate progress in labor; and his experience in handling vaginal breech deliveries.

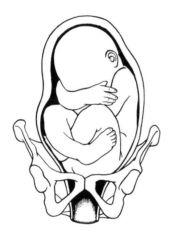

Complete breech.

Frank breech.

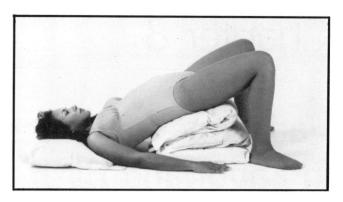

Position for rotating a breech.

Breech presentation may or may not be known before labor begins. If discovered during labor, X-ray pelvimetry may be performed on a first time mother to determine whether her pelvic measurements are adequate. If other complications like a prolapsed cord do not occur, the woman can frequently give birth vaginally. Effective pushing is most helpful in delivering a breech baby. Sometimes forceps are used if the second stage is prolonged.

If you discover during pregnancy that your baby is in a breech presentation, you may be able to **rotate the breech to vertex** by doing the following exercise. Lie on your back on the floor, with pillows elevating your pelvis 9–12 inches. Stay in this position for 10 minutes twice every day. Do it before meals for greatest comfort. Continue this routine for 4 to 6 weeks. If your baby turns, stop doing the exercise or he may turn back to breech again. Once he has turned, do plenty of walking to help him settle further down in the pelvis. Be sure to check with your birth attendant to confirm the change in your baby's presentation.[1]

To be effective, this technique should be started by the thirtieth week of pregnancy, but you may want to try it even if your breech is discovered after that time. One study reported an 88.7 percent success rate.[2] The exercise is also effective in rotating a baby who is lying transverse in the uterus.

It is also possible to turn the baby from a breech or transverse lie by using **external version**. Usually, this procedure is performed in the hospital under the visual guidance of ultrasound. You may be given medication to relax the uterine muscle. This makes it easier for the doctor to manipulate the baby into a head-down position by applying gentle, yet firm pressure to the mother's abdomen (pressing on the baby's head and hip). External version is most successful when done at 36 weeks of pregnancy. After

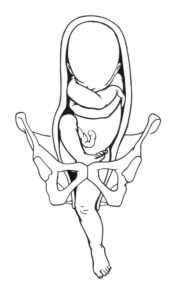

Footling breech.

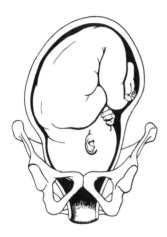

Anterior position.

Posterior position.

37 weeks, the doctor is less likely to be able to rotate the baby since there is less amniotic fluid present. In addition, at that time the baby is larger and may settle into the pelvis. Risks associated with the procedure include initiating labor, soreness to the mother's abdomen and, on rare occasions, shearing the placenta from the uterine wall. It should be performed by a physician who is experienced in the technique.

Position

The position of the baby, as used in obstetrics, refers to the relation of the presenting part to the mother's pelvis. In a vertex presentation the back of the head (occiput) is the point of reference. The most common position during labor is **anterior,** in which the back of the baby's head is towards the mother's abdomen. A less common position, known as **posterior,** occurs when the occiput is against the mother's spine. This position often results in a prolonged labor accompanied by a great deal of back discomfort. (See back labor.) Most posterior babies will rotate to an anterior position prior to the second stage. If not, changing positions may help (knee-chest, side-lying, lying on back with hips elevated). See page 120. A persistent posterior position may result in a prolonged second stage and possibly require the assistance of forceps or a vacuum extractor to turn the head or to deliver the baby.

VARIATIONS OF LABOR

Precipitate Labor

This type of labor is one that lasts three hours or less. The length of labor may sound appealing, but it presents its own special problems. Your contractions will probably be quite intense and you may misinterpret them as very difficult early labor. Because your contractions may be hard to control, your labor partner should remain with you at all times, and use all the comfort measures at his disposal. If left alone, you may experience confusion and fear because of your lack of knowledge of your labor's progress. This can be complicated by the rushing around of the hospital staff upon their discovery of your labor's advanced state. You must have confidence in your own feelings about your body. Be sure to request a vaginal examination immediately upon admission to determine your progress if you suspect your labor is progressing rapidly. Your own control and the directions of a good labor partner are crucial. Relaxation may be difficult, but it is important to your comfort. In addition, using accelerated breathing techniques, along with changing positions and emptying your bladder, should be tried before requesting medication. Your labor is probably almost over!

In some cases, labor progresses so rapidly that you have no time to get to your hospital or birth center. If this happens to you, follow the instructions for emergency childbirth later in this chapter.

Prolonged Labor

A labor that lasts 24 hours or more is termed prolonged labor. Some causes for this type of labor are ineffective contractions, breech presentation, posterior position, a large baby, small pelvis, extreme tension, large amounts of medication given to the mother and malnutrition during pregnancy.

Considerable patience is required during a long labor, along with creativity in the use of breathing techniques, comfort measures and relaxation. Fatigue is most difficult to combat, and dozing between contractions may make it even harder to control labor. If you experience a prolonged labor, you must work together with all of the techniques and comfort measures available to avoid discouragement, tension and fatigue. **Encouragement is essential!** You should **relax** as much as possible to conserve energy. **Walking** is often beneficial in helping to speed up labor. Ask to do this if you have been confined to bed for some time. **Nipple stimulation** will release oxytocin in your system and may help to strengthen contractions.

During a prolonged labor, the fetal condition must be monitored carefully by a nurse or a fetal heart monitor. I.V. fluids are usually given to provide nourishment and prevent dehydration if you have not been allowed to eat or drink. Ultrasound or X-rays may be used to estimate the size of the pelvic outlet and the fetal head to rule out cephalopelvic disproportion, a condition where the fetus' head is not progressing through the pelvis.

In case you do experience a prolonged or extremely difficult labor, be sure that you understand your situation—what is happening to you, suggested procedures and diagnosis. If you have questions, ask your birth attendant. And remember, this is not an endurance contest! If you are too fatigued and cannot cope, consider available alternatives, including interventions and medications.

Back Labor

Back labor is defined as labor felt primarily in the back, producing extreme discomfort during and often between contractions. One out of four women experience back labor to some degree. Back labor may be caused by a posterior position, breech presentation, tension, variations in anatomy, or laboring on your back.

Because discomfort can also be felt between contractions with back labor, you may find it more difficult to rest and relax. Labor may also last longer. Take contractions one at a time and experiment with the following comfort measures:

Get the baby off your back. Try changing positions to remove the pressure of the baby from your back. Do not lie flat on your back, as this places more pressure on it and decreases the blood supply to the baby. Lying on your side, with pillows under your head, uterus and upper leg might provide relief. Or try sitting backwards on a straight chair, or tailor sitting with pillows supporting your arms. You could also roll up the head of the bed, face the mattress in a kneeling position and lean on your folded arms resting on the top of the mattress. Or, sit on the side of the bed with your feet on a chair and lean over on a pillow placed on your lap or on the over bed tray, if one is available.

Other techniques to try are the pelvic rock on all fours and the passive pelvic rock on your side.

Apply heat or cold to back. You may find it comforting to have your partner apply warm or cold compresses to your back. While at home, you can use a hot water bottle. Wash cloths soaked in hot water may be applied after you are in the hospital.

Comfortable position for back labor.

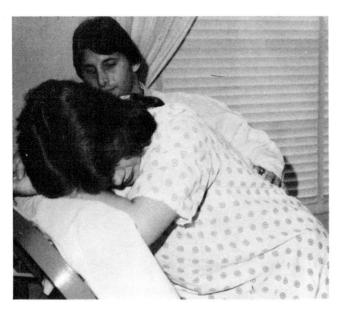

Leaning against head of bed for back labor.

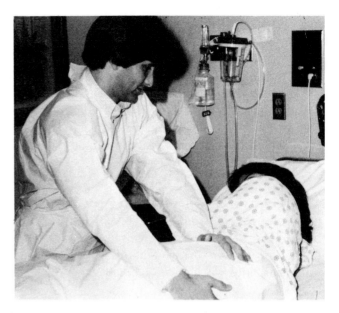

Passive pelvic rock.

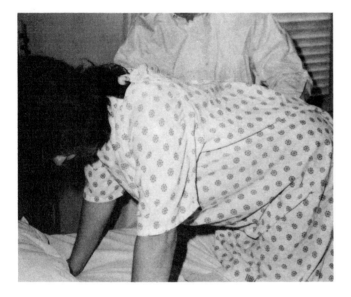

Pelvic rocking to relieve back labor.

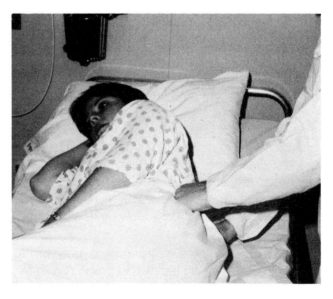

Partner applying counterpressure.

You can apply cold compresses with ice packs, "blue ice" or a frozen can of juice wrapped in a towel. A Tupperware rolling pin filled with cold water or crushed ice, or wash cloths soaked in ice water may be helpful.

Apply counterpressure. Several methods of applying pressure to the back may be helpful. Your partner may use the heel of his hand or fists to press against the area of greatest discomfort, using as much force as is comforting to you. Or, he could kneel on the bed with one knee pressed against your lower back as you lie on your side. You can try lying on your own fists, a roll of toilet tissue or tennis balls placed in a sock. This is especially helpful during vaginal exams when you may be on your back. Also, having your partner massage your back with lotion or powder may be effective.

Other measures that may prove helpful include slow, deep breathing between contractions. This is beneficial in promoting relaxation, as is the use of touch relaxation by your partner. You may need to use the more advanced breathing techniques sooner. An encouraging and supportive labor partner is vital in handling this kind of labor.

INTERVENTIONS

Your birth attendant has various procedures at his disposal which can provide diagnostic information, prevent possible complications and even alter the course of your labor. Any intervention carries with it some degree of risk and therefore should never be used unless medically necessary.

You need to discuss the various interventions with your birth attendant prior to labor, expressing your desires concerning their possible use, and determining at what point he feels their use is indicated. If you are clear on his intentions in advance, misunderstandings will be avoided later, when you are in labor.

Become familiar with *all* of these procedures and the purpose for which each is intended.

Intravenous Fluids (I.V.'s)

An intravenous fluid (I.V.) is a solution which is fed into your body through a vein. It may be indicated in a prolonged labor to prevent dehydration. It is also used during an induction, epidural, spinal and general anesthesia as it provides an easy access for medication if needed. Some physicians use I.V.'s routinely "just in case" a problem arises. During a cesarean birth and the immediate post-surgical period, an I.V. is important to supply fluids and administer medication.

The process involves inserting a needle into your vein and securely taping it in place. A catheter can also be used. (A needle with a thin plastic catheter inside is injected and the needle withdrawn.) Then the solution, usually glucose and water, is continuously infused or dripped into your vein, generally in your arm or the back of your hand.

If you are well hydrated and your labor is progressing normally, I.V. fluids are probably unnecessary. They restrict mobility and decrease your ability to relax effectively. If you do have an I.V. and you desire to walk during labor, you should request a moveable pole. Complications which may result from an I.V. include infiltration (fluid leaking into surrounding tissue) and phlebitis (inflammation of the vein). You may experience some discomfort during insertion.

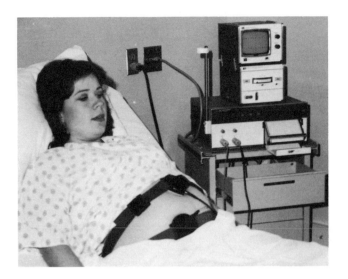

External fetal monitor.

Electronic Fetal Monitor

The electronic fetal monitor (EFM) is a device that measures the intensity and duration of uterine contractions as well as the baby's heart rate. Of special interest to the doctor is the way the baby's heart rate is affected during and immediately after a contraction. The normal fetal heart rate is between 120–160 beats per minute. Any deviation above or below that is a possible indication that the baby is in distress.

Two forms of the monitor may be used during labor: the external and the internal. The **external monitor**, which is used most frequently, consists of two belts that are placed around the woman's abdomen. One measures contraction strength; the other the fetal heart beat. A variation of the external monitor uses electrodes which are directly attached to the abdomen, eliminating the need for one belt. The **internal monitor**, consists of an electrode that is inserted through the vagina and partially dilated cervix and placed beneath the skin of the baby's head or buttocks with a clip or spiral-like projection. The membranes must be ruptured for this type of monitor to be used. A pressure sensitive catheter may also be inserted to measure the contractions, or one belt may be left around the abdomen. Both types of the monitor are connected to a device that records and prints out the information on graph paper.

The external monitor can be used throughout labor since it does not require rupture of the membranes. An internal monitor is used if the membranes have spontaneously ruptured and/or if there is a need for more precise information. A small percentage of babies have developed scalp abscesses as a result of this procedure.

The use of monitors is indicated for women who are considered "high risk" (women with diabetes, high blood pressure, preeclampsia and first pregnancy after the age of 30, etc.). It is also used if a woman's labor is induced or stimulated with oxytocin to determine how well the baby is handling the stress of labor and to assess the strength and duration of the contractions. Some physicians feel that monitoring even low-risk women is beneficial in detecting cord problems or hypertonicity of the uterus. Others monitor all patients, fearing a lawsuit in case a problem arises and the monitor was not used.

Much debate exists about the need for monitoring low-risk labors that are progressing normally. One of the **major controversies** concerns the accuracy of the results obtained from the monitor, especially the external type. Many authorities feel that the only condition that it accurately portrays is when the baby is doing well. The information received on the printout is open to misinterpretation by the medical staff. Sometimes the monitor picks up the mother's heartbeat or stomach and intestinal sounds rather than the baby's heartbeat.[3] Late decelerations of the heart rate (at the end of the contraction) are considered a sign that a baby is in distress. However, there are studies that show that up to 60 percent of fetuses exhibiting that symptom were not in distress at birth.[4]

Skyrocketing cesarean birth rates have also been associated with the increased use of EFM. One study involving 690 high-risk women reported that monitoring did not improve perinatal outcome, but did result in a threefold increase in cesarean births. Dr. McFee, one of the researchers, feels his results refute the growing contention that monitoring should be universal. He showed that frequent listening (every 15 minutes) with a fetoscope by expert nurses is as dependable as EFM in "recognizing continuing abnormal fetal heart rate patterns ominous enough to mandate immediate delivery."[5]

If fetal distress appears to be present, the following conservative measures should be tried by the staff:

1. Have you lie on your left side; lying on your back invites hypotension which affects your baby's oxygen supply.

2. Reduce or stop any oxytocin you may be receiving.

3. Give you pure oxygen to breathe.

4. Apply an internal monitor to verify the accuracy of external monitor readings.

5. Take a fetal scalp blood sample to check the pH level of the baby's blood. Too low a level indicates oxygen depletion which is a true sign of distress.

If the heart rate is not restored to normal within 30 minutes, prompt delivery is needed. Cesarean section may then become necessary.

Another growing concern is that nurses and doctors are losing their ability to evaluate the patient without referring to the "machine." More attention is paid to the monitor tracing than to the woman and her perception of her labor. There is even a tendency for the labor partner to become entranced by the beeps and the read out and forget his main purpose—to support and encourage his partner in labor.

Laboring With the Fetal Monitor

As you have already learned, your mobility and position during labor can have a significant effect on your labor's progress. Therefore, if you choose or are required to be monitored during labor, **change positions frequently** and **avoid lying on your back.** The longer you can stand and walk during labor the more efficient your contractions will be. An upright position widens the pelvic inlet which promotes descent of the baby and dilatation of the cervix. It also helps the uterus to work at maximum efficiency.

If the concept of routine monitoring is disturbing to you, discuss with your physician the possibility of **limiting the time you spend on the monitor.** He may agree to a short period of monitoring upon admission to the hospital (15–45 minutes) which gives him a check on the baby's condition and a printed "strip" of information for his records. Or he may agree to monitor only a portion of the time (15 minutes per hour, 30 minutes every 2 hours). Even just waiting until active labor is well established gives you more time to move about and be comfortable. If an internal monitor is used, it can be disconnected every few hours so you can stand up and move around.

You should continue to change positions frequently, every 20–30 minutes. The monitor may need to be repositioned to pick up the heartbeat each time you move. But your mobility and comfort are of great importance. Don't let anyone tell you that you must stay on your back. This position can cause hypotension and lead to signs of fetal distress in your baby, the very thing the monitor was designed to protect against.

If the **beeping noises** coming from the machine are distracting or annoying, ask that the volume be turned down and possibly that the machine be repositioned so that the read-out isn't in your constant view.

Labor partners: remember to continue your active coaching and support measures. Machines do break and malfunction. If your partner says the contractions are becoming more intense, she knows what she is talking about.

INDUCTION AND AUGMENTATION OF LABOR

Induction

An induced labor is one that is started artificially by either chemical or physical stimulation. Induction is medically indicated in situations where continuing the pregnancy would adversely affect either the mother or the baby. Such conditions include pre-eclampsia, diabetes, postmaturity with a diagnosed aging placenta, Rh sensitization (incompatibility), prolonged rupture of membranes with no labor starting, and fetal death.

A number of techniques can be used to induce labor. The simplest form of induction is known as **stripping the membranes.** This is done by your doctor during a vaginal exam. He inserts his fingers between the partially dilated cervix and the amniotic sac. This irritates and loosens the sac from the uterine wall. Some women feel a burning or stinging sensation or even pain when this is done. Unless labor is imminent, this procedure will not initiate true labor, although it may cause contractions for a time.

Another physical method of induction is **amniotomy,** the artificial rupture of the membranes. This is done by inserting a long hook-like instrument, called an amnihook, through the vagina and partially dilated cervix and making a tear in the amniotic membranes. This is a painless procedure as there are no nerves in the membranes, but it presents some risks. If labor does not begin, both mother and baby are exposed to an increased chance of infection and the use of pitocin. If pitocin does not produce results within 24 hours, a cesarean delivery is usually performed.

Synthetic forms of the hormone **oxytocin** (pitocin or syntocinon) are most frequently used to induce labor. It is usually given through an intravenous drip along with a solution of glucose and water. Pitocin can also be given by injection into the muscles. Because each individual reacts differently to the same drug dosage, this method is difficult to control. The tablet form called buccal pitocin has been withdrawn from the market because the dosage was hard to regulate in that form.

Labor should never be induced simply for convenience because induction results in increased **risks to both mother and fetus.** For this reason the FDA's Obstetric-Gynecologic Advisory Committee voted to withdraw FDA approval of the use of oxytocic drugs for *elective* induction of labor. In natural labor the oxygen supply to the fetus is decreased during each contraction. The long, intense contractions of an induced labor can deprive the fetus of even more oxygen, possibly resulting in fetal distress and a cesarean birth. An overdose of oxytocin, resulting in tetanic or continuous contractions, can cause premature separation of the placenta from the uterus, or even uterine rupture. These conditions would disrupt the oxygen supply to the fetus and lead to an emergency cesarean delivery if a vaginal birth could not be effected immediately. Other maternal side effects include lowered blood pressure, rapid heart rate, anxiety, and swelling. Also associated with the use of pitocin is increased jaundice in the newborn.

Induced contractions tend to start out **much stronger than natural contractions.** The gradual build-up of natural labor is not present. They are more frequent, longer in duration and often peak immediately rather than in the middle of the contraction. This makes labor much more difficult to manage. You must **be on top of the contractions** from the very beginning or you will lose control. Your partner is extremely important in this kind of labor. He must watch the time and/or monitor very carefully so he can prepare you for the start of the next contraction. (If a contraction lasts longer than two minutes, immediately alert the nursing staff.)

Encouragement and support are essential. You will not want to be left alone as panic and loss of control will usually result. Ask a nurse to stay with you if your partner must leave to use the bathroom or get something to eat. Because of the strength of the contractions, you may need to use advanced breathing techniques sooner and for a longer time, which can be very tiring. Your partner's assistance in keeping you comfortable and relaxed will help you conserve energy that you will need for birth.

Augmentation

If your birth attendant feels that labor is not progressing normally, he may want to augment (speed up) your labor. The timetables used to determine "normal" labor are based on averages, and very few women are "average." Before agreeing to any interventions, ask for a little more time, and **try some non-invasive techniques to speed up your labor.** These include a warm shower or bath, a different labor position, walking, loving support (including hugs and caresses, as well as words of encouragement), and nipple stimulation to release natural oxytocin. If anyone in the room is causing you stress, he should be asked to leave.

If these measures do not bring the desired result, your birth attendant may want to perform an **amniotomy.** It introduces the same risks as already mentioned under induction. In addition, it is important to know that amniotomy removes the protective buffer of fluid between your baby's head and the cervix. As a result, babies that go through labor for an extended period of time with membranes ruptured experience more head molding, caput succedaneum and possible cephalhematoma.

Some studies show that amniotomy does not have a significant effect on the progress of labor.[6] Contractions often increase in intensity and duration for a while after the procedure is performed, but the average difference in the length of labor is only 50 minutes.[7] In addition, labor may become uncomfortable and more difficult to control because of unequal pressure during contractions. A drop in the fetal heart rate is also associated with this procedure.

If fetal distress is suspected, amniotomy needs to be performed to insert an internal fetal monitor and/or obtain a fetal blood sample. Otherwise, you are within your rights to reject this procedure.

If amniotomy is done and doesn't produce results, your doctor may start a **pitocin** I.V. drip to

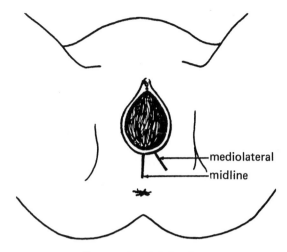

Types of episiotomies.

stimulate the uterus to produce more efficient contractions. Be prepared for stronger and more frequent contractions, the same as in an induced labor. Advanced breathing techniques may also be needed to stay on top of the contractions. The risks associated with the use of pitocin are the same when used to augment labor as they are for induction.

EPISIOTOMY

An episiotomy is a surgical incision from the vagina towards the rectum. It is done to enlarge the vaginal outlet and thus decrease any possible tearing during birth. The incision is usually straight (midline) but can be angled to the side (mediolateral). See illustration. The need for an episiotomy cannot be determined until the baby's head begins to stretch the perineum. If done at this time, when the baby's head is pressing against the perineum, a natural anesthesia results, and you may not feel the incision. You will, however, need a local anesthetic during the repair of the incision following delivery. Some doctors give the local prior to making the incision.

Some authorities feel that the need for an episiotomy is increased by use of the lithotomy position for delivery. With your legs apart and your feet in stirrups, more tension is placed on the perineum, and the chances of tearing are greater. (See Chapter 5 on alternative positions for pushing.) A straight incision heals better than the jagged one caused by tearing, but a few stitches to repair a small tear are preferable to the larger number needed to repair an episiotomy. If an episiotomy is not performed and tearing occurs, it may be superficial in nature, whereas an episiotomy cuts into muscle.

Another reason often presented for performing an episiotomy is to avoid the possibility of a loss of vaginal tone and control which could result in prolapsed organs and a decrease of sexual pleasure for both partners. The opposing argument is that the practice of Kegel exercises during pregnancy and following birth strengthens vaginal muscles and eliminates this problem. Additionally, some experts feel that the severing of perineal tissue during an episiotomy permanently weakens it.

Occasionally, a physician overstitches the repair to "tighten you up" (known as the "honeymoon stitch.") However, stitching too tightly can result in painful intercourse.

Healing of the episiotomy site requires several weeks and involves some soreness and itching. Sitting on pillows or air rings, along with applying anesthetic creams and sprays, will help in alleviating this discomfort.

ROTATION AND EXTRACTION

The forceps and the vacuum extractor are two obstetrical tools used for rotating the baby to a more advantageous position for birth and for assisting in moving the baby down the birth canal. **Indications** for the use of these instruments include a baby's persistent posterior or transverse position, a woman's diminished ability to push because of anesthesia or fatigue, and fetal distress. A regional anesthetic is frequently administered before either of these instruments is employed, and an episiotomy may be required for the use of either instrument.

Rotating a Posterior

If you are told during labor that your baby is in a posterior position, the following procedure may promote rotation to an anterior position. Roll up a blanket and place it beneath the small of your back to increase the angle of your spine. This is uncomfortable for the fetus and will encourage him to change to an anterior position. Alternate this position with side-lying every 15 minutes until rotation is complete.

If your baby is posterior when you begin pushing, you can also push in this position to encourage rotation. Your legs can either be held up by your partner or you can bend your knees slightly with your heels resting on the bed. Once rotation is completed, you can continue pushing in a position of greater comfort.

Forceps

Forceps are large, curved metal tongs which are inserted into the vagina and placed on either side of the baby's head. They are then locked together and can be used for manipulating and extracting the baby. The baby's soft head and facial tissue may be bruised by their application, but they can also serve to protect the head of a premature infant from prolonged pressure while in the birth canal.

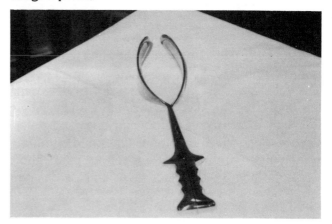

Forceps.

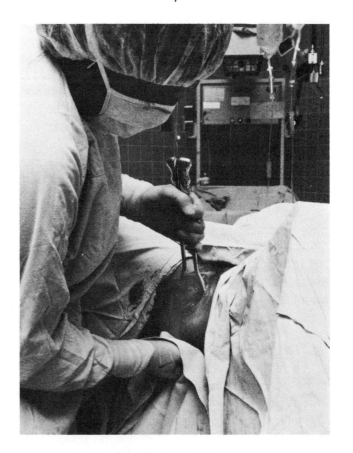

Low forceps delivery.

The dangerous **high forceps** (head not engaged) are rarely used today, being replaced by cesarean delivery as safer for both mother and baby. The application of **mid forceps** (0 to +2 station) presents some risk to maternal tissue and the baby and should be performed by an experienced physician. The procedure of applying **low forceps** at the vaginal outlet to aid in the final expulsion of the baby is more common and carries the least risk to mother and baby.

Cap of vacuum extractor.

Vacuum Extractor

The vacuum extractor is a cap-like device which uses suction to attach to the baby's head. The suction cup fits over a portion of the head and aids in easing the baby out through the contours of the birth canal. The amount of suction can be adjusted by the physician, and as a safety factor, too much tension results in releasing suction on the baby's head.

In rare instances, the vacuum extractor can be applied before the cervix is completely dilated. In these cases, the instrument is valuable in avoiding a cesarean section if fetal distress indicates the need for an immediate delivery. Other advantages of this instrument over forceps include less trauma to the bladder and vaginal tissues, and lowered risk of extending the episiotomy. An anesthetic is not always necessary. The vacuum extractor is used today in some cases which formerly would have indicated the use of high forceps.

Some swelling (caput succedaneum) of the soft tissue on the baby's scalp may result from the vacuum extractor. This normally takes several days to subside. Occasionally a cephalhematoma may occur. This is a lump or swelling on the scalp which is filled with blood. It does not indicate brain damage, but may take weeks to reabsorb.

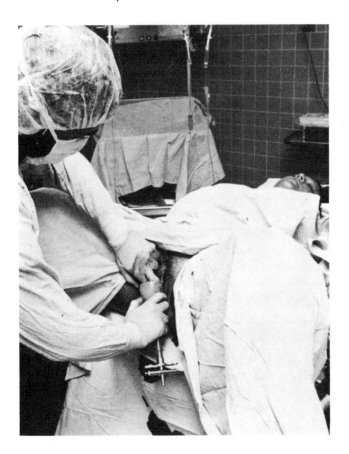

Applying the vacuum extractor.

EMERGENCY CHILDBIRTH

If labor progresses very rapidly or if you fail to recognize that you are in the final phase of labor, your baby may be born at home or on the way to the hospital. In most cases, such a birth is uncomplicated and the baby is born healthy and vigorous. Since no drugs or anesthetics have been given, the baby usually breathes immediately and is very alert.

Nevertheless, you both may feel some uneasiness and fear about handling such a situation. This section is therefore directed to you, the labor partner, to give you support and confidence should you find yourself in the position of being the birth attendant.

Your partner will almost always know if birth is imminent. Take her word for it! She may feel the baby's head coming down the birth canal, have a strong urge to push, or feel a burning pressure. If you are in the car when this happens, resist the temptation to drive fast or take chances to reach the hospital. When it is safe to do so, pull off the road, put the emergency flashers on, get your emergency birth kit (see Chapter 2), and **assess the situation.** Keep your flashlight handy so you can see well. If this is your first baby and his head is not visible at the opening of the vagina, you probably have time to get to the hospital if you are within 15–20 minutes driving time. If it is not your first baby or if his head is visible, it is better to stay where you are. Help your partner get comfortable in the back seat, and let the baby be born. Be sure the baby is breathing well before continuing on to the hospital.

If you are at home, call Rescue or the fire department. They are trained to handle this kind of situation. Wash your hands and arms. **Help your partner get into a comfortable position** on the bed. Place a crib pad, newspapers, blankets or towels under her buttocks to protect the mattress. Do not leave her alone. She will need your calm support to keep from panicking. Let the uterus do all the work. **Once the head is visible at the vaginal opening, coach her to pant until the head is born.** A slow, controlled birth will reduce the chance of tearing the perineal tissues.

As the head begins to emerge, support the perineum with your hand in a clean handkerchief. **If the head is still covered by the membranes, use your fingernail to break them and pull them away from the baby's face** so he can breathe. You can wipe off mucus and fluid with a cloth. **Check to see if the cord is around his neck** and if it is, gently lift it over the head before the rest of the body is born.

When the baby's head rotates to face his mother's thigh, the shoulders are ready to be delivered. Support the baby's head with your hands as your partner **lightly bears down with the next contraction. Do NOT pull on the baby's head,** as it could result in permanent spinal cord injury. Once the shoulders are born, the rest of the body will slide out easily. When completely delivered, **dry the baby's skin, place him on his mother's abdomen with his face down, and cover them both with a blanket.** This permits him to cough and drain any mucus that may be in his nose and throat. You may assist him in this by wiping out his mouth with a clean handkerchief or suctioning gently with a soft rubber syringe. Make sure you compress the bulb before insertion and gently release the pressure.

If he does not breathe right away, vigorously rub his back or the soles of his feet. Don't panic! As long as the placenta is still attached, your baby is still receiving oxygen via the umbilical cord. **If he does not begin breathing within 1½ minutes, you will need to give artificial respiration.** To do this cover both his nose and mouth with your mouth and place your fingers on his chest. Gently puff with only the air in your mouth. You will feel his chest rise slightly. Don't blow hard as forcing too much air into his small lungs could cause them to rupture. Repeat at the rate of one breath every three seconds until he responds. See page 161 for detailed directions on artificial respiration and heart massage.

Do not worry about cutting the cord. This can be done when you reach the hospital or the paramedics arrive. If the cord is long enough, **put the baby to breast** as soon as he is breathing well. His sucking will stimulate the uterus to continue contracting, expel the placenta, and prevent hemorrhaging. The colostrum will also help remove mucus from the baby's digestive tract. **When the cord stops pulsating, tie it with a shoestring.**

Do not pull on the cord in an attempt to deliver the placenta. When it is ready, you will notice the cord lengthening, and the mother may feel pressure and the need to push. If the placenta is expelled before help arrives, place it next to the baby and wrap them together to provide extra warmth. The placenta should be taken to the hospital with

Okay, honey, I'm ready to deliver now!

you in order for the doctor to examine it.

Some bleeding is normal as the placenta delivers and right afterwards. Immediate nursing is usually sufficient stimulation to keep the uterus contracted firmly. **If bleeding seems excessive (more than two cups), massage her abdomen** 2–3 inches below the navel with a deep circular motion to aid in this contracting. Gentle massage of her nipples will also stimulate the release of oxytocin if the baby refuses to nurse.

If birth occurred in the car, you can now continue your drive to the hospital. If you called for assistance at home, wait for its arrival or call your doctor and follow his instructions.

When you arrive at the hospital to be examined, you may want to request immediate rooming-in to avoid isolation of your baby because his birth was outside of the hospital. If all is well, you may feel like returning home within a few hours. Or you may choose to stay a day or two for observation.

LEBOYER DELIVERY

A Leboyer delivery or *gentle birth* utilizes techniques to ease birth trauma and make it a pleasant and soothing experience for the infant. This type of delivery was devised by Frederick Leboyer, a French obstetrician, and popularized in his book *Birth Without Violence*. Dr. Leboyer feels that birth is a traumatic experience for the newborn and that certain routine delivery procedures increase this trauma. Otherwise, why do babies cry and look so unhappy at birth? In his view, the infant moves from a peaceful womb through the "assault" of labor and emerges into a world of bright lights and loud voices. He is held upside down, the cord is cut and he is immediately removed from his mother. Dr. Leboyer feels that a newborn's senses are very acute and that he perceives the intense sensations of birth, often very vividly.

Even if your doctor does not "practice Leboyer techniques," he may agree to incorporate some of the aspects which appeal to you. Below is a description of a gentle birth.

A dimly lit delivery room allows the baby to adjust slowly to the light. Sufficient light is used to allow for observation of the newborn. The bright lights normally used in delivery are blinding to the eyes of the baby who has been in semi-darkness for nine months. Think about being in a dark room for a period of time and then having bright lights suddenly directed into your face. It is no wonder that the baby shuts his eyes tightly.

To avoid chilling, the **temperature of the room** is also made more comfortable for the baby, rather than for the hospital staff. **Talking is kept to a minimum** or a whisper. While in utero, the fetus hears only muted sounds and voices because of the presence of your abdominal and uterine walls and amniotic fluid. Loud voices and exclamations may seem deafening to the new baby's ears.

As the baby emerges from the birth canal, he is **gently lifted up and placed onto your bare abdomen,** facilitating skin-to-skin contact. He is not held upside down by his feet, as this position straightens his spine—exactly opposite of the position he assumed while in utero. He is also not stimulated to cry but allowed to **begin breathing spontaneously.** You can **gently massage or stroke the baby** to soothe him. Suctioning of the nose and mouth is not done unless necessary.

The cord is not cut until it stops pulsating. This allows the baby to continue receiving red blood cells which decrease the chance of anoxia. By not clamping the cord immediately after birth, there is no rush to get the baby breathing since he is still receiving oxygen from the mother, via the cord. As he begins breathing, there is an easier transition from intrauterine life to breathing on his own.

The father may then **place the baby in a warm bath** to simulate returning to the security of the womb. Many babies completely relax and stop crying when they are gently floated in the water. The baby is then dried, wrapped and given to the mother.

Some of the arguments against a Leboyer type delivery are that the baby will be cold, that the inadequate lighting interferes with the assessment of the baby, and that the father may inadvertently drop or drown the baby in the bath water. Opponents of delayed cord cutting state that extra red blood cells are received by the infant resulting in an increase in jaundice. But unless the newborn is held below the level of the placenta or the cord is "milked" (compressing and stroking the cord toward the baby), an equal amount of blood enters and leaves the baby's body while the cord is pulsating.

Physicians who have specialized in this approach and have kept statistics have found no increase whatever in infection, heat loss, undetected distress or other complications attributed to gentle birth procedures.[8] Since the parents are intimately involved during this type of birth, it may also aid in developing strong attachments and enhance the parents' competence in caring for their new baby.

Interestingly, many of the Leboyer techniques are slowly being incorporated into regular delivery room routines. Doctors no longer hold babies upside down by their feet, acknowledging that they do experience all the birthing sensations. Babies are being born more alert as mothers are taking less medication. Stimulation or "spanking" at birth is not needed in these alert babies. They are welcomed into the world more gently with their comfort in mind.

TWINS

Twins occur in one out of 86 births. Fraternal twins are more common and are the result of two eggs being fertilized by two sperm. They may or may not be the same sex and are no more alike in appearance than any other siblings. Identical twins occur less frequently and are the result of one egg being fertilized by one sperm which then separates. Since they carry the same genetic material, identical twins are always the same sex, have the same appearance and the same blood type. They may be mirror images of each other.

During pregnancy, an increased demand is placed on your body as you are carrying two babies, and possibly two placentas or one larger one. The discomforts of pregnancy will be accentuated since there is an increased demand on your circulatory system and your uterus is an increased size.

You have a higher protein and caloric requirement than a woman experiencing a single pregnancy. If these needs are not met, the incidence of toxemia and premature birth increases. A woman carrying twins needs 110–140 grams of protein and at least 3100 calories per day. Women who eat well during pregnancy can deliver twins at term that weigh more than 5½ pounds each. They also do not experience problems with toxemia. It is not uncommon for a woman carrying twins to gain 50–60 pounds if she is encouraged to eat right. (See Chapter 3.)

During labor, if the uterus has been overdistended, some women have a problem with poor or inadequate contractions. This is another reason why a high protein diet is necessary—to insure good muscle tone of the uterus. It is preferable to limit analgesia and anesthesia during labor and birth to minimize the effect on the babies and to prevent excessive blood loss.

At delivery, twins most commonly present with the first baby in a vertex position and the second in breech position. There is usually a 5–10 minute lapse between the delivery of the first and second baby. If the second twin is not in a favorable position for delivery, the doctor may need to place his hand within the uterus to rotate the second twin. This may require some anesthesia for your comfort. Despite the new, sophisticated equipment that is available, 40 percent of twin births are undiagnosed and are a surprise at delivery.

Having twins is no contraindication to breastfeeding. It saves time not having to wash bottles and prepare formula. Some mothers are able to nurse both babies at one time. (See Chapter 11.)

In early months, you may notice that your twins sleep best or are happiest when they are near each other. Even if you place them apart in a bed, they will usually inch their way over until they are touching one another.

As twins mature, many report a special closeness to each other. If one twin is injured, the other may experience pain, even if they are apart. Interesting reports on twins who have been separated at birth found vast similarities in their mannerisms and preferences.

Mothers of twins groups are available to help you cope with this double pleasure.

THE PREMATURE BABY

A baby is considered premature if he weighs less than 2500 grams (5½ pounds), or is delivered before 37 weeks gestation. If born at this time, he is still immature and may have some difficulty adjusting to extrauterine life. Respiratory distress is the greatest concern as his lungs may not be mature. Also, his sucking may be weak, he may have difficulty maintaining his body temperature and he is more susceptible to infection. Tube feedings and an incubator may be necessary until these functions develop.

Because of his size, medication should be avoided during labor to prevent the depressant effects on the tiny fetus. Forceps may be used during the delivery to protect the baby's head as it passes through the birth canal.

If the baby is very small or needs medical attention, he may be placed immediately in a neonatal intensive care unit. The advent of these specialized nurseries has reduced complications and saved many infants that would otherwise be lost. This may delay immediate contact with your baby. As soon as you are able, both you and the father are encouraged to visit, touch, hold and even feed your baby to begin developing attachments. Your colostrum and milk are extremely beneficial and perfectly suited to the needs of your premature baby. Until he is able to nurse, hand express your milk for him. (See Chapter 11.)

FOOTNOTES

Chapter 8

1. Charles Mahan and Diony Young, *Unnecessary Cesareans, Ways to Avoid Them* (Minneapolis, Minn., ICEA, 1980), p. 13.
2. Nancy Wainer Cohen and Lois J. Estner, *Silent Knife* (South Hadley, Mass., Bergin & Garvey, 1983), p. 310.
3. Margot Edwards, R.N., M.S. and Penny Simkin, R.P.T., *Obstetric Tests and Technology: A Consumer's Guide*, p. 7.
4. Edwards and Simkin, p. 7.
5. "One Mother Dies for 8 Newborns Saved with Electronic Monitoring," *Ob. Gyn. News*, Vol. 12, No. 24, December 15, 1978, p. 1.
6. E. A. Friedman and M. R. Sachtleben, "Amniotomy and the Course of Labor," *Obstetrics and Gynecology*, 22:755, 1963, p. 767 (as cited in *ICEA Review*, Vol. 3: No. 2, Summer, 1979).
7. "Amniotomy," *ICEA Review*, Vol. 3: No. 2, Summer, 1979, p. 2.
8. Nancy Berezin, *The Gentle Birth Book* (N.Y., Simon & Schuster, 1980), p. 21.

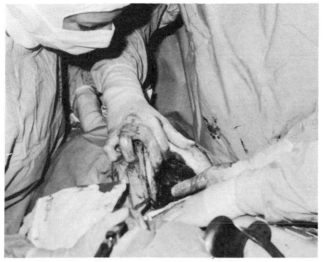

Easing head through incision.

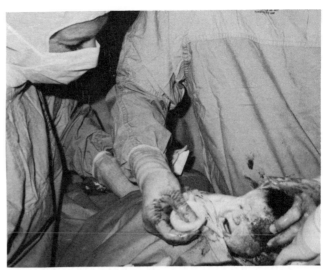

Baby responsive during delivery.

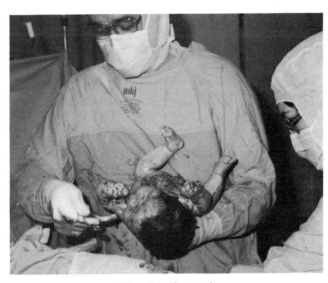

Clamping the cord.

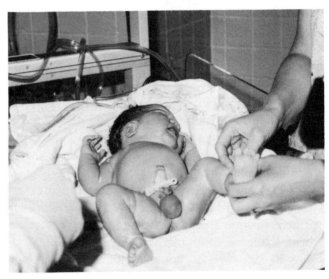

Admission procedures.

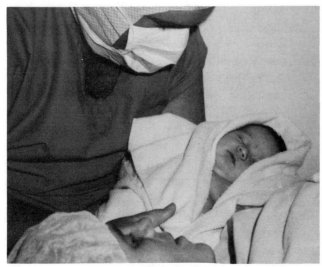

The new family.

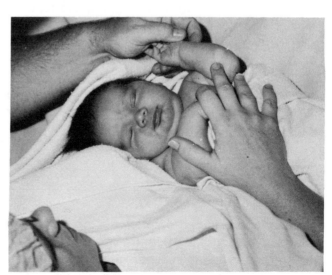

Caressing the newborn.

Husband-Attended Cesarean Delivery

Chapter 9

Cesarean Birth
or "I Wish I Had a Zipper"

Having a cesarean birth means that your baby is delivered through incisions in the abdominal wall and uterus instead of being delivered vaginally. In the hospital it may be referred to as a cesarean section or "c-section." Delivering in this manner is an alternate method of giving birth, one that you need to be aware of as a possibility.

Julius Caesar is usually credited with being the first baby delivered by cesarean section and having the procedure named after him. Actually, it is unlikely that he was delivered in this manner, since during his time babies were delivered surgically only if the mother had died, and it is well documented that Caesar's mother was alive many years later. The term cesarean section probably comes from the Latin word *caedere* which means "to cut." Hundreds of years before Caesar, a Roman law, *lex caesarea*, stated that dying mothers should be operated on to save the infant.

The first recorded successful cesarean (meaning the woman survived) occurred in 1500. It was not until 1882 that Dr. Max Sanger began suturing the uterus rather than removing it. Over the years advances in anesthesia, antibiotics, surgical techniques and pain medication have tremendously increased the safety of the procedure.

Since many cesarean births are not planned, it is important for you to read this chapter carefully so that you will become familiar with the procedures involved in a cesarean delivery and with the possible options available to you if you prepare in advance.

Special classes are provided in some areas and may be required to insure the participation of your support person. The knowledge gained can aid in avoiding an unnecessary cesarean. Additionally, even though a cesarean birth is major abdominal surgery, advance preparation can make it a satisfying birth experience for the entire family.

FAMILY CENTERED CESAREAN BIRTH

A cesarean section is more than an operation. It is the birth of a baby. The way a father and mother feel about their childbirth experience may affect their ability to bond with their newborn. (See Chapter 6.) Being able to see, touch and comfort your baby immediately, begins the bonding process so important to fostering maternal and paternal feelings. Therefore, many cesarean couples desire to share in the miracle of birth, just as couples having a vaginal delivery. George Nolan, M.D., of Women's Hospital, University of Michigan Hospital, states that 100 percent of parents who attended the cesarean birth of their babies indicated a preference of being together for future cesarean births. Fifty percent of parents separated at the time of the cesarean delivery expressed a desire to be together for future cesarean births.[1]

Many fathers wish to participate in this type of birth to comfort and support their wives and also witness the birth of their children. This has met with some opposition from the medical community because it is an operative procedure. However, many obstetricians have witnessed the benefits of husband participation in vaginal births and are very willing to have fathers present during cesarean deliveries.

The biggest obstacle to having your partner present is dealing with the anesthesiologist. Because he does not have to respond to consumer pressure as an obstetrician does (you do not usually choose an anesthesiologist), he is less willing to change. If a cesarean is planned in advance, you will have time to "shop around" to try to find someone willing to meet your needs. In an unplanned cesarean, it is more difficult, but your doctor may be able to help persuade the anesthesiologist to allow your partner's presence. Be aware that you may also have to shop around for a hospital which allows father participation.

Special cesarean classes may be required by certain hospitals in order to have a support person present during delivery. Along with information on the actual birth, you will receive specialized instruction on exercises and postpartum care, as well as breastfeeding hints geared to the cesarean couple.

It is important to obtain the services of a pediatrician who is flexible to your desires. Discuss being able to touch, hold and breastfeed your newborn as soon as possible, even in the delivery room if his condition is good. Of course, if complications arise and the baby needs special care, these requests will be delayed.

Ask your pediatrician to evaluate your baby as an individual and if his condition is good, admit him to the regular newborn nursery, instead of the special care nursery. This will allow your baby to be brought to you for feeding, rather than remaining in a nursery for a prolonged period of time (sometimes 24 hours).

During the birth of their baby, whether vaginally or by cesarean, a couple needs each other's emotional and physical support. Some fathers and mothers have an emotional climax, fulfilled at the moment of birth, and that is a moment that should be shared. During a cesarean birth, your husband can hold your hand, wipe your forehead and talk to you. His emotional support is invaluable. Your attitude becomes so much more positive that you become more relaxed and recovery is faster.

If your partner is not allowed to participate in the birth, both of you may share feelings of resentment and disappointment. If this occurs, it is even more necessary to bond with your baby as soon as possible and to talk to each other about your feelings.

Rooming-in is also desirable for cesarean parents. With help from your partner, you can enjoy all the benefits of having your baby with you. For the first day or two you may wish to delay rooming-in or limit it to the time when you have help available.

This special family centered birth requires you to participate actively with your doctor, anesthesiologist and pediatrician concerning the details of your birth. Your partner should join you for several of your doctor's appointments and talk with him about the surgery, anesthesia and postpartum period in order to make your desires known. Do not take anything for granted or you may be disappointed. Your requests, of course, must be reasonable because this birth involves major surgery and possible risks to you and your baby. Having a doctor who strongly believes in the benefits of family centered maternity care will help to insure the type of birth you desire.

Another source of help is a local cesarean support group. They can also provide important emotional support after your birth. It is often helpful to talk to someone who has experienced a cesarean and knows what you are going through.

INDICATIONS FOR CESAREAN BIRTH

Cesarean deliveries are performed for many reasons. Because opinions vary on these indications, you may wish to request a second opinion if you are told you need a cesarean.

Over 90 percent of elective (planned) cesareans in the U.S. are done because of **previous cesarean birth.**[2] Repeat cesareans have been a policy based on the remote possibility that the old uterine scar may rupture. If the same circumstances that necessitated the first cesarean still exist, or if a new indication is present, then another cesarean is necessary.

Cephalopelvic disproportion (CPD) occurs when the baby's head will not fit through your pelvis. This diagnosis may also be used to indicate a labor which fails to progress, a prolonged labor, an extended period of time since rupture of membranes or weak and ineffectual uterine contractions.

Fetal distress means that the baby is not receiving enough oxygen. It may be indicated by an abnormal fetal heart rate or low fetal blood pH. Meconium stained amniotic fluid, which is greenish in color, may be associated with fetal distress.

If the placenta partially or completely separates from the uterine wall before the baby is born **(abruptio placentae)**, an immediate cesarean is necessary. This is an emergency situation in that the mother may hemorrhage and the baby may lose all or part of his oxygen supply.

A **prolapsed cord** occurs when the umbilical cord protrudes into the vagina ahead of the baby. This condition usually occurs after the membranes rupture and the baby is in a breech position or his head is not well engaged in the pelvis. The baby's oxygen supply is cut off as the presenting part compresses the cord. If you feel this is happening to you at home, immediately get down on your hands and knees, with your hips higher than your head, to relieve the pressure on the cord. Call an ambulance and REMAIN IN THIS POSITION until help arrives. If the cord is protruding from the vagina, place a wet cloth on the cord to keep it moist. Only do this if you can accomplish it without moving from the knee-chest position. When you arrive at the hospital, an immediate cesarean will be necessary.

Placenta previa is a condition in which the placenta partially or completely covers the cervix. The degree of severity determines whether or not a cesarean is necessary. If the cervix is completely covered, a cesarean is mandatory since the placenta would deliver first and the baby would lose his oxygen supply.

If your **baby is in an abnormal position** within the uterus, a cesarean may be indicated. When the baby is lying sideways (transverse lie), a

Knee-chest position for prolapsed cord.

cesarean is necessary since a vaginal delivery is impossible. A baby who is in breech position, buttocks first, may be delivered either vaginally or by cesarean section, depending on several factors. If your physician is experienced in delivering breech babies, he may more readily agree to a vaginal birth. Since the baby's head is larger than his body, some doctors are hesitant about allowing a first time mother to deliver vaginally because her pelvis has not been tried through a previous vaginal delivery. Their rule is *always a cesarean for a breech in a first pregnancy.* Some physicians will attempt a vaginal breech delivery for a first time mother if it is determined that her pelvis is adequate, that the baby is not too large and if her labor progresses normally. See Chapter 8 for more information and exercises to change the position of a breech baby.

When **severe toxemia** is present, the woman may have a stroke or kidney failure. The treatment for toxemia is delivery. Toxemia also affects the welfare of the fetus, thereby necessitating delivery—either by induction or cesarean for the health of both the baby and the mother. See Chapter 3 for information on the prevention of toxemia—a diet sufficient in protein.

If the **woman is diabetic,** early delivery is necessary for the baby's sake. There may be poor placental blood flow, the baby may be an excessive size and he may respond poorly to the stress of labor. If induction is unsuccessful, a cesarean will be performed.

When an Rh negative woman has been sensitized by Rh positive blood, her baby may develop

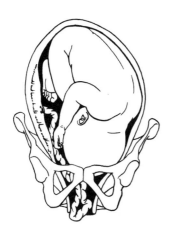
Prolapse of cord.

erythroblastosis fetalis. During the pregnancy, antibodies may pass through the placenta and attack the Rh positive baby's blood cells, leading to anemia and other severe problems which necessitate delivery. With the advent of Rh immune globulin (RhoGam), which can be given to the Rh negative mother during pregnancy and after each birth of an Rh positive infant, this disease is becoming less of a problem.

When active **herpes virus II infection** (of the vulva and/or vagina) is present at the time of birth, a cesarean section is necessary to prevent infection of the baby. This disease can be transmitted to the baby if he comes in contact with an active lesion or even if the membranes have ruptured. It is an untreatable illness which causes death in 50 percent of the infants infected.

FACTORS CONTRIBUTING TO THE RISE IN THE CESAREAN RATE

Cesarean birth rates have skyrocketed in the past ten years. Currently, many areas have rates of 25 percent, with rates as high as 30 percent in some areas.[3] Statistically speaking, this means that if there are ten or more couples in your childbirth class, two or three of you will have cesarean deliveries.

Many factors account for the increase in cesarean births. **A previous cesarean** is the most common indication. Although "once a cesarean, always a cesarean" is no longer true, many doctors continue to follow this philosophy. One reason given by some physicians for the rise in cesarean births is the **threat of malpractice suits** if a cesarean is not done and a "less-than-perfect" baby results.[4]

The **training that obstetricians receive** is changing. Because of the risks involved in the use of forceps, physicians are receiving less training in managing difficult deliveries (breech and fetal distress) in this manner. High forceps deliveries have been almost completely replaced by cesarean section. Some physicians are substituting surgical intervention for a difficult mid-forceps delivery believing it is safer for mother and baby.

Obstetricians' training deals mostly with handling complications and little emphasis is placed on such preventative measures as good prenatal nutrition and mobility of the woman in labor. As a result, many doctors treat all laboring women as potentially high risk, thereby relying on sophisticated equipment such as electronic fetal monitors and also the routine use of I.V.'s. A greater understanding of the hazards of vaginal birth to certain **high-risk babies** and a new ability to recognize those babies have evolved. By utilizing a fetal monitor during a high-risk labor, a fetus' response to the stress of labor can be observed. If fetal distress is noted, immediate surgical intervention can take place.

Some professionals feel that a small percentage of the increase in cesareans may occur because they offer **greater convenience** and **more income for doctors**. Higher fees result from the surgical procedure, longer hospital stay and guaranteed insurance coverage.

AVOIDING AN UNNECESSARY CESAREAN

A cesarean delivery may be necessary to save the life of you or your baby. But an unnecessary cesarean should be avoided at all costs as there are risks involved. It is major abdominal surgery, and as with any surgery, there is a risk of infection, hemorrhage, pneumonia and blood clots, along with increased financial costs, discomfort and a longer recovery. Your baby is also at a higher risk than a baby delivered vaginally. He is more likely to suffer from premature birth, asphyxia and breathing disorders.[5] The resulting problems, intensive care and financial costs can be overwhelming.

The chance of having a cesarean delivery may be increased by certain hospital practices during labor and birth or even by your choice of birth attendant. Be aware of those situations you should avoid in order to prevent an unnecessary cesarean.

Selecting a midwife or a doctor who favors family centered childbirth and who has a low cesarean rate will decrease the chances of your having a cesarean birth.

The **use of pitocin and/or artificial rupture of the membranes** to induce labor may change the type or force of labor contractions, precipitate fetal distress and create potential hazards for the mother and baby.[6] Failure of induction is a common reason for an emergency cesarean section.[7] Labor should only be induced if a medical reason is present. (See induction, Chapter 8.)

In a normal labor, **early intervention** (amniotomy, pitocin, pain medication, epidural anesthesia) may lead to complications that indicate a cesarean delivery. The rule that every baby should be delivered within 24 hours after rupture of the membranes or within a specific amount of time after the onset of labor increases the chance of a cesarean section. Some physicians will closely monitor you for infection (temperature, blood count) rather than routinely perform a cesarean after 24 hours with ruptured membranes.

Your **position in labor** may affect your need for a cesarean delivery. Being permitted to walk about can assist in the normal progression of labor. Walking has been shown to improve the quality of contractions, shorten labor and improve the condition of the baby during labor and delivery. Being made to lie flat on your back can cause supine hypotension and fetal distress.

Although the **electronic fetal monitor** is indicated and beneficial for a high-risk woman, when used routinely for a low-risk woman, it may increase her chance of needing a cesarean delivery.[8] For example, the interpretation of the fetal monitor in the hands of insufficiently trained personnel can be incorrect. They may overreact to abnormalities in the fetal heart tracings which may not actually indicate fetal distress and they might therefore opt for a cesarean delivery. If you are on an external monitor, the internal monitor should be applied to verify a problem if dilatation is sufficient.

Abnormalities in the fetal heart rate tracings can be confirmed by doing a fetal blood test. A blood sample can be taken from the baby's scalp to measure the pH. Not all hospitals are equipped to do this and not all physicians take advantage of it, perhaps because of their lack of knowledge or skill in this area.[9] The equipment needed for this test is very sensitive and requires a skilled technician to maintain and operate it to insure accurate results. Utilization of this test before the decision is made to do a cesarean may help to avoid many unnecessary cesarean births.

The electronic fetal monitor also limits your mobility in labor. Some nurses still insist that you lie on your back so they can obtain a good tracing. This position can lead to supine hypotension and fetal distress.

Epidural anesthesia can inhibit the force of contractions and prolong the second stage of labor, affecting your urge to push and the effectiveness of your pushing. The combined effects of an epidural block may complicate a potentially normal labor and delivery, decrease the baby's oxygen supply because of low maternal blood pressure and, therefore, increase the likelihood of a cesarean delivery.[10] Epidurals may also relax the pelvic muscles and thereby affect the rotation and descent of your baby.[11]

Analgesics and sedatives can slow labor or inhibit the force of contractions, and may cause depression of the baby's heart rate, thereby indicating the need for a cesarean section.

PLANNED AND UNPLANNED CESAREANS

There are two types of cesarean births, planned and unplanned. Most *primary* or first time cesarean births are unplanned. Many of the same routines will occur in both cases but possibly in a different order, and often somewhat more hurriedly in an unplanned cesarean. When dealing with an emergency cesarean, more stress is involved as you do not have adequate time to prepare emotionally. If you are also separated from your labor partner during this time, the trauma of the experience is intensified.

A planned cesarean birth is usually scheduled to occur just before the anticipated due date. Early confirmation of pregnancy and the accurate documentation of fetal growth is essential in determining this date precisely. Because the due date is only an estimate, prematurity is a risk to the baby. Premature babies are more likely to develop respiratory distress syndrome (RDS) and are generally less able to handle life outside the uterus than full-term babies. They are therefore more likely to remain in the hospital for an extended period of time, separated from their mothers and fathers. This increases the new parents' anxiety about the birth experience and inhibits bonding with the baby.

You may request permission to **go into labor spontaneously.** This may be the safest method of indicating your baby's maturity and his readiness to be born and is the least invasive. It has been found that RDS is "four times less frequent in babies that were delivered after labor had commenced than in those that experienced no labor."[12] These labor contractions stimulate the baby's body, better prepare the lungs for breathing and reduce the chance of respiratory difficulties. The contractions also draw up and shorten the cervix. When the incision is made in this area, it is felt to be strongest with less chance of rupture if a subsequent vaginal delivery is attempted. When labor begins, call your doctor at once. **DO NOT LABOR AT HOME!**

The following tests can be used to aid in determining fetal maturity, and therefore lessen the risk of delivering prematurely. (See Chapter 2 for more details.)

A **sonogram** can be done to measure the biparietal (ear to ear) diameter of the baby's head. This can give an estimation of gestational age. Its accuracy depends upon when it is done.

Amniocentesis can be performed to assess the maturity of the baby's lungs. The amniotic fluid is evaluated for the proportions of lecithin and sphingomyelin, substances produced by the baby's lungs. This is called an L/S ratio. The concentrations of these substances change toward the end of pregnancy, with a sudden increase in lecithin occurring after 34 weeks. A ratio of 2:1 or greater indicates lung maturity in the baby, and RDS will rarely occur. A sonogram should be done in conjunction with amniocentesis to locate the placenta and baby.

In certain high-risk conditions, diabetes and toxemia, the placenta begins to deteriorate prior to term. **Serial estriol levels** can be done to determine placental function and fetal well-being as an indicator of the best time for delivery.

PREOPERATIVE PROCEDURES

If this is a planned cesarean birth, you may enter the hospital the day before surgery or you may elect to be admitted the morning of the baby's birth. Some women choose this option since it gives them one more night at home with family members, especially if small children are involved. It also enables them to get a more restful night's sleep in a familiar environment. Though procedures may vary, the following are likely to be required.

Nothing by mouth (NPO) for 8–12 hours before the surgery is necessary to prevent aspiration of stomach contents in case general anesthesia is needed. It is your responsibility to refrain if you elect to be at home during those hours. A light, bland dinner the night before surgery is recommended.

Blood will be drawn for several tests and for typing and cross matching. A **urinalysis** is normally required. Some doctors may also request a **chest X-ray** and **respiratory function tests.** All of these can be done on an outpatient basis.

Your **abdomen will be shaved** in preparation for the surgery, but the area included may vary. A partial prep removes the hair from the abdomen down to the pubic area. A small amount of hair may be visible when your legs are together. A complete prep means that you are shaved from beneath your breasts, between your legs and up to your tailbone. This extensive shaving is unnecessary and adds to your postpartum discomfort. You may be given an **enema** prior to surgery, or you may request to do this at home.

You will be asked to sign a **consent form** for the surgery, anesthesia, and possible circumcision. Read these carefully before signing.

The anesthesiologist will visit you prior to surgery to discuss preoperative medication and anesthesia for the surgery. Be sure to mention any allergies or sensitivities to medication, and discuss your preferences.

If you are admitted to the hospital the night before surgery, you may be offered a **sedative or sleeping pill.** It is your decision whether or not to take it. If you have difficulty sleeping, you may need it. On the other hand, it can make you feel groggy in the morning rather than rested. Whether it is an unplanned or planned cesarean, a sedative or tranquilizer may be offered prior to surgery. Prepared women often feel they do not need this, but rely instead on relaxation techniques. If taken, it may cause both you and your baby to be sleepy at the time of birth. A shot of **atropine** is normally given to dry up secretions. Unless you choose general anesthesia, you may not need this medication.

The two types of **anesthesia** that are used for a cesarean birth are regional and general anesthetics. (See Chapter 7.) Most women and physicians prefer regional anesthesia because it allows active participation of the mother and father and does not depress the baby. Unless an extreme emergency exists, there is adequate time for this type of anesthesia to be administered.

Regional anesthesia includes spinals and epidurals. Their effects are similar, although a spinal provides deeper anesthesia. Upon administration you will feel warm, then tingly and finally numb. With an epidural, you may have some physical sensations such as tugging and pulling as the baby is born. Some women feel that this allows them to experience their babies' birth more completely. Because an epidural is usually administered through a catheter, it can be continuously dosed to give you comfort during the bonding period. Since a spinal is administered in one shot, a general anesthetic is sometimes required for repair of the incision if surgery takes longer than expected and the effects of the spinal wear off.

When the delivery must occur immediately for the health of you or your baby, general anesthesia is used. Because you are unconscious, your partner is usually not able to participate in the birth. Some physicians allow the husband to be present, even in these circumstances, to permit him to bond with the baby and later tell his wife the story of the birth.

You may first be put to sleep with an injection of medication into your I.V., or receive a light (analgesic) dose of oxygen and gas by mask. This light dose of gas is given until the baby is delivered to lessen the effects of the gas on him. You may be aware of voices but will experience no discomfort. After the baby is born, you will be put under more deeply for the repair. When you wake up, you will be in the recovery room and will feel groggy and sleepy. Because of this, the bonding period will be delayed.

SURGICAL PROCEDURE

Depending on the hospital, your delivery may take place in the labor and delivery area or in the surgical operating room. This could be a factor in your husband's participation. Some hospitals have a policy of "no relatives" in the operating room.

Whether your cesarean is planned or unplanned, you may experience some apprehension as you are wheeled in for surgery. Your advance preparation will minimize this. If your husband plans to be present for the birth, he will go to the doctors' dressing room to change into scrub clothes (a mask, scrub suit, cap and shoe covers) as you are taken to the delivery room. Unless you have made prior arrangements with your doctor, your partner will not rejoin you until the operation is ready to begin.

Once you are placed on the table, an I.V. is started in one arm, and that arm is strapped to a board. If you desire to hold your husband's hand and touch your baby once he is born, you need to request that your arms be free, rather than being strapped down. The anesthesia will then be administered, and you may be offered oxygen to breathe through a mask until the baby is born. A urinary catheter is inserted to drain the bladder. This is usually done after the regional anesthesia has taken effect to minimize discomfort. Because of its location, it is important to keep the bladder flat and out of the way to prevent damage during surgery. A blood

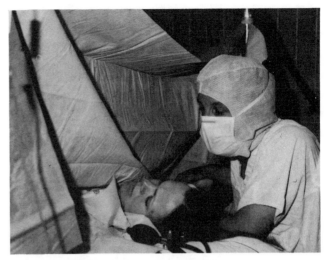

Husband comforting wife during surgery.

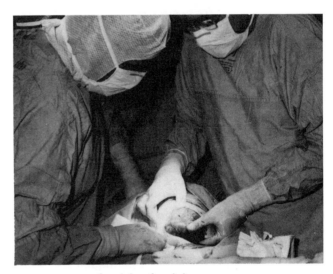

Applying fundal pressure.

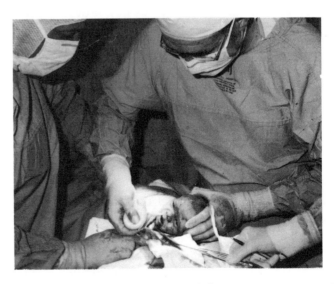

Baby alert during delivery.

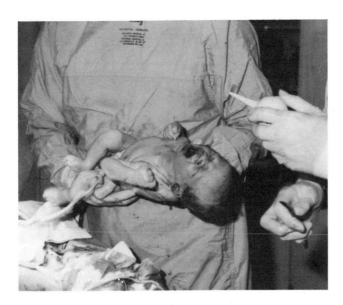

Baby's first cry.

pressure cuff will be put on one arm and electrocardiogram leads may be attached to your chest. Your abdomen and thighs will be scrubbed with a reddish-orange antiseptic solution, a screen will be placed across your shoulders, and sterile drapes will cover this area and the screen. Because of the screen, you and your husband will not see any of the surgery unless you desire. If you want to see the baby emerge, arrange to have a mirror in the room or to have the screen lowered at the moment of birth. Your husband can now enter the room and is seated next to your head.

The surgery now begins. The type of skin and uterine incisions used are influenced by the baby's position, the doctor's preferences, your desires, and the speed with which the baby must be delivered. (See the following section for more details.) The incisions are made and you may hear the suctioning of the amniotic fluid. Within a few minutes, you may feel a tugging or pulling sensation as your baby is born. If fundal pressure is used (downward pressure on the top of the abdomen) to assist in the delivery, a great deal of pressure may be felt. The doctor lifts the baby out, either with his hands or with the help of forceps or a vacuum extractor. Slow-paced breathing helps if you feel uncomfortable at this time. Within moments you will hear your baby's first cry. The cord is clamped and cut and the baby handed to the pediatrician. He will show you your new son or daughter and then examine him. Routine identification procedures are also performed.

(See Chapter 10.) This exam can usually be done within your view which helps to relieve anxiety about your baby's condition.

The placenta is then delivered through the incision, and oxytocin is given through the I.V. to help the uterus contract. Your doctor will examine your uterus, ovaries and tubes. The uterus is now repaired along with the abdominal muscles, peritoneum and skin. Clamps or staples are sometimes used to repair the skin incision. It normally takes about 45 minutes to complete the repair. If you feel nauseated, or experience any other sensations, tell the anesthesiologist.

During this time you may request to touch and hold your baby. If your arms are strapped, you partner may be able to hold the baby next to your cheek. If your partner was not present for the delivery, the pediatrician can bring the baby out for his viewing immediately after the birth. This helps to relieve his anxiety about the condition of you and the baby.

Skin and Uterine Incisions

Two incisions are necessary for a cesarean delivery, one in the skin and one in the uterus. You may be given two different types so that the skin incision may not match the uterine incision. The one in the skin is usually chosen for cosmetic reasons; the uterine incision for medical reasons.

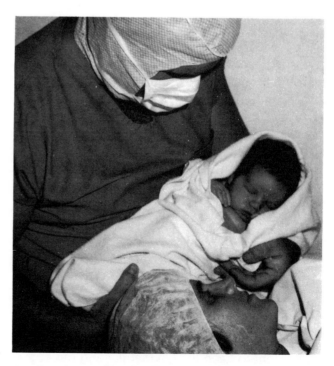

Greeting the new baby.

Skin incisions may be done either vertically or horizontally. The **low transverse or Pfannenstiel incision** is made crosswise along the pubic hairline. This "bikini cut" is preferred for cosmetic reasons because it is barely noticeable. It takes longer to do and gives the doctor limited space in which to work. Therefore, it is not used in an extreme emergency. Discomfort during recovery is less and the wound heals more quickly. A **vertical incision** is faster to make and gives the doctor more room to work. Hence, it allows for a quicker delivery in an emergency situation.

Uterine incisions may also be done vertically or horizontally. The **low transverse cervical incision** is made horizontally in the cervical area. Because it is not in the contractile part of the uterus, it forms the strongest scar with the least danger of rupture and fewest postoperative adhesions. The incision is smaller and is thought to heal more quickly. It is the only incision most doctors will accept for a possible vaginal birth following this cesarean.

A **classical incision** is made vertically in the fundal area which gives the doctor more working room. This is done for a large baby, a transverse lie, adhesions or scar tissue from previous cesareans or when the baby must be delivered immediately. It forms the weaker scar and healing is slower.

SKIN INCISIONS

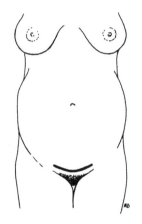

Low transverse.

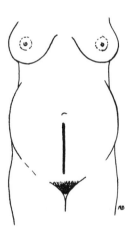

Vertical.

UTERINE INCISIONS

Low transverse cervical.

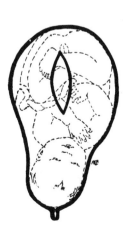

Classical.

RECOVERY ROOM

Once the surgery is completed, you are taken to the recovery room where you will stay until the anesthesia has worn off, about two to three hours. During this time, the nurse checks your blood pressure, temperature, pulse, respiration, and the amount of vaginal and incisional bleeding. If the uterus becomes soft, she may massage it to prevent bleeding. Breathing and relaxation techniques can be helpful in relieving any discomfort. Pain medication is also available if needed. However, if your baby is with you for bonding at this time, you may want to wait to take medication since it may make you sleepy or nauseated.

The nurse may ask you to breathe deeply and cough. This helps to prevent pneumonia and relieve gas discomfort. Splint your incision by holding a pillow firmly against your abdomen, and "huff" if coughing seems difficult at first. (See page 146 for explanation of huffing.)

If you had a regional, feeling will return to your toes and feet first and progressively move up toward your abdomen. If you had general anesthesia, you may be groggy and nauseated upon awakening and feel the need for pain medication.

It is possible to have your husband with you if you recover in the maternity recovery room. Your pediatrician may permit you some bonding time, providing the baby's condition is good. This special time is just as important to cesarean parents as it is for couples who have experienced a vaginal birth. Breastfeeding can also be initiated at this time. (See Chapter 11.)

THE CESAREAN BABY

No two babies are alike, cesarean babies included. One noticeable difference between vaginally delivered and cesarean babies is that the head of the cesarean infant is nicely shaped because it was not molded by the birth process. Because your baby has experienced a surgical delivery, he may need closer observation. Some hospitals require all cesarean babies to spend a certain amount of time in the special care nursery. Since he does not pass through the birth canal, which compresses the amniotic fluid from his lungs, he may have more mucus. This is lessened if you have experienced some labor. If you have received medication or general anesthesia, he may be drowsy.

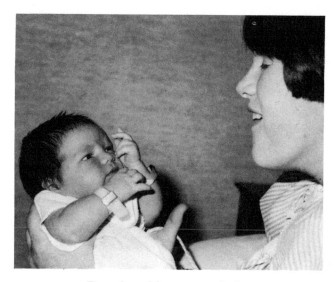

Two-day-old cesarean baby.

As long as your baby's condition is good, you may request that he be placed in the regular nursery to allow earlier contact with him. If your baby was in distress at birth, he may be taken immediately after birth to an intensive care nursery. As soon as you feel able, your husband can take you in a wheelchair to visit the baby in the nursery. Until he is able to nurse, you should pump your breasts to provide him with your colostrum and milk. Even if he is not allowed out of his isolette, it is important for you to touch and talk to your baby.

POSTPARTUM

The average stay in the hospital is three to six days. The I.V. and catheter will remain in place 24-48 hours following surgery. The **I.V.** provides nourishment and adequate fluids until the intestines begin to function again. The **catheter** allows the bladder time to recover from surgery and keeps it empty until you are able to walk to the bathroom yourself.

Your diet will consist of liquids, gradually increasing to a regular diet. Adequate intake of fluids is important for proper kidney function, to prevent dehydration and fever, and to build an adequate milk supply.

You will be encouraged to get up and walk within 24 hours of your surgery. This promotes good circulation, which reduces the chance of blood clots, and it helps to relieve gas. The first time you attempt this will be the most difficult. It will get easier each time you do it. Some doctors order support stockings for their patients.

Even though you have had a cesarean birth, you will still have a **vaginal flow**. You may wish to use beltless pads or attach the napkins to your underwear with safety pins.

You may feel **discomfort in one or both shoulders** as a result of a collection of blood and air under the diaphragm. The pain is felt in the shoulders because of nerve connections between them and the diaphragm. If you had general anesthesia, your throat may be sore as a result of the tube inserted down your throat.

You will experience **abdominal pain** for several days following surgery. As the intestines begin to function, around the third day, you may experience sharp gas pains. Pain medication or analgesics will be available and most often are necessary so you can interact comfortably with your baby. If you are nursing, be sure your doctor orders medication that can be taken safely. Utilize relaxation to maximize the effect that your medication will have for you.

As your incision heals, it will probably itch, possibly continuing for several months. Wearing cotton panties, rather than nylon, may be more comfortable during this time. The clamps are removed from your incision prior to your leaving the hospital. You and your husband may want to look at the incision together before going home.

Rooming-in is especially important for the cesarean couple to aid in developing feelings of attachment to their baby. It is best if you can have assistance since it will be difficult for you to move around for several days. Don't hesitate to ask for help from the nursing staff. Rooming-in also helps breastfeeding get off to a good start. Comfortable nursing positions for the cesarean mother are described in Chapter 11.

Once you get home, you will need household help for the first few weeks. Moving about is desirable, but difficult! Doing housework should not be one of your priorities at this time. Setting reasonable goals and expectations for yourself and your baby makes life much easier for all concerned. Take time to relax and nap when the baby does.

Recovery is more rapid when you concentrate on your health and the baby's welfare rather than entertaining visitors or cleaning the house. Continue with prenatal vitamins and maintain a high level of protein in your postpartum diet. Wound healing requires lots of protein, just like growing your baby did. Nutrition can play an important part in how strongly your incision heals.

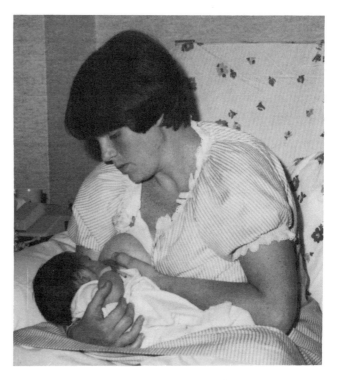

Cesarean nursing couple.

The correct time to resume **sexual relations** varies with each couple. Healing of the placental site, signaled by the cessation of vaginal discharge, and the amount of abdominal discomfort you are experiencing influence your decision. Your doctor's advice and your own desire for sex are also important factors.

While you are not dealing with an episiotomy, you are coping with an abdominal incision which is even larger and more painful than an episiotomy. You may find some of the positions you used during the last months of pregnancy to be most comfortable. (See Chapter 12.) Many women experience a changed "body image." Because of their incision, they worry that they are no longer attractive to their husbands. You may need lots of reassurance that you are still appealing.

An **emotional recovery** from a cesarean birth may take from two to six months. Your feelings may vary from relief that it is over to painful depression. You must be reassured that you did nothing wrong and that you are not inadequate or a failure. Cesarean birth is simply another way to give birth safely. Contact your local cesarean support group for help and information.

EXERCISE AFTER A CESAREAN

First Day

Because you may spend the first 24 hours in bed, it is important that you begin **ankle rotating** and **foot flexing and stretching** as soon as possible after surgery—in the recovery room when sensation returns or as soon as you are alert after general anesthesia. This stimulates circulation and decreases the chance of blood clots. (See First Day exercises in Chapter 12 for descriptions.)

You also need to begin **deep breathing** to expand your lungs. In the recovery room or as soon as you wake up, take ten deep slow chest breaths. Repeat once an hour to loosen phlegm and mucus that may have collected in your lungs during surgery. This is important to do to prevent pneumonia. Along with your deep breathing, "huff" to bring up the phlegm. To do this, take in a deep breath, hold your incision with both hands, and breathe out with a short sharp "ha" sound. This is not as uncomfortable as a cough and will be very effective if you take in enough air first. Don't worry about the stitches breaking. They have been done in a number of layers and are very strong.

To relieve gas and aid in the healing of the incision do the following exercise.

Abdominal Tightening—While sitting, lying down or standing, slowly tighten your abdominal muscles as you *exhale*; hold for one to two seconds at first and gradually increase to five seconds or more. This may be difficult at first, but the increased circulation will aid the healing of the incision, and the muscle contractions actually draw the ends of the incision closer together. The first few days you do this, support the incision with your hands for added comfort.

Log rolling.

Knee reaching.

Though not really an exercise, **proper body mechanics** can ease the strain on your abdomen as you roll over and sit up in bed. To turn to your left side, bend only your right knee and bring it over the left knee. As you turn your body, reach for the left side of the bed with your right arm. (This is called **log rolling**.) Reverse the procedure if you want to turn to the right. From this position you can easily sit up using your arm and shoulder muscles to lift you, as you did during pregnancy, without putting undue strain on your abdomen.

Second Day

If you are still in bed most of the time on the second day, continue **ankle rotating** and **foot flexing**. You should also continue "huffing" until your lungs are clear.

Deep breathing along with the following two exercises will stimulate intestinal activity and reduce discomfort from gas.

Pelvic Rock—Lying on your back or side with knees bent, gently rock your pelvis back and forth, using your abdominal and buttocks muscles.

Kegels—Contract and relax the muscles of the pelvic floor five to ten times at least once every hour.

To begin abdominal strengthening do the following.

Knee Reaching—Sit semi-reclined (at a 45° angle), with the bed raised or your back and head supported by pillows and breathe in deeply. As you exhale, tuck in your chin and reach for (don't touch) your knees with both hands. Breathe in and lower your head to the pillow and relax. Repeat several times. Start slowly and gradually increase the repetitions to ten as you are able. For additional comfort support your incision as you raise your head.

Before you go home from the hospital, check for separation of the recti muscles as described under third day postpartum exercises, Chapter 12. The separation must be restored to normal before doing further abdominal strengthening exercise.

Progress at your own pace with the exercises described for postpartum when your doctor gives his permission. Avoid lifting, straining and undue exertion. Be sure to get plenty of rest to speed your recovery.

VAGINAL BIRTH AFTER CESAREAN (VBAC)

In most countries of the world it is not unusual to experience a vaginal birth following a cesarean. In the past couple of years there has been a surge of new information in this country strongly supporting the position that the majority of women can attempt a vaginal birth after cesarean (VBAC, pronounced *vee back*). Various studies have shown that from 38.5 to 72.5 percent of women who had cesarean births can safely deliver vaginally.[13]

If you had a transverse uterine incision, you may be a candidate for a future vaginal birth. The major concern is the possible rupture of the previous scar while you are in labor. Yet the risk of scar rupture is only 0.5 percent with this type of incision.[14] This number is small, and the actual percentage may be even smaller. This statistic includes not only actual separations of the uterus associated with bleeding, but also those separations of the uterus that were discovered during subsequent cesareans, but in which no bleeding or problems occurred. These separations are called "windows," and may have occurred during the healing process, not as a response to pregnancy or labor.

As long as the indication for your previous cesarean does not recur and no new indications appear, your chances of a vaginal delivery are quite good. Your **choice of birth attendant** is an important factor. You need to discuss his criteria for permitting a trial of labor. Studies show that a successful vaginal birth is possible if the original cesarean was performed for one of the following nonrecurring

reasons: multiple birth, CPD, abruption of the placenta, failed induction, fetal distress, placenta previa, hypertensive problems, abnormal presentation, or prolonged or abnormal labor.[15]

In 1983, the American College of Obstetricians and Gynecologists (ACOG) released a statement supporting vaginal birth after cesarean. Even so, many physicians are continuing to perform routine repeat cesareans. They caution women about the dangers that uterine rupture will pose to them and their children. But they neglect to mention the danger of a repeat cesarean section, when in fact this method of delivery can be more risky than attempting a vaginal birth. Complications can include surgical damage to the bowel and bladder, hemorrhage, infection, poor wound healing, blood clots and anesthesia-related problems.

In addition, a woman who has given birth surgically is more likely to experience depression and report feelings of failure or other negative emotions.[16] Her feelings of inadequacy are greater when she believes that the surgery was performed unnecessarily. After having a VBAC, many women state that they now feel "complete," even if they accepted the fact that the previous cesarean was justified.

Mothers attempting a VBAC require good emotional and physical support since they may receive many negative comments from lay persons as well as professionals. A good source book is *Silent Knife* by Nancy Wainer Cohen and Lois J. Estner. This book provides important medical facts to support your decision, and helps you to attain your goal. It is must reading for cesarean prevention.

FOOTNOTES

Chapter 9

1. George Nolan, "Family Centered Cesarean Maternity Care Policy " (Ann Arbor, Mich., University of Mich. Hospital), p. 1.
2. Diony Young and Charles Mahan, *Unnecessary Cesareans, Ways to Avoid Them* (Minneapolis, ICEA, 1980), p. 16.
3. Nancy Wainer Cohen and Lois J. Estner, *Silent Knife: Cesarean Prevention and Vaginal Birth After Cesarean* (South Hadley, Mass., Bergin & Garvey Publishers, Inc., 1983), p. 8.

4. Young and Mahan, p. 3.
5. Young and Mahan, p. 3.
6. Young and Mahan, p. 4.
7. Young and Mahan, p. 4.
8. Young and Mahan, p. 5.
9. Young and Mahan, p. 6.
10. Young and Mahan, p. 6.
11. Diana Korte and Roberta Scaer, *A Good Birth, A Safe Birth* (N.Y., Bantam Books, 1984), p. 148.
12. M. J. Maiselle et al., "Elective Delivery of the Term Fetus: An Obstetrical Hazard," *Journal of the American Medical Association*, Vol. 238 (November 7, 1977), p. 2036.
13. Young and Mahan, p. 15.
14. Young and Mahan, p. 15.
15. Young and Mahan, p. 16.
16. Susan G. Doering, "Unnecessary Cesareans: Doctor's Choice, Parent's Dilemma," in *Compulsory Hospitalization or Freedom of Choice in Childbirth?*, Vol. 1 (Chapel Hill, N.C., NAPSAC, 1976), pp. 145–152.

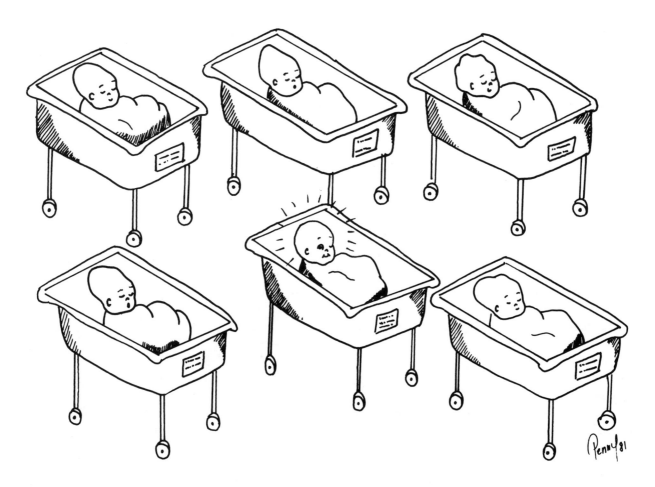

"Can't you tell I'm the cesarean baby?!"

Chapter 10

The Newborn
or "There'll Be Some Changes Made"

YOUR BABY'S APPEARANCE AT BIRTH

The first question most parents ask after learning the sex of their baby is, "How much does he weigh and how long is he?" Babies **weigh** an average of 7–8 pounds and are from 19–21 inches in **length**. Because of the recent emphasis on optimum nutrition, it is not uncommon for babies to weigh more than 8 pounds. These measurements are usually not done until your baby is taken to the nursery. Don't be concerned if your baby loses a few ounces during the first couple of days. This is normal and is usually regained within a week.

Most people are not familiar with the appearance of newly-born babies and expect them all to

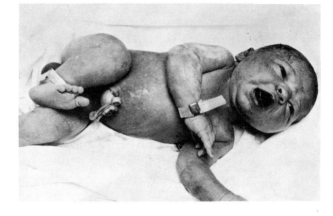

Newborn

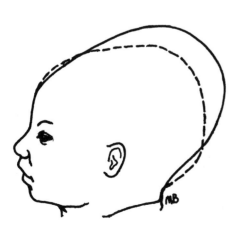

Molding.

look like the *Gerber baby*. You may be surprised or even concerned about your baby's appearance upon delivery. Immediately after birth he **may appear bluish or gray.** Once he starts to cry or begins breathing, you will notice him becoming pinker and pinker. Sometimes his hands and feet may be slightly bluish for a few hours. His head may be misshapen and elongated (like a conehead) as the result of **molding** within the birth canal. This molding occurs from the overlapping of the skull bones which eases his passage during birth. It may take a day or two to become rounder. Sometimes swelling occurs (**caput succedaneum**) which may take several days to subside. If a vacuum extractor was used during the birth, this will be accentuated.

Your baby's **face and genitals may appear swollen or puffy.** This also subsides within a few days. His **nose may be flattened** and his **ears pressed to his head**.

His body may be covered with a cheesy-like coating called **vernix caseosa.** You may only notice it in the creases of his skin or under his arms. The closer to term the baby is delivered, the less vernix he has. This "baby cold cream" protected his skin while floating in the amniotic fluid. Some mothers desire to massage this into their baby's skin to serve as a natural skin conditioner rather than having it washed off. The amount of blood present on the body varies from baby to baby.

PHYSIOLOGICAL CHANGES THAT OCCUR AT BIRTH

Your baby's circulatory system changes at the moment of birth. While in the uterus your baby receives his oxygen from your red blood cells via the placenta. At the time of birth, he begins to expand his lungs and to breathe on his own. Your doctor or midwife may suction his nose and mouth to remove any mucus if necessary. His heart begins to pump blood through his lungs to pick up the oxygen that was breathed in. After the umbilical cord is cut, certain internal blood vessels which carried blood to and from the umbilical cord are no longer needed and become ligaments.

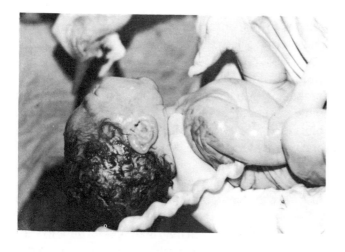

Suctioning the newborn.

CARE GIVEN TO THE BABY AT BIRTH

After you have had an opportunity to hold and soothe your newborn, the delivery room nurse may "borrow" him to perform admission and identification procedures. Since the delivery room is often 20 degrees cooler than body temperature, your baby must be kept warm. During these procedures, he is placed under a warming light, and while in the delivery room he may be placed in a heated isolette. When he is with you and covered with a blanket, this is not necessary since *you* are the best baby warmer!

Your fingerprints and your **baby's footprints** will be recorded by the nurse. If you have brought your baby book with you, ask her to put his footprints in the appropriate place. Both of you will receive an **identification bracelet** which will be checked throughout your hospital stay. This prevents nursery mix-ups!!! Interestingly, mothers who are awake and who bond with their babies right after birth rarely look at the identification bracelet. They know their babies!

Florida state law requires that an **antibiotic ointment** or **silver nitrate drops** be placed in your baby's eyes within one hour after birth. This time may vary from state to state. It is done to prevent blindness if the mother has gonorrhea. It also may prevent other bacterial eye infections. You may request a delay in its application until after the bonding period since eye-to-eye contact is an important component of the bonding process. (See page 102, Bonding.)

An **injection of vitamin K** is given to the baby while he is in the delivery room or upon admission to the newborn nursery. Vitamin K is an important factor in blood clotting and is manufactured by the body in the intestine once certain normal bacteria are present. All babies are deficient in vitamin K as their normal flora (bacteria) is inadequate.

Your baby's first exam in life will be given at one and five minutes after birth. This evaluation is called an Apgar score and shows how well he handled labor and delivery. It also predicts how he will do in the postpartum period. The scoring system was developed by a pediatrician, Dr. Virginia Apgar. A score of 8–10 at one minute means your baby's condition at birth is good, whereas a low Apgar rating alerts the staff to a baby who is in distress and needs careful observation. The rating at five minutes indicates his adjustment to extrauterine life. You can ask your doctor what Apgar score he gave your baby.

APGAR SCORING CHART

Characteristic	0	1	2
Color	Blue pale	Body pink Extremities blue	Body completely pink
Respiratory Effort	Absent	Slow, irregular weak cry	Strong cry
Heart Rate	Absent	Less than 100	More than 100
Muscle Tone	Limp	Some flexing of extremities	Active motion
Reflexes	Absent	Grimace, some motion	Cry

NEWBORN CHARACTERISTICS

At first glance, your baby's **head** may appear too large for his body. It is about one quarter of his body size. The average head circumference is 13″–14″. Since his neck muscles are weak, it is important that you support his wobbly head at all times. Of great concern to most parents are the two **fontanels** or "soft spots." These are areas in the skull where the bones are not joined but instead are held together by membranes. They allow for molding during birth and also for further growth of the skull. The anterior fontanel (on top of the head) is diamond shaped and usually closes by 18 months of age. The posterior fontanel (back of head) is triangular shaped and generally closes by six weeks of age. You should not be overly concerned about harming the baby at these areas because they are covered with a tough membrane called the dura.

Some babies are born with a full head of **hair**, while others are bald. It is common for a baby to lose some or all of this first hair. (Heartburn during pregnancy does not mean your baby will have hair.)

You may notice little "whiteheads" or **milia** over the baby's forehead, nose and cheeks. These are immature oil glands and will go away without any treatment when the glands start to function. Do not attempt to remove them.

Normal "cross-eyed" appearance.

Your baby's **eye color** is usually blue at birth. His permanent eye color is normally determined by six months of age, although changes can occur up to one year. He will blink at bright lights and may not nurse well or look at you if the light is shining in his face. Your baby may appear "cross-eyed" as he looks around. This is because the eye muscles are not well developed. By six months of age, his eyes should be focusing together. If not, your pediatrician will refer you to an ophthamologist (a medical doctor who specializes in eye disorders).

His **tear ducts** may not function for several weeks. You may notice some swelling or discharge as a result of the application of silver nitrate. Some staining around the eyes may be seen if the antibiotic ointment was not wiped off. Small **hemorrhages** in the whites of his eyes may be present because of pressure during birth. These may take several weeks to disappear.

For years, mothers were told that their babies could not see until they were several weeks old. But many mothers continued to feel that their babies did indeed look at them. Recent research has proven that even though **vision** is not perfect, babies *are* able to see, and their best vision is at a distance of 12–15 inches.

Even before birth, your fetus exhibits sensitivity to sound. **Hearing** becomes more acute within several days following birth as the amniotic fluid is absorbed. Loud noises are disturbing to a newborn, while soft soothing voices or sounds quiet him.

The sense of **taste** and **smell** are well developed in the newborn. Your baby may react negatively to someone wearing heavy perfume or smoking. Some research has shown that babies can differentiate the scent of their mother's breastmilk from another mother's milk.[1]

You may notice clusters of small capillaries on the nape of his neck, eyelids or bridge of his nose. They are minute blood vessels, which are close to the skin. These "stork bites" or "angel kisses" usually fade by nine months of age.

Your newborn's **skin** is sensitive to its surroundings. If he is chilled, his skin will appear blotchy and skin capillaries may be apparent. His hands and feet may be slightly bluish. If overdressed or wearing irritating clothing, a rash may develop.

Some babies are covered with fine downy hair called **lanugo.** This is seen more frequently with premature babies and rarely in those born past their due date. It usually disappears within a few weeks. Dry scaly skin is not unusual, with some peeling occurring a week or two after birth.

Dark skinned babies may have purplish-brown discolorations on their lower back. These are called **Mongolian spots** and disappear by one year of age.

As you observe your baby's **breathing**, you will notice it is fast (about 35–50 times a minute), irregular, shallow and abdominal in nature. It may be noisy at night. The **hiccups** you may have felt during pregnancy will continue until the baby's diaphragm matures. His **heart rate** is also rapid

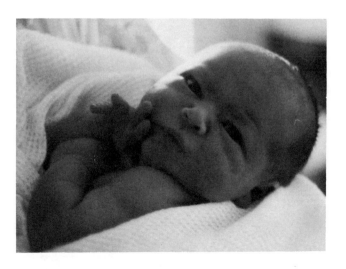

Two-day-old infant looking at camera.

(90–160 beats per minute). When crying, this may accelerate to 180–200.

Both male and female babies' **breasts** may be enlarged as a result of the transfer of hormones through the placenta while in utero. There may even be some secretion of milk (**"witch's milk"**) within the first two weeks of life. These hormones may also cause "false menstruation" or **vaginal bleeding** in female babies. The **genitals** of both sexes can be enlarged or swollen as a result of the hormones. A little girl's clitoris may be large enough for her to be mistaken for a boy at quick glance.

Your baby's **abdomen** is round and protruding. This is caused by poor abdominal muscle tone, as well as relatively long intestines confined to a small area, and possibly swallowed air. The **umbilical cord stump** dries up and falls off in one to two weeks.

A newborn's **arms** and **legs** are proportionately short for his body. His arms are usually bent and held close to his chest with his hands in fists. The position of his legs may be similar to that assumed while in utero and may appear bowed. His **nails** may be very long at birth and need cutting. They are soft and pliable and can be trimmed with baby scissors.

Certain reflexes are present at birth, some of which are vital to your baby's survival. He has been "practicing" many of these while in utero.

His **sucking reflex** is very strong at birth. Any stimulation of his lips elicits sucking motions. It is not unusual to see newborns sucking on their thumbs, fingers or fists. This is just a continuation of what they did before delivery. His **swallowing reflex** was also present prior to birth as he swallowed and excreted amniotic fluid. If you stroke your baby's cheek, he will turn his head in that direction (**rooting reflex**). To nurse your baby, simply allow your breast to touch his cheek.

Your baby is equipped with certain protective reflexes. These include a **gag reflex** to prevent choking and a **cough reflex** to get rid of mucus. **Yawning** is also considered a protective reflex.

Even a newborn is able to make instinctive attempts to protect himself. If his face becomes covered with a blanket, he will flail his arms and move his head to remove the cover. Therefore you need not be overly worried about your baby smothering in his covers. If a limb is exposed to cold, he will draw it

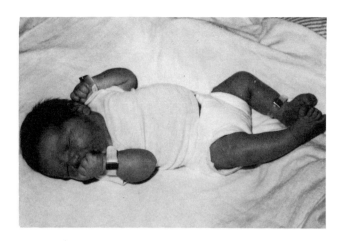

Sucking reflex.

close to his body to warm it. If pinched or stuck with a pin, he will quickly withdraw.

When you place your fingers in your baby's palms, he will grasp them tightly (**grasp reflex**). His grasp may be strong enough to allow you to raise his body up. (Do not try this because he may let go!) If held under his arms in a standing position, he will make walking motions (**stepping reflex**). When your infant is a few weeks old and is lying on his back, you may notice he often lies in a "fencing position" with his head turned to one side with that arm and leg extended while his other arm and leg are flexed (**tonic neck reflex**). If the baby is startled, he will thrust out his arms as if to embrace (**Moro reflex**).

During the first few weeks, a harmless rash (known as **erythematoxicum**) may appear on his body. It resembles a heat rash (a red blotch with a small white raised center), does not appear on the extremities, has no known cause, and is not a reason to be concerned.

Within the first week of life, your baby will have a blood test done to check for several inherited metabolic diseases. Even though these are extremely rare, all can be managed with diet or medication. By early screening, your baby could be saved from serious problems (including mental retardation) if he happens to be one of those rare babies who have one of these diseases. The state of Florida routinely checks for four problems: PKU, hypothyroidism, glactosemia, and maple sugar urine disease. Required tests may vary from state to state.

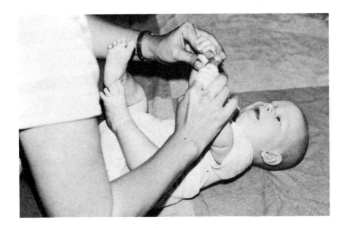

Grasp reflex.

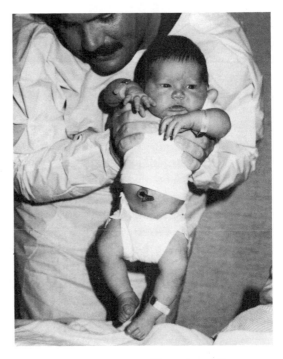

Stepping reflex.

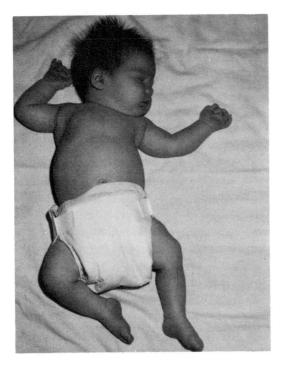

Tonic neck reflex.

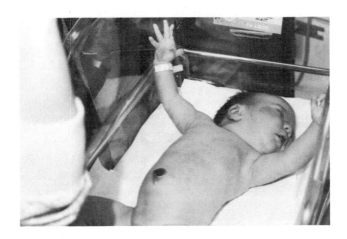

Moro reflex.

COMMON CONCERNS OF NEW PARENTS

Most new parents express some concern over their newborn's appearance or the care involved with a new baby. If you are a first time mother or father, you may feel unsure of yourself and wonder what to do with this little person. This section is devoted to those topics that new parents have many questions about.

Normal physiologic jaundice is a condition which affects 50 percent of all newborns. Your baby has a large number of red blood cells (RBC's) while in utero. After birth, the extra RBC's begin to deteri-

orate and a product of this breakdown is bilirubin. Bilirubin is normally detoxified by the liver and excreted by the kidneys. Because your baby's liver is immature and unable to handle the bilirubin, the excess may produce jaundice, a yellow discoloration of the baby's skin, mucous membranes and whites of his eyes. Physiologic jaundice usually appears on the second or third day of life and usually disappears within a week. Your physician will test your baby's blood to determine the level of bilirubin. Usually no treatment is necessary as this is a normal condition found in newborns.

Certain medications taken during labor, such as pitocin can increase jaundice. If the bilirubin becomes elevated to a high level, your physician may place your infant under a "bili-light," an ultra-violet light which aids in lowering the bilirubin level. While under this phototherapy, his eyes will be covered to protect them from the light. Because phototherapy can cause dehydration and results in separation of you and your baby, it should be avoided if his bilirubin level is not significantly elevated and he is otherwise healthy and vigorous. Frequent feedings and placing the baby in the sunlight can also help the bilirubin level return to normal without the trauma of prolonged separation.

Some physicians encourage mothers who are nursing to supplement with water or eliminate several feedings if the bilirubin is elevated. Breastfeeding does tend to prolong jaundice but is *not* an indication to stop nursing or supplement. Frequent nursings will provide sufficient fluid. True **breast milk jaundice** is rare and can be detected in a laboratory test.

A high bilirubin level can cause irreversible brain damage. Therefore your baby's doctor will observe your infant closely to determine whether the jaundice is normal or pathologic in nature. **Pathologic or abnormal jaundice** usually occurs within the first 24 hours after birth. It may be due to a blood type incompatability (ABO), or Rh factor incompatability. This type of jaundice causes more concern, and treatment may include a blood transfusion to prevent brain damage if other conservative measures do not decrease the bilirubin level.

The most common concern of new parents is how to care for the **umbilical cord stump**. If a clamp was applied at birth, it is usually removed within 24–48 hours. The stump will dry up and fall off within one to two weeks. Some physicians state that only sponge baths should be given until the cord falls off. Others allow tub baths right from birth, quoting studies that show no increase in infection. Keep the cord dry between baths by placing the diaper below the navel and wiping the cord with alcohol two or three times a day. Some slight bleeding may be noted as the cord falls off. If a foul odor, redness or discharge is observed, you should notify the doctor.

A **circumcision** is a surgical procedure that removes the foreskin from the head of the penis. Traditionally, this procedure has been performed on the majority of American male babies immediately following birth. It was thought that removal of the foreskin promoted health and cleanliness and prevented masturbation. Careful studies have shown, however, that circumcision is not necessary for good health or hygiene and that it does not affect masturbation. One argument for routine circumcision states that it prevents cancer of the penis in males and cancer of the vagina or cervix in females, but little evidence exists to support this.[2] The United States remains the only country to practice non-religious circumcision almost routinely.

You should give careful thought *before* your baby is born as to whether you desire to have a circumcision performed on your son. In 1975, the American Academy of Pediatrics stated that there is no valid medical reason to circumcise the normal newborn male.[3] Circumcision is a surgical procedure, and can result in bleeding or infection. In addition, when done on newborns, no anesthetic is used. Recent studies have verified that newborns *do* feel both pain and pleasure sensations. No one knows exactly how much pain is felt by a newborn during circumcision, but most babies scream during the operation.[4]

Some parents choose to have this done so that their sons will not be *different*. However, the number of males not being circumcised is increasing. They are no longer so "different." After examining both the benefits and risks, many parents today are concluding that the practice serves no medical purpose, and they are deciding against circumcision for their sons.

If you are considering this procedure for your newborn, check with your insurance company beforehand to determine their policy for coverage. Many companies no longer pay for routine circumcision of the newborn.

The uncircumcised penis requires no extra cleaning. Just wash, rinse and dry, along with the rest of the baby's bottom. *Do not pull the foreskin back over the head of the penis.* In a newborn, the foreskin is almost always attached to the head, and forcing it back may cause damage. It may be months or even years before separation occurs. If you wish, you may check for separation every few months by *gently* pushing back the foreskin only as far as it goes easily. *Do not force it.* Once the foreskin is fully retractable (separated), you should pull it back gently to wash the penis and then replace it. Your child will then learn to do this for himself when bathing.

If you decide to have your son circumcised, delay the procedure for at least 24 hours to allow him time to adjust to extrauterine life. Following surgery, observe for bleeding, infection or discomfort, and notify your doctor if they occur. Placing your baby on his side rather than his stomach may make him more comfortable. Apply petroleum jelly to the head of the penis and cover with sterile gauze to prevent the diaper from sticking. When washing your baby, gently pull back the small remaining foreskin in order to prevent pieces of scar tissue from growing between the foreskin and the head.

Diaper rash is the result of urine and stools irritating the skin, laundry products in the diapers or some chemicals used in disposable diapers. Some babies have diaper rash while teething. Rashes can be prevented by changing the baby frequently and washing the area with warm water. If he has had a bowel movement, soap and water should be used. Always make sure he is dried well, especially in the folds of the skin. Petroleum jelly or medicated ointment may be applied if desired. Plastic pants should be avoided if possible, and exposing the area to air will also help. Your diapers may need to be rinsed twice to remove all traces of soap, or change your brand of disposables.

Avoid applying powder to the genitals. Especially in girls, this can cake in the creases and irritate sensitive tissues. If you use talcum powder or cornstarch on your baby, first place it in your hand, and then apply sparingly. If shaken onto the baby, it can be breathed into his lungs and cause irritation.

A **rash** may appear on other parts of the body. Prickly heat occurs most often in warm weather or if the baby has been overdressed. Most new parents tend to overdress their new babies. Dress him as you would yourself. If it is 90° outside, he certainly doesn't need a sweater. All baby clothes and bedding should be washed prior to their first use with special baby detergent and a softener that is diluted in the rinse water. This avoids rashes from allergy to strong detergent or from chemicals in new clothes. Softeners that are placed in the dryer do not get rinsed out, are usually perfumed and may cause a skin reaction.

The first **bowel movement** your baby has will be black, tarry and sticky. This is called meconium and was in his intestines in utero. For the first five to six days, his stools will make a transition from tarry black to greenish-brown to brownish-yellow, to greenish-yellow. After the transitional stool, the color changes to milk stools. If bottlefed, they will be soft, yellow and have an offensive odor. The stools of breastfed infants tend to be mushy, loose and do not have an unpleasant odor. The number of stools varies from baby to baby—one to eight per day (small amount with each diaper change) or as infrequently as one every several days, or even one a week if totally breastfed.

Constipation occurs when stools are hard, dry and difficult to pass. It is not related to the frequency of bowel movements. This rarely occurs in totally breastfed infants that have been given no supplements of formula or solids. A change of formula may be necessary if constipation becomes severe.

Diarrhea in an infant requires medical attention to prevent dehydration. Frequent stools that are watery, green in color, foul smelling or contain mucus should be reported to your pediatrician. Be prepared to tell him the number, color and the consistency of the stools. Remember, a totally breastfed baby normally has loose stools, but they are not considered diarrhea unless other signs are present.

Cradle cap appears as flakes, scales or crusts on the baby's scalp or behind his ears. Wash the area daily and brush vigorously with a baby brush. If necessary, a special soap may be prescribed by your doctor.

Spitting up is common in the early weeks. The sphincter at the top of the stomach may be immature and allow some of the milk to escape along with the air as the baby is burped. Be prepared by keeping an extra diaper handy. To minimize the amount of air swallowed, hold the baby at a 45° degree angle while feeding and burp him often. Avoid overfeeding him as this may cause him to vomit. If a nursing mother's let-down is forceful, it may cause the baby to choke and gulp air. You can press down on the areola with your forefinger and middle finger to lessen the ejection, or hand express a small amount of milk prior to feeding.

If a baby is allowed to cry too long before being fed, he may gulp large amounts of air which will cause him to spit up. After feeding, place your baby on his right side to aid digestion. As he matures, the sphincter will become stronger and spitting up will not be a problem.

If your baby frequently **vomits forcefully** either during or right after a feeding, you need to inform your doctor.

Colic is characterized by abdominal cramps or spasms, often with some swelling or hardness of the abdomen. Your baby's knees may draw up as he cries in pain and he may pass gas. Colic occurs most often at the same time each day. Crying can often be soothed by walking or rocking the baby. Placing the baby over your knees with a warm towel under his tummy may help. You can easily warm a towel by placing it in the dryer. Fortunately, colic usually disappears by three months of age.

Trying to cope with a **crying** newborn can be a very frustrating experience for new parents. Crying is your baby's only way of expressing his needs. Many babies experience "fussy periods" which occur at the same time each day, usually late afternoon when you are rushing to make dinner. This time is so typical that in earlier days, mothers aptly named it "grandma's hour "—the time when grandma could help by rocking and cuddling. Don't let anyone convince you that "crying is good for the lungs." Lungs don't need "exercise." Try to approach this crying with as much comfort and calmness as possible since your baby can sense your tension and become more irritable.

Is he hungry? If he has not eaten for two hours or longer, he may need more food. If you are breastfeeding, he may be trying to build up your milk supply with more frequent feedings. Even if your baby has recently nursed, he may be soothed by additional nursing just for comfort. A pacifier can also be used if your baby enjoys it and needs more sucking. If you are bottle feeding, check the nipple to make sure the milk is dripping freely.

Is he uncomfortable? Check for a loose diaper pin, a soiled or wet diaper, or an irritating diaper condition (too tight, rash). Is he underdressed or overdressed? Is the room too hot or too cold? Sometimes clothing that is too tight or rough may make your baby fussy.

Is he lonely? For the previous nine months your newborn has been carried within your warm body while he listened to your heartbeat and other sounds. Once he is delivered, he is expected to be satisfied lying in a hard wooden crib. He may just need to be cuddled and held close to you. A front baby carrier is a tremendous help. Your baby will be happy being close to you and you will have your hands free to do other things.

Has he been overstimulated? Too much handling by visitors or long periods of wakefulness can cause exhaustion in your baby. Motion of any kind can help to calm him down—a stroll, car ride, baby swing or walking. If you are tense, having someone else hold him may do the trick (fathers are especially good). Laying a naked baby (leave a diaper on) on your breast or your husband's bare chest and lightly massaging the baby can help. You can also get into a warm bath with the baby. This accomplishes three things—quieting the baby plus getting two baths done! Have someone available to take the baby out of the tub, or carefully place him onto a towel on the floor while you get out.

Surprisingly, the sound of a vacuum cleaner may be just the trick to quiet your little one. Its constant hum seems to lull and relax some fussy babies.

Crying spells, especially with colic, can cause parents to become angry. Don't feel guilty about that. It will make it easier if you and your husband talk or even laugh about it. Remember that your baby isn't mad at you or doing it purposely.

Your newborn **sleeps** from 12 to 20 hours in a 24 hour day. The periods of sleep and wakefulness vary from baby to baby, depending upon his individual sleep cycles and eating patterns. Some babies seem to be awake all the time. Most newborn babies wake up when hungry and fall asleep after a satisfying meal. This rhythm usually continues throughout the entire day, except for that possible late afternoon fussy period. As the year progresses, the need for sleep lessens. At nine months, most babies need only a morning and afternoon nap. By one year to 15 months, only one nap is usually taken. But remember, each baby is an individual and establishes his own routine.

Some babies may not be lulled to sleep by sucking and have a little trouble falling asleep. He may fuss or cry for a few minutes. Try rocking or singing a lullaby to him. You will find that a good **comfortable rocking chair is a necessity.** Do not give your baby any medication to help him sleep. Such drugs are not good for him and may be dangerous.

Most babies are very versatile and will sleep almost anywhere. It does not make any difference to him where he sleeps. Some babies sleep in cribs, others in bassinets, carriages or their parents' bed. It is a matter of personal preference and what works best for your family. Some people feel that allowing your baby to sleep in bed with you or with a sibling when he is older contributes to making the child feel secure. Many adults do not like sleeping alone and can understand why a baby feels more comforted and sleeps better when in his parents' bed. He will not become perverted by sleeping with you. In many cultures, the entire family sleeps together. It is only our *progressive* society which often frowns on this custom. You should do what is comfortable for you! As he becomes older, he may prefer sleeping in his *own* bed and may just return to your bed when he is sick or frightened. A darkened, shadowy room can be quite scary to a young child with an active imagination.

You may wonder if you are **spoiling** your new baby by giving him plenty of attention. Current authorities feel it is impossible to spoil an infant. He needs lots of love, warmth, tenderness, attention and holding. This is very important for your baby's security and development. If you compare a human baby to other mammals, humans are born more immature and remain so for a much longer period of time. Most other mammals are able to walk very soon after birth. Ashley Montagu, a noted anthropologist, states that a human baby's gestational period is only partly completed when he is born, the other part being completed outside the womb. This is necessary because of the rapid brain development that occurs in human infants. If the baby were not born until later, he would not be able to fit through his mother's pelvis. Therefore, as he was carried within your body for nine months, he needs to be carried and held until he is able to become mobile on his own, which is at least another nine months, according to Montagu.[5]

Your young baby is completely ego-centered. He wants to have his needs met immediately and if they are not, he will let you know! He really doesn't *plan* to fuss or cry as soon as you sit down to dinner or at any other inopportune time.

The needs of your infant include both physical (food, warmth) and emotional factors (comfort, love). Babies who receive only physical care are slower in emotional and physical development than babies who are given plenty of attention and love. Don't listen to people who tell you that you are spoiling your baby by lots of holding and cuddling. If he stops crying when you pick him up, it is because he is happy to see you and needs to be held. Your baby will be tiny for such a short time—enjoy him and give him plenty of LOVE. As he matures, he will

cry less frequently and become less demanding knowing that comfort is coming.

Bathing your baby is one task that does not need to be done every single day. After all, a new baby isn't out playing in the dirt! The one area that you need to be concerned about is the diaper area. Make sure that you thoroughly clean his bottom with soap and water after each bowel movement to prevent diaper rash. Plain water is sufficient for just a wet diaper. Dry the area well, especially in the creases. Taking the baby into the tub with you can be fun. Or you can use one of the many commercial tubs that have a special hammock so you have both hands free. If you wish, you can even use a large sink, being careful to wrap a cloth around the faucet for protection. By cradling the baby in the crook of your arm and holding onto his arm with your hand, you will have a free hand to wash with. Make sure you have all your supplies before you start. **Never leave an infant alone in the bath, even for a second.**

WHEN TO CALL THE DOCTOR

Never hesitate to call your pediatrician about your baby if "something is not right." A mother's intuition is often correct in evaluating her child. Your physician can often calm your fears or suggest appropriate treatment. Below are some common indications for calling your doctor.

A **fever** is a symptom of an illness, not a disease in itself. It can be caused by an infection, virus, reaction to immunization or teething (doctors refute this but mothers don't). Suspect a fever if your baby feels hot, has dry skin, a flushed face and seems listless. His temperature should be taken rectally (lubricate with petroleum jelly) or axillary (under the armpit). When reporting to the doctor, tell him how you took the temperature as the reading varies with the method. For example: if the temperature is 100° orally, when taken rectally it will read 101° and axillary 99°.

Report immediately any temperature over 100.5° rectally in an infant under a month of age or over 105° rectally in any age child. If the fever is above 103.8° rectally, give a non-aspirin fever reducer according to your doctor's orders and a 15-minute tepid (lukewarm) water bath. Dress your child lightly. Do not bundle him up, as this will retain heat.

No medication is necessary for mild fevers because it is felt that moderate temperature elevation stimulates the body's protective immune defenses. Aspirin is not recommended for fever reduction because of its link to the sometimes fatal disease known as Reyes Syndrome. Alert your doctor if the fever does not go down within 24 hours or if your child shows other symptoms.

Repeated or frequent vomiting following a feeding should be reported. **Diarrhea** (loose, watery, foul smelling bowel movements that are green in color) or bowel movements that contain mucus or blood are also abnormal. Vomiting and/or diarrhea are of concern as they can cause dehydration, often very rapidly in a tiny baby. The **signs of dehydration** are loss of tears or saliva (dry mouth), sunken eyes, a decrease or absence of urine, and lethargy. Dehydration is a medical emergency and needs to be treated immediately.

Coughing and a stuffy or runny nose are signs of a cold. A cool mist vaporizer eases breathing. If your baby's nose is congested, your physician may recommend using normal saline nosedrops (dissolve ¼ teaspoon of salt in 8 ounces of water). Place two drops in each nostril, wait a minute, then suction with a bulb syringe (compress bulb *before* insertion). Do this before meals and at bedtime to aid in feeding and sleeping. If your baby has a fever and is also pulling on his ears or is irritable, he may have an **ear infection** which requires medication. **Severe hoarseness, difficulty in breathing or a "barking cough"** also need to be reported.

Alert your doctor if your baby has a **change in his temperment or habits:** excessive crying, unusual irritability, extreme drowsiness, unusually poor sleep, restlessness or severe loss of appetite.

Inflammation or a discharge from the eye may need medical attention. **Body rashes** that are not cured by methods explained on page 156 may indicate a communicable disease or allergic reaction.

Any **twitching, convulsions, or rigidity** should be reported at once. Also, if your child appears to be in **pain**, he may require medical attention.

If your child receives a **head injury,** observe him for a change in mental alertness, extreme sleepiness with difficulty in waking, vomiting, a discharge from the ears or nose, unequal pupils or a skull deformity. Elevate his head and alert your doctor if any of these signs are apparent. When **a limb is injured**, observe and report any deformity, redness and swelling, extreme tenderness or an inability to use the affected limb. An open wound may require suturing. For cosmetic reasons, some parents prefer a plastic surgeon to repair a facial cut.

In case your child **swallows any nonfood substance**, immediately call your doctor or poison control center for instructions.

Immunizations

This important part of your baby's health care protects him from potentially harmful diseases. Some babies have reactions to the vaccines. Symptoms include pain and redness at the injection site, fever and irritability. A rash may appear 6–12 days after the measles vaccine is given. To reduce fever or pain, give your child a non-aspirin medication (acetaminophen) as ordered by your doctor. Be sure to call him if your child has a severe reaction.

A recommended schedule for immunizations is given below.

IMMUNIZATION SCHEDULE

Age	Disease
2 Months	Diphtheria, Pertussis (whooping cough), Tetanus (DPT) injection; oral Polio vaccine
4 Months	DPT and Polio
6 Months	DPT and Polio
15 Months	Measles, Mumps, and Rubella Injection
18 Months	DPT and Polio (may be given at 15 months with MMR)
24 Months	Haemophilus influenzae type B (Hib)
5 Years	DPT and Polio booster
15 Years	DT booster

FIRST AID

Some conditions should be considered emergencies and need to be treated immediately. Below are instructions for handling these life-threatening situations. Read and become familiar with the following procedures so that they will not be confusing to you if you ever need to use them. **All parents should take a course in Infant CPR** (cardiopulmonary resuscitation) to receive firsthand practice on a manikin under the guidance of a certified instructor. It is also important that baby sitters, grandparents and other care givers are trained, as accidents can happen at any time!

Never practice CPR on anyone.

Choking

If an infant or small child is choking and the airway is obstructed, you will need to take action to **dislodge the obstruction.** Signs of obstruction are blue lips, hoarse or crowing breathing, or a child who cannot speak or cough. (If he *is* able to speak or cough, allow him to expel the object on his own. Unnecessary intervention may cause further problems.) **Call for help** if you can. However, if you are alone, do not take the time to use the phone. You are the lifesaver at this time.

Do *not* use blind finger sweeps in the mouth, because this could cause further obstruction. In an unconscious infant or child, look carefully in the mouth for the obstruction. If you can actually *see* it, remove it. If not, take the following steps:

In the case of an **infant**:

1. Straddle the child over your arm, with his head lower than his chest. Support his head with your hand.

2. Give **4 sharp back blows** between the shoulder blades with the heel of one hand. See photo.

3. Turn the child onto his back and give **4 chest thrusts** over the breastbone at the nipple line with two fingers of one hand. (This is done exactly the same as infant CPR. See Photo 5.)

Abdominal thrusts, such as the Heimlich maneuver, should not be performed on an infant under one year of age because of the risk of injury to the abdominal organs.

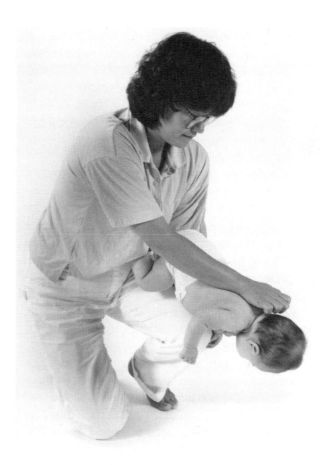

Back blows for infant.

In the case of a **small child over age one**:

1. Place the child on his back, and kneel next to him.

2. With the heel of one hand deliver **6 to 10 thrusts to his abdomen** midway between the navel and the rib cage. These should be rapid inward and upward thrusts. See photo.

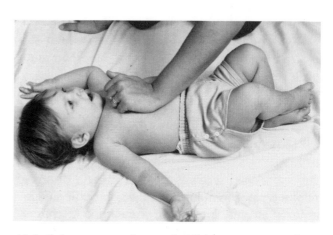

Heimlich maneuver for small child over one year of age.

Heimlich maneuver for larger child or adult.

Larger children can be treated the same as adults, using the Heimlich maneuver.

1. Stand behind the choking person and encircle his waist (between the navel and rib cage) with your arms.

2. Grasp one fist with the other and make 4 quick upward thrusts. See photo.

3. Repeat as necessary to expel the object.

If the victim is not breathing, attempt to **deliver four breaths**. If unsuccessful, **repeat the back blows and chest thrusts (or abdominal thrusts) and breaths** until relief comes. Check for breathing and for pulse after relief arrives. (See next section on CPR.)

It is best to prevent choking by taking precautions beforehand. Although most people realize the danger of such objects as buttons, coins and small toys, many parents are not aware that some *foods* also pose hazards. According to surveys at Johns Hopkins University, the following foods are the most frequent cause of fatal choking in childen under five:

- hot dogs/sausages
- round candy
- peanuts or other nuts
- grapes
- hard cookies, biscuits
- meat chunks or sticks
- raw carrot slices or sticks
- peanut butter (including sandwiches)
- apple pieces
- popcorn[6]

Never leave a baby alone while eating, and make sure that small children are adequately supervised at mealtime. Many choking incidents take place when a child is running or playing with food in his mouth, or talking and laughing while eating.

Artificial Respiration and Heart Resuscitation (CPR) for an Infant or Small Child (Up to One Year)

If a baby or child stops breathing, he is not receiving the oxygen needed to maintain life. If breathing stops, the heart may also soon stop. (Other causes of cardiac arrest include electric shock, drowning and sudden infant death syndrome.) You must act immediately to breathe for him, possibly pumping his heart.

Have someone call for a rescue unit. If you are alone, perform CPR for at least one minute before quickly calling the emergency squad.

Remember A–B–C

Directions:

Airway—Follow instructions for choking. If the airway is unobstructed, place the baby flat on his back. Tilt his head back, placing two fingers of one hand under his neck and the other hand on his forehead. (*Do not* exaggerate tilt, as it may close the airway completely.) (See Photo 1.)

Breathing—Put your ear over your baby's mouth (looking toward his chest) to look, listen and feel for breathing. (See Photo 2.) If all signs of breathing are absent, give 4 quick breaths by placing your mouth over both your baby's mouth and

INFANT CPR

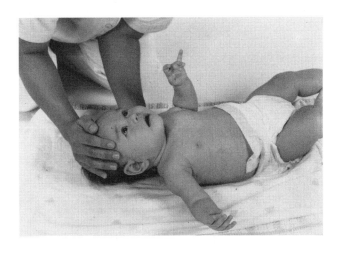

1.   *Tilt head back.*

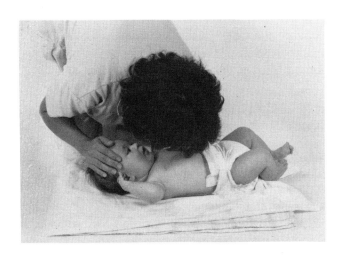

2.   *Look, listen, and feel for breathing.*

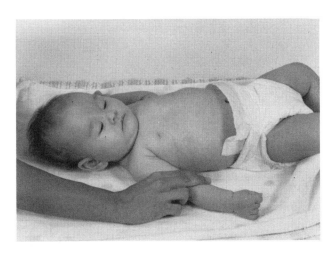

3.   *Feel for pulse.*

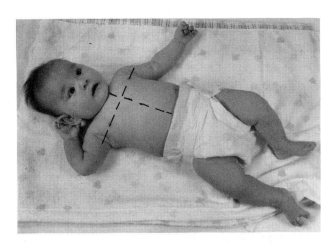

4.   *Place fingers at center of cross.*

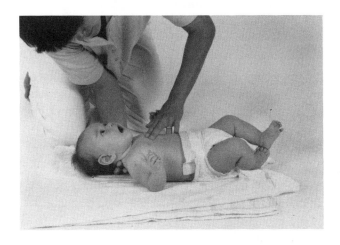

5.   *Perform chest compressions.*

nose and blowing in enough air to cause your baby's chest to rise. **DO NOT BLOW HARD.** Use only small puffs of air. (Blowing too hard may injure the baby's lungs; blowing too softly will not give the baby enough oxygen.)

Next, check to see if your baby's heart is beating by placing the tips of your index and middle fingers at the bend of his elbow and pressing down slightly towards the bone until the pulse is felt. (See Photo 3.) If a pulse is felt but your baby is not breathing, continue breathing 1 breath every 3 seconds, or 20 times a minute. If no pulse is felt, proceed with C.

Cardiac—Place two or three fingers on the middle of the breastbone directly in line with the nipples. (See Photo 4.) Compress area toward backbone only about ½ to 1 inch. Use the other hand to support the back and maintain head position. (See Photo 5.) Compress at a rate of 100 per minute. After every 5 compressions, puff into nose and mouth as your fingertips rise. Try to make the breaths and compressions continuous. After one minute, stop and recheck pulse and look for spontaneous breathing. If no pulse or breathing is found, continue CPR until help arrives.

BABYPROOFING YOUR HOUSE

Before your baby begins to creep or crawl, you should babyproof your house. It is easy to put this off, but if you do, you may find that your baby is rapidly learning to move around, getting into EVERYTHING! The best time to make your home safe for your baby is during your last trimester of pregnancy.

Below is a list of things to do now which will make your home safer. When you take your child to someone else's house, be sure to check for the same hazards.

As you move dangerous items out of the way, replace them with safe, interesting things your baby can play with. A stimulating environment contributes to the development of creativity in your child.

All Over the House

- Protect against electric shock by arranging furniture to cover outlets wherever possible.

- Buy small plastic covers to insert in unused outlets and large box-like covers for those in use.

- Try to hide cords, as babies may chew on them.

- Put tape over unused telephone outlets.

- Turn the water heater thermostat down to 130° to avoid the danger of scalding water.

- Buy safety door knob covers or install locks very high on doors leading to unsafe rooms or outdoors (sewing room, bathroom, garage).

- Many indoor house plants are quite poisonous and should be hung out of reach, put outside or into loving "foster care" until your child is older.

- Have a special utensil set for measuring and applying fertilizer; don't use household utensils.

- Mark sliding glass doors with decals and don't allow playing with heavy toys in that area.

- Keep emergency numbers near or taped to the phone (poison control, rescue, fire, police and pediatrician).

- Put a folding gate at the top and bottom of staircases to prevent climbing and falling.

- Unload and lock up all guns. Never keep guns in a bedroom drawer or purse, or let a small child see you using one.

- Keep ashtrays, pipes, cigarettes, matches and lighters out of reach. A cigarette eaten by a small child may be fatal.

- When visitors or overnight guests are present, be sure their purses and/or suitcases are locked or out of reach of curious hands.

- If your home is over 25 years old or you have second-hand painted baby furniture, the paints used may contain lead. Strip and repaint the furniture and any surface on which your baby might possibly chew.

- Look for the Juvenile Products Manufacturers Association (JPMA) Safety Certification Seal when purchasing baby furniture to insure that the product has met basic safety standards and passed rigorous tests.

- Do not leave your baby in a dropside playpen with the side lowered. He may roll into the space between the pad and the loose mesh side and suffocate. It is best to purchase a playpen with a firm lower edge which prevents entrapment of infants.

- For a free pamphlet on baby furniture safety, write to:

> Consumer Product Safety Commission
> Office of Information and Public Affairs
> Washington, D.C. 20207

Take a **CRAWLING TOUR** of your home to get a baby's eye view. Remove anything that looks potentially enticing and dangerous. A room-by-room checklist follows.

Kitchen

- Put all household cleaners, detergents, bleaches and spray cans out of reach.
- Install safety latches on all cupboards that you don't want little hands to open.
- Put vitamins, waste baskets, glassware, plastic bags and knives in these locked cupboards.
- Put some safe kitchen items (plastic bowls, pots and pans, wooden spoons) in a low cabinet away from the stove for baby to play with.
- Use a gate across the doorway to keep your baby out when you're not there.
- When not using your stove, remove any knobs from the front panel.
- When cooking, turn all pot and pan handles toward the back of the stove.
- Teach your child early what "hot" means.
- Don't drink or pass hot beverages while your child is nearby or on your lap.
- Move pet dishes from the floor when not in use.

Bathroom

- Lock up your medicine cabinet or move all poisonous items out of reach.
- Move the waste basket out of reach.
- Get in the habit of putting your razor up after each use.
- Never leave your baby or small child alone in the tub.
- Avoid taking medication, including vitamins, in front of your child.

- Buy a bottle of syrup of Ipecac at the drug store to induce vomiting in case your child swallows something poisonous. Use it only on instruction from your doctor or poison control center.
- Move perfume, sprays, cosmetics and jewelry out of reach.

Baby's Room

- Buy a crib that has slats 2⅜ inches apart or less.
- Be sure the mattress fits snugly in the crib, with no gaps.
- The lowered crib rail should be 9 inches above the mattress support when the support is placed in its highest position.
- The raised crib rail should be 26 inches above the mattress support when the support is placed in its lowest position. (Cribs manufactured after 1974 meet all these requirements. If you buy a used crib, check for these important features.)
- Place the mattress at its highest position for your newborn; lower it as he grows older. (Once he reaches 35 inches in height or can crawl out of the crib, it is time to move him to a regular bed.)
- For warmth, place the crib along an inside wall, but away from a heater, air vent, or drapery and venetian blind cords.
- Never drape clothes or blankets over the side of the crib, as they could fall or be pulled over the baby's head.
- Never leave your baby alone on the changing table or any high surface.
- Keep pins, cotton balls, oil and powder out of baby's reach and away from other young children as they may try to powder the baby.
- Powder, if used, should be sprinkled into your hand and then rubbed over your baby's body to avoid inhalation of the powder by the baby.

Playroom and Toys

- Toys of your older children that have small parts or sharp points should be kept on a high shelf. Explain to them why these toys are dangerous for the baby.

- Make sure the eyes, nose, and mouth of stuffed toys and dolls cannot be removed. Embroidered features are safest; sewn or glued parts can be pulled off.

Garage or Workroom

- Keep it locked!
- Put all pesticides, paints, and petroleum products (motor oil, gasoline, kerosene) on a high shelf or locked cabinet. Do not store them in any container that could be confused with something else (soft drink bottles, food containers, etc.).
- Keep dangerous tools out of reach.
- Put small items, such as nails, screws and bolts, in closed containers.

Outside

- Remove any poisonous plants from your yard. They include oleander, poinsettia, daffodils, caladium, elephant's ear, dieffenbachia, hyacinth and narcissus bulbs, holly and mistletoe berries, jerusalem cherries, azaleas, daisies, ligustrum, tulips, and rhododendron. The poison control center can identify other poisonous plants for you.
- A backyard pool should be fenced off from the house and have proper lifesaving equipment on hand.
- Take a CPR class with special emphasis on child resuscitation.

AUTOMOBILE SAFETY

Buy an approved car seat that is labeled "dynamically tested," and begin using it the day you bring your baby home from the hospital. Continue using the car seat for your child until he is four years old or weighs over 40 lbs. and can use the adult seat belt. The adult shoulder harness should not be used until he is 4 feet in height.

Automobile accidents are the leading cause of death to young children, ahead of all other types of accidents and all diseases. In addition, injuries from auto accidents are a major cause of epilepsy and paraplegia in children.

In a crash, swerve or sudden stop, your baby could be thrown into the dashboard, windshield or another passenger. Or, he could easily be thrown out of the car. Although your arms are usually the best

Dynamically tested carseat.

place for your baby, *this is not true when riding in a car.* Tests have shown that volunteers holding 17 lb. baby-sized dummies were not able to hold on to the "babies" in impacts at 15 m.p.h. and 30 m.p.h., even though they were prepared for the crash. Even a tiny 10 lb. infant would be thrown forward with a force of 300 lbs. in a 30 m.p.h. impact. That is like falling from a three-story building. Putting him in the seat belt with you is not safe because he would be crushed by the force of your body.

Infants should be placed in a semi-reclined, backward facing restraint which is anchored to the vehicle seat by a lap belt according to manufacturer's directions. When your baby is big enough to sit up without help, you can safely move him to a forward-facing seat, which is anchored securely. Certain models have a raised seat that allows your child to see out the window. This may be more acceptable to him as he grows older.

Remember, no car seat will protect your child from injury unless he is properly secured in it. Take the time to strap him in, even for short trips. Most accidents happen within 25 miles of home.

Never leave your child (or pets) in a car for any amount of time. A car heats up rapidly even with the windows down. There is danger of overheating, accidents and the possibility of your child wandering off.

BABY EQUIPMENT

When you begin looking for baby equipment, you may notice that the advertising appeals to your most tender and protective feelings. It can even attempt to arouse guilt and anxiety in you if you choose not to buy the product. You may be tempted to buy everything you see, especially if this is your first child. Resist buying too much too soon!

The needs of a newborn baby are very simple. In the early weeks, he requires only a car seat, a few nightgowns, diapers and a place to sleep. Other items can be added gradually.

He will quickly outgrow newborn size garments. By four to six weeks he may wear three to six month sizes. If friends ask what you need for the baby, encourage them to buy 12 month or larger size clothing. Otherwise, before you know it, you will have a dresser full of "little" clothes that don't fit and nothing for your baby to wear.

Be sure that all garments you buy or receive are soft to the touch and easy to put on. Babies dislike having their heads covered for more than a second. Also, choose clothing that allows room for growth (extra long hems, straps, etc.).

By spreading out your purchases over an extended period of time, you won't be overwhelmed by the cost. Friends or relatives who no longer need certain items may loan or sell them to you at a fraction of their original cost. Garage sales are another good source of "nice-as-new" furniture, clothing and toys. Babies do not wear out things like older children do. If you purchase a used crib, car seat or other furniture, be sure to check for the safety features mentioned in the Safety Checklist.

Front pack carriers offer good transportation plus a warm place to sleep during your baby's first months of life. As he reaches two to three months of age, you may prefer a stroller for shopping trips or longer excursions. An umbrella type stroller can be used sooner than a straight-backed model as it molds to the shape of the baby's body. The other type requires that the baby be able to hold his head and back erect in the sitting position. Umbrella strollers are also less expensive and can be stored in a small space.

Front pack carrier.

You won't need a high chair until your baby is about six months old. His back and neck will not be strong enough to keep him sitting upright until then.

Listed below are those items which most parents feel are necessary to meet their infant's basic needs.

Sleeping

- A sturdy crib with a firm mattress can be used for at least two years.

- Crib bumper pads protect your baby's head, arms and legs as he begins moving about in his sleep.

- A bassinet provides the small, confined space which most newborns prefer in the first weeks of life, but it is an expensive purchase considering the short time it is used. Achieve the same result by laying your baby crosswise at one end of the crib with a rolled up blanket next to him; or better yet, keep him in bed with you.

- Two crib sheets, one to use and one to wash. Fitted sheets are the easiest to keep on and knitted cotton is the softest.

- 1–2 mattress pads to protect against wetness and absorb perspiration.
- 4–5 receiving blankets to cover baby when sleeping or when going outside on a cool day.
- 1–2 warm blankets

Traveling

- A dynamically tested infant car seat is essential the day you bring the baby home from the hospital. (Your community may have a car seat rental program which loans seats for a minimal fee.)
- Front pack carrier.
- Stroller.

Diapering

- Most new mothers appreciate the gift of 1–2 months' diaper service. Continued use is expensive.
- Disposable diapers are convenient but expensive and are not good for the ecology.
- 3-4 dozen cloth diapers and 4–6 diaper pins. The initial cost may seem high, but the money saved by not buying disposables more than offsets the cost of fuel, hot water and soap needed for using your own washing machine. Gauze and birdseye are the two fabric types available; gauze is more absorbent but also more expensive. Flat diapers are less expensive and dry more quickly, but pre-folded ones are more absorbent and save time.
- Choose a diaper pail that will hold 2–3 days' worth of diapers and water, but not so large that you can't carry it.
- Diaper liners can be used to make clean-up after a bowel movement easier, but also add to your weekly expenses.

Clothing

- 3–6 cotton nightgowns that open and tie at the bottom make diaper changing easier.
- 2–3 one-piece stretch sleepers (6 month size) are great for day and night wear as your baby grows and becomes more active.
- 3–6 waterproof pants if you use cloth diapers. Choose plastic coated fabric pants that snap together at the sides to allow air circulation and lessen the risk of skin irritation.
- Depending on the time of year that your baby is born, you may also want to buy several short sleeve snap-front shirts, a sweater and cap, or a snowsuit.

"I'm sorry, dear, you and the baby will have to take the bus!"

Bathing

- A special baby bathtub can be purchased, but the kitchen sink, lined with a towel, works just as well.
- 3–4 soft washcloths for bathing and wiping little "bottoms."
- Mild bar soap or liquid baby soap for cleaning tender skin.
- Baby bath towels are available but not necessary; those that you already have will work fine.

Optional Items

- A wind-up baby swing to provide movement and diversion when your hands are busy; be sure it is well balanced to prevent tipping.
- A back-pack carrier for shopping trips and excursions with an older baby.
- A playpen to protect the baby from activities of older children, but never to "cage" your baby. If you have baby-proofed your house, you will have little need for one!

PLAYING WITH YOUR BABY

Positive interaction with your baby is a crucial factor in promoting his mental and emotional development. Visual, vocal and tactile stimulation are all valuable aids to his learning. Set aside some time each day simply to play with him; a time when he is wide awake, happy and well fed. Bath time provides a good opportunity for playful interaction. Following are some suggested activities for playing with your baby.

Baby Exercises

Young babies are often quite tense with flexed arms and legs and clenched fists. The first exercises, therefore, should be those which promote relaxation. He will often relax to your gentle touch. These exercises may help him to sleep better and cry less. They are done with your baby on his back.

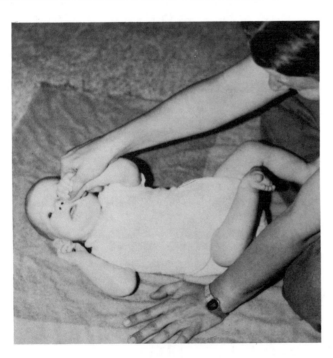

Arm stroking.

Arm Stroking—Take each arm, one at a time, and stroke it very gently, starting at the shoulder and moving toward the hand. Then move the arm gently up and down. As the hand relaxes bring it up to his face and then to yours.

The Hug—After relaxing both arms through stroking, gently draw his hands toward the opposite shoulders. Don't pull on the arms, but wait for them to relax to your touch.

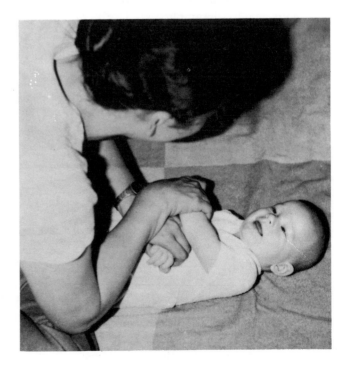

The hug.

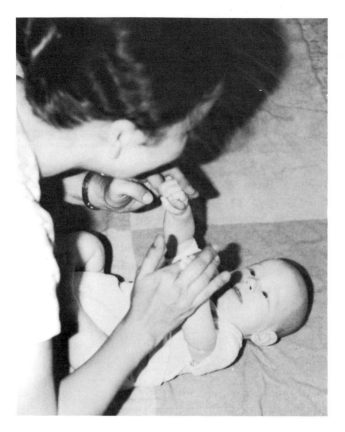

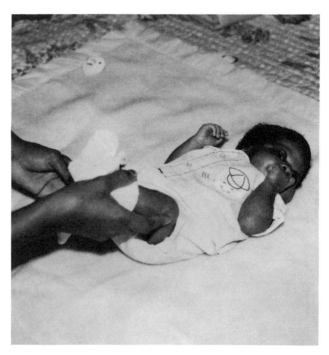

The Bicycle.

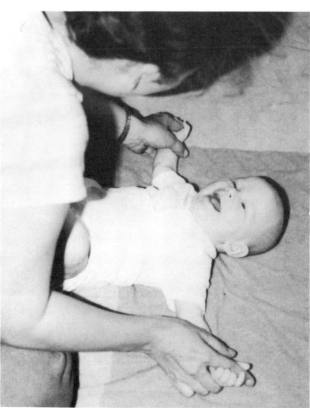

The Cross (top and bottom photographs).

The Bicycle—While holding one of your baby's lower legs in each hand, gently bring one knee up toward his chest, and then alternate with the other knee. Continue this movement as if he were riding a bicycle. This encourages relaxation in his legs.

For a more extensive exercise program, refer to *The Baby Exercise Book* by Janine Lévy.

The Cross—Let your baby grasp your thumbs or hold him by his wrists. Gently stretch his arms forward and then lower them sideways in the form of a cross. This extends and relaxes his arms.

Massage

Massaging your baby's bare skin while talking or singing to him is another way to play with him and encourage relaxation. Wait until he is about one month old before trying this. When massaging him, use vegetable or baby oil on his skin. Your touch should be firm, but gentle, and one hand should always be in contact with the baby. You can use your fingers or the palm of your hand to stroke; your fingertips to tap or pat; and your flat hands to wring (*very* gently!) the legs and arms.

Songs and Nursery Rhymes

Many nursery rhymes have words and motions which help your baby gain an awareness of his body and of language. The following are some suggested nursery rhymes which you can do with your baby beginning around two months of age.

Songs and Nursery Rhymes	Physical Action
Pat–a–cake, Pat–a–cake, Baker's man; Bake me a cake as fast as you can.	(Clap hands)
Pat it, and roll it, and mark it with B, And put it in the oven for baby and me.	(Make rolling motions with hands)
This little piggy went to market;	(Grasp big toe)
This little piggy stayed home;	(Grasp next toe)
This little piggy had roast beef,	(Grasp next toe)
This little piggy had none;	(Grasp next toe)
And this little piggy cried,	(Grasp smallest toe)
"Wee, wee, wee, wee," all the way home.	(Run fingers up leg and tickle baby)
Mousie, mousie, mousie,	(Tap fingers on child's hand)
Up to (child's name)'s housie.	(Run fingers lightly up child's arm or body to his head)
Shoe a little horse,	
Shoe a little mare,	(Pat the soles of the baby's feet)
But let the little colt go bare, bare, bare.	
Brow bender,	(Touch baby's forehead)
Eye peeper	(Touch baby's eyes lightly)
Nose dropper,	(Touch baby's nose)
Mouth eater,	(Touch baby's mouth)
Chin chopper,	(Touch baby's chin)
Knock at the door,	(Tap baby's forehead with knuckles)
Ring the bell,	(Pull baby's ear or hair gently)
Lift up the latch,	(Raise nose slightly)
Walk in,	(Put finger in mouth)
Take a chair,	
Sit by there,	
How do you do this morning?	(Hopefully, the baby is laughing by now!)
Itsy, bitsy spider went up the water spout,	(Walk fingers up baby's arm)
Down came the rain and washed the spider out,	(Move fingers like falling rain)
Out came the sun and dried up all the rain,	(Hold hands together like a sun over baby's head)
And itsy, bitsy spider climbed up the spout again.	(Walk fingers up arm again)

Bath Play

During bath time, you can help your baby learn the names of his various body parts by saying them as you wash each part. You can sing songs such as "Here We Go 'Round the Mulberry Bush," in which you substitute verses like, "This is the way we wash your face, wash your face," etc.

Toys

Your child's toys should be selected according to his age and abilities. Toys which are too advanced for him will not only prove frustrating, but may even be dangerous. For a child under one year of age, toys should be large, simple, brightly colored, light in weight, and have no small removable parts. Household items such as plastic bowls, wooden spoons and pots and pans are fascinating. Other possible choices include squeak toys with noise-makers molded in; sturdy, non-flammable rattles; washable dolls and stuffed animals with embroidered features; and cups, teethers or other smooth items that can be chewed.

The following are additional suggestions for toys you may want to purchase:

Under Two Months:

A mobile—find one that looks interesting from *underneath,* where he will be.
Pictures or decals in his room.

Two to Four Months:

Stainless steel mirror (place it about six inches from the baby's eyes.)
Cradle gym

Six to Eight Months:

Balls
A box with simple objects to put in and take out.
Stacking and nesting toys

Eight to Twelve Months:

Busy bath and other bath toys for pouring or floating.
Collection box of interesting objects too large to be swallowed.

Remember, your baby doesn't need elaborate toys at this age. Although toys can be useful in helping him learn about his world, none compares in interest to him with your face and voice. The time you spend playing with him is most beneficial. Do not let yourself be swayed by appealing advertising claims for expensive or complicated toys for your baby.

FOOTNOTES

Chapter 10

1. Marshall Klaus and John Kennell, *Maternal-Infant Bonding* (St. Louis, C. V. Mosby Co., 1976), p. 12.
2. David Grimes, "Routine Circumcision Reconsidered," *American Journal of Nursing* (January, 1980), p. 108.
3. Sara Katz, "Circumscision," *ICEA Sharing,* Vol. V, No. 1 (Spring, 1977), p. 5.
4. Edward Wallerstein, "The Circumcision Decision," Pennypress, Seattle, Wash., 1980, p. 4.
5. Ashley Montagu, *Touching, The Human Significance of the Skin*, 2nd Ed. (N.Y., Harper and Row, 1978), pp. 39–41.
6. "The Better Way," *Good Housekeeping* (March, 1985), p. 229.

Chapter 11

Infant Feeding
or "Keeping Abreast"

Both breast and bottle feeding can produce babies which are physically and emotionally healthy, but there are differences. Breastfeeding is recognized as nutritionally superior by the American Academy of Pediatrics.[1] The following section discusses the many advantages of breastfeeding and provides factual information on milk production and nursing techniques. Possible problems and their solutions are also covered.

The section on bottle feeding is included to offer helpful hints and suggestions for those who choose that method of feeding.

BREASTFEEDING

Nursing your baby is a natural continuation of the birth process as it completes the maternity cycle. Just as you nourished him prior to birth from the nutrients within your body, you continue to supply your baby with the food perfectly suited to his needs—breastmilk.

Breastfeeding fosters a special relationship, one in which a close physical and emotional bond develops between you and your baby. It is unique in that your baby is totally dependent on you for his nourishment. This giving of yourself is an expression of your love for him, and it can result in many enjoyable and rewarding hours for both of you. Some of your fondest memories will be of the time spent nursing your baby.

Your success in breastfeeding depends greatly on your desire to nurse, as well as the encouragement you receive from those around you. Because of the importance of your husband's support, the decision to breastfeed should be a mutual one. His

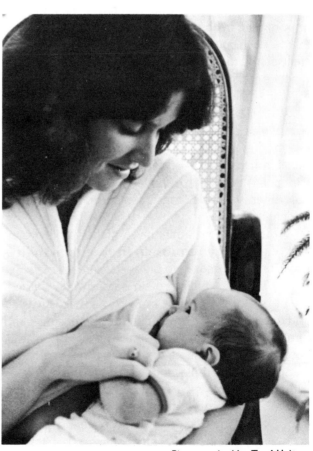

Photographed by Terri Helton

knowledge and understanding can provide you with a source of strength on those "trying" days when you may be tempted to give up. In addition, support from your doctor, relatives and friends is most helpful. Knowing a mother who has had a successful breastfeeding experience or who is a member of La Leche League can be extremely beneficial when questions arise.

Several other important factors can aid in promoting successful breastfeeding. Having knowledge of the production and supply of your milk helps to prevent most problems. Advance preparation of your nipples, while you are pregnant, will decrease soreness which can be discouraging in the early days of nursing. Also, good personal care is a key element in successful nursing—nutritious food and adequate rest are mandatory.

WHY BREASTFEED?

The Optimum Nutrition

Many advantages of breastfeeding, both for you and your baby, have been documented. First, and most importantly, **breastmilk is the ideal food** for your infant. Each species of mammal produces milk especially suited to the needs of its young. Human milk is biochemically suited to brain development, while animal milk promotes muscular development. Cow's milk was meant for baby cows. Formula companies often claim that their product is "most like mother's milk," but none can equal it. Components in breastmilk—enzymes, hormones and even vitamins—have been discovered over the years, and still other valuable constituents probably remain undetected.

Although cow's milk has a higher protein content, the **quality of protein in mother's milk** is superior and is geared to the specific needs of the infant. While breastmilk protein is completely utilized, about half of the protein from cow's milk is wasted and excreted. The **amount of fat** in breastmilk and formula is similar, but breastmilk fat is more readily absorbed. To imitate mother's milk, formula companies have replaced the butterfat of cow's milk with mono and polyunsaturated vegetable oils. However, this substitution also eliminates cholesterol, which investigators are discovering may be necessary for several vital functions. It aids in the ab-

sorption of nutrients and the development of the covering which surrounds and protects your infant's nerves.

Although the **iron content** of human milk is low, it is in a form which is absorbed much more readily than that added to formula or given as a supplement.

For many years authorities stated that breastmilk contained no **vitamin D.** Only recently, that vitamin was discovered to be present—not in the milk fat, where expected, but in the watery fraction, and in the exact amount normally recommended as a supplement.

Additionally, during your baby's first weeks of life, your milk undergoes changes so that the milk he receives is particularly suited to his individual needs. It begins as **colostrum,** a sticky yellowish fluid which contains immunity factors and has a high protein content. It also helps to get rid of mucus at birth and cleanses his intestinal tract. It gradually changes to a thin, white or bluish-white liquid, which contains the exact combination of water, fat, protein, sugar, minerals and vitamins needed by your baby's system.

Breastmilk is raw and fresh. Formula is processed and must be stored and then reheated before use, all of which destroy important nutrients. Breastmilk is unprocessed and is used when its maximum nutritional value can be received by your baby.

Best for the Premature Baby

Breastmilk is particularly important for the premature infant's **sensitive digestive system.** These babies have temporary deficiencies of certain enzymes and frequently have malabsorption problems. Breastmilk is perfectly suited to meet these special needs. In fact, the benefits are so well recognized that milk banks have been established in some cities especially for supplying milk to premature babies.

Because of the premature baby's need to gain weight rapidly, his **caloric intake must be higher** than that of a term baby. Research has found that milk from mothers of premature babies is higher in protein, thereby meeting this higher caloric demand.

If you find that your premature baby is too weak to suck, it is extremely important to **hand express or pump your breasts** in order to provide your milk for him. This will take extra effort on your part, but it is well worth the benefits your baby receives.

Healthier Babies

Because breastmilk is available immediately, your baby's hunger can be eased without waiting for a bottle to be warmed. Breastmilk remains at body temperature, needs no sterilization and **contains antibodies** which help prevent infection. Breastfed babies get **fewer and milder colds** than bottlefed babies and even have **less eczema, ear infections, and diaper rash.** In addition, a breastfed baby is **less likely to be affected by allergies,** either as a baby or later in life. **No baby has ever been found to be allergic to his mother's milk!** (Occasionally a particular food which you have eaten may cause a digestive upset, but the elimination of that food will usually solve the problem.)

In case you have a family history of allergies, it is extremely important to breastfeed and to delay solid foods. Breastfeeding is the best way to prevent severe allergic illness in your children. Your baby should continue a diet of only breastmilk for at least six months. As he gets older, his susceptibility to developing allergic reactions will diminish.

One of the most common causes of allergies is cow's milk. Many babies are switched from formula to formula until one is found (usually a soybean based formula) that is agreeable. In the meantime both baby and parents have suffered!

On rare occasions, a baby is found to be so allergic that he cannot tolerate any formula. In this case, breastmilk is crucial to the infant's survival. If his mother is not nursing him, another source of human milk must be located until she can relactate and build up her own milk supply. This relactation is possible even if several weeks or months have passed since lactation was terminated (or since birth). Some women have even successfully nursed their adopted babies as it is the sucking stimulus which produces milk.

Better Digestion

Digestion is easier for the breastfed newborn because breastmilk fosters the growth of "friendly" bacteria in the intestines. Their presence results in **fewer bowel upsets** and **less diarrhea.** Breastmilk is utilized more completely than formula. Babies fed entirely on breastmilk **rarely get constipated,** whereas formula-fed babies occasionally are constipated, resulting in the passing of painfully hard bowel movements.

Better Teeth

Breastfeeding encourages **good facial development** in your baby. The muscles used in nursing are different from those used to suck on a rubber nipple. Nursing requires more effort and results in superior muscle and jaw development. Bottle feeding is considered to be a major cause of malocclusions and other facial and dental problems in children.[2]

Breastfeeding has also been associated with generally **healthier teeth.** In a study conducted at Oregon State University, children who were breastfed for three months or longer had from 45 to 59 percent fewer cavities than their bottlefed counterparts in the same communities.[3]

Benefits to the Skin

Breastfeeding encourages the close physical contact which is necessary for development. Your new baby needs plenty of love and cuddling and this is easily accomplished by nursing. It is impossible to "prop a breast" (as can be done with a bottle).

You will notice when you hold your baby how soft his skin is. This **softness** is enhanced by breastmilk. Some doctors even claim that they can tell the difference between bottlefed babies and breastfed babies by the feel of their skin.

Long Term Benefits

Evidence exists that other benefits of breastfeeding remain with the infant throughout his lifetime. A study done at the Northwestern University School of Medicine found that bottlefed children (whose ages ranged from birth to ten years of age) had four times as many ear infections, four times as many colds, eleven times as many tonsillectomies, twenty times as many diarrheal infections and from eight to twenty-seven times as many allergic reactions when compared to children of the same ages who had been fully breastfed for six months or longer.[4]

A British study showed that ulcerative colitis in adults is 100 percent more common in patients who were not breastfed past two weeks of age than those who were.[5]

Emergency Situations

During a major disaster, such as a hurricane or earthquake, where the electricity and water supply are often cut off, breastfeeding may be crucial to your baby's survival. In situations like these, nursing mothers can relax in the confidence that their babies will continue to receive the same plentiful and uncontaminated food supply.

Safer Than Formula

Formula may not always be safe. As recently as 1979 and 1980, problems were discovered with two soybean based formulas, Neo-mull-soy and Cho-free. They contained insufficient amounts of an essential nutrient, chloride. As a result, babies suffered metabolic acidosis and possibly retardation and other problems in later life.

In 1950, SMA, another formula, was found to be lacking in vitamin B_6. Children who had been fed this formula suffered convulsions and cerebral palsy because of the negligence.

Contamination is another danger associated with formulas. Enfamil with iron was recently found to be contaminated with bacteria to the extent that it was considered hazardous by the FDA, but it was not recalled! An undetermined number of infants became ill after consuming this formula.

The public has been led into a false sense of security regarding formulas. Millions of dollars have been spent promoting these products and trying to convince women that artificially feeding their babies is just as good as breastfeeding. Formula companies also promote the idea that even if you breastfeed, you will need to use their products "to supplement." No formula company benefits by extolling the advantages and superiority of mother's milk.

Benefits to You

Advantages also exist for you, the nursing mother. Breastfeeding is **cheaper** and **easier** in that there is nothing to purchase and nothing to measure, pour, heat or sterilize. Your baby's sucking is beneficial to you because it **stimulates your uterus to contract** and return to its prepregnant size sooner. In addition, since you burn more calories while nursing—40 calories per ounce of breastmilk (20 calories to produce it and 20 calories in each ounce)—it is easy for you to lose weight without dieting and **regain your shape sooner.** Your body may burn 1000 calories per day just in the production of milk. The extra fat that is deposited during pregnancy will be utilized during the early period of lactation.

Some evidence shows that breastfeeding decreases your chances of ever developing breast can-

cer, particularly if you continue nursing for an extended period. Studies have shown that the **risk of getting breast cancer drastically decreases** when a mother nurses for six months.[6]

Traveling is easier with a breastfed infant since no packing or warming of bottles is required. Nursing mothers have found that taking their baby along is easily accomplished by just grabbing an extra diaper or two. Outings are more relaxed since you don't have to rush home for feedings or worry if the formula is becoming sour without refrigeration. If you wear a blouse or sweater that pulls up from the waist, you'll be able to nurse discreetly almost anywhere.

The emotional advantages of breastfeeding include **more intimate contact** between you and your baby and the **feeling of satisfaction and sense of fulfillment** which you experience while nursing. The production of hormones during lactation is instrumental in your feelings. The hormone prolactin, which causes the secretion of milk, helps you to feel "motherly." It has been found to initiate mothering behavior when given to animals.[7] Prolactin also has a soothing and tranquilizing effect, and thus causes you to **feel calm and relaxed** each time your baby nurses.

Because you must sit or lie down to nurse, **you are assured of getting the necessary rest** you need postpartum.

The return of your **menstrual period is delayed** while you are nursing because the hormone

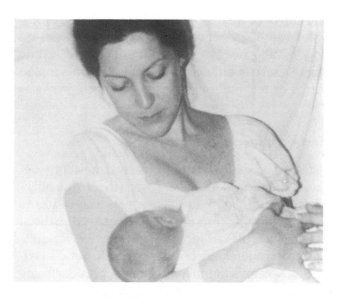

Nursing in recovery.

prolactin suppresses ovulation. Breastfeeding, therefore, is an aid to spacing children. However, another method of contraception should be used along with breastfeeding, because it is not 100 percent effective. The amount of breastfeeding necessary to suppress ovulation varies from woman to woman. It is possible that you could ovulate prior to your first period and thus become pregnant without ever having a period.

For Fathers

Your encouragement is crucial to your wife's success in breastfeeding. Knowledge of the benefits of nursing is important so that you can respond to comments or suggestions from friends or relatives which might tend to discourage her or sabotage her efforts to nurse. Breastfeeding will best aid your child in achieving his full potential mentally, physically and emotionally. Support and encourage your wife in providing these benefits to him.

You will discover that advantages also exist for you, the father of a breastfed baby. For example, those **middle-of-the-night feedings will not be disruptive to your sleep!** Your wife will probably awaken as soon as the baby does, often before he even cries! (The two of them seem to be on the same wavelength. You may often wonder which one of them wakes up first.) These feedings are easiest if the baby is simply tucked into bed with the two of you, allowing your wife to drift back to sleep while the baby nurses. Chances are, the closeness and body warmth will encourage him to fall asleep sooner too.

Another benefit you will certainly notice is that **breastfed babies smell good!** They do not have a "sour milk" smell like formula babies often do, even if they spit up. Their stools do not have an offensive odor, so you'll find that changing diapers isn't so bad after all.

You will also appreciate the **economic advantages of breastfeeding.** Bottles, formula and baby food cost money. Breastmilk doesn't. Some couples have calculated that they saved enough in six months of breastfeeding to purchase a major appliance.

You need not feel left out or unimportant because you are unable to feed your baby. Feeding is just one part of his care. There are many other ways for you to show your love—bathing, holding and

cuddling, rocking and even changing diapers. And you can have the satisfaction of knowing that he is getting *the real thing.*

MILK PRODUCTION

How Milk is Produced

Within your breasts are many grape-like clusters (alveoli) where milk is produced under the influence of the hormone prolactin. Milk travels from the alveoli through the lactiferous ducts until it reaches the 15-20 lactiferous sinuses where the milk is stored. These sinuses are located under the areola, the darkened area which surrounds the nipple. The raised bumps which become prominent during pregnancy are called the glands of Montgomery. They lubricate and protect the nipple.

Each nipple contains 15-20 tiny openings—one from each sinus—through which milk flows. Stimulation of the nipple by sucking, or even by touching, causes the nipple to become more erect for ease in grasping by the infant. It also causes the release of oxytocin into the blood stream. The oxytocin acts on the alveoli to push milk into the ducts and sinuses where it is available for your baby. This process is known as the **let-down reflex,** and it occurs shortly after your baby begins each nursing. Most women feel a sort of *tingling* in their breasts during a let-down, along with a surge of milk from each breast, sometimes strong enough to send a spray of milk as

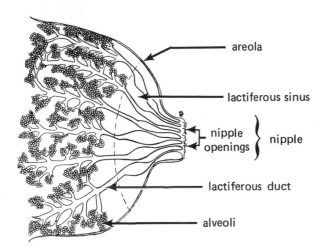

Cross section of lactating breast.

far as twelve inches in the first days of nursing. Occasionally just hearing your baby cry or even thinking about him can cause a let-down. This let-down reflex can be inhibited by emotional upsets, fatigue or tension.

Supply and Demand

Your milk supply is determined by the amount of milk your baby requires. The more he nurses, the more milk you produce. This is why mothers are able to nurse twins. To establish an adequate supply you should **let the baby nurse whenever he is hungry** and avoid the use of supplements—water, formula and solid foods. Wait until your milk supply is well established before introducing any supplemental feedings. Otherwise, you may disturb this perfect demand-supply relationship which nature has devised and thus diminish your milk supply.

You will find that allowing your baby to set his own schedule will be beneficial to you both—he will be more content and you will **avoid breast engorgement and an inadequate milk supply.** As your baby grows, your milk supply adjusts to his growth needs and to his intake of other foods.

Any mother can develop an adequate milk supply for nursing unless she has had a complete mastectomy or a certain type of breast reduction surgery which severs the milk ducts. The **size of your breasts has no effect on milk production.** (Size is determined by the amount of fatty tissue.) Inability

to produce milk is more often because of cultural reasons (negative myths and discouraging social influences), rather than physical ones.

Even if you become ill, with a cold or flu, you should continue nursing. Your baby will receive the antibodies which you are producing to fight the illness, and he will probably not get sick, or else he will have a very mild case.

You need to **maintain a nutritious diet** while nursing. Your body requires increased quantities of protein, vitamins, minerals and calories, so you should continue the diet you established during pregnancy. An added peanut butter sandwich and glass of milk will provide the extra protein and calories. In addition, you need to **drink more liquids.** At least eight 8-ounce glasses of fluid are necessary each day to insure adequate milk production. If you don't like milk, drinking water and fruit juices is fine, and you can get your calcium supply from such foods as cheese and yogurt. You will probably find that you are quite thirsty, so drinking that much should be easy. To make sure however, and to avoid the chance of missing any meals, fix yourself a snack and a drink while your baby is napping. When he wakes up wanting to nurse, grab your snack, and the two of you can relax and enjoy mealtime together. (Having one hand free makes it easy!)

Many nursing mothers find that brewer's yeast is an important supplement to their diet. This is nature's B-vitamin complex concentrate, which comes in powdered form and can be mixed into juices. Brewer's yeast is known for its ability to promote relaxation and to reduce fatigue and irritability. Some women even feel that it actually increases their milk supply.

Be careful to **avoid exhaustion** by getting plenty of rest and relaxation, especially in the first few weeks. Do only those household chores which are absolutely essential—simple meals, clean clothes for your family and light housekeeping. Having a spotless house is not necessary. Pick up the "chunks" or that which bothers you most (dirty dishes, unmade beds, etc.). Remember that your house will still be standing years from now, whereas your baby will only be an infant for a very short time.

Ideally, you will have help during the early weeks from your husband, mother, mother-in-law or a paid employee, so that your time can be devoted to your baby. If you don't have help, you will need to use your time wisely. When your baby goes to sleep in the afternoon, you should use that time for napping, rather than running around cleaning house. Your milk supply and your disposition will benefit.

HELPFUL HINTS

During Pregnancy

Choose your pediatrician carefully. Make an appointment with him well in advance of your due date to discuss your feelings and his ideas about breastfeeding. The early months with your baby will be much easier if you and the pediatrician are in agreement in such areas as the use of supplements, introduction of solid foods and weaning. If you agree on rooming-in and "nothing but the breast" while in the hospital, have him write it on your record.

Prepare your nipples. They need to be "toughened up" in order to reduce soreness when you begin nursing. The simplest way to do this is to wear a nursing bra and drop the flaps. This allows the air to circulate freely, and it creates gentle friction between your nipples and clothing. Massage them with pure lanolin daily while pulling the nipple out and rolling it between your fingers. Rub them gently with a towel after every bath or shower during your last month. Do not use soap on your nipples because it would remove the natural lubrication.

Read about breastfeeding. Buy a book and take it to the hospital with you. See Recommended Book List.

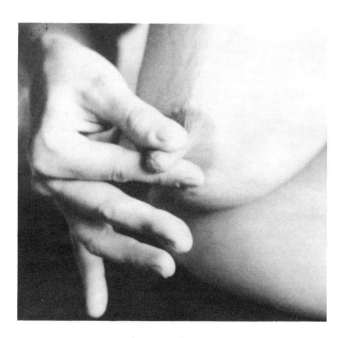

Nipple preparation.

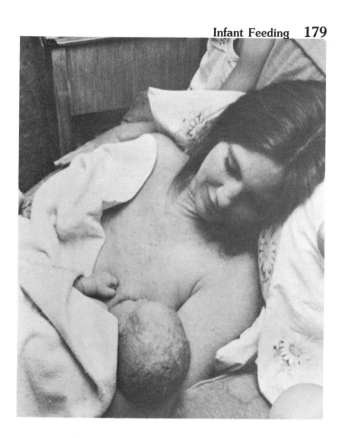

Nursing immediately after delivery.

Begin attending La Leche League meetings early in pregnancy. They offer excellent advice on breastfeeding and mothering.

In The Hospital

Nurse as soon as possible after delivery. The earlier you are able to begin your breastfeeding relationship, the easier it is for you and your baby. An unmedicated baby is usually eager to nurse, and the sooner he begins, the better he will nurse. His sucking reflex is strongest in the first hours after delivery. The longer you delay, the more difficult it becomes. Shield your baby's eyes from the light if it is very bright.

Nursing is easiest if you are **rooming-in.** This way you can nurse your baby when he is hungry, not when the hospital routine dictates. Most breastfed babies get hungry more often than every four hours because breastmilk is digested so quickly. Nursing on demand also results in less breast engorgement and nipple soreness.

If your baby does not nurse well at first, **try changing positions.** You can lie down with him cradled next to you. Or try sitting up with him on a pillow in your lap. Snuggling him close to your breast will prevent unnecessary pulling on your nipple which may lead to soreness. Make sure his head is slightly higher than his stomach. Also, check to see that your breast is not pressing against his nose and restricting his breathing. If it is, pull your breast back with your fingers.

Avoid supplements with the bottle. This would fill him up and decrease his interest in nursing. Because it is easier to get water or formula from a bottle, your baby might get lazy and not want to nurse. Also, since different muscles are used to suck from a bottle and breast, he may become confused. Don't let anybody convince you that there's no need to nurse during this time because "your milk isn't in yet." He does receive rich colostrum in the first few days, and the more he nurses, the sooner your milk will come in.

Do not use soap or drying agents such as alcohol on your nipples. You do not need to wash them before each feeding because they secrete a substance which keeps them clean. If you are requested to wash your nipples while in the hospital, you can use sterile water.

Never force the nipple into his mouth. Simply touch it gently to his cheek and he will turn towards you with an open mouth ready to latch on. Compress the areola with your thumb and forefinger and gently guide the nipple into your baby's mouth. If you want him to stop nursing, do not pull your breast away. His sucking is very strong. To avoid hurting your nipple, break the suction by sticking a finger in the corner of his mouth. You can then pull your breast away painlessly.

Do not restrict the length of nursings to prevent soreness. A baby who is allowed to nurse only every four hours for five minutes on each breast will be hungry and will nurse more vigorously. Also, if your let-down takes a couple of minutes, your actual feeding time will be shortened and will reduce the amount of milk you are supplying to your baby. Rooming-in and nursing the baby often will reduce the chances of sore nipples and a fussy baby.

It is best to **alternate the breast you offer first** at each feeding since the initial sucking is the strongest. This insures building an adequate supply in both breasts. (A safety pin on your bra is a good reminder of which breast to use.)

Do not use nipple shields for sore breasts. They inhibit adequate stimulation of the breasts and thus interfere with milk production. Their use creates more problems than it solves.

Don't be discouraged if you and your baby have trouble getting started with breastfeeding. Remember, this is new for both of you! Have patience. Before long, you'll both be pros.

The First Weeks At Home

Give yourself about six weeks to establish a good nursing relationship. These first weeks may seem hectic and difficult, but any newborn is demanding, breastfed or not. Just imagine having to wash bottles and prepare formula besides! After about six weeks, your life will calm down a bit as you and your baby adjust to each other.

Continue attending La Leche League meetings. Encouragement and support from other nursing mothers can be a life-saver to you, particularly when problems arise.

Feed your baby whenever he is hungry. Because breastmilk is more easily digested than formula, breastfed babies need to eat more often—sometimes as often as every two hours. Also, when experiencing **growth spurts** (usually around three weeks, six weeks and three months of age), their frequency of nursing will increase. Some women say that at these times their babies want to nurse all day. By providing this extra nursing, you insure that your milk supply will respond to his increased need. When the supply has built up sufficiently, his frequency of nursing will return to normal.

Even though your breasts are somewhat engorged at first, after a few weeks your milk supply will even out and your breasts will return to a more normal size. Don't confuse this with "**losing your milk.**" There's still plenty of milk for your baby.

Some babies have **greater sucking needs** than others. You can usually soothe your baby by putting him to the breast. Even if his need is not so much hunger as it is to be held close and to be comforted by the breast, it is still important. You are not spoiling him, simply meeting his needs. It is crucial to his security that you meet his needs as soon as possible. As Dr. Herbert Ratner says, "The quickest way to make your child independent is to take care of his needs when he is dependent."[8]

In the early weeks, your baby may have five or more **bowel movements** a day, sometimes as often as after every nursing, or as infrequently as one every five days. He may even switch from one routine to the other. You will soon know what is "normal" for *your* baby and will be able to recognize variations. The stools of a totally breastfed baby are yellow in color and are mushy or loose. These loose stools do *not* indicate diarrhea unless they are green in color, contain mucus or have a strong unpleasant odor.

You can be sure that you are **producing enough milk** if your baby has six or more wet diapers a day and is receiving only breastmilk. There is no need to give formula supplements or water. He gets plenty of water in your milk (breastmilk is 89 percent water), along with important nutrients, so don't fill him up on just plain water.

Babies are individuals and **gain weight at different rates.** If your baby is gaining weight slower than "average," do not be alarmed as long as he is happy and alert and is a good nurser. Similarly, if he is gaining more rapidly than the average, you do not need to take drastic action. (Averages are determined from both lows and highs.) Even if he appears "fat," do not be concerned as long as his only food is breastmilk. This fat will not remain with him throughout life. Some evidence suggests that this fat is different from the fat formed in artifically fed babies. He does *not* need a reducing diet! Continue nursing him as usual, and he will slim down as soon as he begins actively moving around.

Many women appreciate the support of a **good nursing bra.** You should begin wearing one in the hospital. During the early weeks you may be most comfortable wearing it 24 hours a day—even to sleep in.

If leaking is a problem, place nursing pads or folded cotton handkerchiefs inside your bra. Do not use plastic pads or liners as they tend to keep your nipples wet. After each feeding, leave your flaps down for a few minutes to allow your nipples to dry thoroughly.

A comfortable chair, preferably a rocker, is mandatory. At times you may want to nurse lying down. You can lie on your side with your baby lying next to you so that you can snooze while he does.

You will find breastfeeding **convenient** since it gives you a free hand to do other things while your baby nurses. This is easiest when he is very young and doesn't move around much. You can keep a book, magazine or paper and pen by your chair and catch up on your reading or correspondence. How about your thank you notes for baby and shower

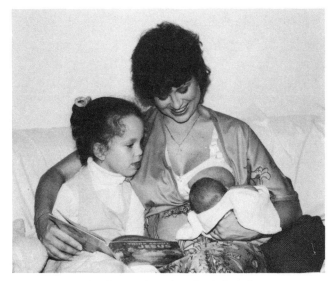
Nursing is a perfect time for being close.

gifts? If you are a list maker, this is a perfect opportunity for that. You can make grocery lists, a "things to do" list, or even Christmas lists. (It's never too early to start!)

If you have other children, nursing is a perfect time for reading to them, talking or just being close. Don't feel that you always have to be accomplishing something while nursing, however. You can best relax by just cuddling, talking or singing to your baby, and enjoying this quiet time with him.

Check with your doctor or La Leche League before taking any **medication or drugs,** even over-the-counter drugs. Some of them do show up in your milk and will affect your baby. Do not take stimulant laxatives. They can be upsetting to your baby.

The National Institutes of Health recommends that you refrain from drinking **alcohol** during lactation since its effects on the baby are not known. Any alcohol which you consume is readily transmitted to your nursing baby in much the same concentration as that in your blood. In addition, heavy alcohol consumption inhibits the flow of milk.

Learn to **hand express your milk** and freeze it for later use. Express the milk by gently squeezing with your thumb and forefinger from the outer edge of the areola towards the nipple. Squeeze it directly into a sterile plastic "nurser" bag. Seal it tightly and place it in the freezer. Because it contains no preservatives, breastmilk cannot be left at room temperature. To defrost the frozen milk, simply run it under cold water until it gets mushy. Then use warm to hot water to take the chill off. Breastmilk may be kept

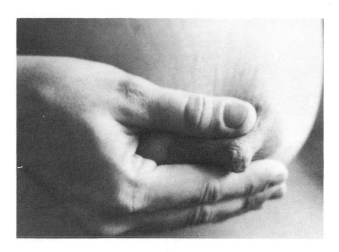

Hand expressing milk.

frozen up to six months at a temperature of 0°F. or less. Once it is thawed, however, it should be used within two hours or discarded. It can be refrigerated fresh for 24 hours.

You will probably find that **you won't want to go out without your baby very often.** You need him almost as much as he needs you! Breastfed babies are very portable and can be taken anywhere. However, it is a good idea to keep some frozen milk on hand in case of emergency or a situation in which you need to be away from your baby during a feeding.

Be deaf to criticism concerning breastfeeding or your method of caring for your baby. Right now your baby's happiness and comfort are most important—not your neighbor's (or your mother-in-law's) opinion. Remember, this is your child to raise in the manner which you feel is most comfortable. Read and become knowledgeable. Then decide what works best for you.

Don't forget to **keep your priorities straight.** Baby's happiness and your rest are tops right now!

POSSIBLE PROBLEMS

Sometimes problems arise in connection with nursing, but they can easily be remedied if you are prepared to handle them.

Sore Nipples

Nipple soreness occurs in some mothers when they begin nursing, even after advance preparation. Many mothers experience tenderness when the baby latches on to a full breast. This generally subsides after the milk lets down. **Nursing very frequently** may reduce or eliminate the soreness. By doing this, your baby will not be so hungry that he latches on strongly. Also, snuggling your baby up close to your breast will prevent unnecessary tugging.

Try not to let your breasts become engorged. This fullness may make it difficult for your baby to "get hold" of the breast, causing him to bite down on the nipple.

Proper position of the baby's mouth on the breast is essential. A major cause of sore nipples is allowing the baby to suck on the tip of the nipple instead of drawing most of the areola into his mouth. Make sure your baby is applying pressure on the lactiferous sinuses rather than the nipple. (See diagram.)

Even if you do experience sore nipples, **continue nursing. Do not use soap or drying agents** on your breasts as this washes away your natural protection. **Expose your breasts to the air and sunshine** to aid healing. **Ice chips** in a wash cloth placed on your nipple may also help.

Remember, this is a temporary condition. With good care and some perseverance, your nipples will be healed in a short time.

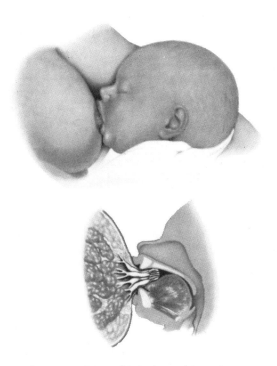

Proper position of baby's mouth on breast.

Lack of Milk

An inadequate milk supply results from a rigid or infrequent feeding schedule, the use of supplements or from low fluid intake. The early introduction of supplements can result in a vicious cycle of diminishing your milk supply—the more supplements you give, the less milk you produce, requiring even more supplements, further diminishing your supply and so forth.

Signs of an inadequate supply include a low weight gain, few wet diapers with dark concentrated urine and an unhappy baby. If these symptoms develop, **nurse your baby often, give no supplements, drink plenty of liquids and REST.** Taking brewer's yeast powder mixed in juice several times a day may also help.

You may think your baby is not getting enough milk if he wants to nurse every two hours. This is very normal in the early weeks and during growth spurts and is no need for alarm as long as he is not showing any of the symptoms listed above. He may just be a baby who needs a lot of sucking.

Engorgement

Breast engorgement occurs when a large amount of milk is in your breasts. Milk remains in the milk ducts and causes a fullness and hardness in your breast tissue. You are likely to feel this when your milk comes in (second to fourth day after birth), when the baby misses a feeding, or when he goes for a longer period (sleeps through the night) between feedings. This situation is temporary. In a short time your milk supply will readjust to meet your baby's demand.

Taking a **hot shower** or placing **hot cloths on your breasts** can relieve the discomfort or swelling by producing a let-down of milk. If your baby has difficulty grasping hold of the nipple, he may become frustrated and cry. **Hand express a little milk** before nursing to make the nipple soft and pliable.

Milk Leakage

Milk leaking or spraying is usually temporary. It can be stopped by **pushing the heel of your hand against the nipple**. Wear nursing pads to guard against wet spots.

Plugged Duct

If you notice a soreness and lump in one area of your

"Oops—looks like it's time to nurse!"

breast, you may have a plugged duct. This is caused by incomplete emptying of the milk ducts by the baby or the wearing of a tight bra. Check your nipple very carefully for a tiny dot of dried milk. When this is removed by gentle cleansing along with **frequent nursing** on the affected breast, the duct will clear itself within 24 hours. Massaging the breasts with firm pressure, from the chest wall towards the nipple also stimulates milk flow.

Alter the position of the baby on the nipple so he is draining all the ducts. Make sure you offer the affected breast first, when his sucking is strongest.

Mastitis (Breast Infection)

If a plugged duct is not taken care of, mastitis can result. You may notice soreness and redness in your breast and have a fever and flu-like symptoms. In fact, in a nursing mother all flu symptoms should be considered a breast infection until proven otherwise.

Continue to nurse your baby frequently to empty the ducts. **DO NOT STOP NURSING!** This would be both an emotional and physical shock to you and your baby. It could actually cause the problem to worsen as you allow the ducts to overfill.

Get plenty of **fluids** and **rest**. Take your baby and go to bed. **Apply heat** to the area in the form of a heating pad or hot water bottle. Your doctor may prescribe antibiotics which can be taken while nursing.

Breast Abscess

Rarely, a breast infection may become a breast abscess, a sore area which is filled with pus. Along with requiring antibiotics, it may need to be incised to allow drainage. This is normally done in the doctor's office and heals quickly. Until the abscess is healed, **hand express the milk from the affected breast and discard it. Continue nursing your baby on the other breast.** Once healing is complete, you can go back to nursing on both sides.

Flat or Inverted Nipples

This is not a contraindication to nursing since the baby applies pressure on the areola to obtain milk. Also, the action of nursing will naturally draw out the nipple. If your nipples are severely inverted, you may wish to use a special shield during pregnancy which encourages the nipple to protrude. The **Woolwich shield** is available from La Leche League. Follow instructions for prenatal nipple care.

BABY RELATED DIFFICULTIES

Your baby's personality or condition at birth may affect your nursing relationship.

A Sleepy Baby

An anesthetized birth may cause your baby to be sleepy and somewhat sluggish about nursing. To combat this, try changing his diaper, **moving him around** and rubbing his back gently. Uncover and expose him to the air. Sit him up. Pat his feet and **talk and play with him. Feed him as often as possible** to prevent weight loss.

A Lazy Baby

A baby who has gotten confused by a rubber nipple may not nurse well. **Avoid giving him a bottle** until he has become well established on the breast.

A Too-Eager Baby

An overly-cooperative baby that nurses too vigorously may gulp too much milk and air. **Partially emptying your breast** by hand before nursing will lessen this problem. Also, taking him off your breast several times and burping him will reduce spitting up and gas discomfort.

If your baby is overly hungry, he may bite down hard and cause sore nipples. **Avoid making him wait** too long before feeding him.

A Weak Nurser

A baby who is a weak nurser may result from a premature birth, cesarean delivery or anesthetized delivery. **Nurse him more frequently** and for longer periods of time. Nurse him as long as he wants. Help him to get started at each nursing by hand expressing some milk into his mouth.

Remember, each baby is an individual and no baby "goes by the book." Avoid comparing your baby to another baby or trying to change him. Meet his individual needs and you will have a happy contented infant. You will be happier too!

BREASTFEEDING FOLLOWING A CESAREAN DELIVERY

The special closeness provided by breastfeeding is particularly important if you have had a cesarean delivery. Since you have not experienced the physical sensations of birth, nursing your infant provides you with the intimate contact and comfort which is essential to both you and your baby. Your breasts will fill up with milk just as if you had delivered vaginally. Because of your need for extra rest, you will appreciate being able to take your baby to bed with you and leisurely feed him without having to get up for bottle washing or formula preparation.

As with a vaginal birth, you should plan to **nurse as soon after delivery as possible**. If you have had a spinal or epidural anesthesia, hold and nurse your baby before the effects of the medication wear off. If you have been given general anesthesia, however, you will have to wait a little longer before getting started.

Your abdominal incision will necessitate finding nursing positions which are comfortable for you. **Experiment with various positions** until you find the one that is easiest. Many women find the side-lying position most comfortable. To do this, use pillows to support your back, abdomen and possibly your upper leg. Place your baby on his side facing you and cradle him in your arm. Pull him in close to you until your nipple touches his cheek. Help him to take as much of the areola as possible. To burp him, roll onto your back and roll him onto your chest, face down. Then roll onto your other side to nurse from the other breast.

Some women prefer a sitting position. If you do, try bending your knees somewhat and supporting your feet in order to lessen the strain on your abdomen. Place your baby on a pillow in your lap and cradle him in your arm. The ''football'' hold is another position that relieves pressure on the abdomen. While sitting, hold the baby in a football carry position with him lying on a pillow at your side, and your hand under his head at your breast.

Continue taking your **pain medication** as needed. Most of these medications do not affect the baby. Check with your doctor to be sure.

Arrange to have **household help** when you leave the hospital. *You* care for your baby as you are able, and let someone else take care of you and the rest of your family.

Don't be discouraged if you and your baby seem to be getting off to a slow start. Remember, this is the beginning of many months of a happy, rewarding nursing relationship.

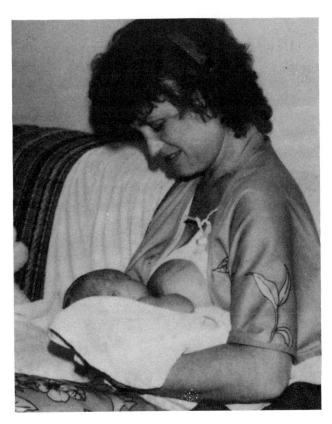

Football hold.

"What do you mean, I can't nurse after a Cesarean?!? I have all the right equipment!"

WORKING MOTHERS

If you plan to return to work after your baby is born, **you can still enjoy a happy and successful nursing relationship**. Your baby will benefit from whatever time you spend breastfeeding, especially during those first days when he receives the colostrum and all of its advantages.

You may be able to arrange to visit and **nurse your baby on your lunch hour** (or have him brought to you). Continue nursing him in the morning and several times during the evening. Your milk supply will even out to meet this reduced demand. You can use either frozen breastmilk or formula to supplement while you are at work.

If at all possible, **delay returning to work** outside the home until your baby is a year old. This is a very important year in his development and one that is very precious to you. Except in extreme cases, the time you spend with him is more beneficial than the income you receive by working, especially after you deduct baby-sitting fees, the cost of formula and extra clothes, and other expenses related to work. You may find the amount left over is not as significant as you thought.

If you must work, **choose your baby sitter carefully**. Find someone who will care for him as you would. A person who keeps only one or two children can provide a more homelike atmosphere, with plenty of cuddling. It also reduces the chance of transmitting disease to your baby, which would further increase your doctor bills.

SPECIAL OR UNUSUAL SITUATIONS

It is possible to breastfeed through unusual situations if you have the proper information to assist you. La Leche League International can provide support for nursing twins, triplets, or a premature baby. They can also supply information on the possibility of continuing to nurse if you need hospitalization for such illnesses as tuberculosis, hepatitis, epilepsy and cancer. Information and guidance are also available for nursing a baby with Down's syndrome or other forms of retardation, cleft palate, physical handicaps or if the baby must be hospitalized. When faced with any of these special cases, it is best to get in direct touch with La Leche League International at the following address:

La Leche League International
9616 Minneapolis Avenue
Franklin Park, Illinois 60131

You will receive specific guidelines and will be put in contact with others who have nursed in similar circumstances. A helpful reference book is *You Can Breastfeed Your Baby Even in Special Situations* by Dorothy Patricia Brewster.

Very few situations exist where breastfeeding is contraindicated. If you have had a double mastectomy or breast reduction surgery in which the nipples have been surgically removed and reattached, breastfeeding would not be possible. Additionally, it is recommended that women who have been exposed to the AIDS virus not breastfeed. Rare cases have been reported of infants acquiring the virus through ingestion of breastmilk.

OTHER FOODS

Breastmilk is a complete food for your baby until around six months of age. At that time, the iron supply he was born with may begin to diminish. Also, his teeth may start breaking through the gums, indicating that nature intended for him to learn to chew. This is usually the time to introduce solid foods. Let your baby be your guide. Some are eager to eat at this time and will reach for food. Others are still not ready and will refuse it. Proceed very slowly. If your baby doesn't want the food, do not force him. Continue offering it occasionally, and when he is ready, he will eat. Do not be overly concerned about quantity. He is just learning how to eat, and it will be some time before he is ready for three "square meals" a day. Mashed banana is a good food to begin with. **Breastmilk should remain his primary source of nutrition throughout the first year**. Refer to *The Womanly Art of Breastfeeding* for more information.

Solid foods should be introduced one at a time. If an adverse reaction results (rash or stomach upset), you will know which food is responsible.

Certain foods are highly allergenic and should be delayed to prevent reactions. Cow's milk should not replace breastmilk until one year of age. Dairy products can be used sparingly after eight months. Orange juice, citrus fruits and eggs should not be introduced until ten to twelve months of age.

You can **avoid the use of expensive, overprocessed commercial baby foods** by taking the nutritious (and non-salted) foods from your table and mashing or blending them for your baby. You can even freeze portions of this mashed food for use later when your family is having a "combination" dish (casseroles, etc.) that includes foods which have not been added to your baby's diet. Freeze these leftover single foods in ice cube trays. When frozen, pack the individual cubes in plastic bags and store them in your freezer. To use, simply defrost to room temperature and serve.

Many women find that blenderizing their baby's foods is unnecessary. You can avoid the expense and trouble of puréeing foods by waiting until your baby is truly ready for **finger foods** (about 8–10 months). At this time he will be able to handle the foods from your table and will enjoy the independence of feeding himself. Offer him small pieces of softened vegetables or tiny pieces of chicken, fish or beef. Foods which you can easily mash between your fingers are good choices. Even baby cereals are unnecessary if you provide packaged cereal such as Cheerios which are low in salt and sugar and easy for the baby to pick up and chew. In this way you will eliminate the hassle of spoon feeding, and mealtimes will be more pleasurable.

The commercial baby food industry has done a tremendous marketing job in convincing mothers that puréed food is a necessary step before table food. They have even invented different levels from "smooth" to "chunky" to prolong the purchasing of prepared foods. Advertising experts have influenced our culture so strongly that mothers feel negligent if they don't use these expensive products. The baby food manufacturers even promote the purchase of small jars of special "baby" fruit juices when the same varieties can be purchased in larger bottles much more economically.

If you do decide to purchase prepared baby foods, look for those with no added salt, sugar, starches or other fillers. Many brands now offer a variety of products which contain only the puréed foods, and no additives. These provide more nutrition, so read the labels carefully. Do not feed your baby right from the jar since his saliva contains enzymes and bacteria which will start to break down the food and prevent you from saving any of it for later use.

Children's Snacks

With so many quality foods available, it is almost a crime to allow your children to form the habit of snacking on packaged cookies and soft drinks. When the highly refined foods are simply not purchased, children readily accept and come to prefer the more nutritious foods. Offer cheese, whole wheat crackers, fresh fruit and vegetables, raisins or other dried fruit or popcorn. Nuts, seeds and popcorn should not be given to children under two.

You can turn your favorite cookie recipes into health cookies by substituting whole wheat flour for a portion of the white flour, substituting honey for refined sugar, and adding wheat germ, brewer's yeast, and powdered milk. They should turn out just right as long as your total dry ingredients equal the total dry ingredients in the recipe. If the batter is too thick, just add an extra egg. Many cookie recipes call for raisins, nuts, peanut butter, or oatmeal, which makes them doubly nutritious.

Soft drinks are devoid of any food element except sugar. They are full of acids, preservatives, emulsifiers, stabilizers, artificial flavoring and dyes. While these have been tested individually for safety, little is known about their combined effect on the human body. They cause tooth decay and take away the appetite for more nutritious foods. They act as a stimulant by causing the blood sugar to soar

temporarily. However, this is rapidly followed by a drop in blood sugar and less energy. Give your child fresh, frozen or canned, unsweetened fruit juice, milk, or water when he is thirsty.

Packaged gelatin desserts are about 85 percent sugar. Unflavored gelatin can be used instead and made with fresh fruit juice.

WEANING

Many women find that their views on weaning change after they begin nursing. Often, an expectant mother will plan to nurse for three months or six months or some other set amount of time. However, once she begins the nursing relationship with her baby, it is so rewarding that she is not anxious for it to end. She knows, too, that breastfeeding is more than just a method of physical nourishment. It is an emotional bond. An abrupt severing of that bond could be traumatic for both mother and baby.

Most nursing mothers find that weaning is easiest for both partners if it is a **gradual process**. Authorities, too, are realizing that weaning is individual and should be determined by each baby's needs. Just as babies begin sitting up, rolling over, walking and talking at different ages, their needs to continue nursing vary. Therefore, ideally, weaning should be **a baby-led process.** You will know when your baby is ready, and it will probably be so gradual that you will hardly even realize it. As he becomes more interested in other activities and in the world around him, and as he becomes more capable of feeding himself from the table and drinking from a cup, his need to nurse will diminish. Of course when he is hurt or ill, he will want to resort to his "baby" ways, and you will be glad that you are able to comfort him through nursing. (In fact, nursing can be a real "life saver" when your toddler is so sick that he doesn't want to eat or drink anything, but will continue to nurse. Nursing can prevent dehydration.) Gradually, however, you will find that he will be asking to nurse less frequently. Your best way to encourage him is not to offer the breast to him but not to deny it when he needs it.

Remember, you are helping him to become an independent human being *at his own rate*. Your months of involvement in the nursing relationship will make you sensitive to your baby's exact needs. Do not let comments from others deny him of this birthright. Our society supports babies remaining attached to the bottle until age two or three. How much better to be attached to a person than a "thing." If you feel that prolonged nursing is best for you and your baby, don't allow public opinion to affect your decision. The nutritional and psychological benefits from nursing will continue, and you will be helping to develop a happy, healthy, well-adjusted human being.

LA LECHE LEAGUE

La Leche League is an organization of women who have successfully breastfed and who desire to help others breastfeed. The organization had its beginnings at a family picnic in Franklin Park, Illinois, in 1956. Two nursing mothers attending the picnic recognized the need of new mothers to receive factual advice on breastfeeding. Previous generations had mothers and grandmothers within their households who could supply this assistance. Our changing family structure had left mothers without good role models, resulting in a lack of information.

Today, La Leche League is an international organization with over 8,500 active leaders in 47 countries. Each chapter meets monthly and covers a series of four topics concerning nursing. If you are considering breastfeeding, you should begin attending La Leche League meetings at least four months prior to your due date in order to complete the series. After your baby is born, you can take him with you to the meetings.

Keep the telephone number of a La Leche League leader handy and feel free to call her at any time if a problem arises. Her knowledge and experience can help ease you through any rough spots.

BOTTLE FEEDING

When you feed your baby, you are providing more than nourishment. He is also receiving love, warmth, intimate human contact and is developing security. **Close physical contact** (especially skin-to-skin) and cuddling are extremely important in the psychological and physical development of your baby.

Propping a bottle or sitting your baby in an infant seat and holding his bottle for him do not provide these necessary elements. Even when your baby is able to hold his own bottle, he should not be left alone, as this can be dangerous and also lead to dental problems. He still needs to be held and cuddled as he is fed.

Make each feeding time special by cradling your baby close to you in the bend of your arm (**the nursing position**) and not rushing the feeding. Talking and singing to him make this a sociable and pleasant time for both of you. **Alternate arms at each feeding.** Babies that are always held on the same side develop different strengths in their eyes. The eye that is closest to your breast will not receive adequate stimulation and will become weak from nonuse.

Types of Formula

The type of formula you use will probably depend upon your pediatrician's preference. Formulas are made from cow's milk or soybeans and modified to make them as similar to mother's milk as possible. Some babies do not tolerate certain formulas and may need a change. They may have problems with constipation or digestive upsets. If your baby is allergic to a cow's milk based formula, your doctor may try a soybean based one. Signs of possible allergy include rash (eczema), diarrhea, chronic cold symptoms, colic or asthma. Occasionally, a baby is so allergic that he can only tolerate breastmilk.

Formula comes in several forms. The single serving ready-to-feed bottle is the easiest to prepare but also the most expensive. Liquid formula concentrate that you prepare should be refrigerated after mixing with water and used within 48 hours. The powdered type does not need refrigeration until it is mixed with water. It should also be used within 48 hours. **Make sure you follow the directions on the can** for dilution and preparation. Adding extra water to "stretch" the formula or not adding enough water is dangerous to your baby's health and development. Formula should be given at room temperature. Overheating will destroy important vitamins.

Basics

Many doctors say sterilization of bottles is unnecessary if you use a dishwasher. Plastic nurser bags are convenient as they are sterile and disposable. Nipples should be cleaned with a brush and boiled to remove any milk residue.

Make sure the hole in the nipple is the correct size. When you shake the bottle upside down, the formula should easily drip, one drop at a time. If it takes your baby a long time (over 30 minutes) to finish the bottle, or if he seems fussy or becomes tired before finishing, the hole may be too small. If he is receiving a lot of air or finishes his bottle very quickly, the hole is probably too large. **Hold the bottle at a 45° angle** so the milk always fills the nipple. Otherwise, your baby will take in a lot of air.

Burp your baby halfway through and at the end of each feeding. If he cried hard before being fed, or if he gulps his milk, he may need extra burping. Placing a diaper over your shoulder will help eliminate stains. Stains can be soaked in a baking soda and water solution or vinegar and water.

Do not place an unfinished bottle back into the refregerator to use later. The baby's saliva is already working on the formula and may promote the growth of bacteria. **Don't save formula for reuse** if it has been out of refrigeration for several hours, it is safer to use the "ready to feed" bottles than worry about the formula spoiling. Contaminated or spoiled milk can cause vomiting and diarrhea. This can lead to dehydration, a serious problem in infants because of their size.

Canned liquid formula should be stored at tempertures below 72 degrees. If it has been stored in a warehouse during the hot summer, it may curdle. Do not use formula which smells "funny" or which separates into layers with a yellow, oily substance on top that cannot be dispersed by shaking.[9] Also, check the expiration date, especially if you buy when the store is having a sale.

After feeding, placing your baby on his right side, his abdomen or in a sitting position (held or in an infant seat) will aid digestion.

OTHER FOODS

The American Academy of Pediatrics has recommended that **babies receive only breastmilk or formula for the first four to six months** of life and continue to receive breastmilk or formula as the **primary source of nutrition for the second six months**.

Skim milk does not contain enough calories to meet your infant's energy and growth needs during the first year. It is also deficient in iron, vitamin C, and essential fatty acids. The high protein and salt content in skim milk puts too much stress on your baby's kidneys. The introduction of any form of cow's milk should be delayed until one year of age because of possible allergic reactions. Approximately 10 percent of children are allergic to cow's milk.

There is no advantage to introducing solids at an early age. The enzymes that are necessary to digest cereal or other food completely are not present in full quantity until the baby is three to six months of age. Before three to four months he is not able to move food from the front to the back of his mouth and most of the food you feed him is wasted. You spend a lot of time catching the food as his tongue thrusts it out and refeeding it to him. Because a baby's gastrointestinal tract is not mature, early introduction of solids can lead to improper absorption and food allergies. It may also lead to obesity in later life as many mothers encourage their babies to finish the jar or clean their plates in order not to waste food.

Solids do not make a baby sleep through the night. Sleeping through the night is a function of neurological maturity and is independent of feeding. It usually occurs between two to three months of age.

BOTTLE MOUTH SYNDROME

Putting your baby to bed with a bottle of formula or juice is not recommended. This allows sugar to remain on his teeth and can lead to **bottle mouth syndrome** evidenced by extensive cavities. Plain water is the only acceptable liquid if you give your baby a bottle in bed. It is preferable to hold and rock your baby as he takes his night bottle and then place him into bed without one. This not only prevents tooth problems but gives him that *extra love and cuddling* which every baby and child need.

FOOTNOTES

Chapter 11

1. *Pediatrics*, Vol. 62, No. 4 (October, 1978) as cited in "Breastfeeding, A Commentary in Celebration of the International Year of the Child," Nutrition Committee of the Canadian Pediatric Society and the Committee on Nutrition of the American Academy of Pediatrics, 1979, pp. 1–11.
2. Karen Pryor, *Nursing Your Baby* (N.Y., Pocket Books, 1975), p. 63.
3. Pryor, p. 63.
4. Pryor, p. 63.
5. Pryor, p. 63.
6. Pryor, p. 39.
7. Pryor, p. 70.
8. Pryor, p. 9.
9. *Parent and Child* (St. Louis Newsletter), Vol. 9:1 (Winter, 1980), p. 4.

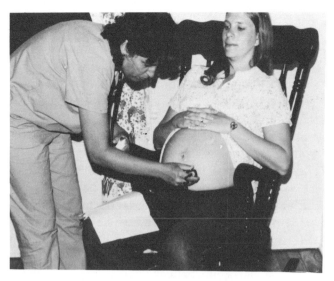

Midwife listening to baby's heartbeat during early labor.

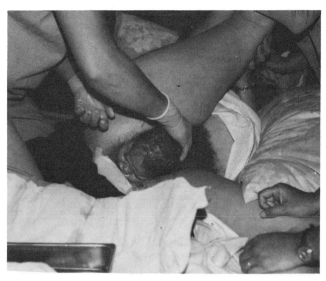

Birth of baby's head.

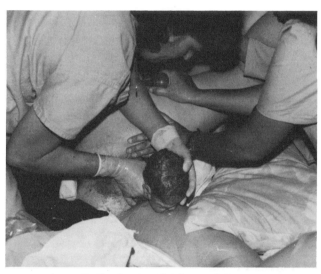

Delivering in sidelying position.

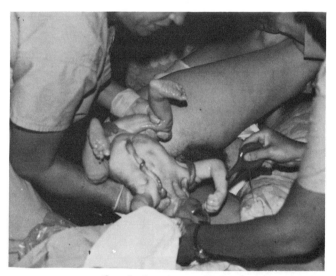

Suctioning the newborn.

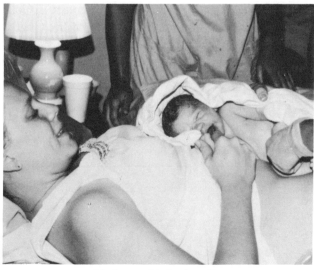

Mother and baby bonding.

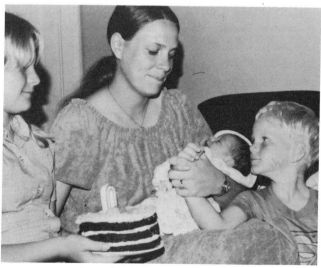

Birthday celebration with siblings one hour after birth.

Birth Center Delivery

Chapter 12

The New Parent

or "It's Been A Hard Day's Night" *

PHYSICAL CHANGES

During your first six weeks postpartum, your body returns to its prepregnant state. You begin eliminating the extra fluid you retained during pregnancy by **frequent urination** and **profuse perspiration.**

Your **uterus** gradually shrinks to its prepregnant size and position (involution). You may be aware of periodic contractions as the uterus becomes smaller. As you nurse your baby, you will feel the uterus contract each time you put your baby to breast for the first few days. Because of this, involution of the uterus occurs faster in breastfeeding mothers.

A **vaginal discharge** is present for three to four weeks as the lining of the uterus returns to normal. It begins as bright red, gradually turning brownish, then light pink and finally clear. If it becomes bright red again after it has cleared, you have overexerted yourself. Slow down, go to bed for the next couple of days and get plenty of rest. If the bleeding is excessive, call your doctor. It may be an indication that you have a postpartum hemorrhage.

Continue the comfort measures used in the hospital for **episiotomy and/or hemorrhoid discomfort** as long as needed. You will find it helps to reduce the strain on the stitches if you squeeze your buttocks together before sitting down or standing up. Also avoid very soft chairs; rather, sit in firm, straight back chairs until the episiotomy heals.

Weight loss will be gradual, sometimes taking months. Remember, it took you nine months to put that weight on, so you can't expect it all to disappear overnight. Nursing will give you added assistance as the production of milk uses approximately 1000 calories each day. Your **abdomen** will be flabby and you may still look like you are four to five months pregnant when you come home. Beginning the exercise program described later in this chapter while you are still in the hospital, gives you a head start on reconditioning the muscles that were stretched during pregnancy.

You may experience both emotional highs and lows during the first weeks after birth. It is not surprising that some women experience **postpartum depression or "baby blues"** since many sudden changes occur. Physically, your body experiences sudden shifts in hormone levels, a thirty percent decrease in blood volume, and contracting and shrinking of the uterus. Pregnancy grew on you month by month, but motherhood (and fatherhood) is thrust upon you very suddenly. One minute your baby is still a part of you and the next he is a separate, unique human being. To further compound the shock, the spotlight shifts from you to the baby. You are no longer the center of attention with much pampering and coddling. In the early days this can make you feel isolated and unimportant.

Your husband may also be affected by these changes. No longer is he the primary focus of your attention. He may feel resentment and jealousy toward the baby if he is not allowed to be an active partner in the baby's care and nurturing. Sudden awareness of the enormous responsibility he has just assumed may overwhelm and frighten him for a time.

According to Dr. Elizabeth Whelan, "more than any other factor, exhaustion is the primary factor in postpartum depression."[1] It is extremely important that you get as much **rest** as possible during the first two weeks at home. Because it will be several weeks before you can fit into your nonpregnant clothes, stay in your nightgown and be comfortable. You will appear to be **recovering** and will be treated as such. If you immediately get into clothes when you arrive home, you will appear fully recovered and will find yourself pushed into hostess and housekeeper roles before you are ready. This will result in fatigue, irritability and a slower recovery. If possible, nap whenever your baby does. In fact, the two of you should spend the first days at home in bed together. Do not feel guilty about this. Your body needs the extra rest at this time.

If you follow these suggestions and the many others that are discussed in the next sections, you can minimize and possibly avoid the down feelings that most women have come to expect following childbirth.

ADJUSTING TO PARENTHOOD

Imagine this scene—you're home with your new baby who's just been bathed, fed, and cuddled and is now sleeping peacefully in a clean and tidy house, while you relax with your feet up, a good book and occasional fond glances at your mate. Lovely, but is it realistic, and *for how long?* No matter what romanticized ideas you may have developed about being a parent, there are times (and many of them) that make it difficult to live up to these ideals. You can't program yourself to have boundless energy, be relaxed and confident, be consistently loving and meet all of your baby's (and spouse's) needs. There is no way to be a perfect parent—**parents are human beings!** The "perfect parent" image we often try to project to those around us—our parents, relatives, and friends—is plainly unrealistic. And if you'll take time to discuss this openly with them, you'll find that they, too, have had some frenzied and anxious moments as new parents.

The adjustments you make after having your baby are similar in many ways to the adjustments you had to make following marriage. New roles are defined; new household tasks are assigned. To help you prepare more realistically for the days that lie ahead, the two of you should sit down and do the following exercise together while you are still pregnant.

Each of you take a piece of paper and draw two circles on it. Label the first circle *Before Baby* and the second circle *After Baby*. Divide the "Before" circle into sections that represent the time in a 24 hour period that you spend in different activities (breadwinner, cook, housekeeper, money manager, companion, lover, gardener, leisure, hobbies, sleeping, etc.). In the "After" circle indicate the amount of time that will be given to these same activities as well as the ones related to the new baby (i.e., diaper folding, bathing, soothing, diaper changing, feeding, etc.).

Compare your circles with one another. Has one partner made more changes than the other? Are your "after baby" circles realistic? Does your partner's involvement in child care activities coincide with your expectations of his/her role as a parent? Discuss any differences in expectations *now* so that after your baby is born you will not have disagreements on who should do what and when. It is fun to save the circles and look at them again after your baby is born.

It should be obvious after doing this exercise, if not before, that the time given to these different roles plus the additional role of parent will be changed considerably after your baby is born.

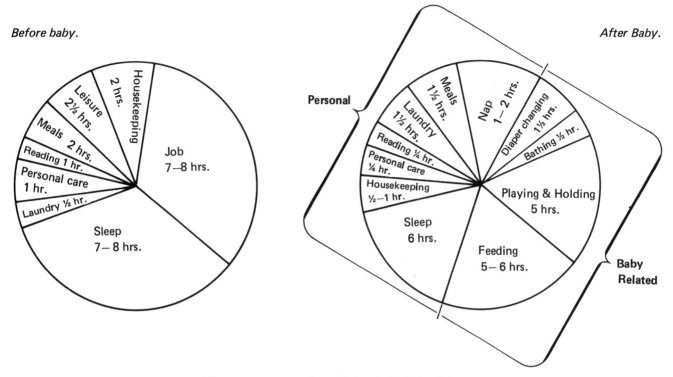

Before baby.

Housekeeping 2 hrs.

Leisure 2½ hrs.

Meals 2 hrs.

Reading 1 hr.

Personal care 1 hr.

Laundry ½ hr.

Job 7—8 hrs.

Sleep 7—8 hrs.

After Baby.

Personal

Meals 1½ hrs.

Laundry 1½ hrs.

Reading ¼ hr.

Personal care ¼ hr.

Housekeeping ½—1 hr.

Nap 1—2 hrs.

Diaper changing 1½ hrs.

Bathing ½ hr.

Playing & Holding 5 hrs.

Sleep 6 hrs.

Feeding 5—6 hrs.

Baby Related

Time management chart: Before baby/After baby.

COPING WITH YOUR FEELINGS

So many **positive feelings** are shared by you as new parents; feelings of personal gratification, challenge and achievement, deepening of love and appreciation of each other. You will enjoy discovering a new dimension in each other as parents, and even closer relationships with your own parents.

It may come as a surprise that you can also experience strong **negative feelings,** which are often followed by feelings of guilt. When you've done simply everything to soothe a fussy baby and he is still crying, when you've gotten up for the third time during the night to feed him, or when the anticipated two-hour nap only lasts for thirty minutes, you may find yourself getting upset or even hostile toward this baby who is so "ungrateful" for all you have done for him. You're not alone! Parents *are* human and have feelings of anger and guilt from time to time whether they admit it or not. But it is not the feelings that present the problems; rather, it is how you handle those feelings and cope with the situation at hand. Often just talking with other new mothers who are experiencing the same feelings and difficulties will help you put the situation in perspective and arrive at a creative solution.

Photographed by Terri Helton

Sometimes it is not your baby that causes these emotions to surface. Instead it is "cabin fever," loss of freedom, lack of intellectual stimulation or lowered self-confidence. Try to find the reason that you feel as you do and then you can work toward a solution. Be sure to share your feelings with your husband. Problems seem less important when they are shared and solved together.

Taking Time to Adjust

Don't have exceedingly high expectations for yourself, your spouse, or your baby at the start. Each of you is adjusting to tremendous changes in your life by virtue of the altered family structure, use and demand of time, and changes in relationships.

The early life with your baby is the most demanding on your time—your time alone and as a couple. **Communication is essential.** Be assured that as you grow as parents and as the baby matures, your lifestyle can and will adjust to what you want it to be.

Simplifying Your Housework

For the first week or two at home, **household help** will ease you through the adjustment period. A relative with whom you feel truly comfortable is a joy! She can prepare the meals, wash dishes, do the laundry and cleaning, and care for older children. This will better enable you to care for yourself and your baby.

If possible, have your husband take vacation time the week after you come home from the hospital. You will appreciate the opportunity to help each other "settle in" and be alone during this time.

Organize your priorities together as a couple and decide to do only those things which the two of you feel are important and necessary. The new baby who needs almost constant physical care is most demanding on your time during the first few weeks. In addition, your own body is undergoing tremendous physical changes that affect your energy level. It often helps to make lists of things to be done. These might include things that MUST be done, things that are *nice but not essential* (do if time permits), things **that can wait** until the baby is older, and *substitutes* that save work. Besides listing jobs in order of importance, you should also consider who will do each job. **Mother can't do everything!**

Although some newborns want to eat nearly every two hours around the clock, the time between feedings will lengthen as they grow older. You will be able to catch up on your housework later. Donna Ewy, a noted childbirth educator and author, suggests that the best gift you can give to your baby is the gift of yourself for the first six weeks of his life.

Finding More Time With Less Time

Become aware of the things in your current lifestyle that are very important to you individually and as a couple. Try to find ways to maintain some of these activities after the baby arrives as it will be impossible to continue all. This simple exercise will help you clarify what these important things are.

Each of you complete the following phrases on a piece of paper. Three things I like to do alone are:

_____

_____

_____

Three things I like to do with my mate are:

_____

_____

_____

Now answer this question: *How will the baby change this?* Trade lists with each other. You may find items missing from your partner's list that you thought were important, as well as things that you didn't realize were important. Decide together which activities are *most important,* what you can *give up for a time* and *how to maintain* the important activities. For example, if you enjoy a good movie but don't want to leave the baby, go to a drive-in. (Nursing babies do very well at any type of theater.) Entertain friends at home for dinner rather than going to a restaurant. Take turns watching the baby for a few hours while the other does something alone. Find specific times for each other that may be different from the times you used to have. Take advantage of baby's nap times for conversation and shared activity, rather than a rushed trip to the grocery store or to finish some yard work.

There are many things that you can do while your baby nurses—make lists, read a book, listen to music, eat or take a nap. Learn to utilize this time in whatever ways are most satisfying to you. Don't feel guilty, however, if there are times when you just want to relax and enjoy this quiet moment.

Parenting Resources

Parenthood is probably one of life's most thrilling adventures and yet, at the same time, you may enter it feeling an array of fears, anxieties and doubts. Be assured that **you both bring many strengths** to this new role of parent.

To become aware of these qualities, sit down together tonight, each of you take a piece of paper and write down three things about *your own* personality that will help you be a successful parent. Trade papers with your partner and write three more things *about him or her* that you see as strengths. Look again at your own paper. See what a good start you have! Qualities like a sense of humor, self-confidence, flexibility, organizational ability, compassion, and an affectionate nature will go a long way to get you over any rough spots during the early weeks and years of parenthood. Build on these strengths to become the kind of parent you want to be.

Becoming aware of **what you liked and disliked about the parenting you received** as a child can also be helpful. Try to remember the things your parents did that you would like to copy. Also get in touch with the weaknesses you saw in the way you were parented. In this way you can avoid being trapped in the same negative patterns you disliked as a child.

Many resources are available to help you in your parenting. They include friends, pediatrician, books, relatives and classes. Talk with others about your new role as parents. Share feelings with friends, compare notes and spend time with them and their new babies. A new parents' group or class may be available in your area and provide wonderful opportunities to share concerns and helpful hints and act as a support group for you. New mothers, especially, benefit from a time out with their babies in an atmosphere of acceptance and common experience.

Making the Most of Those Special Times

Make the most of all the precious, close, happy times you do have with each other and your baby. Feelings are very catching and the baby who is surrounded by loving feelings in the early years is able to give them back later. But most of all, **REMEMBER THAT SENSE OF HUMOR!!!**

A WORD ABOUT SIBLINGS

If you have other children, you should prepare them for the arrival of this new family member just as you are physically and mentally preparing yourself for the birth. The adjustment will probably be greater for them than for you. You did most of your adjusting with your first child.

A new mothers' class.

Advance Preparation

The time to start preparing them depends on the age of the children. Toddlers have no time conception, so talking about a new baby before your seventh or eighth month will only make the wait harder. Preschoolers of three or four can be told when they begin showing an interest in your growing abdomen. They too have limited time conception, so the waiting can seem endless if you start talking about the baby too soon. Older children can be told immediately and involved in the preparations from the beginning.

If your children are going to attend the birth, they will need further preparation. Prepare them for the sights and sounds associated with hard labor and delivery. Seeing a movie is especially beneficial. Have someone available during labor and birth, a friend or relative, who is responsible only for the children. She can feed them, play with them, answer questions and calm their fears as you give birth.

Most children love to look at their baby pictures and hear the story of their own birth. By sharing this story with your child, he will know that the same excitement and anticipation surrounded his arrival as well. **Create a realistic picture of what the new baby will be like.** Many young children expect a ready-made playmate and are greatly disappointed when they see that the baby does little more than eat, sleep, wet and cry. If you have friends who have young babies, take your preschooler to visit so he gets an idea of what babies are like.

If he still sleeps in a crib and you plan to use it for the new baby, **move him to his "grownup" bed** at least two months before your due date. Dismantle the crib and put it out of sight until the baby is born. By doing this, your toddler won't feel that his bed has been taken away from him by the baby. In the same way, don't take away stuffed animals and baby toys and give them to the baby. Let your older child do this when he is ready. He is going to feel that the baby has taken over, as it is. Don't add to his distress by asking him to give up some of his possessions.

During Your Hospital Stay

If possible, **have someone your child likes stay with him** at your home when you go to the hospital. If that's not possible, have him stay overnight with the person who will care for him before your due date so he does not become frightened when you leave him.

Call home at regular times each day to talk to him. Don't be upset if he refuses to come to the telephone. He might feel angry that you have left him. It may be fun for him if you **hide several small toys** or treats around the house, then give him directions to find one each time you call.

Take advantage of **sibling visiting** hours, if available at your hospital. It will ease your child's anxiety about your absence and will give him a chance to meet his new brother or sister.

Home Adjustments

When you come home from the hospital, **let your husband carry the baby** into the house so your arms are free to hold and cuddle your older child. You may be amazed at how BIG he suddenly appears to you. If you like, **bring him home a gift.** Visit and play with him. **Wait until he asks to see the baby,** then satisfy his curiosity by letting him touch, hold, and talk to (and about) this new family member.

Jealousy is a fact of life and cannot be completely prevented. It is usually stronger in children under five because they are more dependent on their parents and have few outside interests. Older children adapt more easily because less of their time and interest is centered on the home. You can lessen these feelings by continuing to **give your preschooler time alone with you** each day.

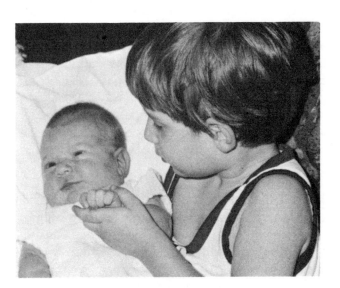

Siblings getting acquainted.

Make the baby's morning naptime his special play time, to do whatever he wants to do. Children also enjoy doing special things with Dad—a trip to the hardware store or lunch at a restaurant can be a special treat for a child of any age.

Other possibilities for decreasing these feelings of jealousy include giving him a doll to play with so he can take care of his "baby" as you take care of yours. Also, having little wrapped gifts on hand to give him when friends bring presents for the baby will make him feel special too. Allowing him to help you with the baby's care, even in little ways, will increase his feelings of importance as part of the family.

If your child shows anger or other **negative feelings** toward you or the baby, encourage him to talk about them. Let him know that you understand these feelings; in fact, that you even feel them sometimes yourself. Assure him of your love, but be firm that striking out at the baby cannot be allowed. Give him a substitute—a punching bag, hammer and peg board—something he can express his anger on other than the baby.

Expect some **regressive behavior** on the part of your toddler or preschooler. If he is not already potty trained, delay starting until the baby is four to six months old. Wet or soiled pants and requests for the breast or a bottle are very common. If you can understand the situation from his point of view, it makes sense. He reasons that if the baby gets so much attention doing these things, he will too! Let him try to nurse or drink from a bottle if he wishes. After a few attempts, he will realize it isn't much fun and will be off doing something else. Use baby's feeding time as moments to share with your older child. Read a book, share a snack, or play a quiet game. In this way, he will feel as important as the baby to you.

Support the side of your child that wants to grow up. Give him a chance to be proud of his maturity and make comments that foster his self-esteem. *"You do that so well." "You are such a help to Mommy."* Remind him there are disadvantages to being a baby—he can't play ball, go to birthday parties, eat ice cream, etc. Have lots of patience and be prepared for the adjustment to take some time.

POSTPARTUM EXERCISES

You should begin exercising as soon as possible after childbirth, certainly within 24 hours. In fact, if your

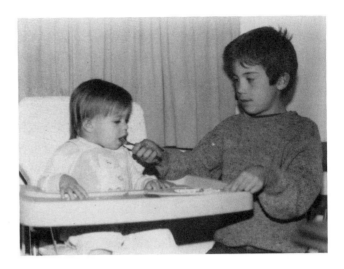

Big brother feeding sister.

perineum isn't numb from anesthesia, begin doing pelvic floor contractions (Kegels) in the recovery room.

The muscle work involved in immediate postpartum exercise is not strenuous or harmful. It will begin to restore tone to your pelvic floor and abdominal muscles, as well as encourage good circulation in your legs. Your doctor may give you a list of exercises to begin after delivery. If not, show him those listed here and get his okay or any modifications that he feels are necessary in your particular situation. They should be started gradually and added to as strength and comfort permit. There is no rush, so **don't overdo!**

Do each exercise series twice a day, repeating each exercise 2–3 times at first and gradually increasing to 5–10 repetitions. Consistency is much more important that the length of a given exercise session.

If you have a cesarean delivery, get your doctor's permission before starting a vigorous exercise program. See Chapter 9 for more information on exercising after a cesarean birth.

First Day

To aid blood circulation and prevent blood clots, do the following two exercises while resting in bed.

Ankle Rotating: While lying down or sitting with legs outstretched, rotate each foot at the ankle in a circle, 3 times in one direction; then 3 times in the other.

Foot Flexing and Stretching: While sitting or lying down with legs outstretched, flex your foot, slowly pointing your toes toward your body. You will feel stretching in your calf muscles. Then point your toes slowly away from you. Do this several times with each foot.

To decrease "flabbiness" and begin restoring muscle tone to the abdominal wall, do the following.

Abdominal Tightening: As often as you think of it, while sitting or standing, pull in your abdominal muscles and hold them tightly for 5 seconds, while you continue to breathe normally. As you become more proficient, increase the holding time to 10 seconds.

To tone pelvic floor muscles, improve circulation and promote healing at the episiotomy site, do the following exercise in the recovery room and every two hours thereafter during the first week postpartum.

Kegel Exercise: Contract the muscles of the pelvic floor and hold for 3–5 seconds as you continue to breathe normally; then relax. Repeat 5–10 times in a series.

Second Day

Continue **Kegels** and **abdominal tightening**, and add the following to promote improved abdominal muscle tone.

Pelvic Rock (on back):   While lying on your back with your knees bent and feet flat on the floor or bed, arch your back and press your buttocks against the floor; then press the small of your back against the floor and contract your abdominal muscles. *REMEMBER to keep breathing* and not hold your breath.

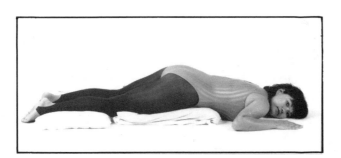

Modified knee chest.

To encourage the uterus to return to its normal position, do the following exercise twice a day.

Modified Knee-Chest: Lie on your stomach with a folded blanket or pillow under your abdomen and upper thighs and another under your ankles; turn your face to one side. Rest in this position often.

Third Day

Check for separation of the recti muscles before doing any further abdominal exercising. This band of muscles runs vertically through the center of the abdomen, is divided into two halves and is joined by connective tissue in the middle. It is not uncommon for these muscles to separate during pregnancy, especially if good body mechanics are not used while lifting.

To check for separation, lie on your back with your legs bent and press the fingers of one hand in a horizontal line into the area of your navel. Slowly raise your head and shoulders about 8 inches. You should feel the bands of muscle on both sides pull toward the center and move your fingers out of the way. If you have three or more fingers in the gap between the muscle bands, you have separated recti muscles. Do the special exercise below to help restore them to their proper position.

Checking for separation of recti muscles.

Head Lifting: Lie on your back with bent knees and cross your hands over the abdomen. Take a deep breath. Then slowly exhale and raise your head off the bed and pull the muscles together with your hands. As you breathe in, slowly lower your head to the bed. Repeat 5–10 times. Do 50 each day.
If you do this every day, the gap should be reduced to the normal ½ inch within a week to ten days. Until

the gap is closed, do *no* exercise that rotates or bends the trunk from side to side or twists your hips. This could pull the recti muscles further apart.

Head lifting.

Second Week

To restore muscle tone to the vagina and give support to the bladder and uterus, continue the following exercise (and also for the rest of your life).

Kegel Exercise: Do a series of 5–10 Kegels, contracting and releasing of the pelvic floor muscles, until you are doing a minimum of 50 a day up to a maximum of 100 a day.

To continue restoring abdominal muscle tone, add the following exercises.

Modified Sit-up: Lie on your back with knees bent and feet flat on the floor, and inhale. As you exhale, raise your head and shoulders and reach for your knees with both hands. Lie back down as you inhale. Repeat 5–10 times. If the recti muscles are still separated, support them as you do this progression of the

Modified sit-up.

Variation of modified sit-up.

head lifting exercise. Variation: As you raise your head and shoulders, reach hands to the outside of the right knee, lie back down and repeat to the left knee. (DON'T do this variation until the recti muscles are restored.)

Pelvic Rock (on all fours):   Pull in your abdominal muscles and buttocks as you press up with your lower back; hold for a few seconds. Then relax. Repeat 5–10 times at least three times a day.

To promote the return of the uterus to its proper position, do the following exercise twice a day.

Knee-Chest Exercise: Get into the all fours position, lower your chest to the floor, and point your elbows out to your sides. Turn your head to one side and spread your knees 12–18 inches apart. Contract and relax the abdominal muscles. Rest in this position for at least 5 minutes.

Knee-chest exercise.

Third Week

To begin restoring your waistline, do the following.

Side Kicks: Lie on your right side with your arms over your head and your head resting on your right

Side kicks.

arm. Keeping your right leg slightly bent, raise the left arm and leg toward the ceiling and touch your hand to your left leg (not toes). Then return arm and leg to original position and extend left arm further to stretch waist and rib cage. Relax. Repeat 5–10 times. Turn to other side and repeat.

To continue abdominal toning, begin this more difficult version of the sit up.

Modified Sit-up II: Do both variations of the sit-up begun during the second week with your hands clasped behind your head. Raise your head and shoulders as in the modified sit-up, pointing your elbows in the same direction of, but not touching, your knees.

Modified sit-up II.

To promote toning of the leg muscles as well as the abdominals and improve blood circulation, add the following two exercises to your routine.

Single Leg Raises: Lying on your back with knees bent and feet flat on the floor, draw your right knee toward your chest. As you inhale, slowly continue raising your leg with your toes pointed toward the ceiling. As you exhale, flex your foot toward your head and lower the leg slowly to the floor in this extended position. Return the leg to the bent knee position. Repeat pattern with the other leg. Do 5–10 times with each leg.

Single leg raises.

Single Leg Sliding: In same position as above, draw your right knee toward your chest while inhaling through your nose. As you exhale through your mouth, slowly return your leg to the bent knee position. Then continue sliding the leg downward, pressing the small of your back against the floor and contracting your abdominal muscles. Slide right leg back to bent knee position and repeat with other leg. Repeat 5–10 times with each leg.

To promote cardiovascular strength and general body tone, begin **walking** briskly around your neighborhood every day.

Single leg sliding.

Fourth to Sixth Week

Continue Kegels, side kicks, leg raises and slides. Increase **walking.**

To help restore your waistline, add the following exercises to your routine.

Hip Rolls: Lie on your back with your arms out to your sides in a T shape. Bring both knees to your chest; then roll your hips, bringing your knees and legs to the floor on the right side. Keep your back and arms flat on the floor as you do this. Bring your hips back to the center; then repeat on the left side. Repeat 5–10 times on each side.

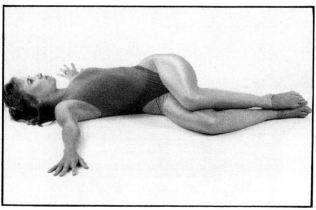

Hip rolls.

To promote greater abdominal strengthening, begin the next level of difficulty when doing sit-ups.

Modified Sit-up III: Cross your arms on your chest as you sit up. You only need to raise your body halfway to the sitting position to benefit from this exercise. Further lifting of your body brings other muscle groups into play.

Modified sit-up III.

After Six Weeks' Checkup

Continue the 4–6 week exercises for at least the next two months and add an aerobic (sustained) form of exercise such as **jogging, swimming** or **biking.**

POSTPARTUM SEX

The time following the birth of your baby is exciting, complicated and busy! Rapid changes are taking place within your body, which is adjusting from the pregnant to the nonpregnant state. As new parents, your relationship will never be the same. Being pregnant and in love is quite different from being parents and in love! After being free and spontaneous as lovers, you are now also parents with new roles, new responsibilities, a whole new life.

The love relationship between you continues to grow in new ways, and part of that love relationship is the enjoyment of sex. You may be confused by what you are told or even by your own feelings as individuals or as a couple. There are a number of considerations that enter into your decision to resume sexual intercourse.

Doctor's Advice

Some doctors advise a delay in sex until after the four to six week postpartum checkup. Others suggest waiting until the vaginal discharge has stopped. This waiting period insures that all healing has taken place at the episiotomy site as well as at the placental site within the uterus. With a cesarean birth, the healing of the abdominal scar is also important. Until these areas are healed completely, there is a risk of introducing bacteria that could cause an infection.

Fatigue

The first few weeks and months with a new baby are the busiest. Your time is really not your own. You never get a decent night's sleep and the days are exhausting. Although the father's routine is somewhat changed, *your* lifestyle is changed even more dramatically. It's difficult to be a good parent around the clock—*but sexy too??* It just doesn't seem possible for awhile!

Hormones

Your body's hormones are active in all the changes involved with birth and breastfeeding and often take some time to get into balance. These hormonal changes may affect your feelings and sexual responsiveness. You may want very much to make love, or may feel turned off by sex for a time.

Pain

Some new mothers find intercourse painful or uncomfortable, especially if it is resumed too soon after giving birth. Some men are hesitant because of concern for their wives. Patience and gentleness are important. Healing must take place at the episiotomy site and in the vagina. If the episiotomy repair is "overcorrected," making the vaginal opening smaller than before, or if there are vaginal adhesions, gentle dilation with the fingers and then with vaginal dilators from your doctor can solve the problem. If your vaginal area is still tender, you may find that the most comfortable position is lying side by side, which takes the pressure off the episiotomy site. A warm bath before lovemaking may also be helpful.

Hormonal changes resulting in decreased vaginal lubrication can also cause intercourse to be painful. This situation may last longer for the breastfeeding mother. This lack of lubrication is easily remedied by applying a water soluble jelly to the penis and vagina. Non-water soluble lubricants, such as petroleum jelly, should not be used as they keep air out and allow bacteria to grow.

Breastfeeding

Some breastfeeding mothers enjoy sex immensely; others don't for awhile. Fathers have feelings about breastfeeding also. Some find it very attractive while others view it as somewhat inhibiting to their sexual feelings.

Breasts are an important part of your sexuality—first to provide nourishment for your baby, and secondly as a source of sexual stimulation and pleasure. If thought of solely for sexual pleasure before the baby is born, it will take both of you some time to get used to the idea of breasts filled with milk. Some nursing mothers do not enjoy breast stimulation, and many couples find new areas of the body for sexual foreplay. At the same time, it's important to know that the baby will not contract an infection if love play includes the breasts, unless the father is ill.

One thing that may catch you unaware is a letdown of milk during love play or orgasm, resulting in both of you getting soaked! This occurs because oxytocin is released at orgasm, which triggers the let-

down of milk. After the initial "surprise" and wondering why "no one told me that," it helps to know that it is normal and natural. It may help to make love after nursing when the breasts are relatively empty (and the baby is more likely to be asleep). Wearing a nursing bra and pads may be more comfortable for you than leaking at a stimulating moment. Towels to keep the bedding dry are also a logical preparation.

Bottle feeding mothers may have uncomfortable amounts of milk within the breasts for a few weeks after delivery. Sexual activity involving the breasts encourages more milk production, so avoiding the breasts in sexual foreplay for a time will be helpful to discourage milk production.

New Responsibilities

The baby's presence as somewhat of a "chaperone," no matter how adorable, can be very inhibiting at times. The spontaneity of your love life may take a dive: "Is the baby going to wake?" "Do we have enough time between feedings?" Sexy feelings hardly get a chance if you're always listening for a cry.

New responsibilities can fatigue both parents, especially during the early weeks of adjustment. Yet tension and fatigue can build if you don't take some time out for yourselves. Change, feed, cuddle and put the baby to sleep and take time to talk together, relax, caress, or shut the door between you and your baby and make love.

Most Important—Feelings

Warmth and affection mean a lot to both of you, especially during the early adjustment period of becoming new parents. A cuddle and hug may mean more than making love for awhile. For lots of couples, a baby arrives before they've had a chance to be completely content with their sexual life together. And the movies don't tell you that it can take years to have a satisfying and exciting sex life.

A new father may feel pushed aside when a baby arrives needing so much attention. Instead of feeling he's gained a baby, he may feel he's lost a lover. He needs reassurance and to be told that your seemingly endless involvement with baby-centered activities does not diminish your love for him. You experience a lot of touching and body contact while caring for the baby all day, but your husband, at work, does not, and he needs this when he gets home. Encourage him to participate in the care of the baby when he is home, and don't forget to give him an extra hug and kiss now and then.

You may find it is quite a change to be at home alone with the baby, especially if you have been employed outside the home up to this time. It is helpful to have reassurance that your new role as a mother is important, even though it has no financial compensation. You require loving and confidence building and need to be told that your body is desirable after childbirth. Bringing home flowers, gifts, dinner, or just saying "I love you" are special ways in which your husband can express his affection. If he takes no special notice of you until you flop exhausted into bed, frustration and resentment can build up. You may react against each other and the difficulties may get worse.

Yet, it would be sad if you miss out on the warmth and affection because you're concerned that it will lead to sex. Try not to put too much emphasis on having sexual intercourse and wondering if "tonight's the night." Loving each other doesn't have to be sexual intercourse or nothing at all. Cuddling in each other's arms, touching, kissing and enjoying each other are very important ways of feeling close.

The main thing is to try to keep in touch with each other's feelings. The concerns that you have as new parents are really not isolated problems, but typical of what you will find throughout your life as a couple. If you can talk about your feelings and needs now, you will find that the understanding of each other will enhance your sexual relationship for the

rest of your life together. The solutions to sexual needs are not difficult to find for couples who will be honest and patient with each other. Talk about your feelings, keep a sense of humor and together look for solutions. After all, you will be friends and lovers long after your baby has grown and left home!!

Fear of Becoming Pregnant

No matter how thrilled you both are with the new baby, the thought of another one right away may be alarming. Thoughts about family planning should be shared between the two of you before the postpartum checkup, and then discussed with your doctor. Breastfeeding is *not* absolutely foolproof in preventing pregnancy. Because of changes in the vagina and uterus, the diaphragm is not appropriate for a time but can be employed later. Birth control pills, even the mini-pill, should not be taken while breastfeeding because the hormones in the pills reach the baby by way of the milk. Menstrual periods must resume with regularity before the rhythm method can be used. A condom and foam or jelly may be best for the first few weeks. The condom should decrease the possibility of introducing infection and the foam or jelly will lubricate the vagina. Remember that all methods are only as reliable as those who use them. Consistency counts!

The following chart was adapted from one compiled by the U.S. Department of Health, Education and Welfare, and is a complete guide to contraception. The intrauterine device (IUD) is not included in the chart as it is difficult to obtain in the U.S.

Father-son interaction.

METHODS OF CONTRACEPTION

Method	"The Pill"	"Mini-Pills"	Vaginal Sponge	Diaphragm with Spermicidal Jelly or Cream
What is it?	Pills with two hormones an estrogen and progestin, similar to the hormones a woman makes in her own ovaries.	Pills with just one type of hormone: a progestin similar to a hormone a woman makes in her own ovaries.	A soft, round, disposable sponge, approximately 2 inches in diameter, coated with a spermicide.	A shallow rubber cup used with a sperm-killing jelly or cream.
How Does it Work?	Prevents egg's release from woman's ovaries, makes cervical mucus thicker and changes lining of the uterus.	It may prevent egg's release from woman's ovaries, makes cervical mucus thicker and changes lining of uterus, making it harder for a fertilized egg to start growing there.	Fits over the cervix and continuously releases spermicide to block sperm and reduce sperm activity for up to 24 hours.	Fits inside the vagina. The rubber cup forms a barrier between the uterus and the sperm. The jelly or cream kills the sperm.
How Reliable or effective is it?	99.7% if used consistently, but much less effective if used carelessly.	97-99% if used perfectly, but less effective if used carelessly.	89–91% effective when used alone. Effectiveness is increased when used with another method such as condoms.	About 97% effective if used correctly and consistently, but much less effective if used carelessly.
How Would I Use it?	Either of two ways: 1. A pill a day for 3 weeks, stop for one week, then start a new pack. 2. A pill every single day with no stopping between packs.	Take one pill every single day as long as you want to avoid pregnancy.	Moisten with water and insert into the vagina before intercourse. May remain in up to 24 hours. Must remain in at least 6 hours after intercourse. Loop is attached to bottom to facilitate removal.	Insert the diaphragm and jelly (or cream) before intercourse. Can be inserted up to 6 hours before intercourse. Must stay in at least 6 hours after intercourse.
Are There Problems With it?	Must be prescribed by a doctor. All women should have a medical exam before taking the Pill, and some women should not take it.	Must be prescribed by a doctor. All women should have a medical exam first.	Removal problems may occur. May have to be removed professionally.	Must be fitted by a doctor after a pelvic examination. Some women find it difficult to insert, inconvenient or messy.
What Are the Side Effects or Complications?	Nausea, weight gain, headaches, missed periods, darkened skin on the face or depression may occur. More serious and more rare problems are blood clots in the legs, the lungs or the brain, and heart attacks.	Irregular periods, missed periods and spotting may occur and are more common problems with mini-pills than with the regular birth control pills.	Users may be at increased risk of toxic shock syndrome. Irritation may occur due to allergic reaction.	Some women find that the jelly or cream irritates the vagina. Try changing brands if this happens.
What Are the Advantages?	Convenient, extremely effective, does not interfere with sex and may diminish menstrual cramps.	Convenient, effective, does not interfere with sex and less serious side effects than with regular birth control pills.	No waiting necessary after insertion. Not messy. May protect against sexually transmitted diseases. Can be purchased without a prescription.	Effective and safe. May reduce risk of cervical cancer.

Spermicidal Foam, Jelly or Cream	Condom ("Rubber")	Condom and Foam Used Together	Periodic Abstinence (Natural Family Planning)	Sterilization
Cream and jelly come in tubes; foam comes in aerosol cans or individual applicators and is placed into the vagina.	A sheath of rubber shaped to fit snugly over the erect penis.		Ways of finding out days each month when you are most likely to get pregnant. Intercourse is avoided at that time.	Vasectomy (male) Tubal ligation (female). Ducts carrying sperm or the egg are tied and cut surgically.
Foam, jelly and cream contain a chemical that kills sperm and acts as a physical barrier between sperm and the uterus.	Prevents sperm from getting inside a woman's vagina during intercourse.	Prevents sperm from getting inside the uterus by killing sperm and by preventing sperm from getting out into the vagina.	Techniques include maintaining chart of basal body temperature, checking vaginal secretions, and keeping calendar of menstrual periods, all of which can help predict when you are most likely to release an egg.	Closing of tubes in male prevents sperm from reaching egg; closing tubes in female prevents egg from reaching sperm.
About 90-97% effective if used correctly and consistently, but much less effective if used carelessly.	About 97% effective if used correctly and consistently, but much less effective if used carelessly.	Close to 100% effective if both foam and condoms are used with every act of intercourse.	Certain methods are about 90-97% effective if used consistently. Other methods are less effective. Combining techniques increases effectiveness.	Almost 100% effective and NOT usually reversible.
Put foam, jelly, or cream into your vagina each time you have intercourse, not more than 30 minutes beforehand. No douching for at least 8 hours after intercourse.	The condom should be placed on the erect penis before the penis ever comes into contact with the vagina. After ejaculation, the penis should be removed from the vagina immediately.	Foam must be inserted within 30 minutes before intercourse and condom must be placed onto erect penis prior to contact with vagina.	Careful records must be maintained of several factors: basal body temperature, vaginal secretions and onset of menstrual bleeding. Careful study of these methods will dictate when intercourse should be avoided.	After the decision to have no more children has been well thought through, a brief surgical procedure is performed on the man or the woman.
Must be inserted just before intercourse. Some find it inconvenient or messy.	Objectionable to some men and women. Interrupts intercourse. May be messy. Condom may break.	Requires more effort than some couples like. May be messy or inconvenient. Interrupts intercourse.	Difficult to use method if menstrual cycle is irregular. Sexual intercourse must be avoided for a significant part of each cycle.	Surgical operation has some risk but serious complications are rare. Sterilizations should not be unless no more children are desired.
Some women find that the foam, cream or jelly irritates the vagina. May irritate the man's penis. Try changing brands if this happens.	Rarely, individuals are allergic to rubber. If this is a problem, condoms called "skins" which are not made out of rubber are available.	No serious complications.	No complications.	All surgical operations have some risk but serious complications are uncommon. Some pain may last for several days. Rarely, the wrong structure is tied off or the tube grows back together. There is no loss of sexual desire or ability in vast majority of patients.
Effective, safe, a good lubricant and can be purchased at a drugstore. Products containing nonoxynol-9 may help protect against AIDS.	Effective, safe, can be purchased without prescription; good protection against sexually transmitted infections and diseases (AIDS, cervical cancer).	Extremely effective, safe and both methods may be purchased without prescription. Good protection against sexually transmitted infections and diseases.	Safe, effective if followed carefully; little if any religious objection to method. Teaches women about their menstrual cycles.	The most effective method; low rate of complications; many feel that removing fear of pregnancy improves sexual relations.

Appendices

Glossary of Terms

abdomen—the area between the ribs and the *pubic bone**.

abortion—any loss of pregnancy before *viability* (28th week), either accidentally (*miscarriage*) or purposefully.

abruptio placentae—premature separation of the *placenta* from the *uterus*.

active labor—the second phase of the *first stage of labor; cervix* dilates from *4–8 centimeters*.

acupressure—the use of fingertip pressure on specific body points for relief of such problems as pain, nausea and fatigue.

adrenal glands—two small glands located on the upper part of the kidneys which secrete *hormones*.

afterbirth—*placenta* and *membranes* which pass out of the *uterus* during the *third stage of labor*.

afterpains —*contractions* of the *uterus* following birth.

AIDS—Acquired Immune Deficiency Syndrome, a viral disease that attacks the body's natural defenses.

albumin—a simple protein.

albuminuria—the presence of protein in the urine, associated with kidney disorders and *toxemia* of pregnancy.

amino acids—building blocks of the protein molecule.

amnesic—a drug which causes loss of memory.

amnihook—instrument used to perform *amniotomy*.

amniocentesis—the removal of a small amount of *amniotic fluid,* usually to determine fetal age and genetic composition.

amnion—the innermost *membrane* of the *amniotic sac*.

amniotic fluid—the liquid contained in the *amniotic sac*.

amniotic sac—the *membranes* composed of two layers, containing the *fetus* and *amniotic fluid,* also known as "*bag of waters*."

analgesic—a drug, gas, or other agent that relieves or reduces pain without causing unconsciousness.

anesthetic—an agent which produces loss of sensation, with or without loss of consciousness.

anoxia—deficiency of oxygen.

antepartum—the period of pregnancy from *conception* to birth; also called *prenatal*.

anus—outlet of rectum, directly behind *vagina*.

Apgar score—evaluation of the infant's condition at one and five minutes after birth.

areola (a reé o la)—the pigmented area surrounding the nipple of the breast which darkens during pregnancy.

auscultation—process of listening to *fetal heart tones* and placental sounds with a *fetoscope*.

baby blues—short period of mild depression after childbirth.

bag of waters—lay term for *amniotic sac* and *fluid*.

barbiturate—a depressant drug which induces sleep.

bilirubin—product of the breakdown of red blood cells, which can cause *jaundice*.

birth canal—the passageway from the *uterus* through which the baby is born.

blastocyst—a stage in the development of the *embryo*.

bloody show—a blood-tinged vaginal discharge seen at the beginning of, or in, *labor*.

bonding—the attachment which a mother and father develop towards their new baby.

Braxton-Hicks—the intermittent and usually painless *contractions* of the *uterus* noticed in pregnancy.

---

*Italicized words are defined in glossary.

209

breech—position of the baby in which the buttocks or feet (footling breech) are presented first.

buccal (buck′ al)—pertaining to a method of administering *pitocin* orally.

caput (ka′ put)—the head.

caput succedaneum (ká put suk se dá ne um)—swelling of the scalp.

catheterization—method used to empty the bladder by insertion of a small pliable tube through the *urethra*.

caudal anesthesia—loss of sensation from hips to toes produced by injection of an anesthetic into the caudal space, which is at the base of the spine.

centimeters—unit of measure used to describe progress in *dilatation* of the *cervix* during *labor*.

cephalopelvic disproportion ("CPD")—a condition in which the baby's head will not fit through the pelvic opening, usually an indication for a *cesarean* delivery.

certified nurse midwife (CNM)—a registered nurse who has completed an accredited midwifery program and is licensed by the state to manage low-risk pregnancies and *deliveries.*

cervix—the narrow neck-like end of the *uterus* leading into the *vagina* which must thin out and open during *labor* to allow the baby to pass into the *birth canal.*

cesarean birth—*delivery* of the baby by means of incisions through the abdominal and uterine walls. ("C-section," "section" are hospital jargon.)

chorion—the outermost *membrane* of the *amniotic sac.*

cilia—hair-like projections which propel the egg through the *fallopian tube* towards the *uterus.*

circumcision—surgical removal of the *foreskin* of the *penis.*

coccyx (kok′ siks)—the small bone at the end of the spinal column; tailbone.

colostrum—sticky, yellowish fluid secreted by the breasts in small quantities during late pregnancy and for several days following birth before the milk comes in.

complete—term used to indicate that the *cervix* is sufficiently dilated and effaced for the baby to pass through, usually 10 *centimeters.*

conception—*fertilization*; the union of *sperm* and egg, resulting in a new life.

congenital—existing at or before birth; hereditary.

contraceptive—any device used to prevent pregnancy.

contractions—tightening and shortening of the uterine muscles during *labor* causing *effacement* and *dilatation* of the *cervix* and contributing to the descent of the baby.

cradle cap—crusting on the scalp of infants.

crowning—term indicating that the presenting part of the baby (usually the crown of the head) is visible at the vaginal opening and no longer slips back out of sight between *contractions.*

delivery—birth; the baby's passage from the *uterus* into the external world through the *birth canal.*

dilatation (dilation)—gradual opening of the *cervix*, accomplished by uterine *contractions*, to permit passage of the baby out of the *uterus.* Dilatation is "*complete*" at 10 *centimeters.*

diuretic—a medication that removes water from the body; "water pills."

due date—estimated date of birth; also called E.D.C. (estimated date of confinement).

early labor—the first phase of the *first stage of labor; cervix* dilates from 0–4 *centimeters.*

eclampsia—a serious *toxemia* accompanied by convulsions and coma. It may occur before, during or after *delivery.*

edema—the presence of excessive amounts of fluid in the body tissues. Some swelling is normal in pregnancy.

effacement—thinning and shortening of the *cervix* occurring before or during *dilatation*, expressed in terms of percentage from 0–100 percent.

effleurage—very light fingertip massage of the *abdomen*, buttocks, or thighs to aid in relaxation in labor.

embolism—presence of air bubble or blood clot in a blood vessel.

embryo—term for the baby during the first eight weeks of life in the *uterus*.

enema—the insertion of a solution into the rectum and colon to empty the lower intestine.

engagement—term indicating that the presenting part of the baby has secured itself into the upper opening (inlet) of the pelvic cavity and is in position to begin its passage through the pelvic bones. This may be felt as *lightening* by the woman.

engorgement—excessive fullness, usually referring to the breasts.

epidural anesthesia—loss of sensation from *abdomen* to toes produced by injection of *anesthetic* into epidural space which surrounds the spinal fluid.

episiotomy—an incision made into the *perineum*, prior to *delivery*, to enlarge the vaginal outlet.

estrogen—a female hormone produced in the *ovaries* and *adrenal glands*.

expulsion—the actual movement of the baby through and out of the *birth canal*. Accomplished by the *contractions* of the *uterus* and the pushing efforts of the woman.

fallopian tubes—two small tubes extending from the *uterus* toward the left and right *ovaries*.

false labor—*contractions* of the *uterus* which are strong enough to be interpreted as true labor but have no dilating effect on the *cervix*.

fertilization—meeting of the *sperm* and egg, normally occurring in the *fallopian tube*.

fetal distress—a term describing a condition where the oxygen supply of the *fetus* is threatened, detected by change in *fetal heart rate* and/or *meconium* stained *amniotic fluid*.

fetal heart tones—the baby's heartbeat, as heard through the woman's abdominal wall, normally 120–160 beats per minute.

fetal monitor—an electronic machine that is used to detect and record the *fetus'* heartbeat in relation to *contractions* of the *uterus*.

fetoscope—instrument used for listening to *fetal heart tones* and placental sounds.

fetus—term used to refer to the baby from the 8th week after *conception* until birth.

fingers—unit of measure used to describe the progress of *dilatation*. One finger equals two *centimeters*.

first stage of labor—the part of *labor* during which the *cervix* dilates to 10 *centimeters*. Includes *early*, *active*, and *transition phases*.

fontanels—soft spots on the top of the baby's head which allow for *molding* during birth.

forceps—a tong-like obstetrical instrument occasionally used to aid in *delivery*.

foreskin—the fold of skin covering the head of the *penis*.

fourth stage of labor—the first hours after birth; the recovery period.

fundus—top or upper portion of the *uterus*.

general anesthesia—inhalation of gas or *intravenous* injection to produce loss of consciousness.

genitals—the external reproductive organs.

gestation—condition or period of carrying a baby in the uterus; approximately 40 weeks long.

gonorrhea—a contagious venereal disease.

gravida—literally, a pregnant woman; used with numerals to designate the number of times a woman has become pregnant. (In her first pregnancy a woman is "gravida I"; in her second, "gravida II," etc.)

heartburn—a burning sensation in the esophagus caused by the seepage of gastric juice from the stomach.

hemorrhoids—*varicose veins* of the *anus*, usually temporary in pregnancy.

herpes virus II—a contagious venereal virus which, if active, has potentially disastrous effects on the fetus during a vaginal *delivery*. It is therefore an indication for a *cesarean* delivery.

hormone—a chemical substance produced by a gland or organ.

hypertension—high blood pressure.

hyperventilation—a possible side effect of improper breathing during *labor,* caused by excessive depletion of carbon dioxide in the blood, characterized by dizziness and tingling of extremities.

hypotension—blood pressure that is lower than normal.

immunity—resistance to a particular disease.

implantation—the attachment of the fertilized egg to the wall of the *uterus.*

incompetent cervix—a *cervix* that begins dilating too early, usually in the second *trimester.*

incontinence—the inability to control the flow of urine.

induction—artificially initiating *labor* by use of medication and/or mechanical techniques.

intrauterine—within the *uterus.*

intravenous (I.V.)—to give a sterile fluid into a vein for purpose of nutrition, hydration or medication.

in utero—within the *uterus.*

involution—return of the *uterus* to the nonpregnant size and position, taking approximately six weeks.

jaundice—yellow discoloration of the skin, whites of eyes and mucous membranes because of a high level of *bilirubin.*

Kegel (keé gull)—refers to a set of exercises devised by Dr. Arnold Kegel to strengthen the *pelvic floor* muscles.

labia (laý bee a)—lips or external folds surrounding the *vagina* and *urethra.*

labor—productive uterine *contractions* which produce *dilation* of the *cervix,* descent of the baby and its *expulsion* into the world.

lactation—the production and secretion of milk by the breasts.

Lamaze (le mahź)—an emotional and physical preparation for childbirth; named after Dr. Fernand Lamaze; *psychoprophylactic* childbirth.

lanugo—fine downy hair on the body of the *fetus* after the fourth month; usually not apparent at birth.

Leboyer birth—a quiet, peaceful *delivery* experience designed to reduce birth trauma in infants; also called gentle birth.

let-down reflex—the involuntary ejection of milk that occurs during breastfeeding.

lightening—shifting of the baby and *uterus* downward into the pelvic cavity, noticed by the mother as a change in abdominal contours.

linea nigra (lińe ah nǐ gra)—the dark vertical line which appears on the *abdomen* during pregnancy.

lithotomy—the standard hospital *delivery* position in which the woman lies on her back with her legs in stirrups.

local—an injection of *anesthetic* into the perineal tissue to numb the *perineum* for *episiotomy* repair.

lochia—discharge of blood, mucus and tissue from the *uterus* after the birth of the baby.

malpresentation—a faulty or abnormal fetal *presentation.*

mammary glands—glands within the breasts that produce milk.

mask of pregnancy—brown pigmentation of the forehead, cheeks and nose seen during pregnancy.

meconium—the dark green or black tarry-like substance present in the baby's large intestine and which comprises his first stools after birth.

membranes—the *amnion* and *chorion* which comprise the *amniotic sac.*

milia—tiny white bumps which sometimes appear on a newborn's face.

miscarriage—accidental *abortion.*

molding—shaping of the baby's head allowing it to adjust to the size and shape of the *birth canal.*

Mongolian spots—temporary purplish-brown discoloration sometimes found on the backs of dark-skinned babies.

Montgomery's glands—small prominences on the areola of the breast which enlarge during pregnancy and *lactation*.

morning sickness—the nausea and/or vomiting experienced by many women in the first *trimester* of pregnancy.

morula (mor' ū la)— the solid mass of cells resulting from the early cell division of the *ovum*.

mucus plug—the heavy mucus which blocks the cervical canal during pregnancy.

multigravida—a woman who has experienced two or more pregnancies.

multipara (mul tip' ar ah)—a woman who has given birth to more than one child; multip.

natal—pertaining to birth or the day of birth.

navel—umbilicus; the site where the *umbilical cord* was attached to the baby.

neonatal period—the first four weeks of life.

neonate—the newborn.

obstetrics—the branch of medicine covering the care of women in pregnancy, childbirth and *postpartum*.

occiput (ok' sip ut)—the back part of the baby's head.

ovaries—the two female glands of reproduction.

ovulation—monthly release of ripe *ovum* from *ovary*.

ovum—the female egg cell; pl., ova.

oxytocin—*hormone* which stimulates uterine *contractions* and the *let-down reflex*.

para—refers to the number of births (para I—first baby, para II—second baby, etc.).

paracervical—an injection of *anesthetic* into the *cervix*.

pelvic floor—hammock-like ligaments and muscles supporting the reproductive organs.

pelvimetry—a method of determining pelvic measurement by X-ray.

pelvis—the bony ring which joins the spine and legs. In the female its central opening encases the walls of the *birth canal*.

penis—the male sex organ.

perineum—the area between the *vagina* and the *anus*.

phototherapy—ultraviolet light used to treat newborn *jaundice*.

physiological—pertaining to the normal functioning of the body.

pit-drip—*intravenous* administration of *pitocin* in a glucose solution.

pitocin—an oxytocic *hormone* used to induce or stimulate uterine *contractions*.

PKU test—procedure in which a small drop of newborn's blood is examined for a specific *amino acid* deficiency.

placenta—the temporary organ of pregnancy which exchanges oxygen, nutrients and wastes between mother and *fetus; afterbirth*.

placenta previa—*placenta* that is implanted in the lower uterine segment; it may partially or completely cover the cervical opening.

position—the way the *fetus* is situated in the *pelvis* of the mother.

posterior—when referring to the baby's position it means the back part of the baby's head is against the woman's spine.

postmature—delivery at 43 weeks *gestation* or more.

postpartum—refers to the time following birth.

postpartum depression—a period of melancholy or "blues" that some women experience after childbirth.

potentiate—to intensify the action of another drug.

precipitate delivery—a sudden and unexpected birth, usually following a very short *labor*.

precipitate labor—a *labor* completed within three hours.

preeclampsia—a severe *toxemia* of pregnancy that if untreated may lead to *eclampsia*.

premature—an infant weighing less than 2500 grams (5 lbs. 8 ozs.) at birth or born before 37 weeks *gestation.*

prenatal—after *conception* and before the birth of the child.

prep —shaving or trimming of pubic hair.

presentation—how the baby is positioned for birth; the part closest to the *cervix* is the presenting part.

primigravida—a woman who is pregnant for the first time.

primipara (pry mip′ ah rah)—a woman who has had her first baby; primip.

progesterone—the *hormone* that is responsible for the building up of the lining of the *uterus* and for maintaining the lining during pregnancy.

prolactin—a *hormone* that stimulates *lactation* and maternal feelings.

psychoprophylaxis—literally "mind prevention"; the technical term used to describe the *Lamaze* technique of childbirth preparation.

pubic bones—the front bones that join the two hip bones to form the pelvic girdle. The pubic bones are connected by a joint that softens during pregnancy.

pudendal block—an injection of *anesthetic* into the pudendal nerves to numb the *vagina* and *perineum.*

quickening—the first movements of the *fetus* felt by the woman, usually felt between 16 and 18 weeks.

relaxin—hormone which relaxes the pelvic ligaments and other joints in the body during pregnancy.

Rh factor—a blood factor found in the red blood cells which is present in 85 percent of the population. When it is absent, the person is Rh negative.

RhoGam—a medication that is given to an Rh negative woman within 72 hours of the birth of an Rh positive baby or an aborted pregnancy to prevent her from producing antibodies which could endanger subsequent babies.

ripe—a word to describe the softening of the *cervix* that occurs when it is ready for the onset of *labor.*

rooming-in—situation where baby and mother stay in the same hospital room for extended periods, rather than just for feedings.

rooting reflex—the instinctive movements of the baby's head and mouth toward a touch on the cheek or mouth.

sacrum—the triangular bone that is situated below the last spinal vertebra and above the *coccyx.*

saddle block—an injection of *anesthetic* into the lower spinal canal which causes numbness from the pubic area to the toes.

scopolamine—a medication used for its *amnesic* effects; also called "scope."

second stage of labor—the time from *complete dilatation* until the birth of the baby.

sedative—a medication that reduces anxiety.

sibling—one of two or more offspring of the same parents.

sperm—the male reproductive cell produced in the *testes.*

sphincter—a ring-like muscle which closes a natural opening, i.e., *anus* and *urethra.*

spinal block—an injection of *anesthetic* into the spinal fluid which produces numbness.

station—the location of the presenting part in relation to the woman's pelvic bones.

striae gravidarum (strī ee)—the pinkish or purple lines seen on the *abdomen* and breasts during pregnancy; commonly called "stretch marks."

stripping of membranes—pulling of the *amniotic sac* away from *cervix* to induce *labor.*

term—the completed cycle of pregnancy, full term being 40 weeks.

testes—the two organs which produce *sperm;* located in the scrotum.

tetanic contraction—a uterine *contraction* that is extremely long and strong; usually associated with induced *labor.*

third stage of labor—the time from the birth of the baby until the *placenta* is delivered.

toxemia—a metabolic disorder of pregnancy. Symptoms include *hypertension,* swelling, and *albumin* in the urine.

tranquilizer—a medication that relieves anxiety.

transition—the last phase of the *first stage of labor;* dilatation of the *cervix* from 8–10 *centimeters.*

trimester—a period of three months.

twilight sleep—a combination of an *analgesic* and *scopolamine.*

ultrasound—use of high frequency sound waves for diagnostic purposes; sonogram, B-scan.

umbilical cord—cord-like structure containing two arteries and one vein that connects the baby and *placenta.*

umbilicus—the *navel* or belly button.

urethra—the tube which carries urine from the bladder to the outside of the body.

uterus—muscular pear-shaped organ of *gestation;* also called womb.

vagina—curved, very elastic canal, 4–6 inches long, from the *uterus* to the *vulva.*

varicose veins—unnaturally distended veins, commonly found during pregnancy in legs, *vulva* and *anus.*

vernix caseosa (ver′ niks kay se o′ sah)—white, cheese-like protective coating covering the baby's skin.

vertex—the top or crown of the head.

viability—ability to survive outside the *uterus.*

vulva—the external female reproductive organs, consisting of the clitoris and the lips or folds on either side of the vaginal opening.

Wharton's jelly—the jelly-like material surrounding the vessels of the *umbilical cord.*

Recommended Reading List

This book has provided you with basic information on many topics related to pregnancy, birth and the newborn. For more detailed reading in these areas, the following books are recommended. Those titles which are preceded by an asterisk (*) are recommended most highly.

If you are unable to locate one of these books in your teacher's library, the public library, or your local bookstore, you may order it directly from either of the following sources:

ICEA BOOKCENTER
P.O. Box 20048
Minneapolis, Minnesota 55420-0048

Birth and Life Bookstore
P.O. Box 70625
Seattle, Washington 98117

PREGNANCY, BIRTH AND CHILDBIRTH PREPARATION

Active Birth, Janet Balaskas and Arthur Balaskas, 1984.

Descriptions of all stages of labor, demonstrating how a woman's choice of position during labor can reduce her discomfort. Includes an illustrated section on stretching exercises.

Birth Reborn, Michel Odent, 1984.

Descriptions of labor positions and delivery methods as used in Odent's famous clinic at Pithiviers, France.

Birth Trap, Yvonne Brackbill, June Rice and Diony Young, 1984.

Discusses benefits and risks of high-tech birthing, including many controversial topics.

Birth Without Violence, Frederick Leboyer, 1975.

Poetic and powerful, with beautiful photos showing techniques for easing the trauma of birth for the baby.

*****Birthing Normally**, Gayle Peterson, 1984.

Holistic approach providing ways to maximize chances of giving birth naturally, without intervention.

*****Birthrights**, Sally Inch, 1984.

Presents arguments for and against obstetrical intervention.

Bonding: How Parents Become Attached to Their Babies, Diony Young, 1978.

Good brief pamphlet on the value of parent-infant bonding and the practical problems faced by most parents in hospitals.

*****A Child is Born**, Lennart Nilsson, Furuhjelm, Sundberg, Wirsen, 1977.

Brilliant photos which capture the mystery of life within the womb from conception to birth, along with up-to-date advice on childbearing methods.

*****Childbirth With Insight**, Elizabeth Noble, 1983.

Encourages self-reliance and responsibility. Goes beyond structured methods and shows how to permit labor to take its natural course.

Children at Birth, Marjie Hathaway and Jay Hathaway, 1978.

A positive report on children's presence during the birth of their siblings, including over 125 photos.

217

Choices in Childbirth, Silvia Feldman, 1978.

A good overview of the many options available to expectant parents for the birth of their child.

Commonsense Childbirth, Lester Dessez Hazell, 1976.

Childbirth from the mother's perspective, with emphasis on the mother's feelings and on her right to control the experience. Detailed examination of home birth, its advantages and risks.

Episiotomy and the Second Stage of Labor, Sheila Kitzinger and Penny Simkin, 1984.

Management of second stage labor, including benefits and risks of episiotomies.

Essential Exercises for the Childbearing Year, Elizabeth Noble, 1982.

Very good presentation of valuable exercises for mother before and after birth. Particularly good information for the mother recovering from a cesarean delivery.

Expectant Fathers, Sam Bittman and Sue Zalk, 1980.

Preparation for pregnancy and childbirth written especially for fathers.

Experience of Childbirth, Sheila Kitzinger, 1984.

Emotional aspects of pregnancy, with emphasis on relaxation.

The First Nine Months of Life, Geraldine Lux Flanagan, 1962.

Basic presentation of fetal development with excellent photographs.

The Gentle Birth Book, Nancy Berezin, 1980.

A practical guide to Leboyer family-centered deliveries.

Giving Birth, Barbara Katz Rothman, 1984.

Exposé of the medical model of birth as compared with the more natural midwifery approach.

*****A Good Birth, A Safe Birth**, Diana Korte and Roberta Scaer, 1984.

Provides the tools needed to experience the best possible birth. Includes documented studies.

Having Twins, Elizabeth Noble, 1980.

Tips on prenatal care and parenting, as well as fascinating facts dealing with multiple births.

Husband Coached Childbirth, Robert Bradley, 1981.

Information for husbands on helping their wives from pregnancy through birth. Bradley method.

Immaculate Deception: A New Look at Women and Childbirth in America, Suzanne Arms, 1977.

Extensive documentation of modern social trends that have deprived parents of control of the birth experience. A good explanation of the reasons that prepared childbirth training has become necessary.

Labor and Birth: A Guide for You, Linda Todd, 1987.

Complete, easy-to-read manual.

Life Before Birth, Ashley Montagu, 1977.

How a mother can affect the physical and emotional development of her unborn child.

*****Making Love During Pregnancy**, Elisabeth Bing and Libby Colman, 1982.

Facts about intercourse during pregnancy. Examines many myths about the subject, and offers good practical information. Extensive illustrations.

Moving Through Pregnancy, Elisabeth Bing, 1976.

Photos and helpful hints on exercise for physical comfort and well-being during pregnancy.

Parent-Infant Bonding, Marshall Klaus and John Kennell, 1982.

A research-based text documenting the fact that early contact with the newborn increases parental feelings of attachment and is a positive influence on the baby's development.

*****The Pregnancy After 30 Workbook**, Gail Sforza Brewer, 1978.

Valuable manual featuring detailed plans on how a woman at any age can manage her pregnancy with self-assurance.

*Pregnancy and Childbirth: The Complete Guide for a New Life, Tracy Hotchner, 1984.

Discusses the pros and cons of all aspects of pregnancy, childbirth and infant care. Explores many controversial subjects.

Pregnancy As Healing, Vols. I and II, Gayle Peterson and Lewis Mehl, 1984 and 1985.

Discusses both the emotional and spiritual aspects of childbearing and the intensely physical experience. Volume I explains holistic prenatal care. Volume II includes discussions of intervention and family roles.

Pregnancy, Childbirth and the Newborn, Penny Simkin, Janet Whalley and Anne Keppler, 1984.

Complete, well-organized guide, emphasizing parental choice.

Preparation for Childbirth, Donna Ewy and Rodger Ewy, 1985.

Easily understood explanation of the Lamaze method. Many illustrations.

Right From the Start, Gail Sforza Brewer and Janice Presser Greene, 1981.

Information and support for a natural birth.

A Season to Be Born, Suzanne Arms and John Arms, 1973.

A masterpiece of photos joined with the truthfulness of a couple's adventure of pregnancy, labor and delivery.

The Secret Life of the Unborn Child, Thomas Verny with John Kelly, 1981.

New and startling information on the physical and emotional influences on the unborn baby.

Six Practical Lessons for an Easier Childbirth, Elisabeth Bing, 1982.

An excellent guide to Lamaze training for couples unable to attend classes. Includes exercises, techniques and illustrations.

Special Delivery, Rahima Baldwin, 1979.

Comprehensive guide for couples wanting to take greater responsibility for their birth experiences at home, in a birth center or in a hospital.

Spiritual Midwifery, Ina May Gaskin, 1980.

Advice on the spiritual and physical aspects of birth. Includes accounts of births at The Farm in Tennessee.

Teenage Pregnancy: A New Beginning, Linda Barr and Catherine Monserrat, 1978.

Brief description of pregnancy and birth aimed at adolescent mothers. Good supplementary materials on exercises and breastfeeding. Extensive illustrations.

Thank You, Dr. Lamaze, Marjorie Karmel, 1983.

Mrs. Karmel's description of her training for and experiences of two deliveries without anesthesia and without pain because of Fernand Lamaze.

Transformation Through Birth, Claudia Panuthos, 1984.

Explores the relationship between a woman's psychological well-being and her ability to experience a healthy and rewarding birth.

We Gave Birth Together, Karen Michele and Elisabeth Bing, 1983.

Color photographs of four couples. Includes dialogue of the work, joy and emotions of childbirth.

Whole Birth Catalog, Janet Isaacs Ashford, 1983.

Compilation of books, products and resources for the childbearing consumer.

Woman-Centered Pregnancy and Birth, Ginny Cassidy-Brin, Francie Hornstein and Carol Downer, 1984.

A feminist approach to birth, emphasizing the woman's right to make decisions concerning her experience. Includes many controversial topics.

CESAREAN BIRTH

The Cesarean Birth Experience, Bonnie Donovan, 1986.

Helpful guide to parents facing a cesarean birth. Emphasis on the involvement of the father.

Cesarean Birth—Risk and Culture, Gayle Peterson and Lewis Mehl, 1985.

Cesarean birth information including discussions of the emotional and spiritual aspects of cesarean delivery.

Cesarean Childbirth, A Handbook for Parents, Barbara Hickernell, editor, 1977.

Compilation of brief discussions by authorities from several fields. Good, basic information.

Cesarean Childbirth, A Handbook for Parents, Christine Wilson and Wendy Hovey, 1980.

Complete guide to cesarean birth including information on emotional and physical preparation and recovery.

*****The Cesarean (R)evolution, A Handbook for Parents and Childbirth Educators**, Linda D. Meyer, 1981.

How to have a family-centered cesarean birth.

Having a Cesarean Baby, Richard Hausknecht and Joan Ratter Heilmann, 1982.

Examines what parents can expect with a cesarean birth. Written from a doctor's point of view.

How to Avoid a Cesarean Section, Christopher Norwood, 1984.

Strategies to avoid unnecessary surgery and steps to get the best medical care if surgery is needed.

*****Silent Knife: Cesarean Prevention and Vaginal Birth After Cesarean**, Nancy Wainer Cohen and Lois J. Estner, 1983.

Powerful, documented information on the cesarean epidemic, including methods for preventing unnecessary cesareans.

*****Unnecessary Cesareans—Ways to Avoid Them**, Diony Young and Charles Mahan, 1980.

Explains what you can do during your pregnancy, labor and delivery to decrease the chance of having a cesarean, and how to have a positive experience if a cesarean is necessary.

For further information on cesarean birth, contact either of the following organizations:

C/SEC
22 Forest Road
Framingham, Massachusetts 01701
(617) 877-8266

Cesarean Prevention Movement
P.O. Box 152
University Station
Syracuse, New York 13210
(315) 424-1942

BREASTFEEDING

Abreast of the Times, Richard Applebaum, 1970.

A pediatrician's advice to nursing mothers, with good practical information.

Breastfeeding, Janice Presser, Gail Sforza Brewer and Julianna FreeHand, 1983.

Complete guidance from pregnancy through weaning. Beautifully illustrated.

Breastfeeding Today: A Mother's Companion, Candace Woessner, Judith Lauwers and Barbara Bernard, 1987.

A comprehensive, up-to-date guide designed for today's woman.

The Complete Book of Breastfeeding, Marvin Eiger and Sally Wendkos Olds, 1987.

Very complete examination of the subject, with much practical information.

*****Nursing Your Baby**, Karen Pryor, 1973.

Valuable and interesting information on the physiology of the breasts and the nursing process.

Preparation for Breastfeeding, Donna Ewy and Rodger Ewy, 1985.

Good presentation of the methods and advantages of breastfeeding, with emphasis on the psychological aspects. Easy reading.

*****The Womanly Art of Breastfeeding**, La Leche League International, 1987.

Complete and practical guide. A must for every woman planning to nurse her baby.

You Can Breastfeed Your Baby Even in Special Situations, Dorothy Patricia Brewster, 1979.

Information on nursing twins and triplets, as well as babies who are adopted, retarded, physically deformed, diabetic, etc. Also provides breastfeeding support for mothers with such conditions as blindness and tuberculosis.

PARENTHOOD, CHILD CARE AND CHILD DEVELOPMENT

*The Baby Massage Book, Tina Heinl, 1983.

Explains the positive physical and emotional effects of massaging your baby. Includes step-by-step directions.

*The Baby Exercise Book, Janine Levy, 1975.

Specific exercises designed to aid your baby's development up to fifteen months of age. Complete with photographs.

Babysense, A Practical and Supportive Guide to Baby Care, Frances Wells Burck, 1979.

A unique guide which answers most of your "how-to" questions and explains both mental and physical aspects of infant development.

Childhood Illness—A Commonsense Approach, Jack Shiller, 1974.

Good background information to help you understand and work with your pediatrician.

*Circumcision: The Painful Dilemma, Rosemary Romberg, 1985.

A balanced critique of current medical research, myths and realities. Includes extensive bibliography.

The Early Childhood Years, The 2 to 6 Year Old, Frank Caplan, 1983.

Discusses the development of the young child.

*The Family Bed: An Age-Old Concept in Child Rearing, Tine Thevenin, 1987.

Explores the pros and cons of siblings' sleeping with one another and with parents.

The First Three Years of Life, Burton L. White, 1978.

Detailed guide to the child's development in the early years.

*The First Twelve Months of Life, Your Baby's Growth Month by Month, Frank Caplan, editor, 1978.

Month-by-month guide to infant development, with detailed charts and many good photographs.

How to Father, Fitzhugh Dodson, 1975.

Focuses on the father's role and experiences in raising children.

How to Parent, Fitzhugh Dodson, 1971.

Practical guide, from a psychological perspective, on effective parenting.

*Living With Your New Baby: A Postpartum Guide for Mothers and Fathers, Elly Rakowitz and Gloria Rubin, 1980.

An excellent guide to understanding and coping with parenthood.

The Mother's Almanac, Marguerite Kelly and Elia Parsons, 1975.

Comprehensive information for the mother of small children, with emphasis on developing a loving relationship.

The New Mother Care, Helping Yourself Through the Emotional and Physical Transitions of New Motherhood, Lyn Delliquardri and Kati Breckenridge, 1984.

Sensible advice to the new mother during the early months.

*Ourselves and Our Children: A Book By and For Parents, Boston Women's Health Book Collective, 1978.

Good exploration of the conflicting demands placed on the adult as parent, spouse and worker.

Parent Effectiveness Training, Thomas Gordon, 1970.

Presents a practical method for raising responsible children with the emphasis on listening skills and acceptance of feelings.

People Making, Virginia Satir, 1972.

Focuses on the importance of the family in human development. Good information on and activities for family interaction.

Practical Parenting Tips, Vicki Lansky, 1982.

Over 1,000 ideas to save you time, trouble and money.

The Private Life of Parents, Roberta Plutzik and Maria Laghi, 1983.

How to be a successful parent without neglecting the other aspects of your life.

*The Second Twelve Months of Life, Frank Caplan and Theresa Caplan, editors, 1980.

Month-by-month guide to development in the second year.

*A Sigh of Relief, The First-Aid Handbook for Childhood Emergencies, Martin I. Green, 1984.

Concise, practical information for dealing with childhood health emergencies. Bold print and illustrations.

Traits of a Healthy Family, Dolores Curran, 1984.

How to build on your family's strengths to produce an even healthier family.

The Well Baby Book, Mike Samuels and Nancy Samuels, 1979.

Preventive medicine from pregnancy through age four.

What Every Child Would Like His Parents to Know (To Help Him with the Emotional Problems of Everyday Life), Lee Salk, 1983.

Adult guide to the child's feelings and perceptions, with practical advice.

What Now? A Handbook for New Parents, Mary Lou Rozdilsky and Barbara Banat, 1975.

Extensive exploration of the problems and fulfillments of new parents.

Whole Child/Whole Parent, Polly Berends, 1983.

Combines practical information with discussions of such spiritual values as beauty, touch and love.

Your Baby and Child, Penelope Leach, 1980.

Comprehensive and sensitive guide to child care and development during the first five years. Beautifully illustrated.

Your Child's Self-Esteem, Dorothy Briggs, 1975.

Guide to helping your child develop feelings of self worth.

Your Second Child, Joan Solomon Weiss, 1981.

Detailed presentation of the impact of a second baby on the family, including discussions of pregnancy, childbirth and sibling rivalry.

NUTRITION

As You Eat, So Your Baby Grows, Nikki Goldbeck, 1986.

A brief guide to nutrition in pregnancy.

The Brewer Medical Diet for Normal and High-Risk Pregnancy, Gail Sforza Brewer and Tom Brewer, 1983.

Specific, proper nutritional management from preconception to weaning.

Diet for a Small Planet, Frances Moore Lappe, 1974.

Good ideas for adequate nutrition for vegetarians.

Feed Me! I'm Yours, Vicki Lansky, 1979.

Helpful information and recipes to make eating fun for your toddler.

The Good Breakfast Book, Nikki Goldbeck and David Goldbeck, 1976.

Offers interesting and appetizing breakfast ideas, including over 400 recipes.

Nourishing Your Unborn Child, Phyllis Williams, 1982.

Practical guide with recipes and menus for good nutrition during pregnancy and postpartum.

Nutrition for Your Pregnancy, Judith Brown, 1983.

Up-to-date scientific information about nutrition and pregnancy presented in a readable format.

Pregnancy and Life-Style Habits, Peter Fried, 1983.

Information on the effects of alcohol, caffeine, nicotine, marijuana, prescription and over-the-counter drugs on the unborn baby.

Supermarket Handbook, Nikki Goldbeck and David Goldbeck, 1985.

Newly revised presentation on getting your nutritional money's worth.

The Taming of the C.A.N.D.Y. (Continuously Advertised Nutritionally Deficient Yummies) Monster, Vicki Lansky, 1982.

Sensible nutrition for school-age children.

*****What Every Pregnant Woman Should Know, The Truth About Diets and Drugs in Pregnancy**, Gail Sforza Brewer and Tom Brewer, 1985.

Discusses the prevention of toxemia and other complications through good nutrition, with emphasis on a high-protein diet. Stresses the dangers of poor nutrition and drugs in pregnancy; includes menus and recipes.

FOR CHILDREN

Amie, Terry Stafford, 1984.

Charming description of a day in the life of a nursing toddler.

Baby, Come Out!, Fran Manushkin, 1972.

Imaginative story for ages 4 to 8 about a baby who refuses to be born—until Daddy gets an idea.

How Was I Born?, Lennart Nilsson, 1975.

Basic, clear presentation of pregnancy, from conception to childbirth. Beautifully illustrated.

Mom, Dad and I Are Having a Baby, Maryann Malecki, 1982.

Picture book to prepare children of all ages to be present at birth.

Nobody Asked Me If I Wanted a Baby Sister, Martha Alexander, 1971.

Realistic tale of a new big brother.

On Mother's Lap, Ann Herbert Scott, 1972.

A young Eskimo boy discovers that even with a new baby, there is still room for him.

*****Our Family Grows**, Renee B. Neri, 1985.

Delightful coloring and activity book to promote involvement of a young child in the plans and excitement surrounding his sibling's arrival.

*****Where Did I Come From?**, Peter Mayle, 1977.

Clear presentation of the physiology of conception, pregnancy and birth, presented with humor. Intended for 8- to 12-year-olds.

*****Where Do Babies Come From?**, Margaret Sheffield, 1983.

Good basic exploration of the physiology of intercourse, conception, pregnancy and birth. Sensitively illustrated with colored drawings.

MISCELLANEOUS

The Art of Natural Family Planning, John Kippley and Sheila Kippley, 1982.

Complete information about temperature, mucus and cervix changes as related to fertility.

The Birth Control Book, Howard Shapiro, 1982.

Concise, unbiased, medically sound contraceptive information.

Ended Beginnings—Healing Childbearing Losses, Claudia Panuthos and Catherine Romeo, 1984.

How to use inner resources to help heal losses from miscarriage, stillbirth, abortion, or from a traumatic birth experience.

The New Our Bodies, Ourselves, Boston Women's Health Book Collective, 1985.

Complete information on all aspects of a woman's biological and psychological health.

The Relaxation Response, Herbert Benson, 1976.

Principles of controlled meditation and relaxation.

Touching, The Human Significance of the Skin, Ashley Montagu, 1978.

Montagu's popular treatise on the importance of touching in all human interaction. Discusses benefits of skin-to-skin contact during breastfeeding.

A Woman in Residence, Michelle Harrison, 1983.

A female doctor-in-training presents her view of the medical profession and its treatment of women.

Woman's Experience of Sex, Sheila Kitzinger, 1983.

Detailed exploration of women's feelings about their bodies; includes many drawings and photographs.

Bibliography

Books

Apgar, Virginia and J. Beck. *Is My Baby All Right?* N.Y.: Simon and Schuster, 1972.

Applebaum, Richard M. *Abreast of the Times.* El Paso, Texas: Applebaum, 1969.

Baldwin, Rahima. *Special Delivery.* Millbrae, California: Les Femmes Publishing, 1979.

Baring-Gould, William and Ceil. *The Annotated Mother Goose.* New York: Bramhall House, 1962.

Beals, Peg. *Parents' Guide to the Childbearing Year,* 6th. ed. Milwaukee, Wisconsin: ICEA, 1978.

Beals, Peg, and others. *ICEA Teacher's Guide.* Milwaukee, Wisconsin: ICEA, 1978.

Berezin, Nancy. *The Gentle Birth Book.* New York: Simon and Schuster, 1980.

Bergerson, Betty and Elsie Krugen. *Pharmacology in Nursing.* St. Louis: C. V. Mosby Co., 1966.

Bing, Elisabeth. *Moving Through Pregnancy.* New York: Bantam Books, Inc., 1976.

Bing, Elisabeth. *Six Practical Lessons for an Easier Childbirth.* New York: Grosset and Dunlap, Inc., 1973.

Bing, Elisabeth and Libby Colman. *Making Love During Pregnancy.* New York: Bantam Books, 1977.

Bogert, L. Jean, and others. *Nutrition and Physical Fitness,* 9th ed. Philadelphia: W.B. Saunders Co., 1973.

Brewer, Gail Sforza. *The Pregnancy After 30 Workbook.* Emmaus, Pa.: Rodale Press, 1978.

Brewer, Gail Sforza. *What Every Pregnant Woman Should Know, The Truth About Diet and Drugs During Pregnancy.* New York: Penguin Books, 1985.

Boston Women's Health Book Collective. *Our Bodies, Ourselves.* New York: Simon and Schuster, 1976.

CEA of Seattle. *Becoming Parents.* Seattle, Wash.: Childbirth Education Association of Seattle, 1979.

Chard, Tim and Martin Richards. *Benefits and Hazards of the New Obstetrics.* Suffolk, England: Lavenham Press, LTD., 1977.

Cohen, Nancy Wainer and Lois J. Estner. *Silent Knife: Cesarean Prevention and Vaginal Birth After Cesarean.* South Hadley, Massachusetts: Bergin & Garvey Publishers, Inc., 1983.

Colman, Arthur and Libby. *Pregnancy: The Psychological Experience.* New York: Seabury Press, Inc., 1978.

The Complete Runner. New York: Avon Press, 1978.

The Consumers Union Guide to Buying for Babies. New York: Warner Books, 1975.

Cooke, Cynthia W. and Susan Dworkin. *The Ms. Guide to a Woman's Health.* New York: Doubleday, 1979.

Davis, Adelle. *Let's Have Healthy Children.* New York: Harcourt, Brace, Jovanovich, Inc., 1972.

Deutsch, Ronald. *The Key to Feminine Response in Marriage.* New York: Random House, 1968.

Dick-Read, Grantly. *Childbirth Without Fear.* New York: Harper and Row, 1959.

Donovan, Bonnie. *The Cesarean Birth Experience.* Boston: Beacon Press, 1978.

Ehrmantraut, Harry C. *Headaches: The Drugless Way to Lasting Relief!* Brookline, Massachusetts: Autumn Press, Inc., 1977.

Elkins, Valmai Howe. *The Rights of the Pregnant Parent.* New York: Schocken Books, 1980.

Ericson, Avis. *Medications Used During Labor and Birth.* Milwaukee, Wisconsin: ICEA, 1978.

Ewy, Rodger and Donna. *Preparation for Childbirth,* 2nd. ed. New York: Signet Books, 1976.

Feldman, Silvia. *Choices in Childbirth.* New York: Grosset and Dunlap, 1978.

Flanagan, Geraldine Lux. *The First Nine Months of Life.* New York: Simon and Schuster, 1962.

Goldbeck, Nikki. *As You Eat, So Your Baby Grows.* New York: Ceres Press, 1978.

Green, Martin I. *A Sigh of Relief.* New York: Bantam Books, 1977.

Guttmacher, Alan F. *Pregnancy, Birth and Family Planning.* New York: The New American Library, Inc., 1973.

Hamilton, Eva May and Eleanor Whitney. *Nutrition Concepts and Controversies.* St. Paul: West Publishing Co., 1979.

Hausknecht, Richard and Joan Rattner Heilmann. *Having a Cesarean Baby.* New York: E.P. Dutton, 1978.

Hazell, Lester. *Commonsense Childbirth.* New York: G. P. Putnam's Sons, 1976.

Hotchner, Tracy. *Pregnancy and Childbirth.* New York: Avon Books, 1979.

Jacobson, Edmund. *How to Relax and Have Your Baby.* New York: McGraw-Hill, 1965.

Karmel, Marjorie. *Thank You, Dr. Lamaze.* New York: Dolphin Books, 1965.

Kieffer, Joyce. *To Have—To Hold.* Harrisburg, Pa. Training Resource Assoc., 1979.

Kitzinger, Sheila. *The Experience of Childbirth,* 4th. ed. New York: Penguin Books, 1978.

Klaus, Marshall and John Kennell. *Maternal-Infant Bonding.* St. Louis: C.V. Mosby Co., 1976.

Klaus, Marshall and John Kennell. *Parent-Infant Bonding.* St. Louis: C.V. Mosby Co., 1982.

Korte, Diana and Roberta Scaer. *A Good Birth, A Safe Birth.* New York: Bantam Books, 1984.

Krause, Marie V. *Food, Nutrition and Diet Therapy,* 4th. ed. Philadelphia: W.B. Saunders Co., 1966.

Leboyer, Frederick. *Birth Without Violence.* New York: Alfred A. Knopf, 1976.

La Leche League. *The Womanly Art of Breastfeeding.* Minneapolis: La Leche League International, 1980.

Lerch, Constance. *Maternity Nursing.* St. Louis: C.V. Mosby Co., 1970.

Levine, Milton and Jean Sebezman. *The Parents' Encyclopedia of Infancy, Childhood and Adolescence.* New York: Thomas Crowell Co., 1973.

Lévy, Janine. *The Baby Exercise Book.* New York: Pantheon Books, 1975.

MacMahon, Alice. *All About Childbirth, A Manual for Prepared Childbirth.* Maitland, Fla.: Family Publications, 1978.

Meyer, Linda D. *The Cesarean (R)Evolution.* Edmonds, Wash.: Chas. Franklin Press, 1979.

Montagu, Ashley. *Touching, The Human Significance of the Skin,* 2nd. ed. New York: Harper and Row, 1978.

Myles, Margaret. *Textbook for Midwives.* New York: Churchill Livingston, 1975.

Nilsson, Lennart. *A Child is Born.* New York: Delacorte Press, 1977.

Noble, Elizabeth. *Essential Exercises for the Childbearing Year.* Boston: Houghton Mifflin Co., 1976.

Oxorn, Harry and William R. Foote. *Human Labor and Birth,* 3rd. ed. New York: Appleton-Century-Crofts, 1975.

Peterson, Gayle. *Birthing Normally,* 2nd ed. Berkeley: Mindbody Press, 1984.

Physicians' Desk Reference, 41st ed. Oradell, New Jersey: Medical Economics Co., Inc., 1987.

Pryor, Karen. *Nursing Your Baby.* New York: Pocket Books, 1975.

Rakowitz, Elly and Gloria S. Rubin. *Living with Your New Baby.* New York: Franklin Watts, Inc., 1978.

Sasmor, Jeannette L. *What Every Husband Should Know About Having a Baby.* Chicago: Nelson-Hall, 1977.

Shapiro, Howard I. *The Pregnancy Book for Today's Woman.* New York: Harper and Row, 1984.

Tucker, Susan. *Fetal Monitoring and Fetal Assessment in High-Risk Pregnancy.* St. Louis: C.V. Mosby Co., 1978.

Verny, Thomas with John Kelly. *The Secret Life of the Unborn Child.* New York: Dell Publishing Co., 1981.

Walton, Vicki E. *Have It Your Way.* New York: Bantam Books, 1976.

White, Burton. *The First Three Years of Life.* New York: Avon, 1978.

Williams, Phyllis. *Nourishing Your Unborn Child.* New York: Nash, 1974.

Wilson, Christine Coleman and Wendy Roe Hovey. *Cesarean Childbirth.* Ann Arbor, Mich.: Wilson and Hovey, 1977.

Worthington, Bonnie. *Nutrition in Pregnancy and Lactation.* St. Louis: C. V. Mosby Co., 1977.

Young, Diony and Charles Mahan. *Unnecessary Cesareans, Ways to Avoid Them.* Minneapolis: ICEA, 1980.

Articles

"AIDS and Pregnancy. " Maternity Center Association Pamphlet. New York.

American Academy of Pediatrics. "Revised First Aid for the Choking Child." *Pediatrics*, Vol. 78, No. 1, July 1986.

"Amniotomy," *ICEA Review*, Vol. 3, No. 2, Summer 1979.

Banta, David and Stephen Thacker. "Electronic Fetal Monitoring: Is It a Benefit?" *Birth and the Family Journal*, Winter 1979.

"The Better Way." *Good Housekeeping*, March 1985.

Caldeyro-Barcia, Roberto. "The Influence of Maternal Bearing-Down Efforts During Second Stage on Fetal Well-Being." *Birth and the Family Journal*, Spring 1979.

Caldwell, Jean. "CVS: An Early Test for Genetic Problems." *American Baby*, Feb. 1985.

Carr, Katherine Camacho. "Obstetric Practices Which Protect Against Neonatal Morbidity: Focus on Maternal Position in Labor and Birth." *Birth and the Family Journal*, Winter 1980.

"Companies Wrestle With Threats to Workers' Reproductive Health." *The Wall Street Journal*, February 5, 1987.

Di Franco, Joyce. "Home Practice Guide." *Lamaze Parents Magazine*, 1986.

"Diagnostic Ultrasound Imaging in Pregnancy." National Institutes of Health Concensus Development Conference Concensus Statement, Vol. 5, No. 1, 1984.

"Diagnostic Ultrasound in Obstetrics." ICEA Position Paper, 1983.

Doering, Susan G. "Unnecessary Cesareans: Doctor's Choice, Parent's Dilemma." *Compulsory Hospitalization or Freedom of Choice in Childbirth?* Vol. 1, 1976.

Dunne, Joanne. "Bendectin and Birth Defects Link Still Unclear." *ICEA News*, Vol. 19, No. 4, December, 1980.

Edwards, Margot and Penny Simkin. "Obstetric Tests and Technology, A Consumer's Guide."

Grimes, David. "Routine Circumcision Reconsidered." *American Journal of Nursing*, January 1980.

Haire, Doris. "The Pregnant Patient's Bill of Rights; The Pregnant Patient's Responsibilities." Minneapolis: ICEA.

Hensleigh, Paul A. "Preventing rhesus isoimmunization." *American Journal of Obstetrics and Gynecology*, Vol. 146, No. 7, August 1983.

Jacobs, Paul. "Caffeine Warning Set for Pregnant Women." *Florida-Times Union*, August 3, 1980.

Jakubovic, A. and others. "Radioactivity in Suckling Rats After Giving C-14-Tetrahydrocannabinol to the Mother." *European Journal of Pharmacy*, Vol. 22, 1973.

Katz, Sara. "Circumscision." *ICEA Sharing*, Vol. V, No. 1, Spring 1977.

Klein, Luella. "Cesarean Birth and Trial of Labor." *The Female Patient*, Vol. 9, 1984.

"Lesser Known Facts." *American Cancer Society Fact Sheet*. Jacksonville, Fla., 1980.

Maiselle, M.J. and others. "Elective Delivery of the Term Fetus: An Obstetrical Hazard." *Journal of the American Medical Association*, Vol. 238, November 7, 1977.

"Maternal Position During Labor and Birth." *ICEA Review*, Vol. 2, No. 3, Summer 1978.

National Women's Health Network: "Certification and Consent Form for Ultrasound Exposure." 1984.

Nolte, Judith. "The First Month." *American Baby, The First Year of Life,* January 1981.

Nutrition Committee of the Canadian Pediatric Society and the Committee on Nutrition of the American Academy of Pediatrics. "Breastfeeding, A Commentary in Celebration of the International Year of the Child." 1979.

"One Mother Dies for Eight Newborns Saved with Electronic Monitoring." *Ob. Gyn. News*, Vol. 12, No. 24, December 15, 1978.

Parent and Child (St. Louis Newsletter), Vol. 9:1, Winter 1980.

"Recent Advances in Research." *Florida SIDS Information Exchange*, No. 5, March 1979.

Shearer, Madeleine. "Complications of Cesarean to Mother and Infant." *Birth and the Family Journal*, Fall 1977.

Shearer, Madeleine. "Malnutrition in Middle Class Pregnant Women." *Birth and the Family Journal*, Spring 1980.

Stratmeyer, M.E. "Research in Ultrasound Bioeffects: A Public Health View." *Birth and the Family Journal*, Summer 1980.

U.S. Dept. of Agriculture. "Composition of Foods—Raw, Processed, Prepared." *Agriculture Handbook No. 8*. Wash., D.C.: Gov't. Printing Office, 1963.

U.S. Dept. of HEW. *FDA Consumer*, HEW Publication No. (FDA) 79-1057. Wash., D.C.: Gov't. Printing Office, May 1979.

Wallerstein, Edward. "The Circumcision Decision." Pennypress, 1980.

Whatley, Nancy and Esther Mark, "Are Enemas Justified in Labor?" *American Journal of Nursing*, July 1980.

Wunderlich, Cherry. "Unborn Males, Children at Risk with Saccharin." *ICEA News*, Vol. 18, No. 3, 1979.

Mail to:

Instructor's Name: _____

Address: _____

CESAREAN BIRTH REPORT

Recognizing the rising cesarean rate, a special birth report has been devised for our cesarean couples. I hope that you will find the time, while still in the hospital, or after you arrive home, to answer these questions. This is for my benefit as an instructor, and as a parent, you can gain understanding of your particular situation. Please feel free to express both your positive and negative feelings. Call me if you have questions or need emotional support. I can also put you in contact with another cesarean couple for additional help.

This report is divided into two sections: one for those of you who had an unexpected cesarean birth; one for those who planned a cesarean birth.

Name_____

Baby is a _____ Born on _____ at _____ M.

Baby weighed _____ lbs. _____ ozs.; measured _____ in. Baby's name_____

Delivered by _____ at _____ Hospital.

Pediatrician_____

UNEXPECTED CESAREAN BIRTH

I. Preparation

A. Was the subject of cesarean birth covered adequately in your Lamaze class? _____

    If not, what else should have been covered? _____

    _____

B. At the time of discussion did you feel this information might apply to you? _____

    How can I insure that couples in future classes really listen to this information? _____

    _____

II. Cesarean Decision

A. How long before the birth was it decided that a cesarean delivery would be necessary? _____

    What was your first reaction to your doctor's decision? _____

    _____

    Labor partner's reaction? _____

B. What was the reason(s) for your cesarean delivery? _____

_____

Was it adequately explained to you? _____

C. If fetal distress was the reason, check how it was determined.

_____ nurse monitoring _____ external fetal monitor _____ internal fetal monitor _____ fetal scalp blood sample

D. If cephalopelvic disproportion was the reason, check how it was determined.

_____ sonogram _____ pelvimetry _____ other _____

E. Did you ask for a second opinion on the need for a cesarean delivery? _____

Explain. _____

F. Indicate which options you used and those that were unavailable to you with these symbols: "U" for used, "N" for not available.

_____ awake for birth   _____ nursing baby soon after birth

_____ partner present   _____ bonding

_____ partial prep   _____ rooming-in

_____ no pre-op sedation

III. Labor

A. I labored _____ hours, was dilated _____ cm., effaced _____ % and baby was at _____ station prior to delivery.

B. Were you permitted to walk around during labor? _____

C. What were your feelings during labor? _____

_____

Your partner's? _____

_____

D. Do you feel that your classes had prepared you for labor? _____

E. Was your partner able to stay with you during labor? _____ If yes, how did he help you? _____

_____

IV. Interventions

A. The following medication was used during labor: _____

When given? _____ Reason for use: _____

How did you feel after receiving it? _____

_____

Was it helpful? _____

B. Membranes ruptured _____ spontaneously _____ artificially.

When? _____

If artificially done, why? _____

_____

How did you feel after it happened? _____

_____

C. Pitocin _____ was _____ was not given. If so, when? _____

and why? _____

_____

How did you feel after it was given? _____

_____

D. A fetal monitor _____ was _____ was not used. It was _____ external _____ internal.

Why used? _____

For how long? _____

How did you feel about its use? _____

_____

E. I _____ did _____ did not have an I.V. When started? _____

Why? _____

_____

V. Birth

A. Delivery occurred in _____ delivery room _____ operating room.

B. If partner was permitted to be with you for the birth, how did you feel about it? _____

_____

How did he feel about it? _____

_____

C. If not together how did you feel? _____

_____

How did he feel? _____

_____

D. I had _____ spinal _____ epidural _____ general anesthesia.

Was this what you wanted? _____

Why? _____

E. What sensations did you experience during the birth? _____

_____

F. What, if any, complications did you have from your anesthesia? _____

_____

G.   The uterine incision was _____ low transverse _____ vertical (classical).

H.   The baby's APGAR score was _____ .

VI. Postpartum

A.   I was able to hold and touch my baby _____ minutes/hours after birth.

My partner was able to hold and touch the baby _____ minutes/hours after birth.

B.   I was allowed to nurse _____ minutes/hours after birth. What problems if any did you experience?

_____

_____

Did you receive support from nurses and pediatrician? _____

_____

C.   Was your partner able to be with you in the recovery room? _____

D.   We were able to bond with the baby _____ minutes/hours after birth. If bonding was not permitted, why?

_____

_____

E.   I roomed-in with the baby _____ 24 hours _____ 12 hours _____ feedings only _____ other _____
_____ When begun? _____

How did you feel about this choice? _____

_____

Were the staff and doctor supportive? _____

F.   How long did you stay in the hospital? _____

What, if any, complications did you experience? _____

_____

G.   When was your catheter removed? _____ Your I.V.? _____

When did you return to a normal diet? _____

H.   Did you have problems with gas? _____ What worked to relieve it? _____

I.   Did you have problems with the incision? _____

_____

Did you and your partner look at the incision before going home? _____

J.   When did you first start walking? _____

K.   What has been the most enjoyable aspect of your cesarean delivery? _____

_____

L.   What has been the most difficult? _____

_____

M. Overall, do you feel that the doctor and the hospital did everything they could to promote a family-centered birth?

_____ If not, what could they have done? _____

_____

PLANNED CESAREAN DELIVERY

I. Preparation

A. How far in advance of the birth were you told you may/would need a cesarean delivery? _____

Did you ask for a second opinion? _____ Explain _____

The reason for this cesarean was _____

_____

B. The tests/methods that were used to determine delivery date were:

_____ labor started naturally   _____ ultrasound

_____ estimated due date used   _____ X-ray

_____ amniocentesis (L/S ratio)

C. Indicate which options you used and which were unavailable with these symbols: "U" for used, "N" for not available.

_____ admission day of surgery   _____ awake

_____ nursing baby soon after birth   _____ partial prep

_____ no pre-op sedation   _____ bonding time

_____ allowing labor to start   _____ rooming-in

_____ partner present

D. Were you permitted a trial of labor for a possible vaginal delivery? _____ If yes, what prevented it? _____

_____

E. If this was a repeat cesarean delivery, what pleased you about it? _____

_____

What displeased you about it? _____

_____

F. What benefits do you feel you gained from being prepared? _____

_____

_____

G. What information should be added to future cesarean classes? _____

_____

II. Please complete Sections V. and VI. under "Unexpected Cesarean Birth."

Mail to:

Instructor's Name: _____

Address: _____

CHILDBIRTH REPORT

It is important for me to know if the classes met your needs and enabled you to experience a joyful childbirth. Your answers to the following questions will be most helpful in evaluating the effectiveness of the classes.

Your name _____ Baby is a _____

Born on _____ at _____ M. Baby weighed _____ lbs. _____ ozs.; measured _____ inches.

Baby's name _____

Delivered by _____ at _____ Hospital/Birth Center.

Please answer the following questions completely and check where applicable.

I. Before Labor

A. I practiced _____ daily _____ couple of times a week _____ once a week _____ other(explain)_____

B. Each practice session was _____ minutes long.

C. My partner practiced with me _____ every session _____ most sessions _____ some sessions _____ none.

II. Beginning of Labor

A. What was your estimated due date? _____

B. Date and time labor actually began _____

C. My first sign of labor was _____ contractions _____ loss of mucus plug _____ ruptured membranes _____ other

   (explain) _____

D. Contractions began at _____ M., were _____ minutes apart, lasting _____ seconds.

E. How did you feel when labor began? _____

   _____

III. Admittance to Hospital

A. I entered hospital/birth center at _____ M.

B. Contractions were _____ minutes apart, lasting _____ seconds.

C. I was _____ cm. dilated and _____ % effaced when I was admitted.

D. I used _____ breathing at this time.

E. I _____ was _____ was not separated from my labor partner during admission.

F. If separated, would you have preferred to be together? _____ Why? _____

   _____

G. What procedures took place during admission? _____

_____

H. How did you feel during admission to your birthing place? _____

_____

IV. Early Labor

A. The early phase lasted _____ hours. The contractions lasted _____ seconds, and were

_____ minutes apart.

B. How did you feel during this phase? _____

_____

C. I used _____ breathing. Was it effective? _____

_____

V. Active Labor

A. The active phase lasted _____ hours. The contractions lasted _____ seconds, and were

_____ minutes apart.

B. How did you feel during the active phase? _____

_____

C. Check the comfort measures you and your partner used.

_____ ice chips	_____ all-fours position	_____ ice pack
_____ wet cloth	_____ effleurage	_____ other (explain)
_____ walking	_____ massage	_____
_____ back pressure	_____ heat to back	_____

D. I used _____ breathing technique(s).

Was it effective? _____

_____

VI. Transition

A. Transition lasted _____ minutes/hours. The contractions lasted _____ seconds, and were _____ minutes apart.

B. Check the following that you experienced.

_____ trembling of legs	_____ nausea/vomiting
_____ desire to move bowels	_____ amnesia
_____ urge to push	_____ belching or hiccups
_____ chills and/or warmth	_____ loss of modesty
_____ cramps in legs/buttocks	_____ irritability
_____ sleepy between contractions	_____ restlessness
_____ not wanting to be touched	_____ panic
_____ wanting to give up	_____ other (explain)

_____

C. How did you feel during transition? _____

_____

D. I used _____ breathing technique(s).

Was it effective? _____

_____

VII. Second Stage

A. I pushed for _____ minutes. The contractions lasted _____ seconds, and were _____ minutes apart.

B. How did you feel during expulsion? _____

_____

C. Did you use Level 1 pushing? _____   How long? _____

Was it effective? _____

D. Did you use Level 2 pushing? _____ . How long?_____

Was it effective? _____

E. In what position(s) did you push and give birth. Mark with a P those used during pushing; with a D for delivery.

_____ semi-sitting (no stirrups)   _____ side-lying
_____ lithotomy (in stirrups)   _____ squatting
_____ on all fours

VIII. Medical Interventions or Complications

A. Was there anything unusual medically or otherwise about your labor or delivery? _____

_____

B. Length of first stage _____ hours. Length of second stage _____ hours.

C. Did you have an enema?   _____ fleet   _____ soapsuds   _____ none

D. I had the following kind of prep:

_____ partial   _____ clip   _____ full   _____ none

E. I _____ did _____ did not have an I.V. If yes, when started?_____

Why used? _____

How did you feel about it?_____

_____

F. Membranes ruptured _____ spontaneously _____ artificially. When? _____

_____

If artificially, why? _____

_____

How did you feel after it happened? _____

_____

G. Pitocin _____ was _____ was not given. If given, when? _____

Why was it used? _____

How did you feel after it was given? _____

_____

H. The following medication was used during labor: _____

When given? _____

Reason for use. _____

How did you feel after receiving it? _____

Was it helpful to you? _____

I. The following medication/anesthesia was used during delivery: _____

_____

When given? _____

Reason for use: _____

How did you feel after receiving it? _____

Was it helpful to you? _____

J. A fetal monitor _____ was _____ was not used. It was _____ external _____ internal.

If yes, why was it used? _____

How did you feel about its use? _____

How long was it used? _____

_____ Intermittent _____ Continuous

K. Did you have an episiotomy? _____

L. Was your delivery assisted with forceps? _____ Vacuum extractor? _____

Reason used: _____

_____

_____

IX. Labor Support

A. Was your labor partner with you during labor? _____ How did he help you? _____

_____

What more could he have done to help you? _____

_____

If not present, would you have liked him to be there? _____

B. Was your partner with your during delivery? _____ How did he help you? _____

_____

What more could he have done? _____

_____

If not present, would you have liked him there? _____

C. How did the hospital staff help and support you? _____

_____

Were they familiar with the relaxation and breathing techniques? _____

Were you satisfied with the support given? _____ If not, why? _____

_____

D. How did your doctor help and support you? _____

_____

Was he familiar with the relaxation and breathing techniques? _____

Were you satisfied with the support given? _____ If not, why? _____

X. Postpartum

A. I was allowed to nurse my baby _____ minutes/hours after birth. What, if any, problems did you experience? _____

_____

Did you receive support from the nurses? _____

B. We had _____ minutes/hours to bond with our baby. How did you feel during this time? _____

_____

If not permitted, why? _____

Was the application of eye ointment or silver nitrate delayed until after bonding? _____

C. I roomed-in with the baby _____ 24 hours _____ 12 hours _____ feedings only

_____ other (explain) _____

How did you feel about this choice? _____

_____

Were the staff and your doctor supportive? _____

D. Was this birth experience satisfying to you? _____

Would you repeat it if you have more children? _____

Comment please! _____

_____

_____

_____

_____

E. Do you feel that this course prepared you adequately for your childbirth experience? _____

_____

F. What changes could you suggest to improve the course? _____

_____

Please add any comments you would like to make. Thank you!

_____

_____

_____

_____

_____

_____

_____

_____

_____

PERSONAL INFORMATION SHEET

Name _____

Address _____

City _____ Zip _____

Home Phone Number _____ Your Age _____ Due Date _____

Dr. or Midwife _____ Place of Delivery _____

No. of children now have _____ Pediatrician _____

Your Occupation _____ Work Phone _____

Labor Partner's Name _____

Address (if different) _____

City_____ Zip _____

Home Phone (if different) _____ Age _____

Partner's Occupation _____Work Phone _____

How did you hear about the classes? _____

What are your expectations from this series? _____

_____

Does your partner wish to be with your during labor? _____ Delivery?_____

Do you plan to breastfeed? _____ Bottlefeed? _____ Undecided _____

Previous labors: (Please fill in where applicable)

	1st	2nd	3rd
Name of child:	_____	_____	_____
Date of birth:	_____	_____	_____
First sign of labor:	_____	_____	_____
Length of labor:	_____	_____	_____
Medications used:	_____	_____	_____
Awake or asleep for delivery:	_____	_____	_____
Where delivered:	_____	_____	_____
Birth attendant:	_____	_____	_____
Breastfed how long:	_____	_____	_____

Additional comments: _____

_____

_____

PERSONAL LABOR RECORD

Use this form to keep a record of your partner's progress during labor. It is not necessary to record every single contraction; only enough to be aware of a change in frequency and duration of the contractions. As the contractions become stronger and closer together, it is more important that you *encourage and support your partner* during contractions. After birth you can use this form to fill out the birth report.

Time Contraction Starts	How Long It Lasts	Effacement, Dilatation, Station (note whenever checked)	Comments (include feelings, breathing patterns used, medication given, time membranes rupture, when interventions are used or started, position change, urination—remind her to urinate hourly)

PERSONAL LABOR RECORD (cont.)

Time Contraction Starts	How Long It Lasts	Effacement, Dilatation, Station	Comments

CLASS EVALUATION
(To be completed the last night of class)

It is important for me to know if classes in "Preparation for Childbirth" have met your particular needs and interests. Your answers to the following questions will be a great help in evaluating the *effectiveness* of these classes.

1. What did you like best about the course? _____

   _____

   _____

2. What did you like least about the course? _____

   _____

   _____

3. What changes would you recommend for these classes in the future? _____

   _____

   _____

4. What things could be added that were not offered at this time? _____

   _____

   _____

5. What things seemed unnecessary that could be left out? _____

   _____

   _____

6. Do you feel you were adequately trained in the relaxation techniques necessary for a Lamaze

   labor and delivery? _____

   _____

7. Do you feel you were adequately trained in the breathing techniques necessary for a Lamaze

   labor and delivery? _____

   _____

8. How have your feelings toward labor and childbirth changed as a result of taking this course?

   (Please explain and be as specific as possible.) _____

   _____

   _____

9. Do you wish to be awake when your baby is born? Please explain your feelings.

   _____

   _____

   _____

10. What books did you read, as a result of taking this course, that are related to childbearing? _____

_____

_____

11. Generally, do you feel that this course was worth the time, money and effort you spent on it? _____

Would you recommend it to others? _____

(Please explain your feelings and reasons.) _____

_____

_____

12. Labor partner, do you wish to be with your partner during her labor? _____

Do you wish to be with her during the delivery? _____ Please explain your feelings. _____

_____

_____

13. How many classes did you attend? _____

ADDITIONAL COMMENTS: _____

_____

_____

_____

_____

_____

Index

PEN